CENTO
CITTÀ

CENTO CITTÀ

A Guide to the "Hundred
Cities & Towns" of Italy

PAUL HOFMANN

An Owl Book

A DONALD HUTTER BOOK

Henry Holt and Company ▪ New York

Published by Henry Holt and Company, Inc.,
115 West 18th Street, New York, New York 10011.
Published in Canada by Fitzhenry & Whiteside Limited,
195 Allstate Parkway, Markham, Ontario L3R 4T8.

Library of Congress Cataloging-in-Publication Data
Hofmann, Paul, 1912–
Cento città.
"A Donald Hutter book."
Includes index.
1. Italy—Description and travel—1975–
2. Cities and towns—Italy—Guide-books.   3. Italy—
History, Local.   I. Title.
DG430.2.H64   1988   914.5'04928   87–28512
ISBN 0-8050-0728-8
ISBN 0-8050-1465-9 (An Owl Book: pbk.)

Henry Holt books are available at special discounts
for bulk purchases for sales promotions, premiums,
fund-raising, or educational use. Special editions
or book excerpts can also be created to specification.
For details contact:
Special Sales Director, Henry Holt and Company, Inc.,
115 West 18th Street, New York, New York 10011.

First Owl Book Edition—1990

The six maps introducing regional sections of Italy were designed
by Otello Scarpelli, Rome.

Photo credits are as follows: ENIT, Rome, for photos on pages
36–41, 94–97, 133–138, 179 (top), 182, 185, 214 (bottom),
215–217, 219, 270–273, 314–319, 348–351.
Edoardo Fornaciari, Rome, for photos on pages 178, 180, 183,
184, 212, 214 (top), 218, 274, 320, 321.

CONTENTS ■

Preface   ix

1. THE SERENE VENETIAS

    Padua   6
    Adria   10
    Chioggia   12
    Trieste   14
    Udine   17
    Cividale del Friuli   19
    Asolo   21
    Bassano del Grappa   24
    Treviso   25
    Vicenza   28
    Cortina d'Ampezzo   31
    Ortisei/St. Ulrich/Urtijëi   33
    Bressanone/Brixen   42
    Bolzano/Bozen   44
    Merano/Meran   47
    Trent   49
    Rovereto   51
    Verona   53

2. THE DYNAMIC NORTHWEST:
    Lombardy, Piedmont, and Liguria

    Como   62
    Campione d'Italia   65

Bergamo 67

Brescia 71

Mantua 73

Cremona 77

Pavia 79

Piacenza 82

Aosta/Aoste 85

Lerici 88

Portofino 90

San Remo 92

3. THE HEARTLANDS: Emilia, Romagna, and Tuscany

Parma 103

Modena 107

Ferrara 110

Faenza 114

Forlì 116

Ravenna 118

Rimini 123

Republic of San Marino 127

Fiesole 130

Pistoia 142

Lucca 144

Pisa 148

Volterra 151

Portoferraio 153

San Gimignano 155

Pienza 158

Siena 162

Montepulciano 166

Chiusi 169

Arezzo 172

Sansepolcro 175

Cortona 186

4. THE HINTERLANDS OF ROME: Umbria, Latium,
the Marches, and Abruzzo

Frascati 194

Palestrina 197

Anagni 199

Tivoli 201

Subiaco 204

Spoleto 207

Foligno 211

Assisi 221

Perugia 224

Gubbio 228

Città di Castello 231

Orvieto 232

Todi 235

Bracciano 238

Viterbo 240

Tarquinia 244

Porto Santo Stefano 247

Rieti 251

L'Aquila 252

Chieti 255

Sulmona 257

Urbino 259

Ancona 262

Pesaro 264

Loreto 267

Macerata 276

Ascoli Piceno 278

Anzio   282
Terracina   284

5. THE MEZZOGIORNO: Southern Italy

Gaeta   291
Cassino   293
Caserta   295
Benevento   298
Capri   301
Sorrento   304
Positano   307
Amalfi   309
Ravello   313
Salerno   323
Cosenza   325
Lecce   327

6. THE ISLANDS: Sicily and Sardinia

Taormina   336
Syracuse   339
Enna   343
Agrigento   346
Erice   353
Monreale   355
Sassari   357

Appendix: Practical Travel Information   361

Photos follow pages 35, 93, 131, 177, 211, 269, 313, and 347.

PREFACE ∎

Whenever Italians want to stress the cultural variety of their nation, or nostalgically mention places where they *really* would like to live, they speak of the Cento Città (CHEN-toh Chee-TAH). The alliterative phrase must be translated as the "hundred cities and towns," because the word *città* means either. The townspeople of Todi (population 16,000) and the 7,000 residents of Asolo, referring to their habitat, say *"città"* the same way as the three million Romans.

With their chain hotels, credit-card restaurants, and packaged sightseeing tours, the capital and other big centers of Italy, including such tourist magnets as Venice, have to some extent become protectorates of the international travel industry. Anyone who longs for an older, more leisurely and genuine Italy had better seek out the cities and towns in the provinces, possibly those off the motorways and tourist-coach circuits.

Each of the hundred places profiled in this book for the benefit of visitors to Italy and armchair travelers alike is distinguished by a personality of its own. Nevertheless they all have many features in common. There will almost always be a central piazza where people meet for an espresso or a glass of wine and, above all, a chat. Foreigners will as a rule feel welcome. They may sit down for a drink or a *gelato,* and will receive friendly and expert advice when they ask, "Where's the best *trattoria* in town?" or "What are your gastronomic specialties and your favorite wine?"

Travelers in Italy shouldn't be shy about striking up conversations with local people even though their Italian vocabulary may consist of only a dozen words. Italians are not snobbish about their language and will encourage a stranger's attempts to communicate; most of them will go out of their way to be helpful—in the provincial cities and towns even more so than in the tourist spots.

If the guest doesn't want just to sit in the piazza or otherwise take it easy, which may be understandable, there is plenty to see and do everywhere: ancient ruins, medieval castles and cathedrals, Renaissance palaces, frescoes and paintings, scenic promenades and celebrated panoramas. Not only the famous galleries of Florence and Rome hold great art; so do many obscure museums in surprising places.

Every now and then the newspapers report that, alas, yet another valuable sculpture or picture has been stolen from a church or a collection in a town one has never heard of before. Fortunately, there is a stunning wealth of historical artifacts and works by great masters still left in musty chapels, rarely visited museums, and odd corners. Many of the Cento Città possess treasures for which the world's capitals might envy them.

Actually, there are many more than a hundred cities and towns that well deserve to be visited in Italy, a country of urban life since the oldest times. More than 300 cities were counted in the era of Emperor Augustus, each with its forum (which may today be the town square), its temples and magistrates. In the Middle Ages each see of a bishop, and a number of market towns, seaports, and garrisons were considered *città*, about 400 in all. Today several hundred of Italy's 8,000 municipalities have an urban character.

Many of the cities and towns in present-day Italy bear names derived from Etruscan, Greek, or, especially, Latin roots. Some were founded on hilltops by the Etruscans or other pre-Roman tribes, then shifted into a nearby valley or plain during the long peaceful periods of the Roman Empire, when ramparts were superfluous in Italy, then moved back to the hills and behind restored walls when barbarian invaders and Saracen and Norman raiders came, and when medieval feuds and pestilence made the plains unsafe.

The hilltowns have long since spilled into the valleys again, and lately they have sprawled out with housing developments, industrial plants, and the service-area clutter of the motor age. But the original settlements of the Etruscans or the Volscians on the hills are still inhabited, and some have even been spared the worst outrages of the mobile consumer society within their archaic walls.

Most of the cities and towns described in this book can look back on a long, and in many cases turbulent, history. The visitor may find residents in, say, Mantua or Urbino who speak about the dukes who in the Renaissance were the local rulers as if they had lived only yesterday. Roman roads, bridges, and aqueducts are still in use in many places, and the pattern of streets and squares follows the ancient layout. The past is everywhere; it is well remembered and often serviceable.

Following an orgy of garish urban reconstruction after World War II, an increasing number of Italians and quite a few foreigners attracted to life in the country began to buy old houses and install modern plumbing and fixtures, usually being careful to maintain as much of the original character as their architects thought possible. Such renovations, at times cosmetically overdone, continue in the Cento Città.

The selection of these particular hundred provincial places is a personal one—I like them best. I have been living in Italy for thirty years as a correspondent for *The New York Times,* serving as chief of its Rome bureau from 1970 to 1976, and I have long known the cities and towns whose descriptions follow. I revisited all of them in preparation for this book.

Readers who are fond of a particular city or town that isn't mentioned will ask, "Why not Montefiascone?" or "Why not Catanzaro or Campobasso?" Italians themselves have not agreed on a catalog of their Cento Città. I would have had to write about 500 cities and towns to do justice to all that might qualify.

Only four of the cities portrayed in this book—Brescia, Padua, Trieste, and Verona—have more than 200,000 inhabitants. They were picked for their singular atmosphere, and knowledgeable Italians with whom I consulted would without any hesitation include all four in their personal list of the Cento Città.

I have tried not to be gushing about natural scenery, architectural magnificence, cultural splendor, and historic achievements. Nor do I avoid aspects that are glossed over in travel folders—shoddily built new neighborhoods marring the approaches to the noble core of some ancient town, oil refineries near bathing beaches, traffic congestion, and large-scale flouting of zoning laws.

Italy today is neither a pastoral idyll nor a museum. It is a resilient society that has become the world's sixth industrial power. Economic development, often helter-skelter, has exacted its price in overbuilding of urban areas, a free-for-all on the roads, and pollution. Places where such drawbacks have lately become overwhelming were skipped.

The Appendix contains practical touring information. The reader is told how to get to each of the hundred cities and towns. Most of them can easily be reached by rail—every day thousands of trains run on the 10,000-mile network of the Italian State Railways (Ferrovie dello Stato, or FF.SS.) and the secondary railways. It is not difficult to find the appropriate information in the Orario Ufficiale, the official railroad timetable, where references and symbols are explained also in English. The volume can be bought at major railroad stations and at many newsstands. For motorists, advisable routes, not necessarily the shortest ones (which may be congested), are indicated.

Local tourist offices, where they exist, are listed with their addresses and telephone numbers. Many of these agencies are able to answer inquiries in English. In writing to them, it is sufficient to have the words "Ufficio Turistico di [locality]" precede the address, as given.

The Appendix also contains addresses and telephone numbers of museums to enable would-be visitors to inquire beforehand about opening hours and admission fees, both subject to change.

I have listed a few hotels and restaurants that I personally found satisfactory, but this information is spotty and subjective. A new management may meanwhile have come in, or a chef may have found another job; performances are not always the same; different travelers may have different experiences. All too often I have observed how the quality of food and service began slipping soon after a favorable rating appeared in a travel publication.

Visitors to any one of the Cento Città will have no trouble finding a place for a meal or somewhere to spend the night. Italians have been in the business of feeding and accommodating strangers for more than 2,000 years; they know how to take care of travelers. So why not, in a new place, trust your instincts and try some *trattoria* or inn that may not be listed in the standard guidebooks but looks inviting?

Although this book does not cover Rome, Milan, Naples, Turin, Palermo, Genoa, Florence, Venice, and other big cities, easy side trips are suggested in the introductions to the six regional sections for city tourists who want to see some distinctive town or get an idea of provincial Italy. Six illustrated maps and the introductions to each section sum up for the newcomer the character, history, and appeal of Italy's main regions. The six-part organization of this book will assist readers whose interest is or has become inclined toward provincial Italy.

1
THE SERENE VENETIAS

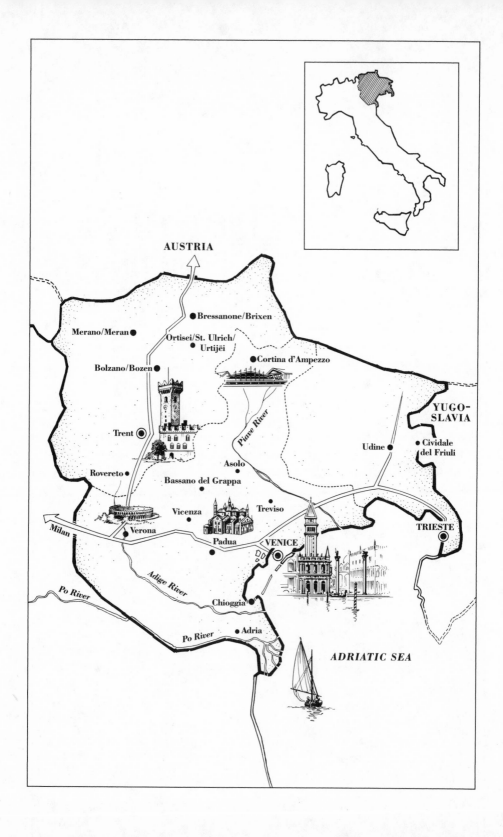

AUSTRIA

Merano/Meran●

●Bressanone/Brixen

Ortisei/St. Ulrich/
Urtijëi

Bolzano/Bozen●

●Cortina d'Ampezzo

Piave River

Trent ◉

YUGO-
SLAVIA

Udine ●

● Cividale
del Friuli

Rovereto ●

●Asolo

Bassano del Grappa ●

Vicenza ●

● Treviso

Milan

Verona ●

Padua ●

VENICE ◉

TRIESTE ◉

Adige River

Po River

Chioggia ●

● Adria

Po River

ADRIATIC SEA

Italian newspapers, particularly their baroquely inclined sportswriters, like to refer to Venice as "*la Serenissima*," "the Most Serene One." The sobriquet is by now as hoary as "Eternal City" for Rome. For centuries, however, this proud and singular oligarchy of merchant-aristocrats that from its impregnable base on a cluster of islands around the Rialto had built a far-flung empire styled itself officially "The Most Serene Republic."

Serene was then understood to mean a posture of calm, self-assured power, something like majesty without the trappings of royalty. Sereneness in the current sense of the word pervades much of the northeastern corner of Italy, which has been ruled, or at least influenced, by Venice. Visitors to the unique city that was once also called the "Queen of the Adriatic" will profit by devoting some of their time to exploring what is known as the Venetias (*le Venezie*), namely the mainland provinces close to it.

The Venetias are fertile plains crisscrossed by canals and often shrouded in fog, with Alpine foothills and, behind them, spectacular mountains on the horizon. Several cities and towns in the soothing lowlands boast neighborhoods skirting some waterway that makes them look like little Venices. Sculptures of the winged lion of St. Mark, the emblem of Venice's patron saint and symbol of Venetian dominance, are everywhere. The way the people on the mainland speak echoes the soft accents of the Lagoon City, a dialect that Italians from more distant parts of the nation don't easily understand.

With Venice overrun by tourists during the summer months, travelers will find a more authentic Venetian atmosphere—including genuine Venetian food—in places like Adria or Treviso.

The Venetian mainland is set apart from the rest of Italy by a flavor all its own, with faintly exotic overtones. History provides the explanation for such lingering separateness. At the height of its power in the fourteenth century, Venice controlled a large share of the trade between Europe and the East. The republic secured the navigation of its argosies and galleys with a string of colonies, protectorates, and naval bases along the eastern Adriatic coast and in the Ionian and Aegean seas all the way to Constantinople. Oriental wares—spices from India, silks from China, and coffee from Araby among them—reached the West first by way of Venice. Eastern splendor inspired the architects who built the churches and marble palaces on St. Mark's Square and the Grand Canal.

The Turkish conquest of Constantinople in 1453, the opening of the route around Africa to India, and the European discovery of America eclipsed Venice's fortunes. And as its role in the eastern Mediterranean and in commerce with the Orient declined, the still immensely wealthy republic turned its attention to the territories it had gradually acquired on the Italian mainland, and expanded them.

At the time of Venice's maritime ventures, its farsighted rulers thought it prudent to shield the island city's rear from envious neighbors—especially Medicean Florence and the ambitious dukedom of Milan—by a defensive belt on the *terrafirma*, its hinterland. Eventually, the Italian areas dominated by Venice stretched as far as Bergamo to the west and the Dolomite Mountains to the north. Such important old cities as Padua, Treviso, Vicenza, and Verona passed under Venetian government, which was generally benign and generated remarkable loyalty to the Most Serene Republic.

Napoleon put an end to Venetian sovereignty in 1797. After his downfall Venice and its hinterland were for half a century administered by Austria, until they joined unified Italy in 1866. Today the imprint of Venice is still noticeable as well in northwestern Italy, in places that only during limited periods, or never, belonged to the Most Serene Republic, like Trent, Trieste, and the towns of Alto Adige, or South Tyrol, a predominantly German-speaking province of towering Alpine peaks, rushing streams, and pleasant valleys.

The Venetias have long been a bulwark of the Roman Catholic Church. Travelers will be struck by the lofty, slender campaniles dotting the lowlands, and the many crucifixes along mountain paths. Significantly, no fewer than three twentieth-century popes came from the area: St. Pius X, John XXIII, and John Paul I.

Paintings by Titian, Tintoretto, and other masters of the glorious Venetian school can be found in many churches, chapels, palaces, and museums on the mainland; Palladio's famous villas are the pride of the countryside between Vicenza and the Venetian lagoon.

When Milan and Turin to the west were already affluent industrial and commercial centers, the eastern portion of northern Italy was still living essentially, and not too well, on farming, shipping, fishing, and tourism, and the area included pockets of outright poverty. Many mainland Venetians emigrated in the late nineteenth and early twentieth centuries overseas and to other European countries in search of a better life than they could expect at home.

Today a huge petrochemical complex rises on the shores of the Venetian lagoon (and, alas, is fouling its air and water). All over the mainland of Venice small and medium-sized industrial plants have sprung up since the end of World War II, turning out anything from ceramics to shoes and knitwear to the signboards that announce flights in international airports. Prosperity and sophistication have come to once-stagnant towns. Elegant stores and boutiques offer locally manufactured clothes, leatherware, and fashion accessories, often at lower prices than those asked in the shops in Venice that cater to tourists.

Cooking is a distinctive and most enjoyable ingredient of Venetian civilization, to be sampled throughout the Most Serene Republic's mainland possessions and beyond. Marco Polo, the Venetian adventurer and explorer, is supposed to have brought back noodles from China, thereby becoming the father of the Italian spaghetti culture. More specifically Venetian is polenta; the usual definition, "cornmeal mush," doesn't do justice to the dish, which comes in many different versions and should never be mushy but should possess an almost grainy texture. Polenta, once the staple food of frugal farmers who rarely saw meat or fish on their tables, now usually accompanies such Venetian delights as liver broiled with onions (*fegato alla veneta*), venison, codfish, or inky squid. Scampi, sole, and other seafood are superlative from Trieste to Chioggia. The red salad from Treviso, *radicchio*, has lately become popular also in the United States.

The best-known Venetian wines are velvety red Valpolicella and white or red Merlot vintages. Try also gentle Soave from the vast vineyards near Verona, rich red Refosco, and dry white Riesling.

Venice is the obvious starting point and base for exploring the region. One suggested trip is to Padua, Adria, and Chioggia (or vice versa). Or visit Trieste, and proceed from there to Udine and Cividale del Friuli. Asolo, Bassano del Grappa, Treviso, and Vicenza are fairly close together, easily reachable from either Venice or Padua.

5

There are good routes also to Cortina d'Ampezzo in the Dolomites and to the towns in South Tyrol, or Alto Adige—Ortisei, Bressanone, Bolzano, and Merano. You can then return to Venice, or go on to Milan by way of Trent, Rovereto, and Verona.

PADUA (PADOVA) ▪

Many travelers are so impatient to get to Venice and so reluctant to leave it that they will hardly spare any time for Padua, only half an hour by train or car to the west. Or maybe they grudgingly stop here just to glimpse the Basilica of St. Anthony, Donatello's statue of Gattamelata outside of it, and the nearby canals and streets before hurrying on.

Old yet lively, Padua deserves more attention. Not only is it a religious shrine but it has for many centuries been famous for its scholarship and art, and today it is the foremost business center of the Venetian region. Much more ancient than Venice, it has long and profitably lived in the shadow of the "Queen of the Adriatic." Today Padua keeps growing far beyond its old bastions and has reached a population of 250,000, while fewer than 80,000 people still live permanently in the Lagoon City. But unlike Mestre, Venice's unsightly outgrowth on the mainland, Padua possesses genuine charm. The arms of the Bacchiglione River, flowing through the city, and a few canals provide Venetian vistas. Religion, pride in history, intellectual achievements, and, yes, money contribute to Padua's self-assured mood.

The city's university is one of the oldest in Europe, and still one of Italy's main institutions of higher learning. Quite a number of doctors who practice in the United States are graduates of its medical school. All of Padua's many thousand students live off campus, a large part of them commuting from Venice and other environs. In the 1970s Paduans were frightened by the extreme militancy of many students and of a few teachers of the local university. Some were arrested and sentenced to jail terms for terrorism. The town-gown tensions have since then eased markedly.

Padua's university was founded in 1222, when a group of professors of law and their students moved here from Bologna, a famous seat of medieval learning. Soon medicine, philosophy, theology, and other disciplines too were taught in Padua. Petrarch and Galileo were associated with the university, and students from all over the continent and the British Isles flocked to it. Shakespeare, in *The Taming of the Shrew*, called Padua a "nursery of arts."

Some time after 1493 the governors of the university bought a stately building at the center, the Hostel of the Bo. A guest house for ambassadors and other distinguished visitors, the place had been named after its business sign in the shape of an ox (*bò* in the local dialect). It became the central seat of the university and still has this function. The chief entrance on Via Otto Febbraio carries an old inscription: "Enter to become every day more learned; go out to be more useful day by day to the country and to Christian society."

The walls of the arcaded courtyard, the staircase, and the principal hall are covered with the coats of arms of university dignitaries from 1542 to 1688, when all available space was taken up. The anatomical theater, built in 1594, with six wooden tiers seating 300 students around a dissecting table, is intact. Near the main hall stands a wooden pulpit with nine steps, from which Galileo lectured on physics between 1592 and 1610.

Diagonally opposite "the Bo" is the Caffè Pedrocchi, a landmark that has recently been restored to its old splendor. When a local entrepreneur, Antonio Pedrocchi, opened it in a neoclassical building in 1831 it was praised as the most eloquent coffeehouse in all of Europe.

With its stone lions and Doric columns, and with the immaculate table linen in its Green, White and Red rooms (Italy's national colors), today the Caffè Pedrocchi is a hangout for well-to-do Paduans. A cappuccino at the standup counter doesn't cost more than it would in any other local espresso bar.

A few steps from the old coffeehouse is the sixteenth-century city hall, with a modern addition. Walk past it to Piazza delle Frutta (Fruit Square). The huge edifice between that piazza and Piazza delle Erbe (Vegetables Square) with a colorful outdoor market is the Palazzo della Ragione (Palace of Reason). The thirteenth-century structure, which looks like an overturned boat, was the seat of the law courts and meeting place of the popular assembly of the free republic of

Padua before the city came under Venice's domination in 1405. The arcaded upper floor forms a single hall, 266 feet long and 89 feet wide, now used for exhibitions, fairs, and concerts.

Farther to the west is the solemn Piazza dei Signori (Square of the Lords) with a column carrying the winged lion of St. Mark, the symbol of Venice, in front of the former palace of the Venetian governor, with a huge clock in a square tower. The sixteenth-century cathedral of Padua and a thirteenth-century brick baptistery are in the same part of the city.

Much more interesting are two churches in the north of Padua's historical center, in a park around the ruins of a Roman amphitheater. The size of its arena indicates the wealth and importance of the city, Patavium, in antiquity. (The historian Livy was its most famous son.) The small Scrovegni Chapel, also known as the Church of the Madonna dell'Arena, boasts the earliest preserved frescoes by Giotto and his pupils. Painted sometime between 1302 and 1306, the celebrated panels tell the history of the Redemption in thirty-four episodes, from the Birth of Mary to the Last Judgment.

The Church of the Eremitani (hermits) on the southern edge of the arena park contains fragments of early frescoes by Andrea Mantegna that were saved when the church was heavily damaged in a 1944 air raid. Mantegna (1431–1506), who came from a town near Vicenza, studied in Padua, married the daughter of the Venetian painter Jacopo Bellini, and became a leader of the Paduan school of painting. His main works are, however, in Milan, Mantua, and other cities rather than in Padua. The copy of a Mantegna fresco of St. Anthony and St. Bernardino holding the monogram of Christ fills the lunette above the main portal of the Basilica of St. Anthony; the detached original is in the Antonian Museum adjoining the church.

Paduans call the large, Oriental-looking edifice enclosing the tomb of St. Anthony simply Il Santo ("The Saint"). Many thousands of pilgrims from all over the world come to see it year after year. St. Anthony, born in Lisbon in 1195, became a follower of St. Francis of Assisi, preached in Africa, and lived in Padua only a short time before his death in 1231. He is nevertheless revered as St. Anthony of Padua, the patron saint of the city, a legendary figure and miracle worker.

His church was built between 1232 and 1307. The sanctuary, floodlit at night, is a Gothic basilica with two slender bell towers, a conical roof and six domes similar to those of St. Mark's in Venice. In the piazza outside, pilgrims buy candles to be lit in front of St. Anthony's altar and take snapshots of one another and of the innumerable pigeons, which expect to be fed by them.

Near the left side of the church's façade rises the monument of Gattamelata ("Tigercat"); this was the nickname of the fifteenth-century condottiere Erasmo da Narni, who served the Republic of Venice as commander in chief of its army for a few years. When the memorial was erected in 1453, ten years after the generalissimo's death, it was the first equestrian statue cast in bronze since antiquity. Donatello, the Florentine artist, represented Gattamelata as a battle-hardened military leader whose life-size figure rides haughtily on a giant horse like a Roman Caesar.

St. Anthony's sepulcher is in the Chapel of the Saint in the left transept of the basilica. High reliefs depict scenes from the saint's life and miracles attributed to him. (In one of the episodes in relief on the chapel walls, St. Anthony discovers a stone instead of a heart in the dead body of a miser—an allusion to the Paduans' reputed passion for amassing money?) The altar, in white and black marble, is cluttered with votive tablets and testimonials from devotees of the saint. There is also a large box for offerings "to St. Anthony."

Artists from the Renaissance to the present time have contributed paintings, sculptures, and other decorations to the basilica. A series of frescoes with sequences from St. Anthony's life by Titian and his pupils adorns the walls of the School of the Saint, the meeting hall of a medieval brotherhood in a large, cloistered structure on the right (south) side of the church. The building includes also the Antonian Museum, containing objects from the basilica. Nearby is the Civic Museum, occupying rooms around the cloister of a former convent, with an archaeological section, a Crucifixion fresco by Giotto that has been detached from the Scrovegni Chapel, and paintings by Jacopo and Giovanni Bellini, Paolo Veronese, Tintoretto, and Giovanni Battista Tiepolo.

The wide open space to the southeast of "The Saint"—with parking lots—has been a recreation and meeting place of the Paduans since antiquity. Known as the Prato della Valle (Meadow of the Valley), it surrounds a park with old plane trees on an oval artificial island, enclosed by a circular canal with four bridges and lined with statues of mythical and historical figures. Old houses stand around the square, which is dominated by the multidomed Renaissance church of the Abbey of St. Giustina, which is about as big as the Basilica of St. Anthony but more austere.

Local tour operators conduct side trips to Petrarch's house at Arquà Petrarca, a village in the hills southwest of Padua, and to the celebrated Venetian villas, many of which were designed by Palladio (*see* Vicenza).

ADRIA ▪

When I visited Italy for the first time, as an eighteen-year-old hitch-hiker, I took an immediate liking to this little town that gave the Adriatic Sea its name. I arrived in Adria from Venice toward the end of the first week of my grand tour and was nearly overwhelmed by the friendliness of the people here. It was the late afternoon of a hot day in July, and I must have looked dusty and tired after marching for hours on the road southward from the rim of the Venetian lagoon. A group of men who were sitting outside a tavern asked me to have a glass of wine with them; they wanted to know where I was coming from, insisted that I share some salami with them, and inquired whether I liked their country. Very much so, I said. When I got going again after about an hour my legs were a bit wobbly, but my Italian had remarkably improved.

A woman stopped me, and said, "Do you have a place to sleep?" I told her I didn't, and was looking for a cheap inn; she directed me to a convent. The good friars put me up in a vacant cell and gave me dinner. I still recall the hard crust of their white bread, their delicious thick soup, and their deep-red wine to wash down their cheese. When I took my leave after coffee early next morning, the friars didn't want any payment, and I put a token silver coin into their almsbox. Adria can't have been seeing many foreigners then.

I never forgot the hospitable town. When I came back many years later, Adria had hardly changed, and it still doesn't see many tourists. It now numbers 20,000 inhabitants, only a few thousand more than when I first was there. And Adria is still suffused with the mainland-Venetian charm that had captivated me the first time—the graceful bell towers of the churches, the plain but dignified low houses along the Canal Bianco (White Canal) with its bridges, the good-natured banter of people who are used to spending a lot of their time outdoors, the singsong of their soft dialect.

The Canal Bianco is one of several manmade waterways in the plains between the Po and Adige rivers; it runs from Mantua to the Po delta, bisecting Adria in the same manner that the Grand Canal, on a much more impressive scale, cuts across Venice. Adria is a little Venice; in fact, it was the Venice of the ancients.

What is now Adria was about 2,500 years ago a thriving harbor city on a sandy island in a lagoon at the estuaries of the Adige and the Po. The Etruscans who settled here between the sixth and fifth centuries B.C. traded with Greece, the Greek city-states in Sicily, and other places around the Mediterranean.

Beautiful Greek vases as well as ancient pottery of diverse origin have been found in and near Adria. Much of this material is on display in the National Archaeological Museum that was opened in 1961. Its address: 1 Square of the Estruscans. Every now and then some old copper coin bearing the inscription "HATR" is dug up some-where around Adria; the letters stand for Hatria, the Etruscan name of the ancient seafaring and commercial city. The arm of the Medi-terranean between Italy and the Balkan Peninsula was for the ancients the Sea of Hatria, the Adriatic.

Today Adria is twelve miles inland. Old sand dunes can still be seen at the approaches to the town, but the silt of the rivers has through the centuries pushed the lagoons and the coast far out to the east.

The lowlands between the Po and the Adige are known as the Polesine, a paradise for fishing enthusiasts and waterfowl hunters. The plains, crisscrossed by canals and dotted with water pockets, have often been flooded in the past, and the high dikes of the two main rivers require constant maintenance. The old Republic of Venice to which the area belonged for hundreds of years set up a special flood-control body, the Magistracy of the Waters, which is still func-tioning.

The administrative center of the Polesine is Rovigo, fourteen miles west of Adria. This quiet provincial capital with a population of 50,000 derives much of its income from the sugarbeet fields all around it and from big sugar refineries in the area. Two brick towers, one tall and the other short and slightly leaning, the remnants of a tenth-century castle in the west of the city, are its main landmarks. From the fifteenth century onward Rovigo was ruled by the Republic of Venice until Napoleon took over. The symbol of Venetian dominance, the winged lion of St. Mark on a column, still stands in the city's main square, Piazza Vittorio Emanuele.

Paintings by Venetian and other masters can be seen in the picture gallery in the building of the sixteenth-century Accademia dei Concordi, a learned society, in the same square. Not far from it, toward Rovigo's modern northern district, is the Church of Our Lady of Succor, generally called La Rotonda ("The Round One") because of its octagonal shape. It was designed by Francesco Zamberlan, a disciple of Palladio. The walls of the interior are all covered with large canvases by Baroque painters, with no space between them, like banks of television monitors. The intention must have been to add a relentlessly visual dimension to worship.

CHIOGGIA ▪

This tightly packed island town is a smaller, older, poorer version of Venice, from which it can be reached by boat in an hour or so. When genre paintings were still much in demand, practitioners of the art used to flock to Chioggia (KYOH-djah) to fill their canvases with fishermen repairing their nets or caulking their boats and women gossiping and doing needlework in seedily picturesque side alleys. Such outdoor scenes still characterize everyday life here, although the genre painters are rare now.

Something has nevertheless changed lately. The once ramshackle fishing village of Sottomarina on a spit of the mainland east of Chioggia, which is linked with it by a bridge, has developed into a beach resort with hotels and other businesses, providing a new source of income for the area. Instead of the painters, camera-wielding guests of what is now called Lido di Sottomarina come to town to snap pictures of its old harbor, its canals with humpbacked Venetian bridges, and its huddling, dilapidated houses on the canals and alleys.

Exploring some corners of Chioggia is like a return into the world of the eighteenth-century commedia dell'arte, with its stock characters and predictable situations caused by the interplay of elementary motives and passions—love, jealousy, greed, envy, pride, cunning, and hypocrisy—of highly articulate people who know one another all too well. True, to savor fully the pungent talk of Chioggia one would have to be a Venetian.

One of the classics of the Venetian theater, Carlo Goldoni's *Le Baruffe Chiozzote* (*The Chioggia Quarrels*), is set in the old town; for its humor it borrows heavily from its peculiar dialect, which is saltier than that of Venice. The comedy, first performed in 1762, is little more than the incessant chatter of the women in a small band of Chioggia fishermen. Checca and Lucietta, Toffolo and Titta-Nanna are jealous of each other, and when knives are pulled as a result of all the gossip, tragedy looms; but then everything adjusts itself and a double wedding is the conclusion. The talk of the women, like the chorus in ancient Greek drama, accompanies whatever action there is.

Chioggia's name is derived from Fossa Clodia, the name of a canal that one of several Roman statesmen and officials called Clodius or Claudius (which one is uncertain) had built. A fishermen's town existed on the island near the canal long before people from the mainland, fleeing from invaders, settled on the Rivus Altus (Rialto) and neighboring lagoon islands in the ninth century A.D., founding the kernel of what was to become Venice. As its power rose, the Republic of Venice took control of Chioggia. For centuries Venice relied on Chioggia for a good deal of the salt, fish, and vegetables it needed. Even today much of the seafood served in restaurants in Venice has been brought in by Chioggia fishermen, and the salad has been grown on the mainland fields south of the old town.

At present Chioggia and Lido di Sottomarina together have about 50,000 permanent residents. Boats from Venice arrive at Piazza Vigo, facing the lagoon, with the winged lion of St. Mark on a column recalling who was once in power here. A high bridge across the La Vena (literally, "The Vein") canal leads to the broad main street with the town hall, the post office, a pawnshop, and a former granary. At the south end of the main street is an interesting group of three brick buildings—the large cathedral, which in the seventeenth century was rebuilt by the Venetian architect Baldassare Longhena; a 197-foot-high campanile; and a small gothic church, San Martino, from the end of the fourteenth century. Another old church, San Domenico, on the town's north side, treasures a representation of St. Paul by the Venetian painter Vittore Carpaccio, dated 1520, reputedly his last work.

TRIESTE ▪

A Latin inscription on a neoclassical building in Piazza della Borsa, the Old Stock Exchange, describes this seaport city as the "ultimate recess of the Adriatic Sea." It is also a far corner of Italy about which surprisingly little is heard or known elsewhere in the nation or abroad. Only ninety miles east of Venice, which is packed with tourists from spring to fall and again at Carnival time, Trieste, in contrast, is today leading a wistful existence heavy with nostalgia for bygone days when the city and its excellent harbor were a bustling, prosperous emporium for Central Europe.

Now many of the dockside cranes are rusting, and the harbor often looks empty. Air traffic has ended Trieste's former role as a home port for big passenger ships, while seaports elsewhere in Italy and in neighboring Yugoslavia, and even such distant competitors as Rotterdam and Hamburg, have taken away much cargo business.

Many of the 270,000 inhabitants of present-day Trieste manage nevertheless to live quite well. They import coffee for roasters and espresso bars all over Italy, write insurance policies for faraway clients, and sell shoes and trendy clothes to Yugoslavians who come from across the nearby border for a day's shopping. The city, with a good university and an international institute of theoretical physics, is also seeking new importance as a center for scientific research.

However, there seem to be more older people in Trieste than can be seen in other Italian cities, and its tempo is markedly slower. People sit for hours in coffeehouses the way they do in Vienna, and don't do in Milan or Rome. Bookstores devote much of their window space to reminiscences about the Habsburgs and their era. Every summer an operetta festival, unique in Italy, features the classics by Johann Strauss, Jr., Léhar, Kálmán, and the other masters of the Danube school of escapist music. The city's cuisine is a cosmopolitan blend of Italian, Viennese, Hungarian, and Balkan cooking.

Yet despite all the lingering influences from Central Europe, nobody can accuse the Triestines of lacking in patriotism. Italian national feeling has always been ardent among them. The process of Italy's national unification was regarded as complete only when the maritime city, together with Trent in the Alps (*"Trento e Trieste!"*) passed under Rome's sovereignty at the end of World War I.

The city's splendid main square, open toward the sea at its northwest side, is called Piazza dell'Unità d'Italia (Square of Italy's Unity). A nearby pier jutting out into the harbor is named after the destroyer *Audace*, which landed the first Italian soldiers in 1918; the pier is now a favorite promenade of the Triestines in summer evenings. Piazza dell'Unità, as it is called for short, is Trieste's administrative, business, and social center. It is bordered on the north by the prefecture (the office representing the central government), on the east by the nineteenth-century city hall, and on the south by the headquarters of the Lloyd Triestino Shipping Company. During the warm months the tables of three cafés take up part of the square. The Caffè degli Specchi on the prefecture side of the piazza is one of Italy's most renowned places for coffee and ice cream.

Walk from the square across Piazza della Borsa to Corso Italia, a main artery from which the ruins of a Roman amphitheater are visible. Steep streets lead up to an old castle and to the Cathedral of San Giusto, consecrated to the patron saint of Trieste, St. Justus. The fortresslike fourteenth-century church, combining the remains of two earlier basilicas, rises on the site of a Roman temple. The five-nave interior is austerely Romanesque, the façade Venetian Gothic.

Downtown, the Theresan Borough northeast of Piazza dell'Unità is a neighborhood of stately buildings with streets in a grid pattern laid out during the reign of the eighteenth-century Empress Maria Theresa. A Triestine author and poet, Carolus von Cergoly, writing in Italian, said that Maria Theresa had "invented" Trieste. Although she never visited the city, she is credited with the enlargement of its seaport, the construction of the neighborhood that carries her name, improvements in public education, and the lifting of constraints that up to then had forced Trieste's Jewish community to live in a ghetto.

The Theresan Borough is bisected by the Grand Canal, an artificial inlet dug to permit ships to sail right into the business center. Today the canal serves as a marina for fishing boats and pleasure craft. A well-stocked outdoor market is held on working days on the south side of the canal. A fish market in a large hall on the waterfront south of Piazza dell'Unità and the Aquarium in the same building give an idea of the rich marine fauna of the Adriatic.

The Civic Museum on the Hill of San Giusto contains antiquities, medieval and Renaissance paintings, and a Chinese and Japanese section that is evidence of Trieste's past maritime and cultural links with East Asia. The Museo Revoltella near the Aquarium is one of Italy's better modern art collections. Close by is a marine museum with exhibits regarding sea life, fisheries, and harbor engineering.

Trieste's many restaurants, some among the best of them confusingly called "Buffet," are a major attraction. Their cuisine is eclectic: richly garnished pasta, polenta from the adjacent Friuli region, mushrooms from Slovenia, scampi and many kinds of fish, Hungarian-style goulash, schnitzel, pork, and venison, all topped off with rich strudels and cakes. A local specialty, eaten mainly in the cold months, is *jota*, a thick soup based on potatoes and sauerkraut.

The wines that Triestines like best are Prosecco from the vineyards of a neighboring town of that name, Merlot, Refosco, and other vintages from Friuli. Trieste is also a brewery city with quite a few beer gardens.

A side trip to Miramare Castle is obligatory. This white structure, in a terraced park on a wooded promontory five miles west of Trieste, is a marvelous piece of kitsch with a romantic history. The castle was built between 1854 and 1860 for Archduke Maximilian and his wife, Princess Carlotta of Belgium, who lived there for four years before the Habsburg prince was persuaded by Emperor Napoleon III of France to accept the crown as emperor of Mexico. Republicans led by the Mexican national hero Benito Juárez captured and executed Maximilian in 1867.

The sad story of Maximilian and his empress is told in various languages in a taped Sound and Light show in the Miramare park on summer evenings. The castle can be visited all year. The rooms that are shown are exactly as they were when the princely couple were living there, with precious furniture, Chinese vases, a billiard hall, a chapel, and many paintings. The route from Trieste to Miramare along the rocky waterfront and the adjoining Bay of Gargano teems in summer with sun worshippers, bathers, and boaters.

UDINE ▪

The administrative center of the Friuli region in Italy's northeast is an insider's tip. Spreading from its central castle hill and green church domes in all directions with long streets and low buildings, Udine isn't exactly overrun by foreign tourists. Its architecture, Tiepolo frescoes, and other art, as well as the cordial ways of its inhabitants and Friulan cuisine and wines, will captivate visitors and may prompt them to stay on for a while, and perhaps explore the surroundings.

The foothills of the Alps are near, and a stupendous panorama of high Alpine peaks and ranges to the north can be seen on clear days from the tower of Udine's castle. Good flat farmland stretches toward south and west.

In May 1976 the northern part of Friuli was devastated by a catastrophic earthquake that took more than 1,000 lives. The destruction was most severe in and near the small town of Gemona, seventeen miles to the north, but many buildings were damaged also in Udine. Reconstruction was quick and thorough; the Friulans have always taken pride in their gusto for hard work and self-help. Today Gemona, on a slope, is a town of new quakeproof buildings, few higher than two stories. Almost no trace of the 1976 disaster is visible in Udine.

Regionalism in the area has increasingly been stressed lately, and the Friulan dialect, hard to understand even for other Italians, is being promoted by Udine intellectuals as an emerging separate language with claims to official recognition.

Udine offers vistas reminiscent of Venetian canals, in those neighborhoods through which branches of the Torre River flow past arcaded houses.

The small hill in the middle of the city that rises from the plain is an artificial mound that Attila the Hun had raised so that he could see Aquileia burn, people in Udine will tell you. Attila did take Aquileia, twenty miles to the southeast, in A.D. 452, and presumably watched the destruction of that once proud city, the "Second Rome." However, geologists have found that Udine's castle hill was not piled up artificially but has existed at least since the Ice Age. The flat space northeast of the elevation, now Piazza Primo Maggio, with old plane trees in a vast park, was once a swamp. Here, according to local lore, Attila's slaves dug up the earth and stones for the Hun king's lookout.

The hill that Attila may or may not have climbed can now be reached over a steep path with porticoes starting from an archway designed by Palladio.

The castle on top, in its present imposing form, was built in the sixteenth century to replace an older structure. It was the seat of the officials representing the Republic of Venice, to which Udine had belonged since 1420. The castle, which was damaged in the 1976 earthquake, contains a council chamber with faded frescoes by Giovanni Battista Tiepolo, the eighteenth-century Venetian Baroque painter. More works by him, by Vittore Carpaccio, and by other Venetian masters can be seen in the Civic Museum, which was reorganized after the earthquake. The Church of Santa Maria, slightly below the castle, was built in the thirteenth century and remodeled in the sixteenth century. A statue of the archangel Gabriel crowns its campanile.

Piazza della Libertà at the foot of the south side of the castle hill, the civic center of Udine, is an admirable Renaissance square. Its city hall, also known as the Loggia of Lionello (after the architect who built it in the second half of the fifteenth century), seems a copy of the Doges' Palace in Venice. A clock tower rising from the nearby Loggia di San Giovanni, of the sixteenth century, features two dark bronze figures, locally known as "the Moors," that strike the hours like those in St. Mark's Square in Venice. Two huge marble statues in front of the clock tower represent Hercules and a fire-breathing mythological giant, Cacus. There are also a Renaissance fountain and the standard column with the winged lion of St. Mark that used to signal Venetian rule.

A brief walk from Piazza della Libertà leads to the cathedral, a Romanesque-Gothic edifice with a Baroque interior and an unfinished six-sided bell tower. Behind the cathedral is the small Church of Purity, with frescoes by Giovanni Battista Tiepolo and his son Giovanni Domenico.

Udine's most famous Tiepolos are in the Archiepiscopal Palace on Piazza del Patriarcato, across a park east of the cathedral. The name of the square recalls the patriarchs of Aquileia, once the paramount Christian prelates in northeastern Italy, who resided in Udine from 1238 to 1752. (After the destruction of Aquileia, the seat of the patriarchate had first moved to Cividale del Friuli.)

The role of the patriarchs of Aquileia in the Roman Catholic Church was eventually taken over by the patriarchs of Venice. Portraits of all the patriarchs, archbishops, and bishops who resided in Udine may be seen in the Throne Room of the Baroque palace. The Tiepolo frescoes, commissioned by the patriarchs, include *The Fall of the Angels* in the staircase, *The Judgment of Solomon* on the ceiling of the Red Room, and *Abraham's Sacrifice* on a gallery ceiling.

The historical center of Udine is surrounded by army barracks and by manufacturing plants that turn out anything from shoes to appliances. The city, population about 100,000, lives well. Its eating places and taverns fill up early. Restaurant menus will almost always feature polenta, the yellow or white cornmeal mush that is the regional staple food. Polenta may accompany fowl, venison, calf's liver, and about any other meat, or codfish; it is also, with red wine butter and fried onions or with tomato sauce, a dish by itself.

The wines are red Merlot and Refosco, "black" or "gray" Pinot, and white Traminer and Tocai, the latter pressed from the local version of the Hungarian Tokay grapes. Full-bodied Refosco, which doesn't travel too well, can be outstanding when drunk in its home region. Udine is the place for doing just that.

CIVIDALE DEL FRIULI ∎

Gathered around its monumental cathedral and central piazza, this quiet town lies amid rolling farmland and vineyards near the foothills of the Julian Alps in a corner of northeastern Italy. Cividale del Friuli has inherited architectural treasures from an illustrious past, and apart from them it is also a most attractive place to stay a few days to savor Italian provincial life of a placidity that has vanished elsewhere in the country.

In summer the banks of the Natisone River, which skirts the old neighborhoods, become the townspeople's riviera for sunbathing and an occasional dip into the cold water. Many streets and riverside promenades afford glimpses of the verdant hills nearby. The pace of small-town life is unhurried.

"Friuli" in the town's official name denotes its region; it is derived from Cividale's resounding appellation in antiquity, Forum Iulii, the marketplace of Julius. The Julius in question was Julius Caesar, who apparently raised the status of an already existing community by proclaiming it a colony of Rome. (There was also another Forum Iulii, now Fréjus in southern France.) As the Roman Empire declined, the town that great Caesar had favored unhappily found itself on a main route of the barbarian invasions. Longobard, and after them Frankish, dukes lorded over the town and its region. Eventually the patriarchs of Aquileia, prelates who wielded also temporal powers, installed themselves here after their original see, Aquileia on the Adriatic seashore, had been destroyed. Forum Iulii had long become Cividale, whose name derives from the Latin word for "citizenship" or "towns-folk" (*civitas*), by the time it surrendered to the Republic of Venice in 1419. Today Cividale has a population of 15,000.

The most important monument in the town and indeed in the entire Friuli region is the Tempietto, or Little Temple, the remains of a church that was built as part of a nunnery 1,100 years ago or even earlier. A flood wrecked much of the edifice later; the surviving front portion with its reliefs and frescoes is a prime example of the primitive art of the Longobards, the Germanic people who overran northern Italy in the sixth century. The ruined Longobard church is on the right bank of the Natisone. A little upstream is the so-called Devil's Bridge, whose middle pillar rests on a rock jutting out from the riverbed. Near the bridge, on the left bank, is the Church of St. Martin, which dates from the eighth century and contains an altar with Longobard reliefs.

Cividale's 500-year-old cathedral is a blend of late Gothic and early Renaissance styles with a campanile added in the seventeenth century. Some Longobard art from the Middle Ages can be seen in the cathedral's solemn interior and in its museum. An archaic church rite, the Emperor's Mass or Sword Mass, is performed in the cathedral at Epiphany (January 6) every year. A cleric, wearing a plumed helmet, carries a missal in his left hand and blesses the congregation with a sword that he holds in his right. The ceremony recalls the investiture of the former patriarchs by their secular overlords, the Germanic emperors. Roman and medieval antiquities and memora-bilia connected with the patriarchate of Aquileia are displayed in the

National Archaeological Museum in the Palazzo Nordis on the cathedral square.

It is in this large piazza that many residents meet at least once every day for an *aperitivo*, espresso, or gelato, and for a leisurely chat. Visitors too will be drawn to the cathedral square before or after a meal in one of Cividale's restaurants, a few of which are remarkably sophisticated. (For the cuisine of Friuli see the description of Udine.) On many evenings the local taverns are crowded with soldiers. The Yugoslav frontier is close, and Italy keeps some of its best troops in this area. The parents, wives, or girlfriends of officers and soldiers account for much of the business in the few local hotels and inns.

ASOLO ▪

Sitting on three gentle ridges like Siena but very much smaller than the Tuscan city, this ancient town with its solemn cypress trees, its everchanging vistas, its memories of past loves, and its well-cultivated sense of exclusivity is to its devotees the most romantic spot on the Venetian mainland, if not in all of Italy. When I once asked a friend what attracted him to Asolo year after year he explained: "The beauty and the quiet for a few weeks at least. I can take a dozen different strolls and look at the marvelous hills and the countryside, the villas and the gardens always from a new angle. By now I know the town house by house, and a lot of its people too. The Asolans are friendly, but they leave you alone. And no mobs of noisy, vulgar tourists." If this sounds elitist, my friend meant to sound so.

English artists and aesthetes have been among Asolo's habitués ever since Robert Browning with his wife, Elizabeth Barrett, a poet in her own right, took a liking to the place and spent long periods in it. Browning was inspired by the town to write *Asolando*. Eleanora Duse (1859–1924), the great actress, lived here for some time and wanted to be buried in Asolo. Her simple tombstone is in the hillside churchyard of Sant'Anna.

A square near the town hall is named after La Duse's narcissistic friend, the poet Gabriele D'Annunzio. Another poet, Giosuè Car-

21

ducci, celebrated Asolo as "town of a hundred horizons." Igor Stravinsky too was captivated by the Asolan atmosphere.

Much earlier in its long history, at the height of the Renaissance, Asolo was even the residence of a queen who presided at a shadow court here. The town, it is true, was no more than a comfortable exile to Caterina Cornaro, who then styled herself "Queen of Cyprus, Jerusalem, and Armenia, and Lady of Asolo."

The daughter of one of the great merchant-statesmen of the Venetian Republic, Caterina was fourteen years old when she was betrothed to Jacques II Lusignan, king of Cyprus, who was to be the last sovereign of the Crusader dynasties in the Levant. Four years, a humiliating wait for Caterina, passed before King Jacques got around to sending for his bride and making her his queen. In Nicosia, the capital of Cyprus, the blonde Venetian beauty found herself in the vortex of cabals and poison plots. In 1473 King Jacques died under murky circumstances, and his widow attempted to hold on to his throne. After a tumultuous reign of fifteen years the Republic of Venice forced her to abdicate and proceeded to control Cyprus directly.

Ex-Queen Caterina was assigned to Asolo as her new realm. She took her part as ruler of the town and its environs seriously, heard court cases, and aided the poor. She would entertain prominent contemporaries, among whom was Pietro Cardinal Bembo, a humanist who wrote *The Asolans* in praise of the town. Gossip in Venice had it that Caterina, who was still attractive, was having dalliances with a series of lovers on the side.

The castle in which Queen Caterina resided is a medieval structure with a massive, rectangular clock tower. The building, which underwent several changes before, during, and after her sojourn, now includes a theater dedicated to Eleanora Duse. Occasional dramatic performances bring spectators from Venice, Treviso, Padua, and other nearby cities.

The battlemented walls on top of the hill overlooking Asolo are the remains of another medieval fortress, known as La Rocca (The Rock). Long stretches of old walls surround the town. Excavations have proved that the hillside was inhabited already in prehistoric times.

The parish church was built during the Middle Ages on the ruins of ancient Roman baths, and was given a thorough overhaul in the

Baroque manner during the eighteenth century. An early Lorenzo Lotto, *The Assumption of the Virgin* (1506), is among the old paintings in the bright interior.

The arcaded north side of the church faces a sloping square with a fountain carrying the symbol of Venetian rule, the winged lion of St. Mark. The water for the fountain is supplied by a still-functioning ancient Roman aqueduct. In the west of the piazza is the Loggia del Capitano or Loggia della Ragione, the former town hall; the two façades of the fifteenth-century building are covered with faded frescoes. The structure, with graceful ground-floor arches, now houses the Civic Museum. It contains prehistoric material, archaeological finds, portraits of Queen Caterina and autographs by her, Browning memorabilia, and an Eleanora Duse room.

The house of the Brownings, at 153 Via Robert Browning near the southern town gate, is distinguished by a fountain on its street wall dated 1571, an Asolo landmark. The water spouts from a faun's head into an ornate stone basin. An enameled sign warns that it is "prohibited to water quadrupeds" at the fountain, although in times of old it must have slaked the thirst of countless horses that had pulled carriages from the plains up into town.

The stately building at 306 Contrada Canova where Eleanora Duse lived is marked by a plaque with a D'Annunzio inscription. Nearby is a small deluxe hotel, Villa Cipriani, with a magnificent view of its descending gardens, the Asolan hills, and the lowlands stretching south.

In the studiedly old-fashioned shops under the medieval arcades of Asolo's few streets and squares, the browser finds boutique bric-à-brac and fancily priced brand-name items.

The eighteenth-century Palazzo Beltramini, which wouldn't disfigure Venice's Grand Canal, is now the mayor's office, administering to the town's 7,000 residents. Many of these live in their villas and houses only some months every year but consider the town their real home. The Asolans seem determined to keep the standoffish character of the place the way it is now. There are comparatively few espresso bars, taverns and restaurants, and none of the bazaarlike souvenir stands that today mar all too many Italian resorts. Tourist coaches are banned from the town and must park at some distance from its southern gate; all other motor vehicles are forbidden to enter Asolo on weekends.

BASSANO DEL GRAPPA ▪

When Italians hear *"grappa"* they think first of a potent, colorless brandy based on fermented grape pulp, and only afterward, perhaps, of a mountain massif in their country's northeast that was fiercely contested in a series of World War I battles. In Bassano one is constantly reminded of either meaning of the word.

From the north the 5,827-foot-high Monte Grappa overlooks the pretty and welcoming town of 40,000 people on the Brenta River. A thirty-seven-mile-long road with many bends leads from Bassano up to an ossuary where the remains of 25,000 Italian and Austro-Hungarian soldiers are guarded, and to a refuge below the summit. The panorama encompasses the Alps and, on clear days, Venice in the southeast.

As for the brandy, Bassano boasts some of Italy's most renowned *grappa* distilleries. Doing honor to their products, which may taste pungently clean or may come herb-flavored, is a local ritual at the end of a meal. The city is famous all over Venetia for good eating and drinking—for its pale and plump asparagus in spring, its polenta, its venison during the hunting season, its trout, and its red Merlot and other local wines in addition to *grappa*.

Bassano's landmark and symbol is the Ponte Vecchio (Old Bridge), a covered timber bridge spanning the Brenta. It is said to have been designed by Palladio (*see* Vicenza), although a wooden bridge existed at the site already in the Middle Ages. Palladian or not, the quaint structure was repeatedly swept away during river floods but was always renewed according to the original pattern, faithfully followed every time. As seen now, the bridge is only a few decades old.

The greater part of the city is on the east bank of the Brenta. The mood in the old neighborhoods, with their arcaded and frescoed houses on narrow streets and picturesque little squares, is unmistakably Venetian. Piazza Garibaldi, in the historic center, has on its north side the restored Tower of Ezzelino. A cruel despot who was born near Bassano, Ezzelino da Romano (1194–1259) was a supporter of Emperor Frederick II, and from his native stronghold made himself lord of Verona, Vicenza, and Padua.

The Civic Museum, southeast of Piazza Garibaldi, is noteworthy for its works by a family of painters who are collectively known as the Bassani. Most highly reputed among them is Jacopo da Ponte, called Bassano (1510–1592). The museum also contains collections of Alpine minerals and plants, archaeological finds, engravings by the famous Remondini print shop that flourished in Bassano in the seventeenth and eighteenth centuries, designs by the neoclassical sculptor Antonio Canova, and scale models of Monte Grappa and the Brenta Gorge.

The old cathedral and other churches in the city also treasure paintings by the Bassano clan. The cathedral was part of the Ezzelino castle complex, which was surrounded by three walls. The village of Romano d'Ezzelino, where the medieval tyrant was born, is a mile from Bassano's northeastern outskirts.

The broad Viale dei Martiri in Bassano commands fine views of the Sette Comuni (Seven Towns) on a high plateau to the left, the gorge of the Brenta Valley at the center, and Monte Grappa on the right. Asiago, the main town of the Sette Comuni, was destroyed during World War I and rebuilt afterward. It is now a summer and winter resort that can be reached from Bassano over twenty-three miles of mountain roads.

Pottery and other crafts that require a sure taste in addition to skills have been practiced in the area for centuries. Today Bassano and its surroundings are dotted with ceramics plants, quality print shops, furniture factories, ironwork establishments, and jewelers' workshops.

Admirers of Antonio Canova (1757–1822) may want to visit his birthplace, Possagno, at the foot of Monte Grappa at altitude 1,080 feet, ten miles northeast of Bassano. Canova's tomb is in a domed church that he had built at his own expense, a copy of the Pantheon in Rome. Many casts, models, and designs of Canova's sculptures can be viewed in the house where he was born.

TREVISO ▪

A French epic poem in the Age of Chivalry praised this city and its region as "joyous and amorous." Treviso still is. Visitors will be charmed by the smiling courtesy of many of the city's inhabitants and will note their unprovincial elegance. They have a reputation for being flirtatious but are also known as reliable. Generations ago, when this area of the Venetian mainland was rural and poor, and many people left to seek their fortune overseas, Trevisans were welcome immigrants to the United States and Latin America because they worked hard.

Now, industrial plants in Treviso's surroundings build machinery and furniture, weave textiles and produce building materials and paper. Many Trevisans are well-off and aren't cagey about showing it. A local schoolteacher reported: "The parents of my pupils often hold down two or three jobs, working like horses. Many have expensive cars, and our parent-teacher meetings in winter are full of mink coats."

With all the new affluence that has come since the 1950s, Treviso—today a city of close to 100,000—still has plenty of atmosphere. Its Renaissance walls and ramparts surrounding the historical center are nearly intact, surrounded by the Sile River and by canals. Thirteen city gates, some of them elaborate archways, and thirteen bridges lead to the new suburbs and to the highways radiating from Treviso. The Botteniga River flows across the old town to join the Sile near the southeastern bastion.

Treviso's waters are not stagnant like the canals in Venice; they keep moving. From the bridges at the center, freshwater fish can be seen playing. In the Middle Ages the mills of Treviso ground most of the flour for Venice, which lies only twenty miles to the south. Old paddle wheels still turn idly in canals at the side of passages in modern buildings, installed there as mobile memorials to Treviso's past as a mill town. Fog is frequent in all seasons.

Treviso was ruled by Venice from 1339 to 1797, and is thoroughly imbued with Venetian culture and customs. However, there are still architectural reminders of earlier communal independence. One of them is the Palazzo dei Trecento (Palace of the Three Hundred), built in 1184, where the Great Council of the town used to meet. The battlemented brick building, with an outside staircase, stands in a right angle to the old mayor's palace, which is surmounted by a tower. The brick structures take up two sides of the central Piazza dei Signori (Square of the Lords), much of which is occupied by the tables and gaudy umbrellas of a pair of cafés in the warm months.

The Loggia dei Cavalieri (Loggia of the Cavaliers) south of Piazza dei Signori is an arcaded, open one-story building from the thirteenth century where city notables gathered. At present it houses a permanent book fair. The city's cathedral, northwest of Piazza dei Signori, is a Renaissance edifice with a classical portico and three green-patinaed domes. An *Annunciation* over an altar is by Titian.

The Civic Museum, a ten-minute walk from the cathedral toward the northwest corner of the town walls, contains a portrait of a Dominican by Lorenzo Lotto (1480–1556), a native of Treviso. Aside from works by other Trevisan and Venetian painters, the museum also includes one of the richest archaeological collections in northern Italy.

Treviso is a city for strolling under the arcades of its many old houses, over the bridges across its rivers and canals, and on its northern ramparts with their panorama of the Alps. As soon as the weather turns mild in spring, espresso bars spill out onto sidewalks and squares, their tables inviting to a rest and a drink or snack. There are interesting old churches, and frescoes—some of them imitating tapestry—on many house walls. The fish market is held on a green island, the Pescheria, in the Botteniga River at the center of town.

Market stands and vegetable stores display *radicchio*, a reddish or purple leafy plant related to endive that is grown on the truck farms around the city and is the pride of Treviso. It has an agreeably bitter taste and is used for salads or grilled, or is cooked like cabbage as a dish by itself or served with beans, rice, potatoes, meat, or fish; it is also put on pizza as a topping. There is even a *radicchio*-flavored *grappa* (the colorless grape brandy of the Venetia and Friuli regions). *Radicchio* is available also in Milan, Rome, and other distant Italian cities, and is flown to New York for sale in specialty food stores, but it is fresher and tastier in Treviso. During a *radicchio* fair in December, restaurants in Treviso feature dishes based on the versatile plant.

Like Vicenza and Padua, Treviso is a convenient base for a tour of the Palladian villas on the Venetian mainland (*see* Vicenza). The nearby walled towns of Castelfranco Veneto and Cittadella are worth a visit too. Only half an hour distant from Venice, and linked with that city by frequent train and bus services, Treviso is a good place for spending the night whenever the Lagoon City is crowded with tourists and hotel space there is scarce.

VICENZA ▪

Few artists have been able to transform their birthplace into a memorial to themselves the way Andrea di Pietro, known as Palladio, did. In Vicenza, which stretches out at the foot of a verdant hill thirty-eight miles northwest of Venice, the cool elegance of Palladian architecture triumphs. The principal street, unbroken across the old town, is Corso Andrea Palladio, and it is lined with buildings by Vicenza's most famous son and by his followers. One of Palladio's most celebrated creations, the Basilica, dominates the city's main square, and La Rotonda, perhaps the best-known of his famous villas, stands amid trees and green fields on the outskirts.

The porticoes, stuccoed columns, and symmetric harmony of many buildings in and near Vicenza will strike Americans as familiar. They should. Palladian neoclassicism was championed in seventeenth-century England by Inigo Jones and Sir Christopher Wren; it strongly influenced Georgian architecture and was transplanted as Colonial style into North America. Thomas Jefferson's Monticello was a remote echo of Vicenza, as are countless courthouses, post offices, and banks all over the United States.

Today's Vicenza, a thriving city of 120,000, is the Italian capital of another applied art, gold working. In and around the city some 600 firms, a few with scores of workers and many others with only a handful, turn out rings, bracelets, chains, and other jewelry. Most of their production is shipped to foreign countries including the United States; as a gold-working center Vicenza supplies such gold-handling cities as New York, London, and Basel. Its periodic trade shows draw buyers from all over the world.

If you are not in the gold business, Vicenza will appeal to you mainly through its noble architecture, although the natural scenery of its surroundings and the warmth of its people also make it an attractive place. The Vicentine cuisine is one of the best in the region. A specialty is *baccalà alla vicentina* (baked codfish with polenta).

Palladio (1508–1580), the son of a carpenter, was fortunate both in having been born in a Venetian-ruled town where members of the nobility were rich and secure enough to build themselves sumptuous residences and in finding a generous patron. Count Giorgio Giovanni da Trissino, a Vicentine humanist, poet, and diplomat, gave the future architect his nickname ("Palladio" is derived from the name of Pallas Athene, the Greek goddess) and enabled him to study classical antiquity in Rome for two years. On his return home Palladio began building country houses for gentleman farmers, and eventually received commissions for city palaces, public buildings, and churches. He spent the last ten years of his life in Venice.

In Vicenza, which is often described as a "Venice without canals," signs identify the buildings by Palladio and by his disciples and successors, Vincenzo Scamozzi and Ottone Calderari. One of the master's finest town houses, the Palazzo Chiericati at the northeastern end of Corso Andrea Palladio, is now the Civic Museum. It contains archaeological and numismatic collections, rare Longobard art, and a picture gallery with works by Bartolomeo Montagna (1450–1523), the founder of the Vicentine school of painting, and by such Venetian masters as Giorgione, Titian, and Tintoretto.

Opposite the museum is the Teatro Olimpico, designed by Palladio for an "Olympic Academy" of humanists, completed by Scamozzi, and inaugurated during the Carnival of 1585 with Sophocles' *Oedipus Tyrannus.* Classical drama is still performed in the theater from time to time. The auditorium, rising in thirteen elliptic tiers to a balustrade with statues, seats 1,200. The fixed stage beyond the semi-oval orchestra pit represents a triumphal arch in honor of Hercules, with three openings showing views of an idealized city of Thebes in perspective with trompe-l'oeil techniques. The ceiling of the covered theater is adorned with stuccowork and frescoes. The Teatro Olimpico sits amid the remains of Venetian fortifications near the Bacchiglione River, which lazily skirts the old town.

Palladio's Basilica in the central Piazza dei Signori (Square of the Lords) is a secular, not a religious, structure. It is currently used for art shows and other cultural events. The Basilica is an opulent marble jacket around a medieval building in the Gothic style that once served as the town council hall; it had been deteriorating for some time when Palladio was called to rescue it. Cutout arcades on two floors, the lower Doric, the upper Ionic, allow glimpses of the older walls behind them. A balustrade on the top carries marble statues. Built as a meeting place for the notables of Vicenza, the Basilica was surmounted, rather disappointingly, by a wooden roof shaped like a boat's hull, keel upward. The roof was destroyed during an air raid

29

in World War II and has been replaced by a ribbed gray-green vault that isn't a better solution than the original.

A 270-foot-high slender tower (Torre dell'Orologio), slightly leaning, on the Basilica's left side was erected in the twelfth century as part of a noble family's residence; it was later purchased by the municipality, which had a large clock installed. Opposite the Basilica and the tower are the frescoed Baroque Monte di Pietà (pawnbrokers' building) and the unfinished Loggia del Capitano, which Palladio designed as the headquarters of the Venetian governor of the city.

The thoroughly Venetian character of the lengthy Piazza dei Signori is enhanced by two columns, one carrying the winged lion of St. Mark, the other a statue of the Redeemer, and by the tables of the outdoor cafés. There is also a statue of Palladio, put up in 1859.

The Gothic cathedral, a few hundred yards southwest of the main square, was built centuries before Palladio's time; a Renaissance choir and dome were added later. Another church, Santa Corona, near the Teatro Olimpico, is noteworthy for paintings of saints by Bartolomeo Montagna, a masterful *Baptism of Christ* by Giovanni Bellini, and an *Adoration of the Magi* by Paolo Veronese.

The hill overlooking Vicenza from the south, Mount Berico, is crowned with a pilgrimage church, Madonna del Monte (Our Lady of the Mountain). It can be reached from the Viale Venezia beyond the small Retrone River and beyond the tracks of the Venice-Verona railway line. Many pilgrims get out of their coaches and walk up along a 2,130-foot-long arcade, stopping at some of its 150 arches on the slope to say prayers. The arcade was built in the middle of the eighteenth century.

The church, at altitude 404 feet, almost 300 feet above the city, was erected in 1668; its architecture is inspired by Palladio's nearby villa La Rotonda. The green-domed edifice, with a red-brick campanile, incorporates an earlier Gothic sanctuary of the Virgin Mary. A vast space with a balustrade in front of the shrine wasn't laid out as a parking lot but is now being used as such. Known as the "Balcony of Vicenza," it commands a view encompassing the city below, with the cathedral and the roof of the Palladian Basilica standing out, the modern districts sprawling toward the north, the farmland and villages beyond them, and the Alps on the horizon.

The Villa Rotonda, started by Palladio in 1550 and completed by Scamozzi, is in a valley about a mile southeast of the Church of the

Madonna del Monte. It is a square structure of identical porticoes with Ionic columns over outside stairs on each of the four sides and a domed hall at the center. Travel agents in Vicenza arrange tours of other Palladian villas in the region. La Rotonda, that paragon of Palladian architecture, has the advantage that it can be reached by public transport (No. 8 bus from the Vicenza railroad station) or even in a pleasant stroll from the master builder's native city.

CORTINA D'AMPEZZO ▪

A large, triangular chunk of pale rock near the ice stadium, which was built for the 1956 Winter Olympics, carries the bronze relief of a broad-faced, long-haired head that might belong to a man or a woman, and the inscription "Déodat de Dolomieu, 1750–1801." No further explanation. Dieudonné Gratet de Dolomieu (his correct name) was a French mineralogist who first studied the section of the Alps about 100 miles north of Venice where some of the most dramatic scenery on earth is found—bizarre towers of veined limestone that rise to heights of 10,000 feet; giant massifs whose sheer precipices glow pink, orange, and violet at sunset; jagged ridges, deep gorges, rushing torrents, icy lakes, and immense vistas. This mountain fastness, the Dolomites, is named after the French scientist; its main town, Cortina d'Ampezzo, is today one of Italy's most fashionable resorts.

Set in a wide, sunny bowl at 4,016 feet, and surrounded by forbidding mountain walls that protect it from the winds, Cortina has been inhabited since the dawn of history. But a hundred years after Dolomieu's death, at the turn of the century, the town numbered only 850 people; today's resident population is ten times that, not counting the thousands who stay in hotels and pensions, in rooms in private houses, or in their own second homes during the summer and winter seasons.

For many of the fat-cat habitués from Venice, Milan, and Rome who think they owe it to their reputation to put in an appearance at Cortina, the thing is to be noted at cocktail time in the bar of the De la Poste Hotel in the town's center, or to be seen strolling up and down the Corso Italia showing off pseudo-Alpine fashions, or to dine in one of the smart restaurants, possibly El Toulà. From Christmas to Easter some of the most beautiful women in Italy flock to Cortina, wrapped in expensive furs. Après-ski is much more important to quite a few of the visitors than schussing on one of the superb ski runs on the slopes during the day.

Yet underneath today's glossy, urban veneer an older, more authentic Cortina can be detected. There are still families in town who speak the Ampezzano dialect at home, a branch of the Ladin language (*see* Ortisei), which most Italians don't understand. The architecture of the oldest houses and the local cuisine reflect Tyrolean and Venetian influences. Even many of the new buildings, of which there are plenty, imitate the traditional Alpine style—broad house-fronts with wooden balconies and wooden gables under sloping roofs. Only at the center of town a few discordant structures stand out, looking as if they had been transplanted from the suburbs of Milan.

In summer, geraniums and other flowers are on about every windowsill and balcony. Some houses are frescoed; the so-called Picture Palace at the north end of the Corso is a private home that was decorated with allegorical paintings by its artist owners toward the end of the nineteenth century.

As for the local cuisine, polenta (cornmeal mush) is a mainstay. Other Venetian specialties like fried calf's liver with onions (*fegato alla veneta*) vie with such Tyrolean favorites as big dumplings or *Speck*, the peasants' specially cured and smoked bacon.

Cortina's landmark is the 215-foot-high neo-Gothic campanile at the center of town, erected in white stone from nearby quarries between 1853 and 1858. The square bell tower adjoins the parish church, which was built in the eighteenth century. Close by on Corso Italia is the local museum, containing fossils, examples of Ampezzano handicrafts, altarpieces and other art from churches and chapels in the area, a historical archive and library, and a collection of modern paintings, drawings, and sculptures.

From the outskirts of the town, several cable cars, funiculars, chair lifts, and ski lifts reach the heights, including the nearly 11,000-foot-high middle tower of the Tofane group to the west and a 7,000-foot ledge on Mount Faloria east of Cortina. The main town of the Dolomites is a natural base for anyone who wants to explore the unique Alpine region or take advantage of its extensive winter sports facilities.

A favorite side trip from Cortina is to 5,300-foot-high Misurina,

9.5 miles to the northeast, a cluster of hotels and a few other buildings facing a shallow lake that freezes over solidly in winter. (It was used as a skating rink in the 1956 Olympics.)

Spring brings a dazzling array of Alpine flowers—campanula, edelweiss, and both blue and white gentian among them—as well as a vanguard of sun-starved visitors from northern Europe. Mountain climbers from all over the world too converge on Cortina to measure themselves against the daunting Dolomites. The town is the head-quarters of a hardy band of professional mountain guides, and, more ominously, of an Alpine rescue service unit.

Cortina d'Ampezzo belonged to the Habsburg monarchy for cen-turies until 1915 when Italy declared war on Austria-Hungary. Em-peror Franz Joseph's forces withdrew from the basin of Cortina without a fight to establish their front on the mountain ridges and passes to the west of the town, which since then has been Italian. Cortina today is part of the region of Venetia, and its Italian character is much more pronounced than that of the other main center of the Dolomites, Ortisei, which belongs to the semiautonomous region of Alto Adige/ South Tyrol. Cortina has become a byword for elegance and sophis-tication, money and ostentation in a heroic natural setting.

ORTISEI/ST. ULRICH/URTIJËI ▪

Two languages, Italian and German, are spoken in Italy's northern-most province, Alto Adige or South Tyrol, but this smiling Alpine town nestling in one of its side valleys is trilingual. Visitors ap-proaching it see a large sign: ORTISEI—ST. ULRICH—URTIJËI. The third word is the town's name in Ladin, the language that many of the mountain farmers, wood-carvers, ski coaches, Alpine guides, cowherds, and innkeepers around here speak among themselves. School children in Ortisei attend classes in Italian, German, and Ladin; some church services are held in the language that only the natives understand; and the local radio stations broadcast regular programs in Ladin.

The language is an offshoot of ancient Latin, with some words and roots from the long-forgotten idiom of the Rhaetians, ancient inhab-itants of the Alps, embedded in it; Ladin is related to the Romansh

33

that is spoken in Saint Moritz and other places in the Swiss canton of Grisons, about 100 miles northwest of here. Some Ladins say their forefathers were soldiers of a Roman legion that was cut off in the Alps during the barbarian invasions that marked the decline and fall of the Roman Empire. A modern larger-than-life statue of a Roman legionnaire with helmet, javelin, and shield stands outside the shop of one of Ortisei's many wood-carvers in the town's main street, Via Rezia.

Whether or not the Ladins of Ortisei and its surroundings are the descendants of a lost legion, their archaic language and traditional folk ways have survived thanks to relative isolation. Ortisei is the main town in the high valley of the Gardena River, which rises in the Dolomites and joins the Isarco, or Eisack. Until fairly recently there were few contacts with the outside world, especially in winter when roads and paths were frequently impassable for weeks at a time. The Val Gardena, then called Grödental, belonged to the Habsburg Empire's Tyrol for centuries. German-speaking Tyroleans called the Ladins in their midst *Krautwalsche*, which may be rendered as "Latins who eat sauerkraut."

During World War I the Austrians pressed thousands of Russian prisoners of war into work gangs to build a narrow-gauge railway from Chiusa (Klausen in German) on the main north-south railroad line in the Isarco Valley up the Gardena Valley to be able to supply their military front facing the Italians in the Dolomites. The Gardena railway was completed in record time, and it kept running long after Austria-Hungary had fallen to pieces and South Tyrol had been ceded to Italy. Motorization and improved roads made the narrow-gauge line obsolete after World War II. A locomotive of the Gardena railway still sits nostalgically on a few yards of preserved track behind Ortisei's Baroque church.

Motorization brought tourists and a measure of affluence to the valley. Mountaineers now send their sons and daughters to work in Ortisei's hotels and stores during the winter and summer vacation periods, and take paying guests into their spruced-up farmhouses.

Increased contact with the outside world has engendered new pride in the Ladin heritage. On some Sundays cattle breeders and farmers who live on the green slopes and work hard all week don their old costumes and come down into Ortisei for some wedding or folklore parade—the men in leather breeches and broad belts with vests or coats over gaudy shirts, the women in billowing skirts, embroidered bodices, and merry aprons, wearing panlike or high hats. A Ladin museum in Ortisei is devoted to the art and culture of one of the lesser-known ethnic splinters in Europe.

The Ladins have for generations led meager, toilsome lives. During the long winter months they would carve crosses, religious statuettes, and toys from the wood of their fir forests. Roman Catholicism is deeply rooted in the area; fresh flowers can be found daily at the foot of the many crucifixes that dot the Alpine paths. Wood-carving in Ortisei is now a cottage industry. Computer-guided machines turn out religious and secular kitsch, from Madonnas and cherubs to Snow White and her dwarves. Much of the woodwork is exported. It takes quite some browsing in the smaller showrooms and shops to find any hand-carved example of the ancient folk art.

With fewer than 5,000 permanent inhabitants, Ortisei, at an altitude of 3,700 feet, is still much more of a genuine Alpine town than is the main center of the Dolomites, Cortina d'Ampezzo, which has long been a chic international resort. Ortisei is a convenient base for serious mountain climbing with or without professional guides. The jagged peaks, sheer rock walls, and overhanging precipices represent challenges to the most experienced alpinist. Less skilled or unambitious vacationers take it easy in Ortisei's several outdoor cafés, frequent the town's swimming pools and tennis courts, hike on one of the many well-marked footpaths up and down the slopes, or ride on one of several funicular systems and chair lifts to vantage points aloft. One of them is Alpe di Siusi, or Seiser Alm, a vast tableland 2,300 feet above Ortisei with an overwhelming view of the 9,500-foot-high rock tower of the Sasso Lungo and an amphitheater of other Dolomite mountains. Cars are banned on the high plateau; the guests of the few hotels and inns awaken in the morning to the tinkling of the bells of grazing cows.

Ortisei's cuisine combines Italian and Tyrolean dishes—spaghetti, *Speck* (the region's celebrated peasant bacon), schnitzel, locally picked mushrooms, trout, fresh salads, and strudel or chocolate cake with whipped cream for dessert.

Much less fashionable than Cortina d'Ampezzo, Ortisei has an informal, cordial atmosphere. The Ladins have a knack for making their guests feel welcome.

*ABOVE: Trieste,
Miramare Castle*

*LEFT: Padua,
Basilica of
St. Anthony*

*OPPOSITE, TOP: Udine,
Piazza della Libertà*

*OPPOSITE, BOTTOM:
Cividale del Friuli*

LEFT: *Merano/Meran*

OPPOSITE, BOTTOM:
*Bressanone/Brixen, Convent of
Novacella/Neustift*

BELOW: *Treviso*

OPPOSITE, TOP: Verona, opera at the Arena

OPPOSITE, BOTTOM: Rovereto

ABOVE: Verona, market in Piazza delle Erbe

BRESSANONE/BRIXEN ▪

The Habsburg Empire seems to have survived in some corners and some moods in this tidy South Tyrolean town. The predominant language among its 17,000 inhabitants is an Alpine German dialect, although Italian is understood by about everyone. A knowledge of standard German comes handy. Most signs and notices in the city are in both Italian and German. The arcaded streets at the center with their wood-paneled taverns and wrought-iron business signs look medieval and convey a sense of old-fashioned order and smugness. There are also espresso bars, supermarkets, *gelato* havens, and Italian army barracks as elsewhere in Italy, but travelers coming from the south may feel they have passed an invisible frontier and have entered another country, one that no longer actually exists, a nostalgic holdover from the world of yesterday.

Bressanone, Brixen in German, lies at 1,700 feet in altitude at the point where the Rienza River joins the Isarco, or Eisack. Protected by high mountains, the city is renowned for its dry, sunny climate. At the turn of the century it was a place where wealthy patients from the north who were suffering from consumptive diseases went for long "Magic Mountain" cures. Today socialites from Milan and Turin check in at sanatoriums here for health-farm treatment.

The city and the sanatoriums on its northern fringe are skirted by one of Europe's major north-south routes, the ancient highway and the modern motor road across the 4,500-foot-high Brenner Pass, one of the most important Alpine gateways, which is only twenty-seven miles to the north of Bressanone.

Travelers have been passing through and stopping over for thousands of years. An unforgotten exotic guest was an Indian elephant, sent by King John III the Fortunate of Portugal to Emperor Ferdinand I as a present. The animal was shipped from Goa, India, to Lisbon and Genoa, and was proceeding overland to the imperial court when its handlers decided, during a harsh winter around the middle of the sixteenth century, to let it rest awhile in Bressanone. They put up at a local inn and parked the huge quadruped outside, maybe in a barn. The two-week stay of the elephant and its crew was a local sensation.

The inn forthwith changed its name to The Elephant, and the owner had the scene of the burghers and farmers from the mountain villages gaping at the pachyderm immortalized in a fresco on the establishment's wall.

Today the inn is a highly regarded first-class hotel. The sixteenth-century building has been completely modernized inside, and the elephant fresco has been gaudily restored. The house—with its restaurant, park, swimming pool, and orchard—alone would be worth a visit to Bressanone. A gargantuan specialty of its restaurant is, appropriately enough, the "elephant platter"—an assemblage of grilled, boiled, and breaded meat cuts, sausages, sauerkraut, and other garnishes that can be ordered for four or six persons.

Bressanone/Brixen is a sort of Tyrolean Rome, the historic religious center of a staunchly Roman Catholic Alpine region. For centuries its bishops wielded also secular power as princes of the empire. The bishop of Bressanone resides today in Bolzano, the capital of the South Tyrol, but visits frequently. The Bressanone cathedral with its twin towers on a pleasant square dates from the thirteenth century; it was rebuilt in the Baroque era. The original Romanesque style has been preserved in the adjacent Chapel and Cloister of St. John the Baptist, which go back to the eleventh century; the chapel and cloister were adorned in later centuries with frescoes of biblical scenes. The vast bishop's palace in a park south of the cathedral features a moat and three-tiered arcaded courtyard and suggests the castle of a Renaissance prince.

The 600-year-old convent of Novacella (German: Neustift), less than two miles north of Bressanone, boasts a cloister with frescoes by the fifteenth-century Tyrolean painter Michael Pacher, and includes a fortresslike circular chapel that looks like a scale model of the Castel Sant'Angelo in Rome. The good monks of Novacella have long been producing their own wine; their vintages may be sampled on the spot.

The shore of the Isarco River south of the confluence with the Rienza invites strolling or jogging. A funicular leads from Bressanone up to the 7,800-foot Plose mountain, popular with tourists and skiers, with a restaurant and a panorama of the Dolomite peaks. Nearby places to visit are Fortezza (German: Franzensfeste), six miles north of Bressanone, a railroad junction noteworthy for its 150-year-old grim Austrian fortress, and a picturesque little town, Chiusa (German: Klausen), 6.5 miles south of Bressanone, dominated by a castlelike nuns' convent on a steep cliff. Bressanone itself is a cozy place to spend a long, restful vacation, preferably in the spring or early autumn.

BOLZANO/BOZEN ▪

The magic hour in this hybrid city arrives toward evening, when the setting sun bathes some spires of the Dolomites, soaring ten miles to the east, in pink and purple light, making them look like giant high-stalked flowers. The inhabitants of Bolzano call this event that occurs on every clear day their "Rose Garden," and the 9,000-foot peaks that bloom at nightfall are indicated by that name in German on the maps: Rosengarten. The Italians call the jagged mountain range more prosaically the Catinaccio (Big Chain).

Hundreds of thousands of tourists from northern Europe pass through Bolzano from spring to fall, but most of them miss the spectacle of the Dolomite towers lighting up because they hurry on to reach Lake Garda or the beaches of the Mediterranean Sea, or to get home again. Always crowded during the day in summer and in the skiing season, the city belongs in the evening hours again mainly to its residents. It may be a good idea to stay on for a couple of days or longer. Despite the large industrial plants on the outskirts, Bolzano is a comfortable place—though not in July or August, when it can be very hot—and it is also a convenient base for mountaineering and winter sports.

High mountains surround the city, which lies at the juncture of three valleys: that of the Adige, or Etsch, River (a valley also known as the Val Venosta, or Vintschgau); that of the Isarco, or Eisack; and the high Valle Sarentina, or Sarntal. The Italians call the ethnically mixed area centering on Bolzano the Alto Adige (Upper Adige); its German name is Süd Tirol (South Tyrol).

The German language, or rather its Tyrolean dialect, prevails among the 225,000 people of what since 1918 has been Italy's northernmost province. However, in its capital, Bolzano, the majority of the population of 100,000 speak Italian. Almost all German-speaking residents are bilingual whereas the number of Italians in the city who understand and speak German is proportionally low. Most signs and notices in the city are in both languages.

The small mountain river from the Val Sarentina, the Talavera or Talferbach, bisects Bolzano. The old town on its left (east) bank has retained its Tyrolean character, with arcaded streets, a quaint market square (Obstmarkt or Piazza Erbe), and many cozy, wood-paneled taverns. The new city on the opposite bank might as well spread out on the modern outskirts of Verona or Rovereto with its Via Roma, Piazza Mazzini, and Corso della Libertà and its southern-style buildings.

A triumphal arch marks the transition between the two Bolzanos and the frontier between two cultures. The monument was erected during the Fascist dictatorship to celebrate the Italian victory at the end of World War I that severed the southern part of the Tyrol, including the Italian-speaking Trent region south of Bolzano, from Austria. The arch also lays claim to the Bolzano area as belonging to the Roman world since the conquest of the Tyrol by Tiberius and Nero Claudius Drusus, the stepsons of Emperor Augustus, in 15 B.C.

A Latin inscription asserts that Italy civilized the local populations "*lingua, lege, artibus*" ("through language, law, skills"). This is true enough, as German-speaking scholars will readily concede, as far as antiquity is concerned; the triumphal arch with its Latin message has nevertheless rankled the Tyroleans of Bolzano for generations. They contend that Mussolini, in anachronistic emulation of Augustus, treated South Tyrol as a colony, ordered substantial industrial investments in the Bolzano area, and moved thousands of workers from the south in to Italianize the city and its region.

Today much of Bolzano's labor force, its sizable military garrison, and many employees of the national government are Italian, while the prosperous business community, big real estate owners, and many professional people are of Tyrolean stock. The pro-Austria, pro-Church South Tyrolean People's Party dominates the provincial parliament and government, which in many matters are able to act independently of the central state authorities in Rome. Italians and Tyroleans in Bolzano each have their own schools and newspapers, and despite their everyday contacts seem on the whole cool to each other. In many stores in the old city customers will be more courteously served if they don't speak Italian.

Most visitors to Bolzano will look for what makes the city different from Verona or Rovereto, and therefore will keep to the left bank of the river. (The Isarco skirts Bolzano on the south, and the Adige on the far outskirts to the west.)

The things to do are to stroll in the medieval arcades of the Laubengasse (Via Portici), look for Tyrolean handicraft products in the stores, and then have a meal of soup with liver dumplings and roast pork with sauerkraut in one of the taverns, accompanied by the light red Kalterersee (Lago di Caldaro) wine from the vineyards around a small lake south of Bolzano.

On summer evenings, linger at a table of one of the outdoor cafés in Piazza Walther. This large square, the social center of the city, is named after Walther von der Vogelweide, the finest medieval poet in the German language. Walther was born somewhere in South Tyrol around 1170, and as a minnesinger—the German counterpart of the French troubadours—drifted from castles to princely courts, lyrically praising chivalry and romantic love.

Bolzano's Romanesque-Gothic cathedral with its open campanile, built after the minnesingers' time, is southwest of Piazza Walther. A richly sculpted Renaissance pulpit in the interior is particularly remarkable. The former convent of the Dominicans near the piazza, now a music academy, has a frescoed chapel from the Middle Ages. Anyone interested in the region's history, folklore, and peasant crafts should also visit the Civic Museum near the market square.

The Ritten, or Renon, a high plateau with villas and clusters of houses amid green pastureland and with a grandiose panorama of the Dolomites, stretches toward the northeast, 3,200 feet above Bolzano. It can be reached by car or funicular from Via Renon, the road that leads from the easternmost part of the city to the Brenner Pass.

A narrow-gauge tram line, built in 1907, crosses the high plateau from a hamlet called Maria Himmelfahrt, or Assunta, to the resort village of Klobenstein, or Collalbo, in forty minutes. The small stations of the Renon tram are in restored period style, to the delight of rail buffs. The terminal of the funicular is at Oberbozen, or Soprabolzano, which is also a tram stop. Many well-to-do Bolzano families have second homes on the high plateau; there are also several hotels.

MERANO/MERAN ▪

A *Last Year at Marienbad* mood hangs over this old Alpine town that since the early nineteenth century has been a renowned international resort. At 11:00 A.M. the municipal band plays Viennese waltzes on its covered stand in front of the ornate Spa Auditorium (opened in 1914), while elderly vacationers and people who come to Merano every year to take the waters promenade along the Passirio River embankment with its meticulously kept flower beds. Meals in the many hotels and pensions are elaborate, and in autumn quite a few guests, undergoing the town's famous "grape cure," dutifully eat their prescribed one or two pounds of the hard-skinned blue grapes from the sun-drenched vineyards that surround Merano. After the long siesta the coffeehouses fill up with ladies who order cappuccino and torte with whipped cream, Vienna-style.

The Spa Center, the health clubs of some hotels, and the new beauty farms administer hot baths, cold baths, mud packs, massages, and more esoteric treatments that are supposed to do wonders for a multitude of complaints from orange-peel thighs to tired hearts.

In the evening one may go to the Civic Theater, an elegant Art Nouveau building near the Spa Center, perhaps to take in a revival of *The Merry Widow*. What's missing is only a couple of Habsburg archdukes. Merano is, not surprisingly, proud of a white marble monument to Empress Elisabeth of Austria-Hungary, who came to the town in 1870 in her quest for perpetual youth.

The empress's statue adorns the Summer Walk on the river's left bank, which is lined with white poplars and evergreens. The Winter Walk on the opposite bank offers arcades overgrown with clematis and wisteria. The Tappeiner Walk, named after a civic-minded nine-teenth-century doctor, runs for 2.5 miles 350 to 500 feet high along the hillside overlooking the town, amid palms, magnolias, and other subtropical flora.

On the last Sunday in September every year, all Italy looks to the town because a national lottery with big prize money is linked to the outcome of the Merano Grand Prix horse race. The grandstand at the racecourse on Merano's southwestern outskirts blooms that afternoon with beauties from Milan, Turin, and Venice, showing off the new fall fashions. When the brief excitement is over, Merano relapses into the world of yesterday, and its habitués start discussing whether they should do the Summer Walk or rather climb up to the Tappeiner Walk.

Yet Merano isn't only a spa in the Middle European grand manner which has retained some of its belle époque splendor and oozes nostalgia. Nor is it just a cluster of opulent hotels around hot springs. It is today a prosperous and well-kept town of 40,000 at the confluence of two Alpine rivers, the Adige, or Etsch, and the Passirio, or Passer, and is blessed with a mild climate and plenty of sunshine. In addition to its celebrated grapes, the Merano area produces also select apples, pears, and other fruit. The town, which is bilingual, has furthermore an industrial park in the Lana suburb on its southwestern fringe, and a big brewery.

Behind the fading glitter of the fin-de-siècle spa, there is the historic Merano, a town that, as Meran, had great importance in the Middle Ages. Three miles to the northwest, at 2,096 feet, there rises the restored thirteenth-century Tyrol Castle, which gave its name to the entire Alpine region. Meran was the capital of the County of Tyrol until 1420, and Habsburg rulers resided in the town also after Innsbruck had taken over that role.

One of the rulers was the fifteenth-century Archduke Sigmund, who married a daughter of King James I of Scotland, Eleanor. The coats of arms of Habsburg and Scotland can be seen over the door to the bedchamber in the Princely Castle in Merano's north.

Nearby is the Civic Museum, containing prehistoric and Bronze Age items found in the area, Gothic wood-carvings and paintings, and products of local peasant arts and crafts. Via Portici, or Laubengasse, immediately south of the Princely Castle, is an arcaded street in the Tyrolean manner with fine shops. The Gothic Church of St. Nicholas at the end of the Via Portici, once the town's cathedral, has a massive bell tower and exterior frescoes.

An outdoor market offering foodstuffs and a wide range of consumer goods is held in an area near the railroad station in the northwest part of town every Friday morning. All around Merano, the many castles, country inns, cable-car and chair-lift systems, and mountain refuges provide a wealth of options for interesting side trips.

TRENT (TRENTO) ▪

A traveler on the motorway between Verona and Italy's northern frontier at the Brenner Pass who approaches this city and sees high-rise buildings and clouds of industrial smoke in a valley surrounded by high mountains may decide to drive right on. It would be a pity, for Trent, with all of the modern housing and the chemical plants on its outskirts, has a distinguished historical core; the city also treats visitors well. It is, furthermore, a base from which to explore the valleys, Alpine lakes, and mountains of its region, the Trentino, including the wild Brenta massif, a southwestern offshoot of the Dolomites, where a few brown bears still roam the woods.

Trent, with about 100,000 people, will strike anyone coming from the south with its comparative staidness and its air of orderly affluence. The architecture and many of the businesses look like those in any other northern Italian city, and yet there is an indefinable difference. Trent with its region belonged to the Habsburg Empire until 1918, and Austrian influences in the way people behave and do things linger on generations later.

There is a grimmer reminder of Austrian domination across the Adige River, which skirts the city on the west. The Doss Trento, a 1,041-foot-high rocky hill under which the motorway passes in a long tunnel, is crowned by a circular marble monument in neoclassical style commemorating Cesare Battisti, a pro-Italian Trentino politician whom the Austrians hanged for high treason during World War I. The memorial, visible from afar, commands a fine panorama of Trent and the mountains on its east.

A pass road across these heights links the valley of the Adige with the Valsugana, the valley of the Brenta River, an ancient trade route between Venice and the Brenner Pass road to northern Europe. Trent, at the junction of the Adige valley and Valsugana routes has since ancient times been an important traffic and commercial center.

Today Trent and its region, staunchly Roman Catholic, function in every Italian election as a reservoir of votes for the Christian Democratic Party, one of the nation's major political forces. The founder of the party, Alcide De Gasperi, came from a town near Trent; as premier of Italy in the years after World War II he was one of the champions of the European Economic Community. After his death in 1954 Trent honored his memory with a monument in its Piazza Venezia, a large park south of the castle.

In contrast to its prevailing conservative climate, Trent was one of the breeding grounds of the left-wing terrorism that bedeviled Italy in the late 1960s and through the 1970s. A newly opened school of sociology in the city attracted radical students, from other regions as well, and some of them turned to conspiratorial violence in the clandestine Red Brigades and similar organizations. However, the plotters staged their urban-guerrilla attacks in other parts of the country while Trent, characteristically, remained quiet.

The central role and the power of the Church in Trent and the Trentino are symbolized by the severe cathedral in the middle of the city. The Lombard Romanesque edifice, built between the eleventh and sixteenth centuries, has rose windows and is surmounted by a modern dome. Its interior, with the tombs of several former bishops, saw the plenary meetings of the Council of Trent, 1545–1563, the great ecclesiastical assembly that was a milestone in church and world history. Convened by Pope Paul III to combat Lutheranism, the council redefined Roman Catholic doctrine and tightened church discipline. The Counter-Reformation of the Church of Rome thus started in this old city in the Alps. A large wooden crucifix in front of which the Latin decrees of the Council of Trent were promulgated is kept in a side chapel on the right of the cathedral. A small building with battlements on the left side of the cathedral, the Castelletto (Little Castle) was the original home of the bishops.

The bishops of Trent resided later in the Palazzo Pretorio, a thirteenth-century building with a 120-foot-high clock tower in the frowning Cathedral Square. After the bishops, various city magistrates, law courts, and military authorities used the edifice. Today the restored Palazzo Pretorio houses the Diocesan Museum, which contains memorabilia of the Council of Trent, together with old paintings, sculptures, and Flemish tapestry.

Via Belenzani from Cathedral Square to the north is an architectural gem. The street is lined with austere buildings in a style influenced by the Venetian Renaissance. Particularly noteworthy are the sixteenth-century city hall and, opposite it, the Palazzo Geremia with an elegant stone balcony.

As prince-bishops, the ranking prelates of Trent also wielded territorial powers during nearly 800 years, and a large castle at the foot of a slope in the city's northeast shows that they were ruling in magnificence. The former episcopal residence, the walled Castello del Buon Consiglio (Castle of Good Counsel) with a moat, stout towers, two arcaded courtyards, and a maze of stairways, corridors, and rooms is a complex dating back to the thirteenth century; it was rebuilt and enlarged during various later periods. Under the Austrians the law courts and a prison took up a part of the castle. Battisti and other Italian nationalists were executed in an enclosure behind the edifice.

Today the castle contains two vast collections: the Museum of the Risorgimento, with exhibits on the Italian struggle against Austrian rule during the nineteenth and early twentieth centuries; and the Museum of Ancient, Medieval, Modern, and Contemporary Art, including archaeological finds from the Bronze Age and the Roman era, and detached frescoes from various epochs.

The interesting Museum of Natural Sciences, specializing in local Alpine animal and plant life and the minerals of the region, is in the Palazzo Sardagna between the cathedral and Piazza Venezia.

Venetian palaces stand in the city cheek by jowl with buildings whose wide, overhanging roofs proclaim their Alpine character. A *trattoria* may be found next door to a beer garden. Menus will list Venetian-style liver with polenta in the same column as Tyrolean smoked pork with sauerkraut. Two civilizations meet here.

ROVERETO ■

This pretty town of 30,000 on one of Europe's major north-south routes is an Alpine crossroads and way station. Coming from the north Italian plains and Verona, the traveler at Rovereto enters the Trentino, a region of high mountains and often narrow valleys with villages that look severe, sometimes even somber. The scenery is grandiose at many spots, but generally less smiling than in South Tyrol, closer to the Austrian border. Arriving from the Brenner Pass, from Bolzano and Trent, visitors at Rovereto get a preview of what awaits them in the south. The valley of the Adige River, here called Val Lagarina, widens; vineyards, orchards, cornfields, and rows of mulberry trees surround the town.

Many holidaymakers turn west in Rovereto to reach the nearby lovely towns at the upper end of Lake Garda (*see* Brescia)—Arco, renowned for its mild climate and subtropical vegetation; Riva, a harbor since ancient times; and Torbole, a picture-postcard fishing village.

Motorists who instead take National Route No. 46 from Rovereto to Vicenza, Padua, and Venice to the southeast find themselves in a few minutes on a road with magnificent vistas and many hairpin turns that will take them up to the Pian delle Fugazze Pass (altitude 3,822 feet). Above it towers the 7,335-foot-high Mount Pasubio, and a marble plaque at the roadside recalls that the area saw fierce Alpine battles during World War I. *Pasubio* is to Italians since then a synonym of military valor.

Rovereto was close to the front lines from 1915 through 1918. The town has not forgotten. The Bell of the Fallen tolls every evening in remembrance of all the combatants of all nations who died in all wars. Cast from Italian and Austrian guns fired during World War I, the bell weighs 35,246 pounds and is the biggest in all of Italy. It is enclosed by a circular structure with a green-patined brass dome, the Torre Malipiero, on a hill overlooking Rovereto from the south. Nearby are an ossuary with the remains of World War I soldiers, and at about 1,000 feet in altitude is the Castello Dante, a castle in which the poet was a guest of Count Castelbarco after Florence had exiled him in 1302.

A fourteenth-century castle perched on a rock ledge in the north of the town, like a sentry guarding the road to Vicenza and Venice, is today the seat of the largest World War I museum in Italy. It contains historical documents, photos, collections of uniforms and equipment, weapons, and a vast specialized library.

Despite all the grim reminders of a war that cost Italy 600,000 casualties, Rovereto is a pleasant place to stay. An old silk-manufacturing center, it has lately attracted some light industry, with plants on the outskirts turning out building materials, electronic appliances, and other products.

In the small historic nucleus of the town below its castle there are a few graceful Venetian-style palazzi. The fourteenth-century Church of Santa Maria del Carmine (St. Mary of Mount Carmel) is now the sacristy of a newer church, built in the seventeenth and eighteenth centuries. Another church, from the fifteenth century, is dedicated to

St. Mark, the heavenly patron of Venice. Rovereto was a Venetian possession until 1517 when it was ceded to Emperor Maximilian I and assigned by him to the Tyrol.

From the central Piazza Rosmini a straight, broad street, Corso Rosmini, runs to the railroad station, providing the townspeople with a stately promenade for their evening stroll. Antonio Rosmini (1795–1855), a Roman Catholic philosopher and educator, was a native of Rovereto.

The Civic Museum offers evidence that the spot was inhabited already in prehistoric times. Other exhibits regard the mineralogy and the flora and fauna of the Trentino region.

VERONA ▪

The marble balcony that Romeo climbed with love's light wings is pointed out to tourists; so are the crenellated house of his family, the Montagues, and Juliet's tomb. The places are all spurious. But who would blame fair Verona for having, since the era of the grand tours that brought rich Englishmen to Italy, invented a sightseeing circuit devoted to the memory of the star-cross'd lovers? Shakespeare, for all that we know, never saw the city in the sun-drenched plain near the foothills of the Alps, or its ocher buildings, orchards, and convents. To choose Verona as the setting for a drama on family feuds and youthful passion was sheer genius.

Today emotions rage in the city of 270,000, mostly in the soccer stadium on Sundays, at the horse market in spring, and on the giant outdoor opera stage in the Arena, the ruined Roman amphitheater, on summer nights. An Italian adage says that the Veronese are *tutti matti* ("all crazy"). Most of them seem merry enough, and a lot of laughter is heard in the city. Yet the authorities warn that Verona has also a serious drug problem. Stay away from the more remote stretches of the high Adige embankments at night.

The Adige River, fed by the snow and glaciers of the Alps, flows majestically through the city in a double loop. Halfway within the arc that the river draws around the historic core looms Verona's chief monument, the Arena. Five hundred feet long and more than 400 feet wide, it held 25,000 spectators and was the largest amphitheater next to the Colosseum in Rome. Only four arches ("the wing" to the Veronese) of the three-story outer wall are still standing. The intact inner ring consists of two orders of seventy-two arches, providing excellent acoustics. Up to 22,000 people find seats on the steps and the arena floor during summer performances, when many busloads of opera fans from all over northern Italy and neighboring countries attend. Most of them leave the same night, drunk on Verdi or Puccini or on the heady local Soave wine.

The Arena, two monumental arches from the first century A.D. in other spots, and a Roman theater on the slope of a hill with solemn cypresses in the city's north are reminders of Verona's importance in antiquity. The city's strategic location at the crossroads where the Adige Valley, one of Europe's principal north-south routes, opens into the fertile and hard-to-defend northern Italian plain determined Verona's destinies throughout history. Conquerors, invaders, and emperors coveted the place, and the Republic of Venice eventually annexed it. The way the Veronese speak today recalls the soft Venetian dialect.

Visitors approaching the center from the railroad station outside the city's obsolete fortifications pass a large, luminous square in front of the Arena, Piazza Bra. The broad sidewalk in front of a curving row of houses in various shades of brown and gray on the left, and the sidewalk cafés—the strip is locally known as the *liston*—is a favorite Veronese meeting place, filled with latter-day Juliets and Juliet-watchers afternoons and evenings.

A ten-minute stroll northward leads to Piazza delle Erbe, a picturesque oval square with an outdoor market. It was the forum (marketplace) in the Verona of ancient times. A small stone canopy on four columns in the center is often described as the town pillory; actually, it had nothing to do with criminal justice but was used by magistrates for ceremonial actions and announcements. The "Erbe" in the piazza's name refers to vegetables, which are still sold under gaudy umbrellas, together with Verona's famous peaches and other fruit, postcards, Shakespearean sweatshirts, and snacks.

"Juliet's House" with the balcony and a marble plaque is at 27 Via Cappello. The street running from the south of Piazza delle Erbe toward the river is named after a dal Cappello family (not Shakespeare's Capulets) who once owned the thirteenth-century building. A fourteenth-century house with a porticoed courtyard at 2–4 Via

Arche Scaligere, east of the Piazza delle Erbe, is touted as the Montague home. Nearby is an authentic monument, the fenced-in group of elaborate Gothic tombs of members of the della Scala family, rulers of Verona from 1260 to 1387. Romeo and Juliet were supposedly subjects of the della Scalas.

Walk for twenty minutes downstream along the embankments to reach "Juliet's Tomb" in a former Capuchin monastery in the Campo di Fiera, the large area in the city's south where the historic horse market is held—now largely superseded by an important agricultural fair with displays of new tractors and other farming equipment. A brickwork crypt, built at the end of the nineteenth century, contains a rough medieval stone trough in which true and faithful Juliet is said to have been laid to rest.

With all the romantic make-believe, visitors shouldn't pass up Verona's genuine sights. One is Piazza dei Signori, a few steps from Piazza delle Erbe. A monument of Dante, who as an exile from Florence found hospitality first in Verona, rises in the middle of the noble square. The old Caffè Dante, with outdoor tables, is a place to linger and look at the elegant Renaissance loggia and the two towers in the piazza.

Then there are famous ancient churches: the twelfth-century cathedral, with an *Assumption* by Titian over a side altar, and a peaceful cloister; San Zeno Maggiore in a quiet square on the city's northwestern outskirts, one of the most beautiful Romanesque basilicas in all of Italy; and several others. Red Veronese marble is used profusely in the ecclesiastical buildings.

The Castelvecchio (Old Castle) west of the Arena is a fortress of the della Scalas built at the southernmost point of the upstream Adige bend, to protect a strategic bridge that represented a route for attack or escape across the river. The fourteenth-century bridge, with brick towers and battlements, was destroyed during World War II, as were most other bridges in the city. They have all been painstakingly restored, mostly with original material retrieved from the riverbed. The Castelvecchio houses a museum with paintings by Paolo Veronese (a native son who became a Venetian), Jacopo and Giovanni Bellini, and various masters of the Verona school, as well as Flemish art showing Venetian influences, medieval jewelry, miniatures, and weapons.

Heavy traffic may make strolling in Verona tiresome at times, but visitors exploring the city will every now and then be rewarded by the discovery of yet another delightful church or palace. Or they might cross the river over the restored Ponte della Pietra (Stone Bridge), which incorporates two arches from a structure of the first century A.D., and walk past the Roman theater to the Palazzo Giusti to see its celebrated garden. This lush terraced park, with flower beds, a fountain, statues, and a leafy wall of trees, has a belvedere commanding a panorama of Verona and, on clear days, the Apennines far to the south across the plain.

Gastronomic Verona is supplied with fresh vegetables and quality meat from nearby farms, and boasts some fine restaurants. On the other hand, business with the many transient guests and the summer opera in the Arena has spawned a slew of places for pizza and other fast snacks. The Veronese wines are golden Soave and red Valpolicella.

If English is heard spoken, it's not always by tourists. The North Atlantic Treaty Organization maintains military installations in the vicinity, and Verona is used to American servicemen.

2
THE DYNAMIC NORTHWEST

Lombardy, Piedmont, and Liguria

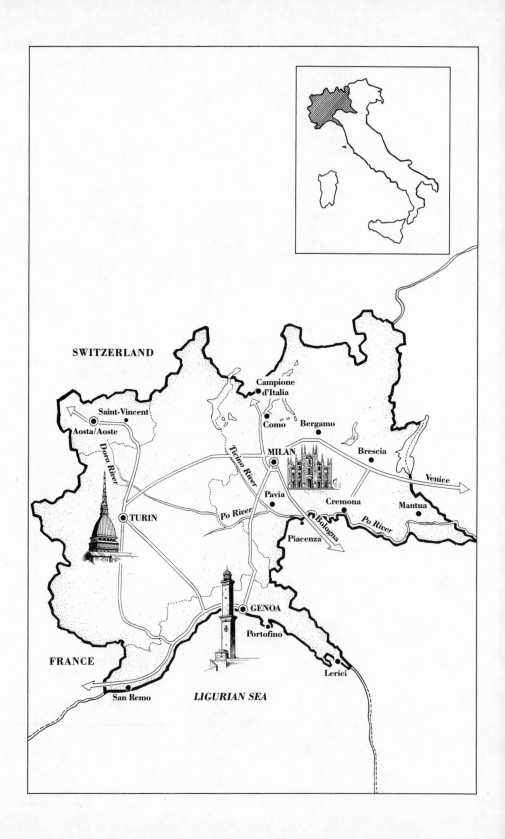

■

Three northwestern regions of Italy with their "industrial triangle" of Milan, Turin, and Genoa are the nation's powerhouse. These large cities with their high-rise buildings and sprawling manufacturing plants are known also for architectural gems, fine-arts collections, and other cultural treasures, yet most visitors come for business rather than for sightseeing or recreation.

From these industrial, financial, and communications centers it is only a short way to any one in a cluster of old towns that have managed, for all the impressive economic development in the region, to retain their distinct individual character. Each is an essential piece of the mosaic that is Italy: Como with its scenic lake views and historic reminiscences, or quiet Mantua glorying in the legacy of past grandeur, or French-speaking Aosta in a majestic Alpine valley, or lovely Portofino with its quaint little harbor and piazza.

Italy's largest river, the Po, unites Piedmont and Lombardy before emptying into the Adriatic Sea between Venice and Ravenna. What geographers call the Po Valley is for the most part a vast plain with thousands of industrial plants scattered in rich farmland.

Through much of their checkered history, however, the regions around Turin and Milan were separated until the movement for the unification of Italy spread in the nineteenth century from the Savoy Kingdom, today's Piedmont and Aosta Valley. Lombardy was long ruled by foreigners—the Spaniards first and the Austrians later—while centuries-old French influence is to this day unmistakably present in Turin and the rest of Piedmont. The French element is so strong in the Aosta Valley that after World War II the Alpine region attained a limited form of self-government.

Genoa was a sovereign republic in the Middle Ages, a rival of other maritime powers at the time in the Mediterranean and, particularly, in the Levant. In Constantinople the Venetians and the Genoese were fierce competitors until the Turks took over. The city that claims Christopher Columbus as its greatest native son and the rocky region hugging its magnificent gulf have furnished mariners since the dawn of history. In small Ligurian towns the visitor is likely to run into some retired seaman who will nostalgically talk about the waterfront of Brooklyn or Sydney, or about his service and experiences on one of the transatlantic luxury liners that were once the pride of Genoa.

The coastal arch that curves eastward is known in Italian as the Riviera di Levante, and the gulf's western shore as the Riviera di Ponente. The Ligurian Riviera is a tiara studded with gems: its string of sea resorts. Lerici and Portofino on the eastern Riviera and San Remo west of Genoa are included in this book for more than their palms, hotels, bathing beaches, and elegant waterfront promenades.

Byron and Shelley loved the Ligurian Riviera; during the Victorian epoch it was fashionable for the rich to pass the winter there. The mountain ranges separating Liguria from Piedmont shield the coast from the cold northern winds, favoring the lush Riviera vegetation. Flowers are everywhere, the olive groves along the coast yield top-grade oil, and vines soak up the sunshine on terraces that climb up the steep, rocky slopes. In summer, cold breezes from the sea make the evenings delightful. No wonder that during the weekends from May to October the Riviera is crowded with people from Turin, Milan, and the other cities in Piedmont and Lombardy.

Traveling in parts of Lombardy and, especially, in the Piedmontese lowlands, one notices extended paddies, where rice has been grown for centuries. Some sections of Piedmont, particularly around the town of Alba, are famous for their truffles.

Not surprisingly, risotto and truffles are the best-known culinary treats in northwestern Italy. Risotto here comes with many different garnishings: meat, seafood, vegetables, mushrooms, and, yes, truffles. Fondue, locally called *fonduta*, is a favorite cheese dish. In Liguria, pesto, the spicy condiment for pasta, is a gourmet's dream.

Piedmont grows two red wines, Barbera and Barolo, that come close to the great Bordeaux vintages. In Liguria ask for wine from the Cinque Terre, five villages in as many coves of the rugged promontory between La Spezia and Sestri Levante. Cinque Terre whites are a perfect match for seafood.

In the Middle Ages and during the Renaissance, stonecutters from Como and Campione helped build cathedrals all over Italy, and they, as well as other craftsmen from Lombardy and Piedmont, were welcomed also in other European countries.

Since the end of World War II northwestern Italy has experienced an influx of uncounted people from the nation's south because Fiat—the Turin-based motor company that is the country's largest private corporation—and other concerns in the industrial triangle needed additional manpower. Today, even in the small towns of Lombardy, Piedmont, and Liguria, there are many families from the tip of the Italian mainland and from Sicily.

The production boom in Italy's northwest is straining its transportation network; trains are often crowded and the highways and motor roads congested. Motorists should drive with extra caution on the cluttered Ligurian coastal roads, which have many bends and tunnels.

Amid all the bustle, there are islands of tranquillity, such as the Upper Town of Bergamo, the Charterhouse of Pavia, or the Ducal Palace of Mantua. Such quiet enclaves serve also as reminders that northwestern Italy has made precious contributions to the nation's culture.

Milan, which likes to call itself the moral capital of Italy (meaning its intellectual center) and which is today a trendsetter for international fashion and design, is the natural starting point for visits to a number of captivating cities and towns all around. Como and Campione d'Italia—the latter by way of Lugano, Switzerland—may be combined in a one- or two-day round trip from Milan, as may Pavia and Piacenza (or, from Piacenza, one can proceed to Parma or Turin). Piacenza belongs administratively to the Region of Emilia-Romagna but gravitates toward nearby Lombardy and Milan. A slightly longer Milan-based trip could include Bergamo, Brescia, Mantua, and Cremona.

Aosta is in itself worth at least a day on the way between Milan and Turin. The old city is now the center of its own semiautonomous unit, the Region of Valle d'Aosta, but it has close links with Piedmont. A three-day trip from Turin to the Italian Riviera can include Genoa. If you don't care for a big, busy seaport, bypass Genoa (although it has its beautiful spots too) on the motorway, or stay on the train if you travel by rail. Three other Riviera towns are singled out at the end of this section.

Piedmont proper, though heavily industrialized, boasts several appealing towns, such as Alba, with its celebrated truffles, or Asti, a byword for sparkling wines—both towns belong to the hundreds of places under consideration for Cento Città status that had to be skipped in this book.

COMO ∎

If one interprets the inverted Y of Lake Como as the shape of a lithe dancer, the city that gave its name to the three-cornered fjordlike remnant of a huge prehistoric glacier is at the tip of the forward foot. From Como's elegant, busy shore promenade only the harbor and a small expanse of water beyond it are visible, enclosed by hills, their lush slopes dotted with villas. At night innumerable lights twinkle from the heights all around. Boats taking off from the Como waterfront for cruises or for one of the towns or patrician mansions along the 118 miles of lakeshore veer northeast after a few minutes, and stupendous vistas open.

The scenery and soft climate of the lake, Larius Lacus of the ancients, and its oleander-scented gardens have been praised by writers and artists since Virgil and two illustrious natives of what was then Comum, the older and the younger Pliny. "Everything is noble and gentle," Stendhal wrote about Lake Como. "Everything speaks of love."

From the beginning of the sixteenth century Como has been the Italian center of silkworm culture and silk weaving. However, silk manufacture has lately declined as artificial fibers have advanced. There are still several silk factories in the city, which has a population of about 100,000.

Many well-to-do families in nearby Milan and other northern Italian cities own second homes in or near Como. Tourists crowd the lake area from early spring to late in October. Yet behind the city's lakefront with its hotels, souvenir shops, and incessant motor traffic there is another, much older and more intimate, Como.

It is enclosed on three sides by old gray town walls with three square towers on their southeast flank. The central tower, the 130-foot-high Porta Torre, was built in 1192 when Como served as a military base of the German emperors and was rivaling with Milan. A bustling outdoor market is now held on most weekdays outside the town walls from the Porta Torre to the railroad tracks that lead to the lakefront.

Between the three stout towers and the modern buildings along the lake promenade old Como huddles in a grid of narrow streets with many frescoed houses. The medieval walls and the street pattern recall the layout of the ancient Roman military encampment that once occupied the site.

The former Cathedral of San Fedele, on a small, picturesque piazza in the old city, was erected in the tenth century in the place of a pagan temple, and it was later rebuilt. It has a Romanesque bell tower, and a rose window on its façade. Opposite are two timber-framed houses that don't seem to have been much altered since the sixteenth century.

Closer to the lakefront, a few hundred yards from the austere Church of San Fedele, is Como's exuberant marble cathedral, or duomo. Built and rebuilt between the twelfth and eighteenth centuries by generations of the lake area's famed stonemasons, the structure combines Romanesque, Gothic, Renaissance, and Baroque elements and is crowned with a high octagonal dome. Seated figures of the two Plinys were placed at either side of the main portal in 1498 when enthusiasm for classical antiquity was at its height. The cathedral interior is particularly splendid during church celebrations, when Flemish and Italian tapestries picturing biblical episodes are hung up between the pillars.

Left of the cathedral's main façade are a Romanesque-Gothic municipal palace and courthouse on arcades, known as Il Broletto, with a balcony from which city ordinances were read, and a square civic bell tower. The streets and squares around the old and new cathedrals are paved with brown flagstones.

Outside the walled district, a few minutes' walk to the southeast beyond the small Cosia River, is the rust-brown Romanesque Basilica of Sant'Abbondio, with square twin towers and, in the interior, four-teenth-century frescoes with scenes from the life of Jesus. The in-ternational railroad line from Milan to Lugano and Zurich passes on the slope above the old church.

The contrast between Como's historic neighborhoods and the modern lakeside quarter is striking. The vast Piazza Cavour, facing the harbor, is bordered by hotels and office buildings; the square was recently found to be subsiding and needed work to strengthen its foundations.

A salient on the left of the bay is taken up by a park with a memorial for war victims, in the shape of one of Como's historic towers, and a modern building in Palladian neoclassical style dedicated to Count Alessandro Volta, the great physicist and inventor who was born near the city in 1745. This Volta Temple was commissioned by a wealthy private admirer and donated to the city in 1927, on the hundredth anniversary of the scientist's death. Volta's tomb is in the cemetery of the village of Camnago Volta in the hillside a mile east of the city.

On the right (northeast) side of the shore promenade is the terminal of cable cars to Brunate, a hamlet at 2,460 feet with hotels and villas, a tall lighthouse donated by Italian telegraph workers on the occasion of the Volta centenary in 1927, and a fine panorama of the lake, with Milan to the south and the Alps to the north.

Como is a convenient starting point for excursions by boat, car, or bus to the many towns and other attractions around its lake. Among them are Bellagio, a resort on a wooded promontory at the point where the lake's three arms meet, with the subtropical parks of the Villa Serbelloni and Villa Melzi; the celebrated Villa Carlotta, with terraced gardens, between Tremezzo and Cadenabbia opposite Bellagio; and the Villa d'Este at Cernobbio, a magnificent mansion built for a Renaissance cardinal and now a deluxe hotel. History was grimly made at the end of World War II in the ironworking village of Dongo on the right shore of the lake's northern arm, when Italian partisans captured Mussolini and his mistress, Claretta Petacci, there as the couple were trying to flee to Switzerland. The two were put up against a garden fence and shot in the village of Mezzegra, diagonally opposite Bellagio, on April 28, 1945; their bodies were taken to Milan and strung up, heads downward, at a service station in the suburban Piazza Loreto. There is a black cross now on the stone parapet near the iron gate where the dictator and his mistress died.

Lecco, an industrial city of 55,000 in the southeast corner of the lake, has a name that is hammered into all Italian high school students, for it is the setting of Alessandro Manzoni's *The Betrothed*, a nineteenth-century novel and a classic of Italian literature that is a perennial in their curriculum. Lecco looks up to the east at Mount Resegone ("The Saw"), a 6,155-foot-high dolomite ridge with eleven sharp teeth.

CAMPIONE D'ITALIA ■

A miniature Atlantic City on the eastern shore of Lake Lugano, this former stonecutters' town and smugglers' lair is now a gamblers' haven and a geographical and administrative oddity. Picturesquely rising from a lakeside promenade, Campione d'Italia can be reached from the city of Como in half an hour—but visitors need a passport or, if they are Italians or nationals of some other European countries, at least an ID card. With a resident population of only 2,000, Campione is a tiny, detached, and prosperous piece of Italy enveloped by Swiss territory.

Passport and customs controls for travelers from Italy are at Chiasso, the Swiss border town four miles northwest of Como, less than an hour's drive from Milan. There are no further formalities at the lakeside point some ten miles farther northwest where the Italian green-white-and-red tricolor again faces the Swiss flag, white cross on red field. Visitors to the Italian enclave who arrive from anywhere in Switzerland undergo no controls at all. Many of them come by boat from the Swiss resort city and banking center of Lugano across the lake.

The town hall of Campione reports to the Italian provincial authorities in Como, but the lone squad car of the Campione police parked outside carries the license plates of Swiss Canton Ticino, as do all other local motor vehicles. All prices in the small town's shops and cafés are listed in Swiss francs, the currency that Campione's business community prefers; Italian lire are nevertheless accepted too, if a trifle grudgingly.

An old photo on the wall of a lakefront espresso bar shows how Campione looked in the 1920s: six houses on a dirt strip, no shore promenade, and an inn-and-billiards. Now the most important building in town is the municipal casino, in pink marble with allegorical mosaics on the outer walls featuring History, Art, and Science. Inside, croupiers in formal dress preside at roulette, baccarat, chemin de fer, and other games of chance that are outlawed in Switzerland and legal in only three other places in Italy—San Remo, Saint-Vincent, and Venice. A hall with slot machines is particularly crowded on weekends. Men are required to wear neckties and jackets in the casino's air-conditioned gaming rooms, restaurant, and nightclub.

During the day the casino of Campione occasionally becomes the setting for conventions and shows, but its most welcome guests are the gamblers who drift in afternoons and evenings. The parking lots are often packed until dawn with luxury cars, many of them carrying Italian license plates.

From time to time the Italian police swoop on Campione and arrest a few alleged mafiosi on charges of laundering dirty money or skimming the casino takes, but business as usual is always quickly resumed. Campione remains a substantial contributor to the Italian treasury department.

Visitors who would never set foot in a gambling establishment will nevertheless like Campione for its pretty views of the lake and of the bizarrely shaped green Mount San Salvatore, which faces the town across the water.

The project of building a funicular to the 4,321-foot top of Mount Sighignola, on whose steep slope Campione nestles, has remained in the concrete-pouring stage and doesn't seem to proceed. The view from the peak is spectacular, but it takes considerable climbing to reach it. The next best thing is to walk up a few hundred feet to the Sanctuary of the Madonna dei Ghirli ("Our Lady of the Swallows" in the local dialect) overlooking the town. The fourteenth-century shrine, with an imposing Baroque portico that was built later and can be seen from afar, commands a panorama embracing much of the four-pronged Lake Lugano, the mountains framing it, and the city of Lugano. A fresco under the arcades of the sanctuary by the fourteenth-century painters Franco and Filippolo de Veris represents the Last Judgment.

The parish church of Campione, near the lakefront and the gambling casino, contains a fourteenth-century triptych of the Madonna with Jesus and angels. The work is a sample of the art of the Maestri Campionesi (Campione Masters), a guild of accomplished sculptors, decorators, architects, and stonemasons who were widely renowned during the Middle Ages and were rivals of a similar school of artists in nearby Como. The Campionesi were called to embellish churches and other buildings all over northern Italy. They worked anonymously at first, but from the fourteenth century on, outstanding stonecutters from Campione started signing their productions. Among them was Jacopo da Campione, who in the second half of the fourteenth century contributed a beautiful Gothic sacristy door to the cathedral of Milan. A ceramic workshop that turns out pottery and tourist souvenirs is about all that remains today of Campione's old fascination with the plastic arts.

BERGAMO ■

The ancient ramparts, towers, domes, and weather-beaten houses of a fortified hilltown, and the broad boulevards of a prosperous modern city in the plain 400 feet below combine to make Bergamo a quintessential corner of Italy. Outside the standard circuits of the international tourist industry, Bergamo has retained an intimate atmosphere of its own. The 130,000 inhabitants of the twin communities, proud of their history and of their recent economic achievements, haven't entirely forgotten their old frugality, but their cordial ways are proverbial.

For three and a half centuries before the Napoleonic era Bergamo was the westernmost stronghold of the Republic of Venice. Although the skyline of Milan with its cathedral and its high-rises, only thirty miles to the southwest, can be seen across the plains of Lombardy from the higher points of Bergamo on clear days, the dialect and traditions of Bergamo still echo those of the Lagoon City, which is about 150 miles away.

Like the Venetians, the people of Bergamo are fond of polenta, or cornmeal mush, as a side dish for all sorts of food, as a main course, or even as a dessert. Farming and small industry, including book printing, make for a balanced, thriving economy.

Bergamo Bassa (Lower Bergamo) developed in the nineteenth century from two large suburbs below the old town with some convents, churches, kitchen gardens, and a large fairground between them. When an architect who was to become a favorite of the Fascist dictatorship, Marcello Piacentini, won a competition to rebuild the lower city's center in the vast urban renewal project of 1922–1924, the pompously monumental neo-Roman style that critics would later call Mussolini Modern was born here.

The main axis of Lower Bergamo is a broad avenue that, as Viale Papa Giovanni XXIII and Viale Roma, leads from the railroad station to a road curving up to the old town. Public buildings, banks, business headquarters, and sumptuous private residences line the streets and squares of the modern center. In the older neighborhoods in the northeast, at the foot of the ramparts protecting the old town, is one of Italy's major picture galleries, the Carrara Academy. It is named after Count Giacomo Carrara, a rich local nobleman who founded an art school and, between 1807 and 1810, had a neoclassical building with an imposing portico erected to house the school as well as his collection of paintings. More art was later contributed by other donors. The gallery boasts an early *St. Sebastian* by Raphael, and works by Botticelli, Lorenzo Lotto, Dürer, Mantegna, Tiepolo, Titian, Canaletto, and other Venetian masters.

Bergamo Alta (Upper Bergamo) can be reached by a funicular from the Viale Vittorio Emanuele II above the upper end of Viale Roma, by car or bus over the Viale Vittorio Emanuele II, and on foot on a rather steep path and stairways from a point near the funicular's lower terminal. Motor vehicles are banned from a large part of the old town.

Quiet Upper Bergamo is enclosed by mighty walls, built by the Venetians in the sixteenth century to replace older fortifications, some of them going back to Roman times. Today the bastions are tree-lined promenades commanding fine views of the lower city and the Lombard plain. Spelunkers are attracted to the caves and underground passages of the bulwarks. The winged lion of St. Mark, in relief on St. Augustine's Gate, greets visitors arriving on the road from Lower Bergamo. The upper terminal of the funicular is in a fourteenth-century palace in Piazza Mercato delle Scarpe (Shoe Market Square).

At the center of the old town is Piazza Vecchia, one of those public spaces in Italy that seem permanent open-air stages. Its dramatic south side is taken up by an arcaded Gothic building, also with a stone lion of St. Mark, the Palazzo della Ragione, which once served as a courthouse and headquarters of the city government. A flight of stairs, open at one side, leads up to the frescoed Hall of the Five Hundred, now occasionally used for art shows. A massive clock tower on the right, 160 feet high, is the symbol of Bergamo's communal independence before the Venetian domination. A Latin inscription piously proclaims: "Where Justice, Charity, Peace, and Love reign, there is God."

A neoclassical building on the square's north side, the New Palace, completed in the eighteenth century, houses the civic library with 100,000 volumes and many illuminated manuscripts and first printings. The graceful fountain in the middle of the piazza, surrounded by stone lions and allegorical figures, was a gift to the city from its Venetian governor, Alvise Contarini, in 1780.

Traditional puppetry is still performed under the arcades of the Palazzo della Ragione on Sunday afternoons in summer. One of the few surviving practitioners of the puppeteer's art will put up Gioppino, the goitrous simpleton from the Bergamasque Alps who is a stock character of local folk comedy, against Arlecchino (Harlequin), the crafty buffoon. The puppet shows in the local dialect are a reminder that the Bergamasque popular theater of the sixteenth century contributed much to the Venetian commedia dell'arte, the satiric plays with improvised dialogue based on standard situations and long-familiar characters.

The archways of the Palazzo della Ragione are themselves like a cutout stage set permitting glimpses of intriguing scenery behind it, the Piazzetta del Duomo (Little Cathedral Square). Probably marking the center of what was the ancient Roman town of Bergomum, the rectangular little square is bordered by religious edifices on three sides. Facing the rear façade of the Gothic municipal building are an 800-year-old church and, wedged into it, a magnificent Renaissance chapel; on the left there is Bergamo's cathedral and on the right a marble baptistery.

The domed chapel with its gaudy ornaments of red and white marble, lacy arches and windows, and statuary and brass railing is the eye-catcher. It was commissioned by a great condottiere as his last resting place. The soldier of fortune was Bartolomeo Colleoni (1400–1475), who was alternately at the service of the dukes of Milan and the Republic of Venice. His famous equestrian statue by Andrea Verrocchio on the Campo Santi Giovanni e Paolo, a small square to the east of the Grand Canal in Venice, proves how high his repute was there. His marble tomb in the Bergamo chapel is surmounted by a gilt wooden statue representing the condottiere on horseback as generalissimo of the Venetian army, his right hand clasping the baton of command. Nearby is a statue of his daughter, Medea, who died before him and is also buried in the chapel. The vault is decorated with frescoes by Tiepolo.

To gain space for his chapel, the high-handed condittiere had the vestry of the old Basilica of Santa Maria Maggiore torn down. What remains of that church is a dazzling mixture of medieval walls in mellow hues, Romanesque and Gothic architecture and ornaments, an octagonal dome, a bell tower, and Renaissance and Baroque decorations in the lavish interior.

The domed cathedral, in a right angle to the Basilica of Santa Maria Maggiore, was begun in the fifteenth century and rebuilt several times. The small circular Church of Santa Croce (Holy Cross) off the southern façade of the basilica has walls of rough-hewn stones dating from the ninth century.

Strolling in the stone-paved, winding streets and little squares of the old town, with their towers, arches, and underpasses, the visitor sees many medieval houses and stately Renaissance palaces. A twelfth-century fortress, La Rocca, built on ancient Roman foundations, overlooks Upper Bergamo. Today it is the seat of a museum of the Italian nineteenth-century struggle for independence and unity and of the World War II resistance movement.

A funicular and a road near a former citadel in the northwest corner of the old town lead up to the 1,631-foot-high San Vigilio Hill, with remains of an old outer fort, which Napoleon had blown up, and a vast panorama of the two Bergamos.

The simple house in whose basement Gaetano Donizetti was born in 1797 is at No. 14 of Via Borgo Canale, a narrow street below San Vigilio. Manuscripts by the composer and other memorabilia are on view in the Donizetti Museum in the Baroque Palazzo della Misericordia (Palace of Mercy) in the old town.

All around the year admirers of Pope John XXIII, the former Angelo Guiseppe Roncalli (pope from 1958 to 1963), flock by the busload to the pleasant village of Sotto il Monte ("Below the Mountain") on a hillside eight miles northwest of Bergamo. They are shown the four-family stone house where the future pontiff, the third of a sharecropper's ten children, was born in 1881, and the church where he was baptized. The diocesan seminary in Upper Bergamo, where he studied for the priesthood, is named after him, as is a main street in the lower city.

With his wisdom and folksiness John XXIII embodied the most likable traits of the people of Bergamo.

BRESCIA ▪

This manufacturing center at the foothills of the Alps near Lake Garda displays the efficiency and affluence of the industrial and postindustrial ages amid the vestiges of a long history. Brescia is a mosaic of diverse elements—ancient ruins, medieval and Renaissance architecture, rich museums, a Mussolini Modern city center, and a thriving economic establishment.

The managers of small and medium-sized iron and steel plants near the city who are known all over Europe as "the Brescians" have successfully defied the continent's state-subsidized industrial giants, and are selling their structural steel far and wide. The Brescia-based Beretta Weapons Company supplies the United States armed forces with its famous handguns. Brescia is also a big name in mechanical products in general and in textiles.

The city's entrepreneurs aren't shy about flaunting their wealth. They live well, own elegant villas on Mount Maddalena, a hill overlooking the city, drive luxury cars, fly in executive jets, and have yachts moored on Sardinia's Emerald Coast or the Riviera. Brescia is self-confident, and many of its 225,000 inhabitants just love to earn and spend money.

The visitor may be impressed by the economic dynamism, but will look also for the historic Brescia, and there is plenty of it. The remains of a temple dedicated to Jupiter, Juno, and Minerva with a columned portico can be seen in Via dei Musei (Museum Street) at the foot of the city's castle hill. According to inscriptions, Emperor Vespasian had the temple erected in A.D. 72 as the capital, or religious center, of what was then called Brixia, a prosperous trading place. The museum, built into the ruins, contains a bronze Winged Victory, gilded busts of members of the imperial house, vases, and other archaeological finds.

The principal landmark, dating from the Middle Ages, is the

Broletto, an austere building with a loggia and the massive Tower of the People at the city center that was the seat of the municipal government until 1421. The Broletto was started a few decades after Arnold of Brescia, a cleric who had become an advocate of church reform, was executed in Rome in 1155. Arnold (*Arnaldo* in Italian), a disciple of the French theologian Abélard, maintained that priests, bishops, and the pope himself must renounce any properties and political power. The puritanical Brescian incited his fellow citizens to revolt against their bishop, and later in Rome he won over the lower clergy with his ideas while two popes, Innocent II and Anastasius IV, "either trembled in the Vatican or wandered as exiles in the adjacent cities" (Gibbon). Under Adrian IV, the only English pope in history, Arnold was burned at the stake as a heretic.

More than 700 years after his death Brescia put a bronze statue of the unfortunate reformer in a space near the old Venetian Gate in the eastern portion of the city walls, renaming the square Piazza Arnaldo da Brescia.

South of the Broletto is Brescia's dual cathedral. It consists of a domed circular church from the twelfth century, known as La Rotunda, and a triumphal Baroque edifice in white marble with a 270-foot-high cupola that seems to overwhelm the older structure.

A few steps northwest of Cathedral Square, and linked with it by an archway, is an urban gem, Piazza della Loggia. The harmonious square is dominated by the city hall, or Loggia, in early-Renaissance style. Palladio (*see* Vicenza) helped in the later stages of its construction. Opposite is a clock tower whose bell is struck by two figures, "the Moors," modeled after the tower in St. Mark's Square in Venice.

South of Piazza della Loggia is a cluster of modern structures around the new Piazza della Vittoria (Square of Victory) in the pretentiously monumental manner of Marcello Piacentini (*see* Bergamo), built after a rundown neighborhood was razed during Fascist rule. Corso Zanardelli south of Piazza della Vittoria is a lively business street.

The hill in the northeast corner of the inner city is crowned with a castle that was erected in the fourteenth century when Brescia was under the domination of Milan. In 1426 the city passed under Venice, and its new masters strengthened the fortress and the city walls, putting up their emblem, the lion of St. Mark, in various places. The castle hill is now a public park, and the old stronghold is a museum devoted to Brescia's spirited fight against Austrian rule. The city was an Austrian possession from the fall of Napoleon to the unification of Italy in 1866.

While the overall impression of Brescia is one of modernity, the stroller will find in inner-city neighborhoods charming old palaces in the Venetian Gothic or Renaissance styles, and a number of churches with paintings by the principal artist of the Brescian school, the highly productive Il Moretto (1498–1555). The real name of the "Little Moor" was Alessandro Bonvicino; influenced by the Venetian painters, he developed his own luminous style. Many works by Il Moretto and by other Brescian painters—Il Romanino (Girolamo Romano) and the accomplished portraitist Giovanni Battista Moroni above all— can be viewed in the Civic Picture Gallery.

Brescia is a good base for visiting Lake Garda, the largest Italian lake, with many romantic views and corners. Desenzano, a harbor, is nineteen miles to the east, linked with Brescia by frequent trains and the Milan-Venice motorway. Cruise boats leaving from Desenzano call at Sirmione, a little town with a castle and the remains of what may have been the villa of the Roman poet Catullus on the rocky tip of a peninsula. Other stops include the resort Gardone Riviera, the beautiful promontory of Punta di San Vigilio, and various scenic spots around the 143-square-mile lake.

MANTUA (MANTOVA) ▪

The best approach is from the north. The traveler coming from Verona crosses rich, level farmland, sees from afar the pipes and cracking towers of a large oil refinery, and unexpectedly reaches the shore of a curving lake. Across the water a high dome, towers of different heights and shapes, the battlemented red-brick walls of a medieval fortress and the tiled roofs and mellow hues of old buildings combine into a panorama almost like that of Venice.

Mantua (Italian *Mantova*, with the stress on the first syllable) is surrounded on three sides by the lake that the Mincio River forms before lazily joining the Po. In ancient times the city's isolation was even more complete because of the marshlands surrounding it. Mantua, a strategic possession, was relatively easy to defend and hard to conquer.

Even today the city seems sheltered. Only a few miles off the Bologna-Modena-Verona motorway, Mantua has been left alone by mass tourism. For that reason too, besides its art treasures in a quaint urban setting and its relaxed mood, it is one of the most likable places in Italy. It is also one of the nation's most prosperous communities; the 65,000 Mantuans are among the Italians with the highest average income.

The farmers in the plains around Mantua are thriving, and the city's entrepreneurs have succeeded in building an industrial establishment of remarkable diversification. Today the area exports steel tubes for various uses, bicycles, toys, ready-made clothing, hosiery, and many other products that sell well all over the world.

The city's fortunes started with Virgil. The Roman poet was born in 70 B.C. as the son of a farmer in what is now the village of Pietole, southeast of Mantua. In his *Aeneid*, Virgil tells a story of Mantua's founding by the Etruscans; the city derives its name from Mantus, an Etruscan deity. All this, however, is legend.

Mantua has always been proud of its great son, the most illustrious poet in the Latin language. A curious relief statue representing a stout Virgil seated on a throne with a self-satisfied expression on his broad Mantuan peasant face can be seen on the façade of the medieval building that houses the city government. At the end of the eighteenth century Mantua laid out a square to honor the poet. A bronze statue of a togaed Virgil on a theatrical white marble pedestal with allegorical sculptures was erected there in 1927.

Virgil's statue and the park surrounding it look out on what is called the Middle Lake, the part of the Mincio bulge that is enclosed by the two bridges leading into the city from the north and the northeast. The Upper Lake is to the west and the Lower Lake to the east of the bridges. A narrow arm of the Mincio, called the Rio, runs from the Upper to the Lower Lake across the city amid vistas like those of a Venetian canal. All that water around Mantua breeds mosquitoes in summer and frequent fog in the cold months.

The heart of medieval Mantua is the rectangular Piazza delle Erbe (Vegetables Square). It is dominated by a massive clock tower flanking the long, low Palazzo della Ragione, the former courthouse, in dark brown brickwork with shops under its arcades. South of the clock tower, a little below the present level of the square, is a round church in the Romanesque style, the Rotunda of St. Lawrence (eleventh century) with only a few windows in its red-brick walls. The interior is austerely bare. The narrow old houses opposite the Palazzo della Ragione are also arcaded. Produce from the Mantuan countryside can be found in the outdoor market in the lively piazza.

It is only a short walk to Piazza Sordello and the Palace of the Gonzagas. That family seized power in Mantua in 1328 and held on to it for more than 300 years. They expanded their city-state's territory in successful wars with Milan and Venice and, as patrons of the arts and science, made Mantua into a shining center of Renaissance civilization. The brilliance was most intense under Francesco II, who ruled from 1484 to 1519, and his wife, the beautiful and cultured Isabella d'Este from Ferrara.

Piazza Sordello is named after a thirteenth-century Mantuan poet who wrote in the Provençal language and was immortalized by Dante in *The Divine Comedy*. The Gothic, arcaded main façade of the Ducal Palace occupies the eastern side of the impressive square, which has a screen of trees at its southern end and accommodates outdoor cafés and the terrace of a restaurant.

From the building on Piazza Sordello the Gonzagas by stages took over the entire neighborhood as far as the embankment of the Lower Lake. They successfully closed off streets and squares, incorporated existing structures into their residence and had new ones built. The result was a maze of 450 halls and rooms, a fortress, and a palace church around several courtyards. In Italy the Gonzaga Palace is, as an architectural complex, second in size only to the Vatican.

The precarious condition of many of the works of art in the palace and a shortage of guards explain why visitors are admitted in guided tours only. During the standard circuit, lasting an hour, sightseers are cursorily shown around some halls, stairways, corridors, and courtyards. Many of the paintings that the early Gonzagas had commissioned or collected were sold off by later members of that family when they needed cash, and are now to be admired in museums in Paris, London, and elsewhere.

In the palace's Hall of Princes visitors see fragments of frescoes by the early-Renaissance painter Pisanello that were discovered only in 1969; he took his themes from the Age of Chivalry. After some rooms with Flemish tapestry, a Hall of Mirrors with rich decorations

75

from the seventeenth and eighteenth centuries, a vast hanging garden high above street level, a diminutive apartment for the court dwarves, and the walled "secret garden" of Isabella d'Este, the guided tour reaches Mantua's pride—the Mantegna frescoes. They are in the Castle of St. George, a fourteenth-century stronghold that controlled the bridge between the Middle Lake and the Lower Lake, and is part of the Gonzaga complex.

Andrea Mantegna (*see* Padua) was first called to Mantua by Ludovico III Gonzaga in 1459, and he returned to the city several times for various commissions. His most famous work still to be seen in the city are the frescoes in the castle's Camera degli Sposi (Hall of the Married Couple). Groups of only up to twenty persons are allowed to view the hall for no longer than one minute at a time because, guides explain, the prolonged presence of crowds may further deteriorate the wall paintings, which are under treatment by art restorers.

The fresco above the hall's fireplace shows the Gonzaga court with Ludovico consulting an adviser, and the ruler's wife, Barbara of Brandenburg, their children, court dwarf, and officious-looking worthies. The figures are realistic and sharply characterized. The scene on the hall's west wall represents the meeting between Ludovico and his son Francesco on the latter's return from Rome as a cardinal. A measure of deference by the father to the son, by secular power to ecclesiastical authority, is subtly expressed. One of the figures in the group is a self-portrait by the heavyset Mantegna, who wouldn't omit an unsightly wart on his nose.

The east and south walls are painted with trompe-l'oeil curtains. The ceiling is a first in Renaissance art, the "eye." Mantegna, solving tricky problems of perspective masterfully, created the illusion of an opening in the roof through which the blue sky and a few clouds are visible while girls, a dark-skinned slave, and cupids seem to be gazing into the hall from above. This pictorial stunt was to be imitated by other artists.

The palace complex includes a noble Renaissance church, the Basilica of St. Barbara, which is usually closed, with a domed campanile. The cathedral of Mantua, with its Baroque façade on the north side of Piazza Sordello, dates from the Middle Ages and was repeatedly, and not very successfully, rebuilt.

The city's most important church is near Piazza delle Erbe, Sant'Andrea; its dome can be seen for miles. The church was started in 1472 from designs by the Florentine architect Leon Battista Alberti and only completed 200 years later. In the splendid interior the first chapel on the left encloses Mantegna's tomb with a bronze bust of the artist, perhaps shaped by himself. The decorations in the chapel, among them a damaged *Holy Family*, were sketched by the master and carried out by pupils.

Mantegna's house, now a museum, is in the south of the city. The Renaissance building with unadorned brick exterior and an interesting round courtyard was built on a plot of land that Ludovico III had donated to the painter.

Farther to the south is the Palazzo del Te, built between 1525 and 1535 as an out-of-town residence for Federico II, the first Gonzaga ruler to have the rank of a duke. *Tè* in Italian means "tea," but the name of the palace has nothing to do with the beverage, being a contraction of "Teieto," as the neighborhood was once called. The opulently decorated building is considered the masterpiece of Giulio Romano, the architect and painter who was Raphael's favorite pupil. The palace is now a museum, which includes a small gallery of modern paintings and serves also as a setting for occasional special art shows.

After the end of the Gonzaga rule in 1707 Mantua passed under Austrian control, and remained a Habsburg possession—with a Napoleonic interval from 1797 to 1814—until it joined unified Italy in 1866. Empress Maria Theresa particularly favored the city. She founded an Academy of Science and Arts and had a fine building south of the Gonzaga Palace erected to house the institution. Now known as the Virgilian Academy, the classical structure includes a splendid lecture hall, the Theater of the Academy, designed by the eighteenth-century architect Antonio Bibbiena.

CREMONA ▪

Owning a Stradivarius, an Amati, or a Guarneri is a virtuoso's dream. The ethereal-sounding violins with one of these precious labels were all turned out in Cremona, near the Po River, between the sixteenth and eighteenth centuries. Now a quiet city of over 80,000 that feels somewhat out of the Italian mainstream, Cremona keeps the tradition of its famous *liutai* (lutemakers) alive. It has an international school where violinmaking is taught, and a Stradivarius Museum. The latter traces the art of building noble violins, violas, cellos, lutes, and other stringed instruments from Andrea Amati (1530–1611) and Niccolò Amati (1596–1687) to the younger Amati's great and eventually wealthy pupil, Antonio Stradivari (1644–1737), and to Giuseppe Antonio Guarneri (1683–1745).

Cremona is also the birthplace of Claudio Monteverdi (1567–1643), the pioneer of grand opera. The city furthermore boasts the most magnificent cathedral in Lombardy next to Milan's Duomo, and in the sixteenth century Cremona brought forth its own style of painting, the Cremonese school.

Besides all this the city's pace is unhurried and its atmosphere delightfully old-fashioned; many streets are lined with medieval red-brick houses and flaking palaces with charming courtyards. Although some industry has lately sprung up on the flat outskirts, Cremona's economy is still essentially farm-based. The city and its agricultural hinterland are renowned for their provolone cheese, salami, pungent mustards, and a kind of nougat known as *torrone*, a word describing the towerlike shape of the confection.

The city's pride and principal landmark is indeed its Torrazzo (Big Tower), the 397-foot-high octagonal campanile of its cathedral, visible for many miles across the Lombard plains. When it was erected in the second half of the thirteenth century it was the tallest tower in Italy. It still is, not counting the 404-foot-high dome of St. Peter's. The extensive view from the top of the campanile embraces the Po and the towns and farmland on either side of the river.

The base of the bell tower is connected with the cathedral by a Renaissance hall and loggia. The huge church was built in the Lombard Romanesque style in the twelfth century, but architects and artists kept making additions for hundreds of years. The main façade in shades of red and pink with flecks of white marble is a medley of styles and tastes spanning four centuries. It has pillars, a rose window with an incongruous gable put above it later, and sculptures of the Virgin Mary, prophets, and saints.

The cathedral interior is dark but can be lit up if a request is made in the sacristy. The frescoes over the arches of the nave are well worth the small expense. They represent biblical episodes painted by masters of the Cremona school, including Boccaccio Boccaccino, Altobello da Melone, Pietro and Gianfrancesco Bembo, Galeazzo

Campi, and younger members—Giulio, Antonio, and Bernardino—of the Campi family. A sequence of Passion scenes is by the Venetian painter Giovanni Antonio da Pordenone, a rival of Titian. South of the cathedral is an octagonal baptistery, also from the twelfth century.

Piazza del Comune (City Hall Square) outside the cathedral breathes an air of civic pride and self-confidence. The battlemented Gothic city hall is from the thirteenth century and was embellished during the Renaissance; it has on its left side an annex that originally served as assembly place for the citizens' militia, and later for the college of jurists. From an open-air café under the loggia one can leisurely study the cathedral façade and observe the people in the piazza, the city's social center.

The large Palazzo Affaitati, a late-Renaissance building in the city's north, with a Baroque courtyard and grand staircase, houses the Civic Museum and Picture Gallery with many works by Cremonese masters. It includes also an archaeological department and a rich numismatic collection. The Stradivarius Museum is in the Palazzo dell'Arte (Palace of Art), also the seat of the violinmaking school, in a southern neighborhood.

The fourteenth-century Church of Sant'Agostino west of the cathedral, in Lombard Gothic brickwork, has frescoes by Cremonese painters and a Madonna by Perugino. Remains of Cremona's old bastions can be seen in the westernmost part of the city. Way beyond them a restored seventeenth-century farmhouse contains a Museum of Peasant Civilization in the Po Valley, with agricultural implements that were used centuries ago and other exhibits regarding past rural life.

Residents of Cremona will tell you that their city was once "as big as Paris." This may be a slight exaggeration. Today Cremona surely is no second Paris, but it is one of the most prosperous places in all of Italy.

PAVIA ▪

The forty-minute car trip from the southern outskirts of dynamic Milan across lonely flatlands and along a superannuated canal is a plunge into the past. Pavia has today barely 90,000 inhabitants, many of whom commute to jobs in the nearby metropolis with its population of nearly two million. Yet the small city that has become a satellite of Milan treasures the memories and trophies of an illustrious past. Pavia was a great name in the early Middle Ages; it competed for centuries with Milan and served as the royal capital of the Ostrogoths and the Longobards.

Entering the city at its Milan Gate, the motorist beholds the red-brick Visconti Castle, the gloomy symbol of Pavia. It was built in the fourteenth century by Galeazzo II Visconti, lord of Milan, to assert his dominance over the rival city that he had just obtained from the German emperor. The fortress, with a vast courtyard, was surrounded by a moat and a huge hunting park enclosed by a thirteen-mile wall. The castle is now a museum, comprising a collection of Romanesque sculptures and architectural fragments, a gallery of paintings from the fourteenth through eighteenth centuries, and a natural-science section.

Castle Square opens into the Strada Nuova, Pavia's north-south axis, which slices across the closely packed inner city. The famous university is about halfway on the east side. Law was taught in Pavia since the eleventh century; Galeazzo II founded the university in 1361. Its present building, with five courtyards, was started in 1490 and much enlarged in the eighteenth century by the architect who built the La Scala opera house in Milan, Giuseppe Piermarini. Many of the university's faculty and students live in Milan.

The Strada Nuova runs to the Ticino River, which skirts the city's south. The Ticino rises near the glaciers below the St. Gotthard Pass, traverses the Italian-speaking canton of Switzerland that has taken its name, flows through the Lago Maggiore, and joins the Po five miles southeast of Pavia.

Cross the river on the Ponte Coperto, a 600-foot-long covered stone bridge from the fourteenth century containing a chapel, or on the modern Ponte della Libertà (Freedom Bridge) one-third of a mile upstream. From the right bank of the Ticino there is an impressive view of Pavia's skyline with its old towers and the dome of its cathedral.

The cupola of the cathedral, a vast edifice west of the Strada Nuova, is 300 feet high; Bramante, the architect of the Renaissance popes, was a consultant during the construction of the church. The 256-foot-high massive tower on the cathedral's left side antedates it by at least 150 years. The elongated Piazza Vittoria to the north is surrounded by arcades. Produce from the surrounding countryside is offered there during market hours.

The oldest neighborhoods of Pavia, a maze of medieval houses on narrow streets, huddle between the cathedral and the river. On a little square in this district, east of the Strada Nuova, rises a twelfth-century church in the Romanesque style, San Michele. An earlier Church of San Michele on the same site saw the coronations of medieval German emperors as kings of Italy. (They used to receive the imperial crown at the hands of the pope in Rome.)

Small industrial plants and the big Necchi sewing-machine and appliance factory ring the city. Some sightseers coming from Milan don't bother to go all the way to Pavia, although the stern city deserves a prolonged visit, but stop at the Certosa, one of the world's most famous monasteries.

The Certosa, or Charterhouse, of Pavia, seven miles north of the city, is a gem of Renaissance architecture and art surrounded by forests and rather melancholy flatlands. It was founded by Duke Gian Galeazzo Visconti, the dour, power-hungry son of Galeazzo II, in 1396 in what was then the northernmost part of the castle park. Formally a unit of the Carthusian order, which is based in the renowned monastery of La Grande Chartreuse near Grenoble in the French Alps, the Certosa was meant chiefly as a monument to Gian Galeazzo and Visconti power. The huge complex took more than two centuries to develop. It comprises a church, a palace for the dukes of Milan and distinguished visitors (now a Carthusian museum), and monastic buildings around a great cloister and three smaller courtyards, as well as vast walled gardens.

Visitors enter a forecourt flanked at right by the Ducal Palace, on the left by the monks' former pharmacy and their wine presses. The space is dominated by the multicolored, richly decorated church façade at the center. It was designed by Giovanni Antonio Amadeo (1447–1522), a prominent Lombard architect and sculptor. The ornaments of the unfinished façade include many statues in niches, and reliefs picturing biblical episodes, scenes from the life and funeral of Duke Gian Galeazzo, and highlights of the Carthusian order's history. Guides point out a stone portrait of Amadeo, holding an architect's pair of compasses.

The interior of the church shows the transition from the Gothic to

81

the Renaissance style. Sculptures and other decorations abound. The majestic tomb of Gian Galeazzo is in the right transept under a fresco by Ambrogio Borgognone showing the duke presenting a model of the church to the Virgin Mary.

The grand cloister with its 122 arches is surrounded by the prior's quarters and twenty-four monks' "cells," each consisting of three small rooms and a little secluded garden on the ground floor and a bedroom and little loggia above them. Among the smaller courtyards the Cloister of the Fountain, with terra-cottas and graceful marble columns around a Baroque waterbasin, radiates peaceful charm. A stock remark by visitors is that "there is much to be said for the monastic life—if it's in the Certosa."

PIACENZA ▪

The approaches are unpromising. The Po, Italy's longest river, sullenly flows beneath railroad and highway bridges, and the traveler wouldn't guess that a city of more than 100,000 inhabitants spreads out less than half a mile from its moody right bank. The Autostrada del Sole (Motorway of the Sun), from Milan to Rome, skirts Piacenza's northeast across flatlands dotted with industrial plants. The old national highway that was originally the Via Aemilia of the ancient Romans once ran straight across the city, but has long been diverted along its former moats to bypass the center. A huge power station rises across the tracks from the railroad station. One's first reaction is: Let's get out of here!

During the 1930s Piacenza seemed destined to become an industrial boom town, an Italian Pittsburgh or Houston in miniature, when prospectors struck oil nearby. It was the first oil field in energy-starved Italy. However, the Piacenza oil wells soon ran dry, and the city suffered heavy damages during World War II. Postwar discoveries of methane in the area did spur industrial development, but the gas fields too are by now nearly exhausted, and the industries around Piacenza depend on other power sources. The farmers in the well-tilled plains all around still contribute much to the city's prosperity.

The Piacentini, as the inhabitants are called, are cordial toward strangers, but seem surprised that anyone should come not for business but just to visit their city. Piacenza makes no particular effort to attract tourists, although it has impressive Gothic architecture, a Renaissance castle, scores of severe palaces, remarkable churches, convents, and squares, and fine museums.

Stretches of the sixteenth-century brick walls that enclosed the old city in an irregular octagon, four miles in circumference, are still visible. Walk through narrow, busy shopping streets to the geometrical center of the octagon, Piazza dei Cavalli (Horses' Square). The name refers to the two equestrian statues in the piazza, in front of the Municipal Palace. They represent the Dukes Alessandro and Ranuccio Farnese, father and son, of the Roman noble family who ruled Piacenza, together with nearby Parma, from 1545 to 1731. Both bronze monuments are the works of a Tuscan, Francesco Mochi or Mocchi. His statue of Ranuccio, erected in 1620, is more conventional than that of Alessandro, put up five years later to the left of it, a Baroque masterpiece distinguished by the dramatic movement of the elder Farnese's flowing cloak and his charger's serpentine mane.

The thirteenth-century municipal building behind the statues is popularly known as the Gothic Palace. The arcaded ground floor with pointed arches carries a huge assembly hall, which receives light through round-arch windows and a rose window. The roof is crowned with small towers and high battlements. The self-assured, defiant architecture is suffused by a spirit of communal independence that was soon to be broken by despotic rulers.

To the left of the Gothic Palace is the Palace of the Merchants' College, an elegant, arcaded seventeenth-century building, now the seat of the city council. From the Middle Ages far into the era of the Farnese dukes, the merchants' college was an influential body comprising the representatives of the city's well-to-do weavers, ironmongers, cheesemakers, jewelers, and other tradesmen.

In the second half of the sixteenth century, thriving Piacenza was a business and financial center of European importance. Four times every year bankers and brokers from various countries, some 200 big-money persons on average, congregated in the city on the Po during its periodic trade fairs to settle the accounts of their far-flung credit operations. Fernand Braudel, the French historian, says that the fairs functioned as a clearinghouse at a time when Piacenza was a big name in world finance. The ducal city was then economically under the tutelage of Genoa, the paramount commercial power of the epoch. When the Republic of Genoa declined, Piacenza's role in international money affairs was taken over by Antwerp.

The low-slung neoclassical Governor's Palace on the northeast side of Piazza dei Cavalli, opposite the Gothic Palace, has on its façade a two-story-high sundial and a perpetual calendar, both installed at the end of the eighteenth century by a local savant who admired Sir Isaac Newton.

Piacenza's cathedral, on a smaller piazza southeast of the city center, was built in the twelfth and thirteenth centuries; it combines Lombard Romanesque and Gothic elements. Walk around to admire its elaborate choir. The high campanile carries a lofty iron cage, put up there to expose to public contempt persons found guilty of sacrilege. Local scholars believe that the cage was never actually used because pillorying on the ground level was thought to be a more effective punishment.

A gilt bronze angel has crowned the cathedral's bell tower since 1341, beloved especially by the people in the countryside around Piacenza. The "golden angel" was toppled during a World War II air raid; it was restored in 1964, as a plaque opposite the church records, thanks to the generosity of local benefactors and the Famiglia Piacentina of New York, a hometown association.

The Farnese Palace in the north of the city, close to the Po, was begun in 1558 by Giacomo Barozzi di Vignola, who was later to succeed Michelangelo as chief architect of St. Peter's in Rome. Only half of Vignola's project in Piacenza was ever built, also because the Farnese dukes eventually established their main residence in Parma. The huge unfinished structure, which conveys a sense of cold pride, today houses the municipal collections. They include a collection of Etruscan and Roman antiquities, one of medieval weaponry, a numismatic department, a number of historic gala coaches, and an art gallery with many works by the Farnese court painters of the seventeenth and eighteenth centuries. A famous exhibit is a bronze model of an animal's liver with Etruscan inscriptions, dug up in 1877. This "Etruscan Liver" is believed to have been the professional prop of a soothsayer some 2,500 years ago.

The Farnese Palace adjoins surviving parts of an older fortress, the squat Citadel, with a round tower, built in the fourteenth century by the Visconti dukes of Milan who had subjugated Piacenza before the Farnese family.

A noteworthy modern art collection, the Ricci Oddi Gallery, donated to the city by a local nobleman, is in a new building in the south of the city center. Twenty-five halls contain 700 works from the second half of the nineteenth century to about 1910, including some by such non-Italian artists as Klimt.

The modern neighborhoods of Piacenza are mainly in the south of the city. On the highway to Parma, on the southeastern outskirts, is one of Piacenza's most characteristic institutions, the Collegio Alberoni. The sober three-story buildings, featuring endless corridors around a large courtyard, a magnificent staircase, and a rich library and a church were commissioned by Giulio Cardinal Alberoni in 1746. The immensely wealthy prince of the church, a native of Piacenza, served successively as a diplomat of the Farnese dukes, as prime minister of King Philip V of Spain, and as papal legate in the Romagna region and in Ravenna and Bologna. The elite college that he founded has in more than 200 years prepared thousands of young men for the priesthood and produced many outstanding prelates.

Astronomical, seismographic, and meteorological observatories were added to the college after its founder's death. The institution also includes a gallery of works of art collected by Cardinal Alberoni. Outstanding among them are an *Ecce Homo* by Antonello da Messina, dated 1473, paintings by Flemish masters, and Flemish tapestries.

The Alberoni College sums up the essence of a singular city: solidity, understated wealth, and earnestness.

AOSTA/AOSTE ■

Three tongues are spoken in this severe-looking city in the northwestern corner of Italy near Europe's highest mountains: Italian, French, and a dialect related to the Provençal language, the *langue valdôtaine*. Aosta is the capital of one of Italy's four semi-autonomous regions, which comprises the valley of the Dora Baltea River, a tributary of the Po, and a dozen high side valleys. (Italy's other territories with a measure of self-government are Trentino–Alto Adige/ South Tyrol, Sicily, and Sardinia.)

In the Valle d'Aosta and its administrative center, street signs, announcements to the public, and broadcasts are in Italian and French;

both languages are taught in the schools. French, Swiss, and Italian cooking blend in the local cuisine. The region's medium-fat fontina cheese plays a big role in pasta dishes; sausages, polenta, and the dried meat of the chamois are other Aostan specialties.

France and Switzerland are each only about an hour's car ride away from Aosta. The 15.5-mile tunnel under Mont Blanc, and the Great St. Bernard Tunnel, which is four miles long, have made motor travel between Italy and the two neighboring countries much easier, and possible even in deep winter. However, quite a few drivers seek the thrill of the old roads over the 7,178-foot Little St. Bernard Pass into the Savoy region of France, or over the great St. Bernard (8,110 feet) into Switzerland's Upper Rhone Valley whenever the two historic Alpine gateways are not snowed in. The friars of the 1,000-year-old hospice on the Great St. Bernard still keep a kennel full of St. Bernard dogs.

The new road tunnels and the proximity of such winter and summer resorts as Courmayeur, at the foot of the Mont Blanc massif, and Saint-Vincent, with its licensed gambling casino, have during the last few years swelled the transit movement through Aosta, which lies at the junction of the region's main roads. Traffic congestion in and around the city is often daunting.

The Aosta Valley, with its snow-capped peaks and majestic glaciers as a backdrop, and with its icy mountain streams, pastures, vineyards, and many medieval castles, seems at times overrun by holidaymakers from Italy's "industrial triangle," Milan-Turin-Genoa, and so is the region's capital. If you decide nevertheless to stop in Aosta, you will be rewarded by the discovery of one of the most Roman cities anywhere barring Rome.

The very name of the place echoes its classical origins: the name Aosta—or, in French, Aoste (pronounced "Aust")—is derived from that of its founder, Augustus. After his general Aulus Terentius Varro vanquished the Celtic tribe of the Salassi in the area in 25 B.C., the emperor settled 3,000 veterans of the Roman elite corps, the Praetorian Guard, at the spot, a widening of the Dora Baltea Valley that strategically controlled the nearby mountain passes. The new fortified encampment was called Augusta Praetoria Salassorum, the headquarters of the Praetorians in the land of the Salassi.

The walls of the Roman garrison town, erected more than two

millennia ago, still stand almost in their entirety. They form a rectangle, 792 by 625 yards, enclosing the core of Aosta. Most of the Praetorians' watchtowers along the walls were transformed during the Middle Ages into the private fortresses of counts and barons. From 1032 onward Aosta was a fief of the counts of Savoy, ancestors of the family that provided unified Italy with its kings from 1861 until the proclamation of the Italian Republic in 1946.

One gloomy former defense structure in the southwestern part of the Roman walls is known as the Leper's Tower. It was the setting for a once-famous romantic novel by the French diplomat and writer Xavier de Maistre. *The Leper of Aosta* (1811) describes the author's meeting and conversations with Pier Bernardo Guasco of Aosta, a real-life person, who in the story was locked up in the tower for thirty years after having been found to be stricken with leprosy. The book, combining emotional humanitarianism with a message of Christian resignation, was a signal literary success in its time. A major street in Aosta is named after the French writer.

Rue Xavier de Maistre starts from the Central Piazza (or Place) E. Chanoux where the ornate, arcaded city hall stands. In a right angle to Rue de Maistre is Via delle Porte Pretoriane (Street of the Praetorian Gates), leading toward the eastern access to the walled center, with two of the original three arches preserved. Proceeding in the same direction on Via Sant'Anselmo, one reaches the imposing Arch of Augustus, a triumphal gateway that might well stand in Rome. Farther on, beyond the little Buthier River, the arch of a Roman bridge sticks out of the ground. Another noteworthy ruin from imperial times is the Roman theater, northwest of the Praetorian Gate, with a 72-foot-high stage wall nearly intact.

Between the eastern walls and the Arch of Augustus stands Aosta's principal monument from the Middle Ages, the Church of St. Ours, with a massive square tower that incorporates stone blocks hewn by ancient Roman masons. The church is said to have been founded in the eleventh century by St. Anselm, a native of Aosta who was bishop of the city before becoming abbot of the Benedictine monastery of Bec in Normandy and eventually archbishop of Canterbury (from 1093 to 1109). A serene Romanesque cloister adjoins the church; the sculptured capitals of its columns delight connoisseurs.

The Priory of St. Ours, on the south side of the complex, is an elaborate Renaissance building with an octagonal tower. Nearby is the Regional Archaeological Museum, where much pre-Roman and Roman material may be viewed.

Aosta's cathedral, northeast of the central square, is essentially a Renaissance edifice with some older parts still discernible, including Roman columns and an early Christian altar in the crypt.

Aosta, which now has 40,000 inhabitants, has long spilled beyond its Roman military core, and at an altitude of around 1,900 feet it spreads out in the floor of the Dora Baltea Valley, here nearly two miles across. Factories working high-grade iron ore from the nearby Cogne Valley, along with other industries, are on the outskirts; mountains rising as high as 12,000 feet surround the city. Travelers who arrive from the Great St. Bernard Pass enjoy a fine view of Aosta for a few miles before descending to the city. In the opposite direction is the winter resort area of Mont Pilaz (Italian: *Pila*), at about 4,500 feet. It can be reached from Aosta over a ten-mile road with many bends, and it commands an even grander panorama of the city and the Alpine chain to its north.

LERICI ▪

Hotels here are named after Byron and Shelley, and business signs make much of the "Gulf of the Poets." Lerici and its twin, San Terenzo, keep cashing in on the English romantics of the early nineteenth century who felt inspired by the scenic bay southeast of La Spezia. That natural deep-water harbor then wasn't the important naval base it is now, and there were no oil refineries and industrial plants all around it. The sea in which Shelley eventually drowned was much more limpid than it is today.

Yet despite its closeness to the now rather unlovely city of La Spezia and the cluttered industrial hinterland of the naval base, Lerici has retained some of the beauty that charmed the poets. Its bay is framed on its left by an old castle on a rock and on its right by another hillside castle; it looks out on the marble promontory of Portovenere and the two small islands that, like the tips of sunken mountains, extend it into the sea—Palmaria, with its Blue Grotto, and tiny Tino. Behind Lerici's seaside promenade there is the maze of an old fishermen's town enclosed by steep hills, an amphitheater with tiers of villas amid pine trees.

Liguria and Tuscany meet and blend in Lerici, the old seaport over which the area's maritime powers in the Middle Ages, Genoa and Pisa, went to war repeatedly until the Genoese prevailed. For many centuries the main pursuits of the people in Lerici were fishing and trading. Today very few of its 15,000 permanent inhabitants still sail far out, beyond the offshore islands, to cast their nets. Many residents commute to jobs in La Spezia or in the even nearer industrial sprawl surrounding the town of Sarzana.

The hundred or more craft that at any time crowd Lerici's small harbor are mostly pleasure boats. A local environmental group is crusading against plans to add marina space by extending the breakwater. The project, its opponents argue, would transform Lerici's old harbor into a foul-smelling pond. The existing breakwater serves now also for rounding out the seafront strolls that most visitors and many local people ritually take every day, preferably toward sunset when the breezes spring up.

Vacationers sun in the cramped bathing concessions but are reluctant to go into the water, which seems more oily than salty. The shore promenade offers the usual amenities of Riviera resorts—café terraces, *gelaterie*, restaurants, *pizzerie*, shops selling beachwear and souvenirs, and towering palms. The real Lerici starts some fifty yards from the water. It is a town with its own life and—as the many wall posters with partisan messages show—vigorous local politics. At the height of summer it is pleasurable to walk in the old streets into which the sun rarely penetrates. Going back to the seafront one passes a town landmark, the striking Romanesque campanile of the Church of San Rocco, which itself is humdrum.

San Terenzo, a five-minute ride by car or bus northwest of Lerici, duplicates its main features. Although the two towns on the bay are close together and form an administrative unit, it is not advisable to walk from one to the other. The shore road, hugging a cliff, lacks sidewalks for some stretches, and motor traffic is heavy. The stroll between Lerici and San Terenzo must have been much more pleasant in the days of the English poets.

Shelley's last home, marked by a plaque, was a villa on the road between the two towns, now a part of San Terenzo. He sailed for Livorno on July 1, 1822, to visit friends, and on the voyage back drowned in a storm off Viareggio on July 8. His body was washed ashore later, and was cremated in Byron's presence. The ashes were taken to the Foreigners' Cemetery near the Pyramid of Gaius Cestius in Rome.

PORTOFINO ∎

On some weekends at the height of summer it takes at least an hour to drive the three miles from Santa Margherita Ligure to Portofino on the only road leading to the former fishing village whose very fame is threatening to smother it. Once arrived, often with the radiator boiling, the motorist finds the town's sole parking lot packed, with hardly enough space left for turning around to inch back to Santa Margherita.

Having a yacht helps getting into Portofino during its dizzy season, although the chances are there will be no slot available in the marina unless arrangements—at staggering fees—have been made well ahead. Most of the visitors come from Genoa, Rapallo, and other places along the Riviera in boats that various shipping companies operate from morning to night. These excursionists write innumerable postcards, use up all the film in their cameras, and leave again after a few hours. They may not even have managed to conquer an outdoor table at one of the dozen cafés and restaurants surrounding the small harbor and piazza.

How can the rich and the would-be sophisticates who think they must put in an appearance in Portofino stand such mobbing? They entertain one another on board their yachts or on the terraces of their villas and cute apartments, or frolic in the swimming pool and bar of the deluxe Hotel Splendido high above the road from Santa Margherita. They may eventually show up in the piazza facing the harbor when the families from Genoa and Milan, the German motorcyclists, and the backpacked Dutch hikers have departed. Astonishingly, with all its summer crowds, Portofino still exercises snob appeal.

Why include such an oversold Riviera resort in the Cento Città? Go there, if you can, on some clear, sunny day between late October and March—there are always at least a few. No more than a thousand people will be living in off-season Portofino, yet the place will seem a little seaport town rather than a mere village. There will be leisure to take in the blend of perfect maritime convenience and exceptional beauty that distinguishes Portofino. The small natural harbor is a sheltered cove near the rocky tip of a lushly overgrown promontory that protects the Gulf of Rapallo like a giant breakwater. Big fish must once have played here, for the ancient Romans called the spot Portus Delfini, Dolphin's Harbor.

The houses that line the port—most of their façades only two windows wide, and painted in pastel pinks, yellows, and greens—are from the eighteenth and nineteenth centuries, but Portofino was surely continuously inhabited since the Romans. Richard Lion-Heart sailed from here in 1190 for the Third Crusade. A waterfront plaque records a visitor with a more frivolous reputation: "The writer Guy de Maupassant sojourned at Portofino for several days in 1889 aboard his sailboat *Bel Ami*."

Stairways near the tribute to *Bel Ami* and its author-skipper lead up to the crest of the promontory where Portofino's parish church stands. On a pole outside, a banner with a red cross on a white field flutters in the breeze. It is the Cross of St. George, the same that appears, together with the crosses of St. Andrew and St. Patrick, on the Union Jack. Relics of St. George, England's patron saint, are treasured in the church, and for that reason Portofino has always meant a lot to the British. According to tradition, St. George was a Roman soldier believed to have died a martyr's death for his Christian faith at Nicomedia in Asia Minor in A.D. 303. How his bones, or some of them, reached Portofino is not known. He was considered the heavenly protector of soldiers, and the English Church adopted him as the patron of the realm during the Middle Ages.

An outer wall of the parish church carries tablets commemorating prominent former residents. There are several English names. "Elizabeth Countess Carnarvon, 1857–1929, Benefactress of Portofino," one inscription reads. Another one praises "Jeannine Watt, Widowed Von Mumm, 1866–1953, who saved Portofino from destruction ordered by the invading armies, March 1945." It seems that the Nazis, just before their surrender to the Allied forces in northern Italy, had intended to blow up much of Portofino, but were prevented from carrying out their design. The parish church did suffer some war damages, but has long been repaired. One tablet is devoted to Alexander Clifford (1909–1952), a British journalist and writer who lived

91

for some time at the Castelletto (Little Castle) near the church with his wife, Jenny Nicholson, a daughter of Robert Graves. Both were my friends.

Yet another plaque on the church wall recalls that Guglielmo Marconi, the inventor of wireless telegraphy, "from his yacht *Elettra* in Portofino turned on the lights of the World's Fair in Sydney, Australia, on March 26, 1930."

Walk around the church to a parapet on the other side from which a panorama of the tormented coast and the breakers can be enjoyed. Only footpaths lead from Portofino up to the hills of the promontory, which is a rocky mass about three miles long by three miles wide jutting out into the sea. The highest point, Portofino Vetta, with a hotel and restaurant at 1,476 feet, can be reached by road from Santa Margherita, east of Portofino, or from Camogli or Recco to the west of it. A part of the promontory has been designated as a national park in an effort to protect its flora and wildlife.

SAN REMO ■

Myriads of carnations, tulips, roses, and lilies frame this lush city on a wide bay near the French-Italian border, which is protected from the cold north winds by a chain of hills and favored by a soft, sunny climate with little rain. San Remo has three facets: it is a medieval Ligurian town crouching on a steep hill between the beds of two torrents as if forever afraid of pirate raids from the sea; it gives the impression of the fading opulence of a Victorian resort now outshone by more glamorous places beyond the frontier; and it features the splendor of the flower plantations that, terrace above terrace, climb up the natural amphitheater between the coastal city and the motorway higher up that links Genoa with Monte Carlo and Nice.

A century ago San Remo was a world-famous byword for elegance in the sun. English lords, German royalty, and Russian grand dukes wintered here. They paraded in their equipages with their liveried servants up and down the Corso. The fancy seaside promenade, flanked by tall palms and luxury hotels, is still called Corso dell'Imperatrice (Corso of the Empress) after Czarina Maria Alexandrovna, who spent ten weeks in the city in the winter of 1874–

1875, welcomed by King Victor Emmanuel II and honored by the visit of a Russian naval squadron in the bay.

San Remo has also a Russian Orthodox church (where the last sovereigns of the operetta kingdom of Montenegro, Nicholas I and his wife, Milena, are buried), a Corso of the English, a French Street, and a Goethe Street. Many rich foreigners used to own hillside villas, and some still do. However, the nearby Principality of Monaco and the French Riviera have taken much business away from San Remo since the end of World War II.

Several scores of hotels, pensions, and rest homes offer accommodations from the luxury category to the plain. Some of them are closed from October to Christmas, and during the remainder of the winter they cater mainly to elderly guests. In the belle époque few visitors came in summer; now San Remo fills up when the bathing season starts, and the fine beaches east and west of the small harbor and the old Genoese Fort of Santa Tecla become crowded.

A special clientele is drawn to San Remo around the year by the gaming tables and slot machines in the Municipal Casino, one of Italy's few legal gambling places (others are in Saint-Vincent in the Aosta Valley, at Campione d'Italia in an enclave on Lake Lugano, and in Venice). The imposing San Remo casino, in a park on the central Via Matteotti, was built in 1906. It has lately been under investigation for corruption and racketeering scandals that have rocked the city; allegedly the Mafia tried to muscle into the gaming operations.

But San Remo's 60,000 inhabitants aren't really as dependent on the casino as the populations of some other international gambling spots are. The city plays host to participants in conventions and symposiums, at Carnival time every year it stages a famous parade with floats and merrymaking, and each February it launches young hopefuls and new songs in its pop music festival, which receives worldwide radio and television coverage.

When cold and snow grip the northern parts of the continent, San Remo ships tons of fresh flowers, harbingers of the coming spring, by chartered aircraft to them. The gardeners of San Remo and its surroundings also supply a good deal of the flowers sold all over Italy. Every weekday morning from autumn to spring the vast Mercato dei Fiori (Flower Market) off Corso Garibaldi to the west of the old city is filled with sweet fragrances, riotous colors, and brisk trading.

OPPOSITE, TOP:
Lake Como

OPPOSITE, BOTTOM: *Pavia,*
Visconti Castle

ABOVE: *Lerici, from the*
park of Villa Bibolini

RIGHT: *Bergamo,*
Colleoni Chapel

Portofino

OPPOSITE:
San Remo

The old town is locally known as La Pigna ("The Pine Cone") because of its shape. The neighborhood is a maze of narrow alleys, furtive cats, stairways, gloomy passages, dilapidated walls, and arches with which rickety houses seem to be holding each other up. The Church of San Siro at the foot of the medieval quarter, in Romanesque style, is 700 years old. High above the upper fringe of the old town, the Baroque domed Church of Our Lady of the Coast commands a panorama of San Remo and its bay.

The local cuisine, especially in the hotels, is influenced by neighboring France. A specialty is the Genoese garnish for pasta dishes that is known as pesto—a greenish sauce made with the region's excellent olive oil, finely crushed basil, sometimes other herbs, and garlic, also Parmesan or pecorino cheese and pine nuts. Much of the seafood that can be had in San Remo no longer comes from Ligurian waters but from faraway fisheries. Instead, the wines served in the city are usually heady whites from the terraced vineyards along the coast.

San Remo is the largest of the resorts on the Riviera di Ponente, the rocky Ligurian shoreline west of Genoa, and is a natural headquarters for day trips to its many beauty spots. To the west are the fishing port of Ospedaletti, the elegant resort of Bordighera, and the frontier town of Ventimiglia. East of San Remo, beyond the industrial seaport of Imperia, such towns as Diano Marina, Alassio, Albenga, and Finale Ligure form a string of vacation spots with many hotels, second homes of families from Genoa, Turin, and Milan, marinas, restaurants, and nightclubs. A little off the seafront with all its concrete, glitter, and noise, some traces of the old days, when the people of the coastal towns lived frugally, mainly by fishing and by harvesting their olive trees, may still be detected—perhaps in the occasional old house that has not yet been cunningly restored, or in the stories that the headstones of the graveyards tell.

The views along the Riviera di Ponente, often spectacular, are generally better from the Via Aurelia (National Route No. 1), which the ancient Romans hewed from the live rock, than from Motorway A-10 with its many tunnels. There is heavy traffic on either highway.

3
THE
HEARTLANDS

*Emilia, Romagna,
and Tuscany*

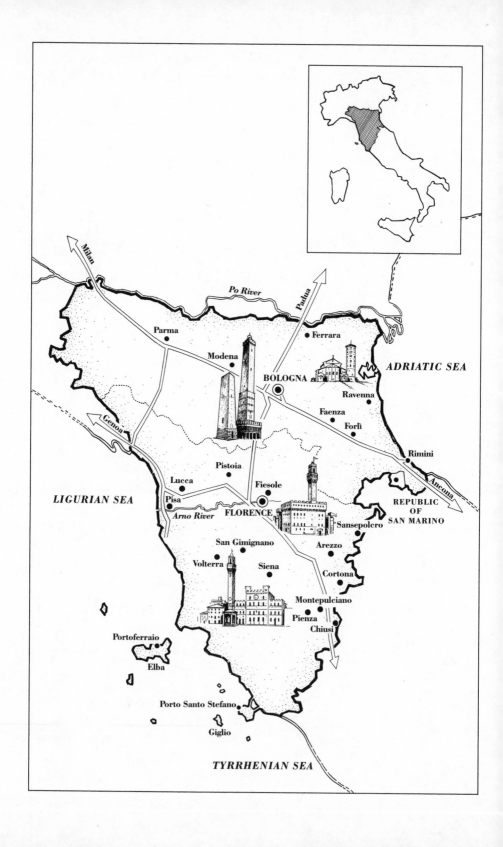

MILAN

Po River

Padua

Parma

Modena

Ferrara

BOLOGNA

ADRIATIC SEA

Ravenna

Genoa

Faenza

Forlì

Rimini

Pistoia

Lucca

Fiesole

Ancona

Pisa

FLORENCE

Arno River

LIGURIAN SEA

Sansepolcro

REPUBLIC
OF
SAN MARINO

San Gimignano

Arezzo

Volterra

Siena

Cortona

Montepulciano

Pienza

Chiusi

Portoferraio

Elba

Porto Santo Stefano

Giglio

TYRRHENIAN SEA

Much of what people abroad regard and love as the quintessence of Italy is to be found in the vigorous regions on either side of the upper Apennines, the peninsula's rocky spine.

Here the traveler is enchanted by a highly civilized landscape of fertile, well-cultivated plains and gentle hills with rows of pines and olive trees leading up to stately villas, and is dazzled by a succession of cities and towns, each distinguished by its special character, and many crammed with noble old buildings and great art.

Europe's oldest university is still thriving in Bologna. Italy's greatest poet, Dante Alighieri, was a Florentine. And it was in Florence too, soon after Dante's time, that the revolution in learning and the arts that eventually came to be called the Renaissance gathered strength.

In the nineteenth century, the two composers who for most music lovers embody Italian opera were born here—Verdi in Emilia and Puccini in Tuscany. Italian cuisine achieves daily triumphs here in celebrated gastronomic shrines, simple country inns, and many private homes; and some of the country's best vintages grow north and south of the Apennine ranges. Since the end of World War II the people of Emilia, Romagna, and Tuscany have attained enviable prosperity through a successful mix of farming, handicrafts, and industry. Can one blame them if they consider themselves somewhat special Italians? Emilia and Romagna are related by history, culture, and dialect, but their inhabitants stress their separate identities. Today the two areas are one administrative unit known as Region of Emilia-Romagna.

Emilia is mostly lowlands watered by the Po River and its tributaries. Once fragmented into city-states and small feudal holdings, much of the region became dominated by the papacy. Today small and medium-sized industrial plants are scattered over land devoted mainly to flourishing agrobusiness. Many local people work alternately on farms and in factories; most still have strong roots in the countryside, and are proud of them.

Emilians have a reputation for industriousness, but they are also proverbially fond of good food and drink, and of other sensual pleasures. Cordiality is their outstanding characteristic. Romagna stretches to the Adriatic Sea alongside the crest of the Apennines. It too belonged for centuries to the Papal States. The Romagnoli, as the inhabitants are called, were in the past known for raging passions and blood feuds; they are still noted for their fiery tempers. Mussolini was a native of the region.

In Tuscany, a sophisticated Etruscan civilization developed long before the ancient Romans conquered the region's hilltop cities and the Arno Valley. Etruscan strains seem to linger on in the ethnic makeup, parlance, and manners of present-day Tuscans. In the Middle Ages and the Renaissance, once-independent city-states like Pisa, Siena, and Arezzo were annexed by the Republic of Florence, which eventually was transformed into a grand duchy that survived until the unification of Italy in the 1860s.

Tuscans, who take pride in speaking what is often considered the purest Italian, are articulate, often argumentative, and seem to possess an innate sense of elegance. Other Italians may find them a trifle supercilious.

Ever since World War II the Communist Party has been firmly entrenched in the "red belt" of Emilia, Romagna, and Tuscany. Italian Communists are by no means averse to the good life or luxuries: They often dress smartly, drive flashy cars, and may run their own businesses along capitalist lines, exporting shoes, ready-to-wear clothes, or wines to the United States. They may reject the United States in theory, but they will be hospitable to individual Americans. Hundreds of expatriates from the United States and Britain own permanent homes in Tuscany, and many others rent villas or converted farmhouses for a season. Foreigners usually get along famously with the local people.

The cities and towns of Emilia with their rich rural hinterland are renowned for their cuisine. Pasta reigns supreme on the region's tables, with plump tortellini, golden fettuccine, and succulent lasagne among the specialties. Parma ham and Parmesan cheese are justly famed outside Italy, as is the region's salami. Steaks are better in Tuscany than anywhere else in Italy.

In the places described in this section, the local wine—often of high quality—may still be served in the straw-corseted flasks that used to be common throughout Italy but have lately been disappearing, replaced by plain glass bottles or, worse, flasks enveloped by plastic imitations of natural straw.

The vineyards of Tuscany yield exhilarating Chianti, which is much more satisfying if drunk on the spot rather than after it has traveled over long distances, however fancy the label may look. In Emilia ask for Lambrusco, a sparkling wine that should have an evanescent flavor of violets. Albana and Sangiovese too are interesting wines in Emilia-Romagna.

The highways, motor roads, and railroad line—all following the ruler-straight Via Aemilia of the ancient Romans—that link Milan with the Adriatic Sea at Rimini represent the main axis for exploring the towns of Emilia and Romagna. The sovereign, tiny Republic of San Marino is close to Rimini.

Visitors to Florence should not pass up a side trip to at least one or the other of the nearby towns—Fiesole, Pistoia, Lucca, Pisa, and Volterra. A brief ferry ride from the Tuscan coast to Portoferraio, on the Isle of Elba, takes the traveler to the territory over which the exiled Napoleon reigned before he tried to regain his empire. The island is noteworthy not only for its history but also for its magnificent scenery.

Set aside time also for many-towered San Gimignano, that precious jewel among Tuscan towns, and for proud Siena. Easy and highly recommended trips from either Florence or Siena may take in Pienza, Montepulciano, Chiusi, Arezzo, Sansepolcro, and Cortona; each one of these towns offers its particular blend of landscape, art, and civilization.

From Bologna, there are several choices for one- or two-day trips, circuits that would include Parma and Modena; Ferrara, Ravenna, and Faenza; or Faenza, Forlì, Rimini, and San Marino.

PARMA ▪

Statistically, the Parmigiani, as the 180,000 inhabitants of this friendly city are called, enjoy some of the highest individual incomes among Italians. Yet Parma's affluence is understated, its wealth is often

103

spent on refinement rather than ostentation. In politics, the city in the fertile plain at the edge of the rounded slopes and ridges of the Apennines has been strongly left-wing since World War II. If you happen to be asked to the home of a local Communist Party member, you may discover that he is a collector of paintings or old furniture, owns a record library with hundreds of labels, is a bibliophile, serves old French cognac, and in intellectual conversation proves familiar with American literature.

Parma owes its prosperity to the inherited skills of its artisans and workers, to a streak of perfectionism, and to a healthy mix of high-quality farming and small and medium-sized industry in its territory. For many generations the area has been renowned for its Parmesan cheese, its delicately cured ham, and its violets. Today Parma markets its dairy products and pasta all over Italy, and exports shoes, other leatherware, and casual clothing to the United States.

Busy though the city is with making money, its inveterate enthusiasm for opera hasn't diminished. Verdi was born in the village of Roncole (now officially named Roncole Verdi), thirty miles northeast of here; Arturo Toscanini was a native of Parma; and Parma's Teatro Regio (Royal Theater) has traditionally awed conductors and artists because of its demanding audiences.

Parma's fanatics of bel canto will mercilessly heckle and boo a singer who doesn't live up to their exacting standards. In memorable operatic debacles of the past, infuriated devotees of lyric drama have been known to run hapless tenors literally out of town by chasing them all the way down the "infamous kilometer" (actually a little less, half a mile) from the Teatro Regio to the railroad station.

The classical Teatro Regio is one of the legacies from the benevolent reign, from 1816 to 1847, of the unforgotten Duchess Marie-Louise (Maria Luigia to the Parmigiani). A Habsburg princess who had become empress of France when Napoleon took her as his second wife in 1810, Marie-Louise was given the Duchy of Parma, Piacenza, and Guastalla for her lifetime after his downfall. She was twenty-four years old when she arrived in Parma while her and Napoleon's little son, the "King of Rome," remained in Vienna.

The many memorabilia in the Glauco Lombardi Museum near the opera house, which is devoted to Marie-Louise and her time, include a bracelet with a lock from the head of her son, the "Eaglet," and paintings of him. After Napoleon's death Marie-Louise remarried twice.

The city and the princely court depicted in Stendhal's great novel *The Charterhouse of Parma* (1839) are largely fictional; the charterhouse, or convent, is imaginary. However, the French writer did live in Parma for some time, and loved it.

Today Parma is hugged by a vast area of workshops, industrial plants, and modern housing, but the center has retained its old, noble character, with streets that look alike and are mostly straight. The Via Emilia, the road from Rimini to Piacenza that follows the ancient Roman route, runs from southeast to northwest across the middle of the city, becoming successively Strada della Repubblica and Via Massimo d'Azeglio. Heavy traffic is diverted over belt roads that retrace the old fortifications.

The central, rectangular Piazza Garibaldi with the city hall and outdoor cafés is a favorite meeting place of Parmigiani. The main architectural sights are a few blocks to the north.

Motor vehicles are banned from Cathedral Square and its surroundings. This restful island in the heart of Parma, with its well-coordinated group of old ecclesiastical buildings, is suffused with the pale pinks and faded reds of their marbles, stone, and bricks. The Romanesque cathedral, from the twelfth century, has a majestic façade with three tiers of small columns and, on its right, a Gothic campanile.

The inside of the cathedral dome is decorated with Correggio's *Assumption of the Virgin*. The famous fresco, with its sense of movement and its exuberance of bright colors, was the master's supreme gift to the city where he spent most of his life. His real name was Antonio Allegri; he was born in the nearby town of Correggio in 1494. He and his pupil Francesco Mazzola, nicknamed Parmigianino ("the little Parma man"), greatly influenced Baroque art.

The imposing baptistery on the square to the right of the cathedral consists of five stories with columns. The outside of the octagonal structure with three doors is adorned with sculptures having biblical and symbolic meanings, the inside with frescoes and reliefs.

Other Correggio frescoes (*Christ in His Glory, The Vision of St. John the Evangelist*) may be seen in the Church of San Giovanni Evangelista. The early-Renaissance basilica, with a Baroque façade, rises on a small square behind the cathedral, adjacent to a monastery with two beautiful cloisters.

Celebrated paintings by Correggio, Parmigianino, and other Italians, as well as an early El Greco (*The Healing of the Blind Man*), are to be found in the National Gallery in the Pilotta Palace. This sprawling, gloomy building, named after the game of pelota that was played at the site, was built west of the cathedral by the Farnese family, who ruled Parma as vassals of the pope from 1545 to 1731. The palace was never finished.

The entrance ticket to the gallery entitles visitors to see also the Teatro Farnese, a huge theater built entirely in wood into what was the tournament court of the palace. The architect was a pupil of Palladio who imitated the master's much-admired Teatro Olimpico in Vicenza. Holding 4,500 spectators, the Teatro Farnese was at the time of its completion, in 1628, the largest of its kind in the world. The structure was destroyed in a World War II air attack, and has since then been restored, with some of the original woodwork incorporated. Present-day safety regulations do not permit the wooden theater to be used for shows or large gatherings.

The Farnese Palace houses other collections as well: a museum of antiquities with a prehistoric section, in addition to Etruscan and Roman material; a rich library with many old manuscripts; and a museum devoted to the master printer Giambattista Bodoni (1740–1813) who in 1768 founded a ducal print shop in the palace and there designed his beautiful typefaces, turning out graphic work that appealed to Parma's perfectionists.

The old Farnese residence looks out on the small Parma River (locally called Il Torrente, "The Torrent"), a tributary of the Po. On its west bank, opposite the palace, is a public park, once the formal garden of the dukes of Parma, with a graceful palace on the right side (rebuilt after grave damage during World War II), a pond, and an outdoor café.

The sightseer who strolls back to the center might stop at a Baroque church, the Madonna della Steccata, on a small piazza. Frescoes by Parmigianino and the tombs of the Farnese dukes and of Count Neipperg, Marie-Louise's second husband, are inside.

The best restaurants are between Piazza Garibaldi and Cathedral Square, and it is advisable to be there no later than 1:00 P.M. for lunch and 8:00 P.M. for dinner. Eating is serious business in Parma.

The local penchant for perfectionism triumphs in cooking, and can be best observed if the visitor is fortunate enough to be asked for a meal in a private home. Quite a number of men in Parma have taken up cooking as a hobby and are proud to prove their expertise. This doesn't seem to be anything new. A Parmigiana recalls: "Grandfather's tortellini and his boiled beef were famous."

Local restaurants with high ratings in the guidebooks have lately yielded to the temptation of overloading pasta dishes with cream, salmon, or other garnishings. Less pretentious eating places offer reliable fare, best to be enjoyed with the region's fizzy Lambrusco wine, the color of Parma's violets.

MODENA ∎

This industrial city in the middle of rich, flat farmland means to Italians at large three things above all else: succulent sausages, expensive fast cars, and the nation's military academy. The foreign visitor will appreciate Modena's much-vaunted though rather heavy cuisine, and should find enough time to inspect its remarkable buildings and museums.

The inner city is separated from the sprawling suburbs by broad boulevards and parks at the site of old fortifications. Traffic on the belt routes and in the center is dense most of the time. Modena has about 180,000 inhabitants; they have a reputation for doing reliable and skillful work, as well as for earthiness, hospitality, and fondness for robust food and wine.

The historic city core is compactly built up, with mostly narrow streets. Via Emilia, on the route of the ancient Roman road from Rimini to Piacenza (the Via Aemilia, named after its builder, the consul M. Aemilius Lepidus), cuts across the center from southeast to northwest. Arcades are almost as common here as in nearby Bologna.

The old city's hub is Piazza Grande (Great Square), which seems gratifyingly ample amid all those tightly packed neighborhoods. The earnest twelfth-century cathedral and its high campanile, both slightly leaning, face the old law courts and city hall at the east side of the piazza. The church, considered one of the outstanding Romanesque buildings in Italy, is praised for the rhythm of its architecture, with high columned galleries and stone reliefs picturing biblical scenes, allegories, miracles, and episodes from Arthurian legend on the outside.

The brickwork interior of the cathedral contains twelfth-century sculptures representing the Passion by anonymous masters from the north Italian lake region. The bell tower at the north side of the church, 335 feet high, is the city's exclamation point, floodlit at night. It is known as the Torre Ghirlandina (Garland Tower) because of a bronze ornament on its weather vane.

The Cathedral Museum deserves a visit on account of its eight metopes, bas-reliefs that originally adorned the exterior of the church. The highly accomplished sculptures, featuring grotesques and allegories, are the work of a nameless artist, the "Master of the Metopes," who created them around 1130.

Proceeding on the busy Via Emilia from the cathedral toward northwest, one reaches a square, the site of the city's former Gate of St. Augustine, with the eighteenth-century Palace of the Museums. The huge building holds collections that are mainly legacies of the House of Este, the noble family who ruled Modena from the thirteenth century for more than 500 years. The Este Library on the first floor is one of Italy's largest. Among its treasures are a fourteenth-century Dante manuscript with miniatures, and the fifteenth-century prayer book of Borso d'Este, duke of Ferrara, Modena, and Reggio nell'Emilia, illustrated by Taddeo Crivelli of Venice and other miniaturists.

The Este Gallery on the top floor of the building contains many paintings by Emilian artists from the fourteenth to the eighteenth centuries, including Correggio, Parmigianino, and Guido Reni, as well as Tintoretto and other Venetians. The gallery has furthermore an unfinished portrait of Duke Francesco I d'Este by Velázquez, drawings by Dürer, sculptures and products of artistic handicraft commissioned by Este dukes, and 36,000 ancient and modern coins and medals.

A museum of medieval and modern arts and crafts, and an archaeological-ethnological museum with prehistoric, Greek, Etruscan, Roman, and extra-European material are under the same roof.

The Ducal Palace in Modena's northeast is an imposing structure from the seventeenth century with a vast courtyard. It is now Italy's West Point; all Italian army officers are trained and commissioned here. The large public park east of the castle includes a botanical garden with a herbarium containing specialized collections of ferns, lichens, and fungi.

Tired from all the sightseeing, the visitor will head for one of Modena's celebrated eating places. Foremost among them is the Ristorante Fini on a small square, Largo San Francesco, in the southwest part of the inner city. It is something like a national institution for savoring *zampone* or *cotecchino*, or both, from the steam table. Either kind of pork sausage is replete with fat that oozes out during the required long simmering. *Zampone*, the principal culinary specialty in Modena, is a pig's front trotter stuffed with seasoned pork forcemeat. The story is that it was invented in 1511 when Julius II, the warrior pope, was beleaguering Modena, and the city's inhabitants were devising new ways to preserve food for what might be a long siege.

Cotecchino, a pork sausage in a casing different from a trotter, is eaten by many Italians all over the country at least once annually: at New Year's, accompanied by lentils that are supposed to represent coins—a symbol of hoped-for riches.

The Fini family, almost as famous as the House of Este, has been selling *zampone* and *cotecchino* in Modena since 1912. The attractively old-fashioned shop of the sausage dynasty's founder, Telesforo Fini, is still in business at 139 Via Canal Chiaro. The Finis have long operated their restaurant and have more recently branched out into the hotel and catering industries.

The wine that traditionally washes down rich Modena food is Lambrusco. This is a light, sparkling red with a faint flavor of violets that is produced in the plains around the city. Lambrusco has lately become popular also in the United States. However, it doesn't travel too well, and it should be drunk at its home grounds for a thorough appreciation of what its devotees call its "generosity." If you have stopped in Modena for a meal, don't try to resume your journey right afterward; a long siesta or a good night's rest will be in order.

Among Modena's guests there are always a few racecar drivers, Grand Prix officials, or motor buffs; the headquarters of both the Ferrari and the Maserati automobile works are in the area. Some customers come to watch for themselves how the cars they have ordered are being handcrafted to their specifications, and to take delivery of them in person.

The Ferrari factory and racing stable, creations of the legendary Enzo Ferrari, are at Maranello, a town ten miles south of Modena on National Route No. 12, near the foothills of the Apennines. Every racing event anywhere in the world causes feverish tension in Maranello and Modena because Ferrari cars are usually among the entrants, and often finished as winners before cars with Japanese engines began triumphing in the Formula One contests. The Maserati works are on the eastern outskirts of Modena.

Visitors to Modena who care for cultural history rather than for Formula One car racing might want to take a side trip in a direction almost opposite to that of Maranello, also on National Route No. 12: to Mirandola, nineteen miles northeast of the city. The graceful old town of 25,000 is the birthplace of Count Giovanni Pico (1463–1494), the humanist who as Pico della Mirandola was one of the most brilliant figures of the Renaissance. A friend of Lorenzo de' Medici the Magnificent, Pico mastered an astonishing amount of his epoch's learning during his short life. The old palace of the Pico family still exists and may be visited. About halfway between Modena and Mirandola, also on National Route No. 12, is the village of Sorbara, which reputedly produces the finest Lambrusco.

FERRARA ▪

This is the biking capital of Italy. Amid rich farmland flat as a kitchen board, quiet Ferrara with its long streets, some of them lined with poplars or other trees, seems made for the bicycle. Housewives fasten a basket in the front of their bicycles when they ride out to do their shopping; workers and professional people pedal to their jobs and offices; and young people who haven't yet graduated to motor scooters mount their two-wheelers for a romantic outing to the lonely banks of the Po, Italy's largest river, which placidly flows three miles north of the city to the Adriatic.

Ferrara, with some chemical industry on its outskirts, is economically stagnant, and markedly calm. Too calm for the young among its 150,000 inhabitants. "The action is in Padua or Bologna," a Ferrarese student said. Either city is about one railroad hour distant.

Some visitors may find Ferrara, which 500 years ago was one of the liveliest capitals in Europe, melancholy or outright sad today—a cultural has-been, a retirees' haven, a provincial backwater. Others will be charmed by its architecture and art treasures and by the courtesy of its people. The number of attractive girls and women in Ferrara is striking. The city can be stifling hot in summer, even at night, but it is no longer plagued by mosquitoes to the extent it was until a few decades ago. A brackish canal south of the city walls, which date from the Renaissance, is a reminder of a former system of waterways that linked Ferrara with the Po and the Adriatic. Spring and fall are the best times here.

Everybody's first stroll is to the castle at the city's center. The domineering red-brown complex with its four square towers, floodlit at night, is surrounded by a water-filled moat; it is a bulky monument to the House of Este. This Teutonic-descended family ruled Ferrara and its territory from around the middle of the thirteenth century to 1597 (the clan's name was derived from the small town of Este, their early fief, thirty miles north of Ferrara).

Niccolò II d'Este had the castle built in the years after 1385, following a local revolt against his cruel tax collectors; the idea was to protect Ferrara's rulers from their own subjects.

Visitors to the castle today are shown a dungeon at the base of the Lion's Tower, the northeast corner of the fortress, and its oldest portion, which saw the last acts of a family tragedy in 1425. Niccolò III d'Este kept his young wife, Parisina Malatesta, and his own bastard son Ugo in chains in that prison after surprising them as adulterous lovers, and soon had them both beheaded. (The somber affair inspired Renaissance novels, dramas by Lope de Vega, Gabriele D'Annunzio, and others, a poem by Byron, and operas by Donizetti and Mascagni.)

The implacable lord who had his wife and son put to death lived to play host at the Ecumenical Council of Ferrara in 1438, which in vain sought a reconciliation of Byzantine and Roman Christians to end the East-West schism. Niccolò III's successors were humanists, and they were eventually recognized as dukes by the emperor and the pope. The brilliant court in Ferrara attracted artists and intellectuals from all over Italy; members of the Este family were patrons of Ludovico Ariosto and Torquato Tasso, the most famous Italian poets of the sixteenth century.

Duke Ercole I, who ruled from 1471 to 1505, expanded Ferrara toward the north. He called on a renowned architect, Biagio Rossetti, to lay out new neighborhoods with palaces and houses on streets in a regular pattern, as well as parks—an early example of rational urban planning that made Ferrara, as local scholars like to say, "the first modern city." It had a population of 100,000—many more than Rome—and was considered one of the most civilized places in the world when Ercole's son, Alfonso I, took Lucrezia Borgia as his second wife.

Lucrezia, the daughter of Pope Alexander VI, a Spaniard, had two marriages behind her already. She must have been at the height of her beauty when she arrived in Ferrara in 1501, barely twenty-one years old. In a culinary tribute to her blond hair the chef of the ducal kitchen whipped up a new dish for the welcoming banquet: golden fettuccine.

In Ferrara Lucrezia lived down the scandalous reputation that had preceded her from Rome. As duchess, from 1505 to her death in 1519, she not only presided with dignity over a refined court but seems even to have been popular with the citizenry. In 1597 Duke Alfonso III died without a son from any one of his three marriages, and the papacy incorporated Ferrara, which it had long coveted, into the States of the Church. The city's dream of greatness was over.

Today a part of the castle is occupied by the offices of the provincial authorities. Visitors may see the Este rooms, including the game hall with ceiling paintings by Camillo Filippi and his sons Sebastiano and Cesare showing athletes at exercise. A gallery links the castle with the city hall, the rebuilt original residence of the Este family.

The nearby cathedral, from the twelfth century, has a triptych façade with three orders of arcades, one above the other. Walk around to the right side of the huge building to have a look at a long row of other columns and arcades over the old shops of artisans, and at the unfinished early-Renaissance bell tower, which leans slightly. The Cathedral Museum contains two of the best paintings by Cosimo Tura, the fifteenth-century master of the Ferrarese school, *St. George* and *The Annunciation.* There is also a statue of a sweet-looking Virgin Mary holding the infant Jesus with her left arm and a pomegranate in her right hand, by Sienese sculptor Jacopo della Quercia.

A plaque on the wall of the archdiocesan seminary to the left of the cathedral records that Nicholas Copernicus won a degree in canon law here in 1503. His clerical professors could not have suspected that the young Polish scholar would revolutionize mankind's perception of the cosmos.

Stroll up Corso Ercole I d'Este, a street without stores that is the main axis of Rossetti's Renaissance city addition, to the so-called Palace of Diamonds on a side street. The popular name of the building, a Rossetti masterpiece, refers to the 12,500 faceted marble blocks of its exterior, which look like gems. The luminous palace houses the National Picture Gallery, essentially a collection of works by Renaissance artists of the Ferrarese school; Tura, Dosso Dossi, Il Garofalo (Benvenuto Tisi), and the Filippis, father and sons, are the outstanding painters.

Nearby is the House of Ariosto. The poet had the two-story brick building erected for himself and lived there during the last years before his death in 1533. It was bought by the City of Ferrara in 1811. The Latin inscription on a tablet, composed by Ariosto, is famous: "A small house, but suited for myself, subject to no one, not mean, and built with my own money." There is little to see inside, only some old tables and chairs.

Unlike Rossetti's Ferrara, the old town south of the castle has twisting streets. The synagogue at 95 Via Mazzini is a reminder that Ferrara was home to an old Jewish community. A plaque outside commemorates the Ferrarese victims of the Holocaust. The fate of Ferrara's Jews under Mussolini is the theme of Giorgio Bassani's novel, *The Garden of the Finzi-Continis*, which was made into a film by Vittorio de Sica.

The straight Via delle Volte, cutting through a maze of buildings under a long series of archways, was a kind of medieval service lane for the crowded neighborhood.

Palazzo Schifanoia, in the city's southeast, built in the fourteenth and fifteenth centuries, was a hideaway and pleasure château of the Este rulers. (*Schifanoia*, literally "evade boredom," may be rendered as "carefree.") The noble mansion, which saw a good deal of Este court life and intrigues, is today a museum. Its centerpiece is the Hall of Months, with Renaissance frescoes featuring twelve seasonal and allegorical scenes, those for January, February, May, October, and November being badly damaged, however. Collections of bronzes, ceramics, and coins can also be seen.

An important museum of Greek and Etruscan antiquities occupies another Renaissance palace south of the Palazzo Schifanoia. On view is one of the world's major collections of Athenian painted vases. They were found in more than 4,000 tombs excavated during the last few decades in the area of what was Spina, an Etruscan seaport near the Po estuary about thirty miles east of Ferrara. Other exhibits are Etruscan bronzes and earthenware, objects made from amber imported from the Baltic countries, and glassy perfume boxes from Egypt. Spina flourished between the sixth and third centuries B.C. and, as the artifacts in the museum prove, traded with faraway peoples. It was no backwater 2,500 years ago.

FAENZA ▪

At least once a year, in spring or summer, the craftsmen of this pottery town gather in the arcaded main square to compete in fashioning the widest plate or tallest cup out of a small lump of clay. Faenza, an old traffic hub where the highways between Bologna and the Adriatic Sea and between Florence and Ravenna cross, has a Viale delle Ceramiche (Ceramics Avenue) and an International Ceramics Museum. Many street signs are made of the glazed, decorated material that is known in English and French as faïence, a word derived from the town's name. Italians, attracted by foreign labels, instead call this kind of earthenware *maiolica*; the word is a corruption of the name of Majorca, the Spanish island where such pottery was also made.

In Faenza, which has slightly over 50,000 people, at least seventy commercial workshops turn out pottery that is fired, coated with a thin layer of enamel containing salts, refired, decorated with hand-painted flowers or other ornaments in brilliant colors, and baked again. A vocational high school, the State Institute of Ceramic Art, makes sure that the old skills won't die out. Pottery manufacturers existed in Faenza as early as the twelfth century and reached the peak of their fame in the fifteenth and sixteenth centuries. Vast assortments of faïences can today be found in local stores, while the workshops around the city welcome special orders, which may take weeks or even months to fulfill.

The municipal ceramics collection, founded in 1908, was damaged during World War II, and has been reorganized and expanded into an International Ceramics Museum since then. Its many exhibits include Faenza pottery from the fifteenth century onward, similar products from other Italian areas, artifacts from antiquity, pre-Columbian and Middle Eastern earthenware, votive tablets and other religious folk art from various epochs and regions, and ceramic works by such modern artists as Chagall, Matisse, and Picasso.

Pottery apart, Faenza is a pleasing town also in other respects, but the heat on summer days can be stifling. Large parts of the walls and ramparts that were built in the Renaissance around the oval urban center still exist. The Via Emilia, on the route by which Roman legions marched from the Adriatic to Gaul, cuts straight across Faenza, but much of the modern through traffic is diverted over belt roads.

Two communicating squares that are really one elongated public space, Piazza del Popolo and Piazza della Libertà, form a monumental town center. Piazza della Libertà is dominated by the unfinished façade of the cathedral, one of the most noteworthy Renaissance churches in the entire Romagna. It was designed and begun in 1474 by Giuliano da Maiano, a member of a Florentine artist family; construction work went on for decades and was never completed. Benedetto da Maiano, a relative of the chief architect, contributed six reliefs to adorn the chapel to the left of the high altar, where, according to tradition, the third-century bishop of Faenza, St. Savinus, is buried.

In the adjoining Piazza del Popolo, the Renaissance town hall on the west side faces the thirteenth-century governor's palace in the east. Loggias surmount the long rows of ground-floor arches, giving the piazza a theatrical character. The clock tower is a faithful reconstruction of a campanile from the beginning of the seventeenth century that German troops blew up in 1944. An elaborate fountain in the piazza, with bronze lions, eagles, and dragons, is also from the seventeenth century.

The municipal picture gallery is noteworthy for its works by Faentine masters and other artists of Romagna in the fifteenth and sixteenth centuries. A new Museum of the Neoclassical Era in a state-owned eighteenth-century palazzo is a collection of stuccowork and furniture from the beginning of the nineteenth century, when the Empire style was dominant.

On weekends some Faentines drive to their villas at Brisighella, a picturesque old town at altitude 377 feet on a slope in the foothills of the Apennines eight miles southwest of Faenza. From the hilltop, a thirteenth-century castle with a tower overlooks the little town (population 8,500) and the valley of the Lamone River, whose farmers were renowned as tough soldiers in the Renaissance. The castle was recently restored and is now the seat of a small museum of farm implements used in the area in the nineteenth century.

FORLÌ ▪

Medieval and Mussolini Modern architecture blend curiously in this lively provincial capital in the heart of Romagna. Il Duce was born near here, and during his twenty-year dictatorship he always favored Forlì. Many new buildings and neighborhoods in the city's southeast, with their neo-Roman arcades and a Piazza della Vittoria (Victory Square) with heroic statuary, look like translations of Fascist rhetoric into stone.

Today, leftists control city hall, and they seem determined to run Mussolini's pet city as a showcase of efficient local government. Forlì is notably clean, public services function well, and nobody sees anything wrong if the owner of some small mechanical factory with a dozen or so workers, one of the many capitalistic enterprises in the area, supports the Communist Party.

Forlì, which has 110,000 inhabitants, looks prosperous; a young fellow who shows off his new Porsche, driving slowly on Corso della Repubblica, hardly makes a splash. Corso della Repubblica and its curving extension into the center of the city, Corso Garibaldi, are crowded with laughing and chatting groups of youngsters in the late afternoon and the evening; this is the good-natured Forlì version of hangin' out. Corso Garibaldi, a pedestrian mall with elegant stores, is also the main shopping street.

The vast Piazza Aurelio Saffi between the two Corsos is the spacious main square of Forlì. Trapezoid-shaped, it is dominated by the Romanesque-Gothic Church of San Mercuriale, dedicated to Forlì's first bishop, St. Mercurialis, who died at the beginning of the fifth century. The old building, with a rose window over the portal, was gravely damaged during World War II, and has recently been repaired. Its Romanesque campanile, 246 feet high, is Forlì's lofty landmark.

Forlì's city hall, a low-slung building dating from the fourteenth century, with a dignified façade that was renovated in 1826, takes up the entire west side of the piazza opposite the church. A smaller Renaissance structure in the south of the square, the Palazzo del Podestà, was the governor's residence. The massive post office facing it and the buildings in the piazza's southeast corner, where Corso della Repubblica starts, bear the imprint of the Fascist era.

The cathedral of Forlì is east of the main square. It too had a high bell tower, but the retreating Germans blew it up in 1944 and it has not been rebuilt. The Renaissance portico of the cathedral seems too grand for the rest of the building, which was erected in the fourteenth century and thoroughly repaired and altered in 1844. To the left of the church is the attractive Piazza Ordelaffi—named after a family that once ruled the city—with a convent and a seventeenth-century palazzo that will look familiar to anyone who has seen Domenico Fontana's Lateran Palace in Rome. Forlì's little Lateran now serves as the prefecture for the provincial authorities.

The municipal picture gallery in a former hospital from the eighteenth century houses an important regional art collection. However, one of the city's greatest sons, Melozzo da Forlì (1438–1494), a disciple of Piero della Francesca, is represented with only one work, painted as an apothecary's business sign.

An archaeological museum in the same building contains Bronze Age finds and material from the ancient Roman market town Forum Livii. The name Forlì is a corruption of the Latin name, which presumably referred to C. Livius Salinator, a Roman consul in the beginning of the second century B.C. His surname, Salinator, recalled the fiscal inventiveness of one of his ancestors, also a consul, who introduced a salt tax. The inhabitants of the city are to this day called Forlivesi; thus, usage has saved the *v* in *Livius*.

The former hospital also has room for an ethnological collection, which gives a good idea of folklore and handicrafts in Romagna before the industrial age.

An old brickwork fortress with round towers in the southern tip of the city center was built by the military architects of the Holy See in the fourteenth century. Cesare Borgia, son of Pope Alexander VI, used it as a stronghold while he was attempting to build a state of his own as duke of Romagna. One of his lieutenants and 200 archers held out in the Forlì citadel in a last stand for three months when

117

Cesare's fortunes brusquely declined after his father's death in 1503.

National Route No. 9 *ter* starts from the fortress, and quite a few young neofascists and nostalgic admirers of Mussolini take it. The highway leads to Predappio in the foothills of the Apennines where Il Duce is buried. The left-wing town administration of Predappio doesn't discourage the pilgrimages by political adversaries: They are good for business. Mussolini was born in the village of Dovia near Predappio in 1883, the son of a blacksmith and a schoolteacher. Years after Communist partisans captured and shot the dictator in northern Italy in 1945 (*see* Como), his remains were transferred to the family tomb near his birthplace.

A quick side trip to Cesena, twelve miles southeast of Forlì, is advisable. This city of 90,000 sees plenty of traffic, as it lies at an important crossroads: The old highway from Milan and Bologna to the Adriatic coast (the Via Emilia) intersects here with the route from Ravenna to Arezzo and Perugia.

The Rocca Malatestiana on a hill in the southeast of Cesena is an intimidating medieval fortress, built in 1380 when the Malatesta family (*see* Rimini) was in control of the city. Cesare Borgia also lived for some time in the citadel; he had chosen Cesena as the capital of his proposed duchy. The ruined stronghold and its park now serve as the setting for summer theater. One reaches the citadel over a monumental stairway at the right side of the handsome city hall on the large, elongated Piazza del Popolo, Cesena's main square. To the north, at the center of the city, is the Biblioteca Malatestiana, one of Italy's oldest libraries, in a structure built for a scholarly member of the Malatesta clan in 1452. The complex, which includes an old Franciscan cloister, houses an archaeological museum as well.

An attractive Renaissance church, Santa Maria del Monte, overlooks Cesena and the Savio River from a mountain spur to the south of the city.

RAVENNA ▪

This venerable city, once the residence of Roman emperors and barbarian kings, has long seemed overwhelmed by its history; now it is struggling against the hazards of the industrial age. Oil refineries, a petrochemical complex, and an oil-fueled power plant, all near an artificial seaport on the Adriatic coast a few miles east of Ravenna, have caused increasing air pollution. Smog and acid rain are shriveling the pine groves praised by Dante and Byron, and gnawing at the buildings that have weathered many centuries. Extraction of methane gas and water from the subsoil has lowered the terrain in a process comparable to the much-lamented subsidence of Venice. At the moment of this writing, environmentalists are fiercely opposing a project to build a huge coal-based power plant near Ravenna.

The plains around the old city are dotted with new factories that turn out anything from packaging material to furniture. Ravenna's population now stands at 140,000, almost four times more than fifty years ago.

Despite the present industrial boom and the ecological worries, Ravenna is an enduring memorial to past greatness and is the foremost western outpost of Byzantine art. Surrounded by vast, modern suburbs, the historical core has moods of nostalgic charm in a few corners where private motor traffic is now banned.

The luminous mosaics from the fifth to the seventh centuries in Ravenna's Christian shrines are world-famous. The city boasts also the tombs of a powerful Germanic king, Theodoric, and of Italy's greatest poet, Dante.

Ravenna is the largest center of Romagna, the region that derives its name from the circumstance that it remained under Roman control when most of Italy had been overrun by barbarian invaders. The Romagnoli have a reputation for being hot-blooded, outgoing, and stormy lovers; they are given both to practical jokes and to endless vendettas. Inhabitants of Ravenna will play elaborate tricks on one another: Someone in a merry company will get dead drunk, and his friends may take him by car to a faraway place like Verona or Milan to dump him in a public park there; on coming out of his stupor, he won't know where he is and will be utterly confused.

Ravenna's importance in antiquity and in the early Middle Ages was due to its nearly impregnable position between the Adriatic Sea and a belt of lagoons and marshes. The swampland has long been drained and is now good farming soil, but rivers, canals, and lagoons still hug the city. Emperor Augustus made Ravenna the home base of his Adriatic fleet, one of the two major naval stations of imperial Rome (the other one was Misenum near Naples). Ravenna's harbor suburb was called Classis ("fleet"), a name that as Classe has been preserved to this day, denoting a strip of pine groves behind the beaches.

At the beginning of the fifth century, when Rome was continually threatened by invaders, the emperors of the West withdrew to Ravenna. The Germanic kings who ruled most of Italy after the fall of the empire in A.D. 476, Odoacer and Theodoric, also resided here. When Justinian, the emperor of the East, recovered Italy in the first half of the sixth century, Ravenna became the seat of the imperial viceroy, the exarch. Pepin, king of the Franks, handed Ravenna and its district, the exarchate, over to the pope in 755.

Ravenna's mosaics alone warrant a visit to the city. Some of the most ancient of them are in the Baptistery of the Orthodox, an octagonal brick structure with a cylindrical tower near the city's eighteenth-century cathedral. The baptism of Jesus on gold ground and the twelve apostles on blue ground are represented at the summit of the dome. The lower parts of the walls are adorned with golden foliage on blue ground with figures of the prophets in the corners.

Other fifth-century mosaics are to be found in the Mausoleum of Galla Placidia in a grassy space in the northwest of the historical center. The small, cross-shaped building was intended to be the resting place for the adventurous and scheming daughter of Emperor Theodosius the Great who was first the wife of a barbarian king and then of Emperor Constantius III, and eventually acted as regent for her son, Emperor Valentinian III. Galla Placidia died in Rome in A.D. 450, and her remains were never taken to the mausoleum that had been built during her lifetime; her large sarcophagus is empty. The mosaics, on dark blue ground, represent Jesus as a young shepherd in a golden tunic, as well as apostles, evangelists, and saints amid rich decorations. Dim daylight filters into the mausoleum through alabaster windows.

Nearby, in the same green area, stands the Church of San Vitale, an octagonal brick edifice with flying buttresses from the sixth century. The interior contains celebrated mosaic portraits of Emperor Justinian and his much talked-about empress, Theodora, both with their court attendants. Above them, Christ between two angels hands the crown of martyrdom to St. Vitalis, according to tradition a Roman soldier who died rather than forswear his faith.

The adjoining former Convent of San Vitale houses in its two cloisters the National Museum of Antiquities with prehistoric and Etruscan finds, Roman sculptures and inscriptions, Byzantine sarcophagi, and artifacts from various periods that were recently dug up in the area of the ancient seaside suburb of Classis.

About halfway on Via Roma, the old city's north-south axis, is the Church of Sant'Apollinare Nuovo with a round tower in brickwork, its windows with one arch at the base, two arches higher up, and three arches at the top. The interior of the church is dominated by grandiose mosaic friezes from the sixth century. The left side, below which the women of the congregation worshipped, carries a realistic representation of the suburb and harbor of Classis with three ships and two lighthouses; twenty-two virgins following the Magi proceed from the seaport town to pay tribute to the Mother of God, seated with the infant Jesus on a throne between four angels. The frieze on the right side of the church, reserved for men, shows the city of Ravenna with the arcaded and curtained palace of Theodoric and twenty-six saints or martyrs approaching Christ the King. Mosaics picturing biblical episodes decorate the upper walls.

The Basilica of Sant'Apollinare in Classe, three miles south of the city center, near the pine groves, is the best-preserved of Ravenna's ancient churches, the burial place of a venerated early-Christian archbishop, St. Apollinaris. To the left of the church rises a round tower that seems to have been copied from Sant'Apollinare Nuovo. Much too close to the right of the church are a hotel and restaurant in modern brickwork imitating the ancient one, and a service station. A twentieth-century bronze statue of Emperor Augustus, "Founder of the Harbor of Classis," stands outside a little park in front of the campanile.

In the solemn interior of the church, twenty-four columns of Greek marble separate the nave from the aisles, where ten sarcophagi of prelates from the fifth to the eighth centuries are lined up. The brilliant mosaics in the apse represent St. Apollinaris surrounded by twelve lambs; his flock, amid trees, flowers, rocks, and birds, are on a green background. Above this scene is an allegory of the Transfiguration: a large golden cross on blue ground and stars with Moses and Elias on either side, and God's hand reaching out of dense clouds, pointing to the cross.

The ancient art of mosaic-making, still alive in Ravenna, is taught at the mosaic school of the local Academy of Fine Arts. The workshops of Ravenna's commercial *mosaicisti* (mosaic artists) copy segments of the famous Byzantine works, restore damaged old friezes or pavements, make framed mosaics as souvenirs, and fill special orders. You may commission religious images, portraits of loved ones, ornaments, or inscriptions (like "WELCOME" for your doorstep) in colored stones and glass, and have them shipped to any address.

The Academy of Fine Arts has its seat in a building around an elegant Renaissance cloister off Via Roma. Its art gallery contains many paintings by Romagna masters of the fifteenth and sixteenth centuries and by other Italian artists.

The Mausoleum of Theodoric the Great (454–526), king of the Ostrogoths and "Governor of the Romans," is on the northern outskirts of Ravenna near the highway to Venice. The monument, which attracts above all German tourists, is a massive ten-sided structure crowned by a flat dome, a single block of bright Istrian stone thirty-six feet in diameter. The burial chamber holds an empty porphyry sarcophagus and is surmounted by an upper-floor chapel with a ledge on which the altar rested. When the Byzantines under Justinian's general Belisarius captured Ravenna, they took the remains of the Germanic king, a heretic in their eyes, out of his tomb and scattered them.

Ruins of the palace of Theodoric that is pictured in the mosaics of Sant'Apollinare Nuovo have been dug up behind the Church of San Vitale. Instead, the façade of an old brick building near the Church of Sant'Apollinare Nuovo that is locally called the Palace of Theodoric probably belonged to troop barracks.

Another famous tomb, that of Dante, is behind the Church of St. Francis and its convent in the city center. An exile from Florence, the poet had eventually found a haven in Ravenna under the protection of its lord, Guido Novello da Polenta, and died here in 1321. His remains are now in a marble urn above a sarcophagus in a chapel in the classical style that was built in 1780. The city authorities decreed long ago that Dante's resting place and its surroundings should be a permanent "zone of silence," but the quiet is all too often shattered by urban noises and troops of sightseers, especially in summer. A Dante Museum was opened in the former Franciscan convent in 1921, the six hundredth anniversary of the poet's death. Early editions of *The Divine Comedy*, illustrations, inscriptions, and other memorabilia can be seen in the collection.

A few blocks to the west, on a square now called Piazza Kennedy, is the Palazzo Rasponi, where Lord Byron lived from 1819 to 1821. In his *Don Juan*, the English poet wrote: "I pass each day where Dante's bones are laid." Byron preferred Ravenna to any other place in Italy, surely also because of his notorious liaison with a local beauty, Countess Teresa Guiccioli.

Extended ruins near the railroad station and a canal in Ravenna's northeast belong to what is known as the Rock of Brancaleone, a fortress built by the Venetians in the second half of the fifteenth century.

During the warm months, the coast east of the city, from Marina Romea to Lido di Classe, is a crowded strip of seasonal hotels, restaurants, bathing concessions, and camping sites. After the barbarians and the Byzantines, the beach people have invaded Ravenna.

RIMINI ■

What is an outrageously overbuilt Adriatic resort doing in a book like this—a place where on summer weekends bathers jockey for every square inch of beach while loudspeakers incessantly tout skin lotions, blare jingles, and call out the names of children who get lost in the crowds?

Rimini is the cluttered powerhouse of what Italians call their vacation factory, an almost uninterrupted string of bathing concessions, hotels, pensions, condominiums, seafood restaurants, pizza parlors, *gelaterie*, and dance spots lining the thirty-five miles of flat, sandy coast from Ravenna to Cattolica. Rimini, together with its outposts along more than ten waterfront miles, is the centerpiece of this "Romagna Riviera."

One of the biggest holiday machines around the Mediterranean, the Rimini strip packs in millions of guests from June to September, and they spend many millions of dollars, much of it in foreign currencies. Swarms of sun-hungry vacationers from Germany, Switzerland, Austria, the Netherlands, Britain, and the Scandinavian countries keep flocking to Rimini year after year.

A large part of Rimini's Italian and foreign summer clientele is made up of middle-class and lower-middle-class people who are attracted by cheap rates in the countless family-run hotels and pensions bordering the coast three and four rows deep. In the typical Rimini beachside establishment, father serves at tables and will clown with patrons between taking telephone calls from Frankfurt and Amsterdam; mother sees to it that there are enough lasagne and roast chicken for everyone; the daughters make up the rooms before kitchen duty; and the sons carry luggage, do lifeguard service, and help in many other ways. Everybody in the family pitches in, nobody minds working long hours during the season, and the owner would much rather press yet another cousin or uncle into service than hire costly outside help.

The guests from Milan and Dortmund, from Bologna and Zurich, love the lasagne and the Albana and Sangiovese wines, the cordial family atmosphere, and—quite obviously—Rimini's seaside bustle; and visitors often make reservations for next year's season when they depart.

Many of the holidaymakers on Rimini's congested waterfront strip never catch a glimpse of the old town west of the railroad tracks. Rimini existed for thousands of years before Mussolini sent Italian workers and children by the trainload to the Romagna Riviera in the 1920s and thereby started mass tourism. The city beyond the tracks is the real Rimini, a quiet provincial center from fall to spring when the waterfront is deserted and windswept. In the long evenings, bored youths hang out in espresso bars and *pizzerie* in the old town, boasting to one another about how many German or Swedish girls they bagged last summer, and showing off nostalgic postcards from their conquests.

Federico Fellini, who was once one of the local boys, has evoked the special Rimini ennui in his films. Everybody in town seems to be waiting for the big time next summer. Quite a few of Rimini's 130,000 inhabitants live all year on the money they make during the hectic beach season.

Off-season Rimini is a good place for anyone interested in history, and for devotees of the painter Piero della Francesca.

A triumphal arch at the southern ramparts and a Roman bridge at the opposite side of the city center, spanning the arm of the Marecchia River, which a few hundred yards downstream becomes a fishing harbor, attest to Rimini's importance in antiquity. Ariminum, as it was then called, was a crucial seaport and road junction, a frontier fortress defending Rome from the Gauls. When Caesar crossed the Rubicon near here in 49 B.C. he technically invaded Roman territory and precipitated the civil war with Pompey.

Scholars still dispute which one of various small streams in the area was the Rubicon, the official frontier between Italy proper and Cisalpine Gaul. The prevailing theory is that Caesar, after "computing how many calamities his passing that river would bring upon mankind" (Plutarch), defied the Roman Senate by leading his legions across what is now the Pisciatello, nine miles north of Rimini. The trouble is that the modern name of that measly river, in summer just a trickle if not dried-up altogether, suggests in colloquial Italian a bed-wetting child. In any case, crossing the Rubicon wasn't a military feat but a symbolic decision. Julius Caesar is unforgotten in Rimini, and many children are still christened Giulio or Cesare or Giulio Cesare.

Rimini's Arch of Augustus is the oldest such structure from Roman times that is still intact. The travertine arch was erected in honor of Emperor Augustus in 27 B.C. An inscription praises him for the repair of the Via Flaminia, the strategic highway from Rome to the Adriatic coast that C. Flaminius had built in 220 B.C. From Ariminum onward, the Via Aemilia, built by the consul M. Aemilius Lepidus around 187 B.C., ran to what is now Piacenza, and later to the present city of Aosta. The five-arched stone bridge across the Marecchia was begun under Augustus and completed under his successor Tiberius; now known as the Ponte di Tiberio, it is still in use. Look west for a good view of the Apennine ranges.

After the fall of the western half of the Roman Empire, Rimini was ruled by Byzantines and Longobards in the early Middle Ages. In the thirteenth century it became the power base of a redoubtable local family, the Malatestas. (Their ominous name, originally a sobriquet, means "evil head.") Despots of Rimini and soon also of other parts of the Romagna and of neighboring areas, the Malatestas hired out as commanders of mercenary troops; became allies successively of the emperor, the papacy, Florence, Milan, and Venice; were patrons of the arts and of humanistic scholars; and always gave their contemporaries a lot to talk about.

Dante in his *Divine Comedy* (Inferno, canto v) has immortalized a Malatesta family tragedy that occurred in 1283 or 1284. Giovanni lo Sciancato ("the Lame") Malatesta, nicknamed Gianciotto, then lord of Rimini, discovered that his beautiful wife, Francesca Polenta of

Ravenna, was the lover of his brother Paolo il Bello ("the Fair"), and put them both to death. The Francesca da Rimini episode has inspired several dramas, including one by D'Annunzio (1901), an orchestra piece by Tchaikovsky, operas by composers from Mercadante to Zandonai, and many paintings, including two by Dante Gabriele Rossetti and Jean A. D. Ingres.

Outstanding in Rimini's line of tyrants was Sigismondo Malatesta (1417–1468), a fascinating and notorious Renaissance figure. One of the great condottieri of his times, he surrounded himself with savants and poets, favored the arts, sponsored debates with Rimini's learned Jews, boldly professed a pagan philosophy, and all the time committed monstrous cruelties and crimes. Pope Pius II, a Tuscan and a humanist (see Pienza), excommunicated Sigismondo, had him burned in effigy in Rome, and made war on him. Yet the learned pontiff also wrote grudgingly that "Sigismondo knew history and had a great store of philosophy; he seemed born to all that he undertook."

Sigismondo's enduring monument in Rimini is the Church of San Francesco at the center of the old town, which he had rebuilt as the Tempio Malatestiano (Malatesta Temple), a memorial to himself and to his mistress and fourth wife, the intellectual Isotta degli Atti. Sigismondo commissioned the Florentine architect Leon Battista Alberti to remodel the Gothic church, which dated from the thirteenth century, in the Renaissance manner. Alberti drew inspiration for his new façade from Rimini's Arch of Augustus; the inscription on the church front proclaims Sigismondo as the patron of the renewal project, with the year, 1450.

The interior of the church is lavishly decorated with the often recurring emblem of Sigismondo—a trumpeting elephant (signifying Fame) and the Malatesta rose—with the interlaced letters SI, which may be read as "Sigismondo" or as "Sigismondo-Isotta." Sigismondo's tomb is at the right of the entrance; Isotta, who died in 1470, rests in the third side-chapel to the right. Portrait reliefs of Isotta that had originally adorned the pillars were later chiseled off, and a Latin inscription extolling her "beauty and virtue" was covered with a bronze tablet identifying her tomb only by her name. Another inscription meaningfully paraphrases Ecclesiastes: "A time to speak, a time to keep silence." The Tempio Malatestiano is now Rimini's cathedral.

The second chapel on the right contains a portrait of Sigismondo that Piero della Francesca painted in 1451. The work, in part restored, has badly deteriorated, but it is an important part of the della Francesca canon. The master represented the tyrant of Rimini kneeling before his heavenly patron, St. Sigismund, the sixth-century king of Burgundy. The Malatesta castle is in the background, a brace of hounds, one white and the other black, are on the lower right side. Sigismondo's hawklike face is among the better-preserved parts of the painting.

During World War II the fresco was detached from the wall for safekeeping; afterward it was put back into the chapel. What is left of the Malatesta castle that Piero della Francesca painted into his portrait of Sigismondo can be seen in the southwest of Rimini, near the city hall.

REPUBLIC OF SAN MARINO ▪

This sovereign state not quite double the size of Manhattan, which claims to be the world's oldest republic, is an Italian Disneyland built around some genuine relics from the free communes of the Middle Ages. What's authentic and what's make-believe is not always easy to tell in San Marino. Most of the three million tourists who spend a few hours in the vest-pocket country every year don't care. They snap photos with pseudo-Ghibelline battlements as a backdrop, they buy Japanese cameras and crockery with Renaissance ornaments, they put the tiny state's gaudy mail stamps on picture postcards, and they sample the local Muscat and Sangiovese wines in one of the many taverns.

From the teeming "Romagna Riviera" (see Rimini), up to 50,000 people make the twenty-minute trip to San Marino by coach or car on some summer weekends. About halfway on the four-lane motorway they pass a little guardhouse from which a white-and-blue flag greets them. Nobody needs to open bags or show documents at the frontier between Italy and the San Marino enclave; travelers who like exotic entries in their passports may ask for a rubber stamp, which will read "REPUBBLICA DI SAN MARINO."

The republic's coat of arms represents three plumed towers on three hills over the Latin motto "Libertas" ("Freedom"), surmounted

127

by a crown signifying sovereignty. Mount Titano, on which the town of San Marino is perched, has indeed three peaks with a bulwark on top of each, visible from afar. The three towers and some of the crenellated walls that run up and down the craggy mountain date from the Middle Ages, but they have been repeatedly repaired and rebuilt; mock-medieval ramparts have recently been added to support new buildings and protect ample parking lots hewn out of the living rock.

The lofty capital of the miniature republic numbers 5,000 inhabitants. Some 14,000 other Sammarinesi, as the citizens are called, live in eight villages and hamlets around Mount Titano. Travelers on the roads winding up the mountain pass new villas, houses, and hotels in vivid colors, a modern convention center, tennis courts, a roller-skating rink, and a pit for clay-pigeon shooting.

Higher up, where the slope gets steeper, huddle the old quarters with stairways and crooked alleys, ancient and not-so-ancient bastions, buildings in slate-gray stone with brown-tiled roofs, and small terrace gardens. To the east one can glimpse the Adriatic Sea, while the panorama on the opposite side is a succession of green Apennine ridges that fade into a bluish haze.

The town faces south and is protected from cold north winds by the 2,438-foot-high summit of Mount Titano with the Rocca Guaita (Guaita Rock), the oldest fortress, over a precipice. The stronghold was built in the twelfth century, or maybe even earlier. A brisk south wind sweeps through the town on many days all year round. In winter, San Marino is often snowed in, and the rare visitor is made especially welcome.

The Church of San Francesco near the gate that opens into the old town was built in the fourteenth century by stonemasons from Como. It contains paintings by Girolamo Marchesi da Cotignola and by the Baroque master who is known as Il Guercino. Higher up is the neoclassical Basilica of San Marino, erected from 1826 to 1838 over the reputed grave of St. Marinus, replacing an old church that had been torn down. The saint after whom the town and the state are named was, according to legend, a stonecutter from Dalmatia who at the beginning of the fourth century sailed across the Adriatic with a band of fellow Christians to flee the persecutions ordered by Emperor Diocletian. Marinus—the name means "man from the sea"—and other fugitives are said to have founded a hermitage in the wilderness of Mount Titano, and the little community later developed into a republic. Recorded history knows of a convent of St. Marinus that existed on the mountain as early as the ninth century.

A few steps from the basilica is the heart of the old republic, Piazza della Libertà (Liberty Square), with the government palace. The free-standing building, in steel-gray stone, looks severely medieval with its Gothic arches, battlements, and bell tower; it is in fact less than 100 years old. San Marino's sixty-member parliament, the Great and General Council, and the republic's executive and judiciary bodies meet in the palace.

A bust of Abraham Lincoln in the grand staircase looks down on officials who enter the council hall. He is revered in this corner of the Apennines almost like St. Marinus and Giuseppe Garibaldi, the hero of Italy's nineteenth-century unification who once found a refuge here. San Marino named Lincoln an honorary citizen in 1861, and the president of the United States acknowledged the gesture with a letter declaring: "Although your dominion is small, your State is nevertheless one of the most honored in all history." Thousands of Sammarinesi and their descendants live in America, especially in New York, Detroit, and Sandusky, Ohio.

A statue of Liberty, represented as a togaed, flag-carrying maiden with a sword on her side and a civic crown on her head, has been standing in the square since 1876; she is thus ten years older than her much larger sister who holds up her torch over New York Harbor.

Piazza della Libertà with its fine vistas is the setting for elaborate pageantry on April 1 and October 1 every year, when San Marino's two chief executives, the captains regent, are installed for their six-month terms. The two dignitaries act jointly as the republic's head of state. When, in 1981, one of the pair was a woman for the first time in history, a special robe and cape in black velvet and white silk had to be designed for female captains regent.

On ceremonial occasions the male incumbents of the top office wear a sixteenth-century costume with a corselet, breeches, black stockings, and a velvet beret, and carry a short dagger. Members of San Marino's volunteer armed forces—the Fortress Guard, the Noble Guard, and the Militia—parade in eighteenth-century uniforms during the installation ceremony, which always attracts crowds of tourists.

The feast day of St. Marinus, September 3, is observed with a competition of San Marino's crossbowmen. They shoot iron-tipped missiles at a target more than 100 feet from their emplacement in a rocky range. A Museum of Ancient Weapons is housed in the guardsmen's hall of the second fortress, Rocca della Fratta, the citadel on the middle peak of Mount Titano. The collection includes medieval armor, halberds, early artillery pieces, and other old firearms.

Specimens of San Marino's coins and many sets of its postage stamps are displayed in the modern Philatelic-Numismatic Museum in the suburb of Borgo Maggiore at the foot of Mount Titano. A funicular links Borgo Maggiore and its heliport with the summit of the mountain. The republic's monetary system is based on the Italian lira currency.

The sale of postage stamps to tourists and collectors is still a major source of revenue, but San Marino has recently experienced something like an industrial boom. In addition to the pottery and wrought-iron articles with which local souvenir shops overflow, new manufacturing plants in the lowlands turn out building materials, paints, yarns, and other products.

Italy has long prevented San Marino promoters from opening a gambling casino or operating a television station, and had enough leverage to make such vetoes stick. The Sammarinesi, on their aerie overlooking the Adriatic, nevertheless have become quite prosperous. And lately the Italian government told the minirepublic it might relent on gambling and television.

FIESOLE ▪

This very old hilltown is famed above all for its panorama of Florence, its "daughter," in the Arno Valley below. The daughter outgrew the mother already in antiquity, and in 1125 the Florentines destroyed much of Fiesole in a quarrel between hostile neighbors. Rebuilt, the town has since then led a dreamy existence on the margins of the proud city on the Arno, and has contributed much talent to Florence's glory.

In the nineteenth and twentieth centuries many expatriates from Britain and other countries made Fiesole their home, and quite a few foreigners live here today. With nearly 15,000 residents, three times the number of fifty years ago, the town is to some extent a bedroom community from which people commute to jobs in Florence, only a brief bus ride away.

However, Fiesole has retained its separateness and a quiet atmosphere of its own. Despite its recent growth it is not overdeveloped; happily, the construction of new housing has been restrained. Unlike many other scenic spots in Italy, Fiesole has still plenty of greenery and has been spared concrete monsters. It is far less garish than, for instance, the modern quarters of Tivoli near Rome.

Although there is so much to see in Florence, visitors to that city won't waste their time if they put aside half a day for a side trip to Fiesole, and maybe to the nearby village of Settignano. If, on the other hand, you have the good fortune of being able to be at leisure in Tuscany, it might be a good idea to set up headquarters here in the fresh air 800 feet above the region's congested capital. Communications with the center of Florence, its railroad terminal, and the motorways are excellent.

The hilltown's attractive center is Piazza Mino da Fiesole, named after the fifteenth-century sculptor, one of several natives who over the centuries won fame in Florence. The square, a long rectangle, is bordered on its north side by the medieval cathedral and is dominated by a steep hill on its west; it looks out on other hills with villas, houses, gardens, and clusters of pine and olive trees in the east. Florence is not visible from the piazza.

Walk behind the cathedral choir toward the archaeological area with its vast Etruscan and Roman remains. The Etruscans took control of the hills, already inhabited by a prehistoric tribe, in the seventh or sixth century B.C. Etruscan Faesulae (the Latin form of an older name) reached the height of its power in the fifth and fourth centuries B.C., protected by cyclopean walls around its shrines and dwellings. In the third century B.C. Rome conquered the place. Etruscan settlers from Faesulae founded Florence around 200 B.C. Later, veterans from Roman legions were allotted houses and land on the hillside.

The fenced-in excavation site, gently descending from behind the cathedral, can be visited. It is delimited in the north by a 700-foot stretch of intact Etruscan walls. A Roman theater from the first century B.C., a semicircle 111 feet in diameter, has twenty-three rows of stone seats, the four lowest ones set apart for prominent spectators. To the left of the theater are the foundations of a temple originally built by the Etruscans and later taken over and altered by the Romans.

131

OPPOSITE: Parma,
opera house

RIGHT: Ferrara,
Este Castle and
Savonarola Monument

BELOW: Parma,
cathedral and baptistry

ABOVE: *Ravenna, Basilica of St. Mary in Porto*

BELOW: *Faenza, locally made candlesticks in the Ceramics Museum*

OPPOSITE: *Rimini, Arch of Augustus*

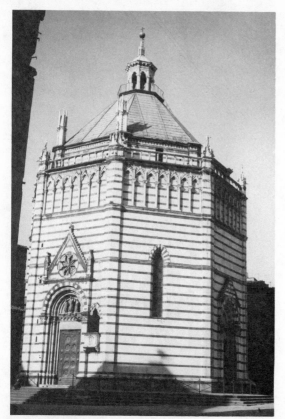

*LEFT: The baptistry
at Pistoia*

*BELOW: Roman theater
at Fiesole*

*OPPOSITE: Lucca,
Guinigi Tower*

Pisa, cathedral and Leaning Tower

An elaborate complex of Roman baths rose to the right of the theater. Some walls, arches, pools, and the location of two stoves that heated the water can be seen.

Inside the archaeological enclosure, in a neoclassical building near the entrance, is an Etruscan-Roman museum. The material displayed in three rooms includes a fragment of a bronze sculpture of the emblematic Roman she-wolf from the first century B.C. Outside the excavation area, adjoining the cathedral, is the Bandini Museum, named after an art-loving churchman. It contains terra-cottas from the celebrated Florentine workshop of the della Robbia family (fifteenth and sixteenth centuries), and paintings by such Tuscan masters as Ambrogio Lorenzetti of Siena (fourteenth century).

Fiesole's cathedral, in austere early-Romanesque style, dates from 1028. A group of white marble sculptures with a bust of the fifteenth-century bishop Leonardo Salutati and high reliefs representing the Madonna and saints over a sarcophagus is by Mino da Fiesole, and is considered one of his masterpieces. Bicci di Lorenzo (1375–1452) painted the *Madonna with Saints* on gold ground over the main altar. The cathedral's slender, square campanile went up in the early thirteenth century; its battlemented parapet was put on top in the eighteenth century.

A very steep street, about 500 yards long, leads from the stately episcopal palace, in front of the cathedral portal, to a terrace with stone benches that is locally known as *la banchina* ("the little bench"); it commands an overall view of Florence. Coin-operated telescopes permit in-detail viewing of the cityscape below, with Brunelleschi's majestic dome of the cathedral standing out, and the hills and ridges on the horizon south of the Arno Valley. In the foreground, right underneath the terrace, is an abstract steel sculpture commemorating three members of the Italian carabinieri force who were executed by the Nazis in Fiesole in 1944.

A few steps farther up, to the right, is a Franciscan convent. It was built at the beginning of the fourteenth century on the site of a fortress that crowned the hill's summit (1,132 feet high) in Etruscan and Roman times. The Gothic convent church, with walls in coarse stone, was enlarged in the fifteenth century, and Renaissance masters decorated its interior. Note particularly a *Conception of the Virgin* by Piero di Cosimo (1480) on the left side of the nave, and a restored

Annunciation by Raffaellino del Garbo (around 1500) behind the main altar. The convent includes two charming little cloisters and a small museum with Egyptian and Etruscan antiquities and exotic material brought home by missionaries. A restful little piazza outside the church opens into Fiesole's terraced public gardens with many old trees.

Back in the main square, have a look at the little town hall from the thirteenth century. Next to it is the equally small Church of Santa Maria Primerana, which was founded in the tenth century and rebuilt more than once through the ages. Two equestrian statues of Garibaldi and King Victor Emmanuel II stand in front of the town hall.

From Piazza Mino da Fiesole, take the street left of the town hall to the scenic road that leads across clumps of pine trees to the village of Settignano (584 feet high). Bernard Berenson, the American art critic and authority on Renaissance painting, lived here in the Villa I Tatti for many years until his death in 1959. Named after a family of Fiesole, the old mansion with its Italian gardens is now the seat of the Harvard Institute for Renaissance Studies. Works of art collected by Berenson, a library of 100,000 volumes, and an archive with reproductions of many thousands of paintings blend into a unique setting in which fellows of the American-sponsored institution conduct their researches.

Another international scholarly center, the European University Institute, is housed in the Badia Fiesolana, an ancient Benedictine abbey on the slope west of Fiesole, less than a mile from the town. The former abbey can be reached from the main street linking Fiesole with Florence. At the turnoff is the Church of San Domenico with a Dominican convent and a cluster of other houses. In a side chapel of the church, left, is a fresco of the Madonna with saints by Fra Angelico da Fiesole (1387–1455); the painter-friar lived in the convent for some time before moving on to Florence.

Half a mile southeast of the hamlet of San Domenico, near the small Mugnone River, is the Villa Palmieri, an old estate that scholars have identified as the site where Boccaccio had the narrators of his *Decameron*, seven young women and three men, spend the first few days after fleeing the plague in Florence in 1348. The place was "on a small hill, on all sides somewhat distant from our roads," Boccaccio reports, "surrounded by little meadows with marvelous gardens, with

141

wells of the freshest water, and with bows of precious vines."

Some of the bucolic mood of *The Decameron* seems to linger in the villas and the little roads between ivied garden walls around Fiesole.

PISTOIA ■

Pistols may or may not have been first made, in the sixteenth century, in the city whose name resembles theirs; its skilled craftsmen have at any rate been renowned since the Middle Ages. Pistoia, with a population of 100,000, is today an important manufacturing center where railroad cars are built and textiles woven. It's a good place to shop for all sorts of hardware and clothing. Only twenty-three miles northwest of Florence, Pistoia is outside the international tourist circuit, and despite its architectural riches and Renaissance art it is no museum city. It gives, on the other hand, a good idea of the vitality of present-day Tuscany.

Visitors will do well to travel from Florence in one of the frequent railroad trains rather than by car because it is at times a hopeless enterprise to look for parking space in bustling Pistoia. The Porrettana (National Route No. 64, by way of Porretta Terme), skirting the city's west, was an important link between Florence and Bologna before the Autostrada del Sole (Highway of the Sun, Motorway A-1) was built. The old road across the Apennines may now see many fewer long-distance trucks than it did in the 1950s, but the local motor traffic has enormously increased because of industrial development and economic prosperity and has invaded even Pistoia's center.

Well-preserved walls enclose the inner city in the shape of a trapezoid, with a fortress and park at the point closest to Florence, and bastions in the three other corners. Pistoia lies in the plain where the small Ombrone River joins the Arno. The city has long, straight streets and looks out at the foothills of the Apennines to the north.

Piazza del Duomo (Cathedral Square) is the geometrical center of the trapezoid and the heart of Pistoia. The large cathedral combines Pisan Romanesque with Florentine Renaissance elements, reflecting the dominant artistic trends in the region between the twelfth and sixteenth centuries. The 220-foot-high bell tower was originally built as a fortified lookout around the year 1200; three tiers of columns in the Pisan manner were added when the structure later became a church campanile.

A terra-cotta relief over the cathedral's entrance, showing the Virgin Mary surrounded by angels, is by Andrea della Robbia, a member of the famous Florentine family of sculptors who received important commissions from thriving Pistoia at the beginning of the sixteenth century. The Baroque interior of the church will not be to everybody's taste.

The octagonal baptistery in the piazza opposite the church is a noble Gothic building from the fourteenth century with an outer pulpit for open-air sermons. The neighboring courthouse (Palazzo Pretorio) is also from the fourteenth century, with a modern top floor. Symmetrically opposite is the city hall. The building, started in 1295 and completed a hundred years later, houses a museum with a painting of the Madonna by Ridolfo Ghirlandaio, son of the more famous Domenico, and paintings by masters of the Pistoia school from the fourteenth to the sixteenth centuries. An arch joins the city hall with the cathedral, reinforcing the architectural unity of the piazza.

The Ospedale del Ceppo northeast of Cathedral Square is one of the oldest and most renowned hospitals in Tuscany. Giovanni della Robbia and assistants from his family's Florentine workshop decorated the portico with a long frieze, in colored and glazed terra-cotta, representing the Seven Works of Mercy—caring for the sick, consoling the afflicted, and so on. Figures of Charity and other personified virtues separate the edifying scenes of the panel.

Above all, the number and magnificence of churches will strike a stroller in Pistoia. Among them is the Sanctuary of the Madonna dell'Umiltà (Our Lady of Humility), west of the cathedral, with a dome by Giorgio Vasari, the sixteenth-century architect, painter, and art historian. The Church of Sant'Andrea in the northwest of the city is a twelfth-century edifice in the Pisan style with an unfinished façade. The columned pulpit in the interior with bas-reliefs of biblical episodes is one of the major works by Giovanni Pisano, of the Pisan dynasty of sculptors. San Bartolomeo in the east of Pistoia is a Romanesque church, also with a remarkable pulpit, dating from 1250.

The twelfth-century Church of San Giovanni Fuorcivitas (St. John's Outside the City) is well inside the fortifications surrounding the urban nucleus; its name refers to the much smaller Pistoia of the early

Middle Ages. The Pisan Romanesque building was damaged during World War II but has been repaired. A terra-cotta *Visitation of Mary* in the interior, on the left side, was supplied by the della Robbia studio in Florence.

There are few vestiges of Pistoria, the city's ancestor in antiquity, originally a string of Roman bulwarks against the Gauls who had overrun northern Italy. Catiline was defeated and slain in Pistoria in 62 B.C. after his famous conspiracy to seize power in Rome had collapsed and he had fled to the north in search of help from the Gauls.

LUCCA ■

When an association of Europe's walled cities and towns was first proposed after World War II, everybody here liked the idea at once. Nothing much came of it, but to Lucca the intact belt of bastions, ramparts, gates, and moats isn't an anachronism and a nuisance to motorists, but remains an essential part of its identity.

Local patriotism, a degree of insularity, and often unconfessed sense of being a little superior to the rest of the people in the region, are Lucchese traits. "It's our city's wall mentality," a history-minded native told me. The Christian Democratic Party, which likes to describe itself as Italy's bulwark against communism, makes an impressive showing in Lucca in every election. By contrast, the left-wing vote in nearby Florence and Pisa, as in the rest of Tuscany, is always among the strongest in the nation.

Lucca's walls, 2.6 miles in circumference, have helped maintain the architectural integrity of the city core. Comparatively few modern buildings break the harmony of the old houses and palaces inside the walls. Church steeples and other towers overlook the uniformly red-tiled roofs.

Suburbs stretch out in all directions beyond the fortifications, and they keep growing. A majority of the about 90,000 inhabitants of Lucca live today outside the walls, some of them in comfortable or even luxurious villas with parks and swimming pools. Yet there is still a cachet about having a place—perhaps in a Renaissance house that has been modernized internally—in *Lucca dentro,* "inner Lucca."

No enemy has ever challenged the red-brick ramparts that Lucca built at staggering cost between 1544 and 1650. The fortifications, which were equipped with hundreds of guns, rose thirty feet high at some points, and effectively sealed off the city during floods of the Serchio River, which skirts it in the north.

At first the walls had only three gates; three more were opened much later. The Gate of St. Peter on the city's south side, one of the original ones, bears Lucca's Latin motto: *"Libertas"* ("Freedom").

The city, wealthy through its silk manufacture and silk trade, didn't conquer liberty but bought it. Lucca paid 300,000 florins to Emperor Charles IV in 1369 as cash price for its independence. Earlier, the city had been torn by the feuds between hostile factions that were chronic in medieval Italy, and was made to feel military pressure from outside, first from Pisa, then from Florence.

Once freedom had been purchased, Lucca was governed most of the time by a coterie of leading merchants. The tiny Republic of Lucca managed to maintain its independence until 1799, when Napoleon invaded Tuscany. He installed his sister, Elisa, as a duchess in Lucca. There is still a Piazza Napoleone in the city.

After Napoleon's fall Lucca remained a dukedom, ruled by a branch of the Bourbon family until 1847, when it was incorporated into the Grand Duchy of Tuscany. The fortifications were never demolished: They were too bulky, and the citizens loved them anyway.

Today a circular avenue on top of the bastions, shaded by stately chestnut and beech trees, girds the center of the city. A stroll on the Passeggio delle Mura (Wall Promenade) will take an hour and a half to come full circle, and provides gratifying views of the city. Some of the former guard rooms and dungeons in the wall basements are used for art events.

From the Wall Promenade near the Gate of St. Peter one can see the Romanesque campanile of Lucca's cathedral. The church itself, from the thirteenth century, is one of Lucca's major sights. Its façade is asymmetrical; it has three superimposed arcaded galleries, a standby of Pisan architecture, over three arches, each with different spans, leading to a richly decorated porch.

Inside the church is a marble sculpture of St. Martin and the Beggar from the thirteenth century that formerly adorned the façade (it has been replaced there by a copy). The paintings in the cathedral include *The Last Supper* by Tintoretto and *The Holy Virgin Among Four Saints* by Domenico Ghirlandaio.

An octagonal sanctuary in the left aisle of the cathedral holds a relic that has been venerated since the Middle Ages, the Santo Volto (Holy Effigy). It is a crucifix in cedar wood that is said to have been mysteriously transferred to Lucca from the Holy Land, and through the centuries has been credited with miraculous powers. The features of Jesus are blackened by long exposure to incense and the smoke of candles. On September 13 every year, at sunset, the crucifix, crowned and wrapped in gold-embroidered cloth for the occasion, is carried around the city in a solemn procession.

To many visitors the most touching monument in the cathedral is the tomb of Ilaria del Carretto by Jacopo della Quercia. Ilaria was the second wife of Paolo Guinigi, lord of Lucca. She died young in 1404, and is represented serenely resting on her sarcophagus, her head on two marble cushions, a pug dog at her feet gazing at its lifeless mistress. Reliefs of classical-style putti holding garlands of fruit decorate the sarcophagus underneath. "A lesson of love," Ruskin called the marble group.

Another important church is San Michele, with a profusely decorated façade of four rows of columns and arches towering above the central nave. The piazza on the south side of the church was the forum of the ancient Roman Luca, a stronghold where Caesar, Pompey, and Crassus, the triumvirs, met for a power-play conference in 56 B.C. Piazza San Michele is still the heart of the city.

The former palace of the mayor, a dignified Renaissance building with a ground-floor loggia, is opposite the church. Nearby, on Via del Poggio, is the brick house where Giacomo Puccini was born in 1858, marked by a marble plaque. (The composer is buried in Torre del Lago, a lakeside resort fifteen miles northwest of Lucca, where he had a villa and died in 1924. A festival featuring performances of Puccini operas is held there every summer.)

The third church not to miss is San Frediano, near the north walls. The Romanesque edifice is dedicated to an Irishman, St. Frigidianus or Finnian, who was bishop of Lucca from 560 to 578. The church contains the tomb of one St. Richard, an Irish or Anglo-Saxon chief who died in Lucca in 729 while making a pilgrimage to Rome. The remains of Lucca's patron saint are the chief object of veneration in the ancient church. She is St. Zita, a servant maid whose reputation for charity and holiness inspired legends; after her death in 1278 she was mentioned by Dante in his *Divine Comedy*.

A short walk from the Church of San Frediano leads to an oval square that was once a Roman amphitheater, 262 feet long and 176 feet wide. The rickety old houses that surround the former arena were built on the ruins of the ancient circus structures, incorporating walls and arches that had remained after the depredations during the Dark Ages—an example of how current everyday life cohabits with ancient history in Italy.

A little farther is a red-brick tower with trees growing at the top, a landmark almost at the geometrical center of the city. The tower is part of the dilapidated fourteenth-century palace of the Guinigi family, masters of Lucca from 1392 to 1430. A large villa that Paolo Guinigi had built for himself in the west of the city, near the walls, has recently been restored and is the seat of Lucca's National Museum. It contains archaeological material, medieval wood-carvings, and paintings by Italian and Flemish masters, none exceptional, from the thirteenth to the eighteenth centuries. Another picture collection is in the Palazzo Mansi, on the city's opposite side, with paintings from the fifteenth to the eighteenth centuries and, among other exhibits, the equipment of Lucca's last weaver's workshop.

Piazza Napoleone, near the cathedral, is dominated by the elegant façade of what the Lucchese still call the Ducal Palace. The building was started in 1578 by Bartolomeo Ammanati, one of the architects of the Pitti Palace in Florence, and for more than two centuries housed the government of the Republic of Lucca. When Napoleon's sister and, later, the Bourbon dukes moved in, a royal staircase was built and the state rooms were redecorated. Today the palace is the seat of the provincial authorities, but the Swiss Hall, named after the Switzers who were the republic's mercenaries, and a few other splendid rooms can be visited.

The main delight in Lucca is wandering about the city, despite the noise echoing in the narrow streets and the fierce heat in summer. The produce of the fertile countryside all around is displayed in Lucca's markets and food shops. For many Italians Lucca rates a detour just to pick up a few bottles of its vaunted olive oil—among the country's best—maybe combined with a meal in one of its restaurants. The Lucchese like their evening stroll in the medieval Via Fillungo with its new boutiques and the Antico Caffè Caselli, since the days of Puccini a meeting place of artists and intellectuals.

PISA ∎

The Leaning Tower is media shorthand for all of Italy the way the Statue of Liberty is for the United States, Mount Fuji for Japan, and the Eiffel Tower for France. To Pisans the marble monument that has since the Middle Ages been numbered among the wonders of the world is like a beloved old relative who is still going strong, but whose health is nevertheless being watched with some apprehension. The city is relieved when it learns that in a given year the tower's inclination has increased only by less than a millimeter (0.04 inch), and that there are good reasons for hope that the 800-year-old landmark will continue leaning without falling down, far into the twenty-first century and maybe even beyond.

Yet Pisa isn't just its famous tower. The city's galleys sailed the Mediterranean far and wide in the eleventh and twelfth centuries, when Pisa ruled an empire that for some time included Sardinia, Corsica, the Balearic Islands, and even scraps of North Africa. Defeated by its maritime rival, Genoa, and later conquered by Florence, Pisa sank into provincial torpor that was to last for centuries. Today the city is groping for new prominence in a field that isn't the tourist business: It is well on its way toward emerging as an Italian science center. Its ancient university, in which Galileo taught mathematics, now leads nationally in computer studies, and its Scuola Normale, founded under Napoleon, is an elite college. Pisa has lately turned out theoretical physicists and other scientists who eventually made their name in the United States.

There are more bookstores in Pisa than in most other Italian cities of 100,000 or so, and there are a lot of young people to be seen. Among them are also off-duty paratroopers of a crack unit, recognizable by their wine-red berets, that is stationed in nearby Livorno (Leghorn). The tough paras are no friends of Pisa's radical students, and weekend rumbles between members of the two camps are no rarity. Politically, the city that once took a leading part in some of the Crusades against the infidel is today heavily left-wing.

Pisa, which is a railroad hub and a junction of important highways, suffered much during World War II. Since then the bridges across the Arno River have been rebuilt exactly as they were before, and all other damages have been repaired. The embankments (Lungarno) present again a remarkably harmonious scenery; the usually languid river, the bridges, and the decorous buildings, all of about the same moderate height, blend into a cityscape reminiscent of Florence.

The Lungarno, alas, no longer invites strolling since it bears a heavy traffic load. Some of the streets and squares in the center are closed to motor vehicles. On Piazza Garibaldi, the spot where Pisa's most important bridge (Ponte di Mezzo) links the northern and southern halves of the city, a municipal ordinance warns: "NO DOG-WALKING IN THIS ZONE." It is, however, a place for meeting people and engaging in outdoor chats.

Corso Italia and Via Oberdan on either side of the Ponte di Mezzo, forming Pisa's narrow axis, are the main shopping streets. Wandering off into the side alleys, visitors soon find themselves in quiet neighborhoods with marble churches and Renaissance palaces, where little seems to have happened in centuries.

Piazza dei Cavalieri in the heart of the city was the forum in antiquity and the place where the seafaring Republic of Pisa had its government in the Middle Ages. Remodeled in the Baroque era, the piazza is today one of Italy's noble squares, with a church of the Knights' Order of St. Stephen, after which the piazza is named, and the Cavaliers' Palace, now housing the Scuola Normale. Piazza Santa Caterina, a larger, oblong square in the city's northeast with a Pisan Gothic church, is now unfortunately a parking lot most of the time.

The long streets closer to the old fortifications that still surround the historical center are calm and distinguished, with few of the houses taller than three or four stories. The high-rises and industrial buildings are on the outskirts near the roads and railroad lines to Florence, Genoa, and Rome.

The unique group of marble buildings—Cathedral, Baptistery, Leaning Tower, and Campo Santo (cemetery)—is an island of respectful quiet in the northeastern corner of Pisa, protected on two sides by the crenellated city walls. The calm may be broken some mornings by the shouts of children who play at the foot of the tower, but they are not allowed onto the lawn, one of the greenest and best kept in Italy.

The first encounter with the campanile that is so familiar from all the pictures and alabaster models one has seen is a surprise. Isn't it shorter and plumper than one had imagined? As for leaning, yes, the tower does a lot of that. One hundred eighty-one feet high, it is in fact fifteen feet out of the perpendicular. Scientific apparatus on the ground floor keep probing the spongy subsoil and the campanile's imperceptible movements, confirming the continued subsidence of its foundations toward southeast. Luckily, the sinking process—which had started already during the tower's construction—has lately slowed down, even despite some occasional earth tremors. An international search by engineers and architects for methods to prevent the Leaning Tower's eventual collapse has so far remained inconclusive. Nobody seems to be in any hurry.

Visitors may climb the 292 steps to the top, which commands a panorama encompassing the city and the Arno, the airport and the pine groves between Pisa and the sea, the Apuan Alps with their marble quarries, and the Pisan Hills to the northeast. On the tower's stairs one feels drawn to the leaning side as if by an invisible hand, and is reminded that Galileo used Pisa's bizarre belfry for experiments to investigate gravitation. He is also said to have been prompted by the swaying of the bronze lamp near the episcopal throne in the cathedral to start research into the physics of the pendulum.

The cathedral is the prototype of the Pisan style in church architecture that recurs in various places in Tuscany and beyond—white marble with dark-colored bands, blind arches under tiers of arcaded galleries with columns, plenty of sculptural decoration.

The cathedral, the baptistery, and the rectangular marble cloister of the Campo Santo, the burial place on the north side of Cathedral Square, contain many works by members of the Pisano family. To appreciate fully the wealth of bronze and marble panels, reliefs, and sculptures that this dynasty of Pisan artists created in the thirteenth and fourteenth centuries, as well as the works by other sculptors and painters in the three marble structures, a detailed guidebook and some leisure are needed.

Students of art will want also to visit the Museum of Sinopias on the south side of Cathedral Square. Sinopias are preliminary drawings for frescoes; the Pisan collection is one of the largest of its kind anywhere. Catalogs of the displays in the baptistery and in the Museum of Sinopias are available on the spot.

The National Museum, in a former Benedictine monastery on the right embankment of the Arno, holds art by Pisan and other Tuscan masters from the fourteenth century to the eighteenth.

The city has good hotels and eating places that range from the plain and honest to deluxe. Florence is nearby, and the fashionable bathing beaches of Viareggio are even closer. One could imagine living pleasurably in proud, and somewhat dreamy, Pisa.

VOLTERRA ▪

Alabaster and grand views brighten up this austere hilltown between Siena and the coast of Tuscany. Statuettes, cups, lamps, and other articles in the soft white material that abounds in the area are on sale everywhere here, cheaper than in souvenir shops in Florence. White dust fills the air and covers the pavement outside the many alabaster workshops. Some windowpanes in the 700-year-old cathedral are of translucent alabaster. The gypsumlike material that the Volterrans have quarried and worked through the ages comes also with yellow or brown streaks, and is occasionally painted over by the local artisans.

Volterra, encircled by the impressive remains of Etruscan walls and by a much narrower girdle of medieval ramparts, is very old and somewhat forbidding. A penitentiary in its citadel adds to the town's somber aspects. The main square is almost sullen in its severity.

Fortunately, there are the vistas from the plateau on which the town sits, at a height of 1,785 feet. From many points one sees the coastal plain and the Tyrrhenian Sea to the west, glittering salt pans a few miles away, and the hills and valleys of the Tuscan Apennines.

The Etruscan walls up and down the slopes have a circumference of four and a half miles. Built with huge sandstone blocks, they enclose an area almost three times as vast as medieval Volterra covered. In Etruscan and Roman times the town was doubtless important; today it has a population of some 15,000. Volterra's Etruscan-Roman past is forcefully evoked by the Porta all'Arco (Gateway at the Arch) in the town's south, a twenty-foot-high archway of massive yellow and gray rectangular blocks. Three human heads of *peperino* stone, their features long corroded, stick out from the semicircular arch.

Volterra's principal square, the cobblestoned Piazza dei Priori or Piazza Maggiore, faces the Gothic town hall, Palazzo dei Priori, a brick building with battlements and a short tower. Two stone lions on high pedestals on either side of the façade look grimly into the piazza. The third floor houses a small picture gallery with an *Annunciation* by Luca Signorelli and works by painters of the Florentine school. Ask to be allowed up the tower: On a clear day the panorama is immense.

The cathedral, behind the town hall, dates in its present shape from the thirteenth century, when an earlier church was rebuilt in the Pisan Gothic style. Frescoes by Benozzo Gozzoli adorn the Chapel of the Madonna on the left side. Opposite the church façade in Piazza San Giovanni, west of the main square, is a thirteenth-century octagonal baptistery with a Renaissance altar and font.

One of Volterra's major attractions is the Guarnacci Museum, named after an eighteenth-century scholarly churchman who willed his vast antiques collection and library to the town. More than 600 funerary urns and chests, dug up from a nearby burial ground, are on view. Most of them are of Volterran alabaster bearing reliefs that depict horse races, banquets, and other scenes from merry Etruscan life as well as episodes from Greek mythology. Another recurrent theme in the reliefs that still moves the beholder two millennia and a half later is the sad farewell of the deceased who starts the journey to the underworld while relatives and friends stay behind on earth. The museum, in the former Palazzo Tangassi, contains Roman antiquities as well.

The citadel, a few minutes from the Guarnacci Museum, is a combination of two fortresses, one built in the fourteenth century, the other in the fifteenth century when the Florentines were already ruling Volterra through a governor. The promenade on the south side of the fortifications, Viale dei Ponti, affords fine views.

Substantial ruins of a Roman theater near the Porta Fiorentina (Florentine Gate) in the city's north show that the town, then called Volaterrae, was well-off in classical times, although it is rarely mentioned in Roman literature.

A road across the northwestern suburb of San Giusto leads in about a mile to a deep ravine known as Le Balze; it was formed by erosion and is still widening because of occasional landslides. The wild scenery contrasts with the gentle contours of the Tuscan hills all around.

Volterra, off the well-trodden routes, seems a little world by itself. Volterrans are generally serious-minded and intensely proud of their history, their art, their grim palaces and towers, and their alabaster. This is a town with character.

PORTOFERRAIO ▪

Napoleon spent only 298 days on the Isle of Elba before embarking on his last adventure, which after the Hundred Days would end at Waterloo. The people of Portoferraio, the island's main town, have never forgotten the son of nearby Corsica who spoke their language and took an unexpected interest in their problems during the short time he was their sovereign.

The former capital of the short-lived miniature realm now sees many thousands of holidaymakers pass through from spring to fall. Some of them stop to visit the Napoleonic places, but most hurry on to the hotels, villas, camping sites, and beaches elsewhere on the triangular island. Few stay in Portoferraio, a picturesque, lively town of 12,000.

On the bay west of Portoferraio's harbor are the blast furnaces and rolling mills of old steelworks, a cement plant, and loading platforms. Iron has been mined on Elba for more than 2,500 years; possession of the metal-rich island was the economic base of Etruscan power from the sixth to the fourth century B.C., until the Romans took over. Today the island's open-pit mines are nearly exhausted, and current worldwide overproduction of iron and steel does not make it profitable to furrow deep for Elban ores. While industry is declining on Elba, tourism is booming.

Portoferraio means "Iron Harbor." The visitor who arrives in its horseshoe-shaped little port is impressed by the sight of the town rising in tiers like an amphitheater, enclosed by walls left and right that climb from the waterfront to two Renaissance strongholds, Fort Falcone (Falcon) and Fort Stella (Star), at 200 to 240 feet above the

153

sea. This was the scenery Napoleon saw when he disembarked from the British frigate *Undaunted* on May 3, 1814, and was presented with the symbolic key of the town by the mayor.

The former master of the continent, reduced to ruling over a rocky island about the size of Manhattan and Brooklyn combined, chose for himself and his mock-imperial court two modest buildings linked by a low structure, overlooking the town and the harbor from a point between the two forts. This Casa dei Mulini (House of the Mills) can be visited today. It includes a central hall that Napoleon had hastily built; he held audiences and receptions there with Count Henri-Gatien Bertrand, a French general who had followed him to Elba, acting as "Grand Marshal of the Palace."

The frescoed halls and rooms of the Casa dei Mulini contain period furniture and Napoleonic memorabilia, including that key of Porto-ferraio, ceremoniously handed to the blue-coated emperor on his arrival, and his books, which he later donated to the town. Two cannon that the dethroned monarch had had brought into position in the small garden behind his new residence are still there. From the garden wall, cliffs drop to the sea north of the promontory on which Porto-ferraio is built.

Napoleon took his responsibilities as ruler of a dwarf state that the powers of the victorious grand coalition had quickly set up for him surprisingly seriously. He had the two citadels on either side of his residence reinforced; hoisted the flag he had designed for himself (three bees on a red bar across a white field); toured the island on horseback or in his brig, the *Inconstant*, to inspect the villages, the mines, and the vineyards; and had the thousand soldiers that he had been permitted to take with him to Elba build new roads. On the *Inconstant* he eventually sailed to Cannes on February 26, 1815, the start of the Hundred Days.

A requiem mass for Napoleon is said in the sixteenth-century Church of Misericordia (Mercy), about halfway between the town hall near the waterfront and his former residence, every May 5, the anniversary of the emperor's death on the Island of St. Helena in 1821. A plaque on the Portoferraio town hall commemorates the onetime sovereign of Elba.

Piazza Vittorio Emanuele II, a square with plane trees near the town hall, is the social center of present-day Portoferraio. The island's climate is mild, and the piazza fills up also on sunny days in the winter months. The slightly fizzy Elban wine, which is white, can be sampled in one of the taverns between Piazza Vittorio Emanuele II and the harbor.

Napoleon buffs will want to visit a former storehouse that the emperor had adapted as his summer residence, but rarely used. Known as the Villa Napoleone, it is at an altitude of 249 feet, amid trees and shrubbery, on the slope of the 1,214-foot-high Mount San Martino, nearly four miles south of Portoferraio, and can be reached on a good road. Harking back to his expedition to the Pyramids in 1798, the emperor had the second-floor dining room decorated as an Egyptian hall; a Latin wall inscription reads: *"Ubicumque Felix Napoleon"* ("Napoleon is happy anywhere").

A villa built by the Russian Prince Anatol Demidoff, son-in-law of Napoleon's youngest brother, Jérôme Bonaparte, in 1852 below the emperor's summer residence, now houses a small museum with Napoleonic relics, books, paintings, prints, and other items connected with the era of the French Empire.

SAN GIMIGNANO ▪

This is the quintessential museum town. With its towers—some of them leaning—of various heights and shapes, its Gothic palaces and frescoed churches, and its fortress at the loftiest point of its steep hill, San Gimignano looks today much as it must have appeared to Dante in 1300 when he ceremoniously visited it as an ambassador from Florence.

In 1928 the Italian government designated the entire "Town of the Beautiful Towers" as a national monument. Any new constructions or architectural changes require special permits, which are seldom granted. While most other towns in Tuscany, and Florence itself, are today ringed with new housing developments and industrial plants, San Gimignano has been spared such a concrete belt around its old walls; its population increase has been moderate during the last fifty years, from 4,500 to 7,500 residents.

All year round, and especially from early spring to late fall, the town fills up with tourists during the day, most of them arriving by coach or car from Florence. Evenings in San Gimignano, when almost all of the visitors have gone again, are quiet. The early-morning hours are glorious. A special treat is to view the town from a vantage point on the road to Poggibonsi off the southern tip of San Gimignano when the rising sun lights up its stone towers, its burnt-sienna roofs, and its houses in lighter shades of brown above olive trees, vineyards, and gardens.

Those margins of time without guided-tour crowds justify staying on in San Gimignano for a few days or maybe even longer to savor its medieval architecture and atmosphere, laze in its squares, and contemplate unhurriedly the great frescoes in its churches and the treasures of its Civic Picture Gallery, one of the most important of Tuscany's minor art collections.

San Gimignano's thirteen square towers, some of them moss-flecked and grass-topped, are the survivors of at least fifty (some sources say seventy-two) such structures that gave the town a porcupine skyline in the Middle Ages. As in other faction-torn communes in northern and central Italy and in medieval Rome, the bristling towers were private fortresses of powerful families who withdrew to them during the frequent periods of street fighting.

Born as a fortified way-station on an ancient road between Lucca and Siena, the hilltown was named after St. Geminianus, a bishop of Modena who was credited with having saved the castle from being overrun by Attila's Huns. The town that since the tenth century grew around the castle and the cathedral (twelfth century) appears to have prospered despite repeated wars with Volterra, about ten miles to the southwest. San Gimignano remained independent until 1353, when it passed under Florentine control; it had by then 13,000 inhabitants, but quickly lost its importance, also because the trade routes in Tuscany were changing. Henceforth bypassed by commerce and history, the townspeople kept tilling their farms and gardens around their hill until San Gimignano found a new vocation: luring tourists.

The tallest of the thirteen towers rises above the People's Palace, the town hall. This 174-foot bell tower, the Torre del Comune, was built at the end of the thirteenth century and commands a bird's-eye view of the racquet-shaped town with its dozen other towers, its rust-brown roofscape, its medieval walls and gates, and the green countryside.

Nearby, opposite the cathedral, is the thirteenth-century Palace of the Podestà (the *podestà* was the town governor), with a clock tower that is affectionately called La Rognosa ("The Mangy One"). A town ordinance in 1602 forbade private builders to exceed its 167-foot height. A few steps farther north, at the beginning of the sloping Via San Matteo, are twin towers that seem an early scale model for the World Trade Center in lower Manhattan. A narrow four-story house with two windows on each floor nestles between the two towers, almost three times its height, which were erected by the Salvucci family.

The Salvucci were the leaders of the Ghibelline faction, forever antagonists of the Ardinghelli clan, which headed San Gimignano's Guelph party. The savage feuds between the two irreconcilable camps contributed to the town's decline.

The cathedral, known as La Collegiata (The Collegiate Church), was enlarged during the Renaissance and is noteworthy above all for its frescoes from the fourteenth and fifteenth centuries. The interior wall behind its restored façade is adorned with a *Martyrdom of St. Sebastian* by Benozzo Gozzoli (1465) beneath a *Last Judgment* by Taddeo di Bartolo (1393). Sienese artists decorated the aisles during the fourteenth century: Bartolo di Fredi with episodes from the Old Testament (right) and Barna da Siena with Passion scenes (left).

Early frescoes by Domenico Ghirlandaio, who was later to become the teacher of Michelangelo, ennoble the Chapel of Santa Fina at the right side of the church. St. Fina, or Seraphina, was a devout girl who had religious visions; after her death at the age of fifteen in 1253 various miracles were attributed to her. One of Ghirlandaio's frescoes depicts the girl saint's funeral with the towers of San Gimignano as a backdrop.

The Museum of Sacred Art in a medieval building on a small rectangular square to the left of the cathedral contains sculptures by Benedetto da Maiano, who designed the altar in the Chapel of Santa Fina (1475), and precious church objects from various periods.

The Civic Picture Gallery in the town hall boasts a *Madonna with Two Saints* by Pinturicchio (1511), an *Annunciation* by Filippino Lippi, the talented son of the more famous former friar Filippo Lippi, as well as paintings by various other Tuscan masters from the thirteenth through fifteenth centuries.

The town hall's council chamber on the third floor (second floor, in Italian reckoning) is known as the Hall of Dante because the poet, in his role as Florentine ambassador, in a formal oration on May 8, 1300, urged the notables of San Gimignano to send delegates to the

157

meeting of a proposed Guelph League. The hall was frescoed by thirteenth- and fourteenth-century artists; Benozzo Gozzoli retouched and completed some of the wall paintings in 1467.

Famous frescoes by Benozzo Gozzoli are to be found in the disused Church of Sant'Agostino in the northwestern salient of the town walls. A sequence of seventeen scenes depicts the life of the church's patron, St. Augustine, from his childhood when his mother, St. Monica, took him to school until the year 430, when the bishop of Hippo and Father of the Church lay in state.

San Gimignano's life today, as in times past, centers on the Piazza della Cisterna, close to Cathedral Square. It is nearly perfect in its rhythm—slightly inclined, it is framed by towers and ancient houses of varying height, with arched doorways and shops, and with a thirteenth-century cistern in its middle. The octagonal waterbasin after which the square is named rests on a base of similar shape with five steps, and is surmounted by a stone architrave on two columns. The piazza is paved with herringbone rows of bricks in geometrical patterns. Potted plants and the tables and plastic chairs outside the espresso bars provide dabs of gaudier colors in the architectural composition of browns.

A medieval washhouse and fountain outside the Porta delle Fonti (Gate of the Fountains) in the northeast of the town walls must also have been a social center of sorts in past centuries. On the opposite side of the town, at an altitude of 1,089 feet, is a ruined castle, La Rocca (The Rock), surrounded by a park. What can be seen now are a tower and other remnants of a five-cornered fortress that the Florentines built on the site of a much older citadel when they took control of San Gimignano. The tower and parapets of La Rocca afford a panorama that is most beautiful in the afternoon sun.

PIENZA ∎

A humanist pope more than four centuries ago dreamed of transforming his humble birthplace into the ideal city. Pienza, the creation of Pius II, may not have become quite what he had in mind, but the town of barely 3,000 inhabitants is an enduring monument to a great

Renaissance figure, an architectural gem, and also one of the most charming places in Tuscany today.

Enea Silvio Piccolomini, the future pontiff, was born in 1405 in what was to become Pienza, into a disgraced noble family from Siena which had exiled itself to the obscure village. The place was then known as Corsignano, and hadn't really lived down its old reputation for being a lair of brigands who would rob pilgrims on their journey to Rome. Boccaccio in his *Decameron* mentioned Corsignano as the refuge of a Sienese (not a Piccolomini) who had reason not to show his face in his native city for some time.

In his early years Enea Silvio was a brilliant author who, among other things, wrote an erotic novel in Latin, *De Duobus Amantibus Historia (Story of Two Lovers)*, a celebration of adultery. As a secretary to high churchmen he attended some sessions of the Council of Basel, 1431–1449. He entered the service of the future Emperor Frederick III, who crowned him poet laureate in 1442. At the age of forty the writer-diplomat became a priest. His career was dizzying: canon in Trent, bishop first in Trieste and then in Siena, cardinal, pope in 1458.

Gibbon, referring to an earlier pontiff (Urban II), wrote that there was no more exquisite gratification "than to revisit in a conspicuous dignity the humble and laborious scenes of our youth." Pius II was not yet fifty-four years old when he savored that pleasure during a stopover in his birthplace on his way to Mantua.

The moving welcome that the villagers gave the pontiff, and maybe other sentimental reasons too, prompted him to decide on the spot that Corsignano should become a model city, to be named, after himself, Pienza. He picked a Florentine architect to build a cathedral, a palace for his own family, a city hall, and other edifices. The man chosen as Italy's first urban planner was Bernardo Gambarelli, called El Rossellino, a disciple of the great architect Leon Battista Alberti. Rossellino had already made his mark by building the innovative Rucellai Palace in Florence from designs by Alberti.

Pius II appropriated 10,000 gold florins for the Pienza project, a respectable sum for the epoch. Funds were to be raised in part by the Holy See, in part by the cardinals whom the pope told to commission palaces of their own in the nascent city. Some members of the Sacred College went into debt to comply with the pope's wishes while others simply dragged their feet.

The astonishing thing is that it took Rossellino and his workers only four years to complete the cathedral and most of the other structures that Pius II wanted to see. Less surprising is the fact that the architect presented the pope with a whopping cost overrun: He had spent 50,000 florins without bothering to inform the head of the Church. Bankers in Florence or Siena must have helped finance the urban project. Pius II praised the contractor for concealing from him the giant expenditures before the results were visible and even gave Rossellino 1,000 gold florins and a scarlet gown as tokens of pontifical favor.

The papal money was well spent. The arrangement of Rossellino's buildings around Pienza's central square, Piazza Pio II, is one of the great compositions of early-Renaissance architecture.

Today's visitors who arrive on one of three highways—from Montepulciano, Siena, or Rome—first see the rust-colored town of Pius II and Rossellino from afar on a little ridge across olive groves, sunflower fields, vineyards, and rows of cypresses. From the main gate in Pienza's west, flagstone-paved Corso Rossellino leads to the noble piazza, a trapezoid. The town's neatness is striking.

The cathedral, with an octagonal campanile at its left, is in sandstone and warm, porous travertine; its dignified Renaissance façade bears Pius II's coats of arms, the keys of St. Peter over a cross surrounded by a wreath pattern. The bright interior of the church is noteworthy for the absence of frescoes and other decorations except five panels by Sienese masters picturing the Virgin Mary with the Infant Jesus and saints. Pius II forbade further ornamentation on the grounds that it would only detract from the church's exceptional luminosity.

The foundations of the cathedral rest on unstable soil. Consolidation efforts, by injection of concrete and other techniques, have been going on for several decades.

The Piccolomini Palace adjoining the cathedral recalls the Rucellai Palace in Florence. The south side, with three tiers of loggias looking out on a hanging garden and on the wide valley of the Orcia River, is particularly felicitous. Some halls of the building that may be visited contain period furniture, paintings, tapestries, sculptures, weapons, and other Piccolomini treasures. Some years ago thieves made off with a *Madonna* attributed to the Sienese Renaissance painter Matteo di Giovanni.

A graceful fountain with two columns joined by an architrave in front of the Piccolomini Palace was also designed by Rossellino. The townspeople call it the "dogs' fountain," although a horse would have a better chance of getting at the water in the high stone basin.

The east side of the Piazza Pio II is taken up by the palace of the cathedral chapter, now housing a museum of sacred art, and by the Borgia Palace. The objects in the museum include Etruscan vases and other archaeological finds from the Pienza area, Flemish tapestries, liturgical vestments worn by Pius II, and a splendidly painted and pearl-encrusted cope, made in England in the thirteenth century and presented to Pius II by Thomas Palaeologus, despot (ruler) of Morea in Greece.

The adjoining Borgia Palace was built for Cardinal Rodrigo de Borja, who was to become Pope Alexander VI in 1492. To save money while fulfilling Pius II's desire, the wily Spanish cardinal took over a former Gothic courthouse and had it rebuilt in the new style, with an additional floor put on top. The original pointed arches, walled up and painted over, can still be discerned on the lower two stories. The building served later for centuries as the residence of the bishops of Pienza.

The arcaded city hall with a battlemented clock tower is on the north side of the piazza. Next door is a small brick building that was used by Pius II's nephew and secretary; it now houses an espresso bar and tobacconist on its ground floor. On Corso Rossellino, opposite the Piccolomini Palace, rises the large, unfinished palazzo of Cardinal Ammanati, a favorite of Pius II. Cardinal Gonzaga, who had to borrow money from his father, the duke of Mantua, had a comfortable residence with a walled little garden built for himself near the Borgia Palace.

Today, wash is often seen hanging from Cardinal Gonzaga's former garden wall, and other laundry usually festoons Via del Bacio (Kiss Street) and Via dell'Amore (Love Street) above the town's southern ramparts, which afford a panorama of the Orcia Valley and the hills beyond it that cannot have changed much since Pius II's day. The romantic street names, nevertheless, are modern.

The Romanesque-Gothic Church of San Francesco, adjacent to the north front of the Piccolomini Palace, was already old when the future Pius II was born. It is noteworthy for a painting of the Madonna attributed to Luca Signorelli and for fourteenth-century frescoes de-

161

picting episodes from the life of St. Francis of Assisi. To the left of the medieval church is a Renaissance cloister. A quarter of a mile outside the town walls, to the west, stands a Romanesque church with a round tower; it contains the font where the future head of the church was baptized.

Pienza has every reason to be grateful to its pontifical patron. The harmonious architectural cluster keeps drawing a steady trickle of visitors. The well-being of the town, however, rests on another pillar besides the tourist business—its famed *pecorino*. This sheep cheese, which owes its delicate aroma and flavor to the rich pastureland around Pienza and to expert curing, is appreciated well beyond Tuscany. A cheese fair is held in Pienza in early September every year.

SIENA ▪

A few cities in the world have lent their names to describe colors, but "Siena" alone labels a pigment that is found here, is widely used in art, and at the same time is one of the city's main characteristics. Raw sienna (the usual English spelling), a yellowish brown, is the color of the earth of the three elongated hills on which the Tuscan city is built; burnt sienna, a reddish brown, is the mellow color of its Gothic palaces and towers.

Burnt sienna, tinged with gold at certain times in a sunny day, is the predominant hue of Piazza del Campo, the center of Siena and one of the loveliest public spaces anywhere.

One should visit this city of fewer than 70,000 at least twice: once on July 2 or, even better, August 16, because the Palio horse race is held and all Siena is gripped by a fever of factional tensions; the other time with plenty of leisure to enjoy its buildings and its art, watch everyday life in the sidewalkless narrow streets which slope up and down, stroll along its well-preserved ramparts, sip Chianti wine from the nearby hills, and gaze at the Torre del Mangia. This brick tower crowned by a travertine aerie reaches into the sky like an outstretched arm; it is Siena's incomparable landmark.

The two annual races always attract many thousands of visitors from all over Italy and from abroad, bringing much business to the city, and helping to sell tons of *panforte di Siena*, a cake of flour, dried and candied fruits, and sugar that has long become a standardized industrial product. However, the Palio is not only for tourists; it is also still an intensely parochial affair, unleashing old passions that most of the year lie dormant. The name is derived from the Latin word for "banner" (*pallium*): A standard with a picture of the Virgin Mary is the prize in the contest that has taken place most years since 1659.

Siena returns one of the strongest votes for the Communist Party of any city in Italy in election after election; yet the Madonna trophy is still doggedly fought over in the historic race.

Carabinieri reinforcements move into Siena a week before each Palio, in August even more than in July because the year's second race brings more people and is more hotly contested than the first. Men who look like plotters huddle in the squares and taverns. Dark glances and taunts are bandied. Peasant horses are led down the crooked streets amid approving or disparaging murmurs, and trial runs are staged. Scuffles break out here and there, usually quelled promptly by the Carabinieri.

The Palio is a contest among the seventeen *contrade*, or wards, that have survived of the thirty-nine into which the city's three main districts—corresponding to the hills in the shape of an inverted Y—were once divided. The inhabitants of each *contrada* identify emotionally with their neighborhood, with its claims to special fame (for instance, the beauty of its girls or the ardor of its men) and with its special emblem. The *contrade* are named after a two-headed Eagle, a Wave with a crowned dolphin playing, a Panther, a Giraffe, a Tower, a Duck, and other symbols.

Each ward enters a horse for the Palio, but only ten of them, chosen by lot, may actually run. The horses come from the excellent farmland around Siena and are trained by riders whom the leaders of the *contrade* have chosen. Rumors of trickery and underhanded deals fill the city. The mood is taut, and the Carabinieri are on alert.

The day of the Palio starts with out-of-towners pouring into Siena while each participating *contrada* leads its horse to its own church for a blessing. If one of the animals misbehaves on sacred soil, it's auspicious, and everybody but the priest applauds.

The Palio starts around 6:00 P.M. The track, covered with a layer of sienna earth, is enclosed by wooden barriers that are padded with mattresses at danger points. It follows the contours of Piazza del

Campo, which is shaped like a fan, and has always been the scene of the contest. Race officials, civic authorities, and paying guests sit in grandstands along the buildings surrounding the piazza. Tapestries hang from balconies and windows, all crowded with onlookers. The vast space inside the track is packed with people.

Proceedings begin with a parade of the seventeen *contrade*, each with its emblem (Eagle, Wave, and so on), around the square. The 500 or so marchers in the pageant wear Renaissance costumes and look surprisingly authentic. Flagbearers flourish gaudy banners, throw them into the air, and catch them again. The representatives of the wards are followed by a float drawn by four oxen, displaying the city standard with Siena's white-and-black coat of arms, a large bell, and the prize banner with the Madonna image. Halberd-toting municipal officers escort the float.

There is much nervousness when the actual race is on, and there may be a few false starts. At last the ten unsaddled horses, mercilessly whipped by their riders, gallop three times around the piazza, jostling one another and sometimes crashing into the paddings. Wild shouts rise from the throng. In three minutes it's all over. The winning *contrada* gets the Madonna banner and parades with it to its neighborhood for an evening of feasting and fireworks. The winning horse is a guest of honor at an outdoor banquet. The Carabinieri remain watchful because partisans of rival *contrade*, charging foul play, may turn spoilsports.

Return to Piazza del Campo sometime between fall and spring when fewer tourists are in the city. You may even find a free table outside one of the restaurants facing the city hall. The square marks the spot where spurs of Siena's three hills meet, and it descends slightly toward the center; it is self-contained like an outdoor theater. The square has always been the seat of civil rule in Siena, clearly distinct from church power, which is concentrated in Cathedral Square, to the east.

The Gothic city hall (Palazzo Pubblico) with the slender, soaring Torre del Mangia on its left may be visited. The complex is a lasting monument to the medieval Republic of Siena, which stubbornly defended its independence until Florence, with the help of Spanish soldiers, at last conquered it in 1555. Siena's farmers, craftsmen, and traders continued thriving, and its shrewd bankers lent money to the popes in Rome.

The decorations in the city hall's state rooms include fourteenth-century frescoes by Ambrogio Lorenzetti, allegorically depicting Good and Bad Government, and an often-reproduced fresco showing the Sienese general Guidoriccio da Fogliano riding out from a palisaded castle. The scene with the arrogant horseman, a condottiere from northern Italy, is supposed to have been painted in the fourteenth century by Simone Martini, but the attribution has lately been challenged.

Anyone interested in the arts should stroll the few hundred yards from Piazza del Campo southward to the National Picture Gallery in the battlemented Buonsignori Palace. Its collection of several hundred works embraces the Sienese school of painting from the tender, two-dimensional figures on gold-leaf background by Duccio di Buoninsegna and other Byzantine-inspired primitives of the thirteenth and early fourteenth centuries to its decline in the Baroque age. The gallery contains important works by Il Sodoma (Giovanni Antonio Bazzi), a native of Lombardy who was influenced by Leonardo da Vinci and who worked in Siena at the height of the Renaissance.

Duccio's famed *Maestà*, a painting of the enthroned Virgin Mary with angels and saints, is in the Cathedral Museum. The cathedral, on the highest point in Siena (1,047 feet above sea level), gives an idea of the wealth and the limitless ambitions of the medieval Sienese. Begun in 1229, the present church was at one time in the early fourteenth century intended to become the transept of a much larger edifice that would have been one of the hugest structures in the world as it was then known. The proposed giant building was never finished, but some arches of what was to have been its nave can still be seen.

As eventually completed at the end of the fourteenth century, the cathedral has a façade in white, black, and pink marble, with three gables. The pavement in the interior, with mosaics and graffiti by various Renaissance artists, is without paragon; most of the biblical and mythological representations are covered with wooden flooring except for a few weeks in summer. The church, its library, and its museum dazzle the visitor also with their sculptures by the Pisanos and Donatello, frescoes by Pinturicchio, and many works by other masters.

Descending from the cathedral to the north, strollers will notice signs directing them to the House of St. Catherine. She was the fourteenth-century daughter of a dyer and became a Dominican nun, experienced mystical visions, and eventually contributed to bringing the papacy from Avignon in France back to the Vatican. The Roman Catholic Church has proclaimed St. Catherine of Siena as co–patron saint of Italy, jointly with St. Francis of Assisi. It is typical of Siena that the frescoed Church of St. Catherine, below the medieval mystic's birthplace, is used by the Duck *contrada* for its horse blessing before the Palio.

One would like to stay on and on in Siena to explore its many palaces and churches with their wealth of art, to hear the Italian language spoken with greater purity than almost anywhere in the nation, and to take side trips to the little towns, abbeys, villas, and inns all around. The heart of Italy beats here.

MONTEPULCIANO ▪

This silver-shaped town on a ridge in southern Tuscany is essentially a mile-long street rising in a loop to the cathedral in an airy piazza at its highest point. What a street! It is "one of the liveliest, most colorful, most extraordinary streets in Italy," wrote the late Guido Piovene, a writer from the Venetian mainland. "It seems that in a street like this our people still live happily, in a folklore of baroque flavor."

There is little of the Baroque in Montepulciano's architecture, though; the town is in fact a Renaissance primer. Its lifeline is bordered with edifices that the likes of Sangallo the Elder and Vignola designed. It starts as Via Garibaldi from the fortified gate at the low north end of the town, and changes names as it ascends and winds. The function of the street as the throbbing artery of a well-to-do community of about 15,000 remains the same throughout. The throbbing is all too often done by motor scooters and cars jockeying for a place to park.

The main street has no sidewalks, and just enough space for one-way traffic between parked vehicles on either side. Pedestrians, who abound, have to watch their step. On my last visit I saw a pretty young policewoman with long blond hair trying hard to keep cars moving while bantering with admirers on foot. If you rashly drive into town, you will have to proceed all the way to the main piazza, and return through a maze of congested one-way lanes.

At the beginning of the main street, near the northern gate, rises a Corinthian column carrying an upward-looking stone lion (called the Marzocco), the symbol of Florentine power. Montepulciano pledged loyalty to Florence already in 1202, later passed reluctantly under Siena, and from 1551 until Italy's unification in the nineteenth century was again ruled by Florence. Cosimo I de' Medici, grand duke of Tuscany, formally proclaimed Montepulciano a "noble city."

Proceeding on the main street, the stroller arrives at the receding Church of Sant'Agostino, whose early-Renaissance façade by Michelozzo incorporates Gothic pointed arches as if to show in textbook manner the transition from one major style to the next. The main portal is surmounted by a relief representing the Virgin Mary with John the Baptist and St. Augustine.

Opposite the church is a medieval brick tower, the Torre Manin, with a larger-than-life wooden figure of Pulcinella on top. The black-masked, white-costumed clown is a stock character of the commedia dell'arte. The Pulcinella of the Torre Manin strikes the hours on a bell hanging from a tripod with a cross.

If you ask what the wooden clown in front of the church means, you will be told that the townspeople of Montepulciano have for hundreds of years enjoyed comedy and melodrama, usually performed by amateur actors out of their midst. The local name for the town's brand of outdoor popular theater is *bruscello*, derived from the Tuscan word for the branches of the trees under which the stage was often set. *Bruscello* spectacles featuring legends or episodes from local history are still enacted in the town's main square at the height of summer, but the trees are missing there.

The town's market hall, close to the Church of Sant'Agostino, has the distinction of having been built by Giacomo Barozzi, known as Vignola, who was to succeed Michelangelo as the chief architect of St. Peter's in Rome. A little farther, on the left side of the main street, is a palazzo with a set-back façade by Antonio Sangallo the Elder.

From the main street, all the way up, short side alleys (*vicoli*) branch out eastward toward arches or parapets that afford intriguing glimpses of the countryside deep below the town. Some espresso bars and restaurants and many private homes are privileged with similar glorious views from their back windows.

The last stretch of the main street before turning into a rising curve around a dismantled citadel is called Via del Poliziano. At No. 1 on the left side (now housing an antiques store) is the fourteenth-century brick building in which Politian, the Renaissance poet, was born. His real name was Angelo Ambrogini; his surname, Il Poliziano in Italian, was derived from the Latin name of his native town, Mons Politianus.

He was a sixteen-year-old lad living with his uncle in a poor neighborhood of Florence, translating Homer into Latin, when Lorenzo de' Medici the Magnificent discovered his early brilliance and took him into his household. Politian taught Latin and Greek to Lorenzo's children, one of whom would become a great pope, Leo X. The humanist from Montepulciano also befriended Michelangelo, Botticelli, Pico della Mirandola, and other artists and scholars of Lorenzo's circle, and won lasting fame with his verses.

From Via del Poliziano it is only a short walk to Piazza Grande with the cathedral and town hall, 1,985 feet above the valleys near the town. The cathedral on the south side was designed by Bartolomeo Ammanati in 1570; its broad façade remains unfinished, lacking the customary marble coating and ornamentation. Fine works of art are behind that rough exterior: a triptych from 1401 by Taddeo di Bartolo over the main altar, showing the Death, Assumption, and Coronation of the Virgin on gold ground; a *Madonna of the Pillar* by the Sienese painter Sano di Pietro (1406–1481); a fourteenth-century baptismal font; and a marble altar by Andrea della Robbia (1435–1525).

The town hall, on the west side of the piazza, a fourteenth-century building with battlements and a watchtower, suggests a somewhat shrunken replica of the Palazzo Vecchio in Florence. The magnificent panorama from the top of the tower embraces Siena to the northwest and Lake Trasimeno to the southeast.

Opposite the cathedral is the imposing Palazzo Nobili-Tarugi, a large, arcaded Renaissance building, probably designed by Sangallo the Elder and completed by junior members of his family and disciples. To the left of the palace is an early-sixteenth-century fountain with mild-looking lions holding up the Medici coat of arms with its six spheres, flanked by two griffins, on the architrave joining its two

168

columns. The Palazzo Contucci on the fourth (east) side of the square was built from plans by the older Sangallo.

A masterpiece conceived by Sangallo the Elder, the Church of the Madonna of San Biagio, rises in isolation on the western slope of Montepulciano's hill. The sanctuary can be reached on foot in fifteen minutes from a gate in the west side of the town walls, or by car in five minutes on the highway skirting the ridge of Montepulciano in the east. Cypress trees, bushes, and green meadows surround the church, which despite its much smaller size has some of the grandeur of St. Peter's in Rome. Sangallo's plans called for a structure on a ground plan shaped like a Greek cross; he foresaw a dome and two detached front towers with four tiers of columns in the Doric, Ionic, and Corinthian styles and a composite of all three. The church was built between 1518 and 1545, but the right tower remained uncompleted, never rising above the first, or Doric, section.

A presbytery, full of charm with its two-story loggia, looks at the church from a little distance. The older Sangallo also designed the little stone fountain between the sanctuary and the presbytery.

The vineyards around Montepulciano produce *vino nobile*, "noble wine." These strong, dense, ruby vintages differ markedly in character from the Chianti grown only twenty miles to the northwest; they are heavier and more stolid than the genial Chianti.

CHIUSI ▪

The sign at the steep crossroads reads: "The City of Porsena Welcomes You." The street leading up to the ancient cathedral is called Via Porsena.

Porsena? Even in a country where history is a palpable presence everywhere, the pedigree of Chiusi is remarkable, for this town of 10,000 on the southern fringe of Tuscany was mightier than Rome 2,500 years ago. Its semilegendary Etruscan king, Lars Porsena, conquered the upstart city on the Tiber, and either reinstated King Tarquinius Superbus, an Etruscan whom the rebellious Romans had overthrown, or ruled over them himself for a while before he permitted them self-government as an aristocratic republic.

The name Porsena may really have been an Etruscan title, and much of the story of Lars may be a myth, but scholars agree that Clusium, which was much later to become Chiusi, was already a powerful and civilized community around 500 B.C. A great Etruscan past speaks through the celebrated painted tombs in the town's immediate surroundings and through the treasures of its archaeological museum. Besides, Chiusi is the kind of place where one would like to spend some time.

Uncounted travelers on the route between Rome and Florence have read the signs "CHIUSI–CHIANCIANO TERME" from the window of their railroad coach or their car, and noted the cluster of motels and service stations around the junctions where the tracks and highway to Siena branch off to the west. One wouldn't suspect that only a few miles from this prosaic traffic hub a beauty spot is hidden.

The visitor may even walk from the railroad station to the City of Porsena; it takes about forty minutes. The road leads past the entrance, now closed by an iron gate, to the early Christian catacombs of Santa Catarina, which were used as a burial place from the third to the fifth centuries. Farther up, stairways provide shortcuts. A municipal bus service links the railroad station with the old town in ten minutes.

The historical Chiusi, with steep, narrow streets, is perched on a 900-foot-high hill that the Etruscans, who were accomplished hydraulic engineers, pierced with drainage galleries and reservoir caves in all directions. Much of this maze is still unexplored, although treasure hunters have for centuries been searching for Lars Porsena's tomb. Pliny the Elder, citing the first-century-B.C. writer Varro, mentions that the Etruscan king who played such a decisive part in early Roman history rests in an underground labyrinth below the city of Clusium. The royal sepulcher has never been found.

The old town is an aerie commanding marvelous vistas. From the little Piazza Olivazzo (which, true to its name, is fringed with olive trees) a sweeping view of the wide Chiana River Valley opens. This sluggish stream is something of a geographical curiosity because it was a tributary of the Arno in prehistoric times before changing its course toward the south to feed, as it does now, the Tiber. A malarial swamp in the Middle Ages, the Chiana Valley was later reclaimed by a drainage system and transformed into a gratifyingly fertile area.

The eye rests on an expanse of green fields through which the Rome-Florence railroad line and the Autostrada del Sole (Motorway of the Sun, A-1) cut.

From another belvedere across the small town an unmistakably Tuscan panorama may be enjoyed—soft-contoured with olive groves, small towns, and isolated buildings nestling on the slopes, and more hills, with perhaps a clump of pine trees or even a single pine on top, all the way to the horizon.

Chiusi's architectural sights are identified by handwritten Italian signs on large boards that, not quite successfully, imitate unrolled parchments. The town's cathedral, dedicated to the martyr St. Secundianus, is an austere twelfth-century reconstruction of an early Christian basilica that rose on the spot. The portico has severe Doric columns. The Romanesque church contains fragments from the older building and the tomb of St. Mustiola, a young woman relative of Emperior Claudius II who was martyred in Clusium in 273. The cathedral museum is noteworthy for its illuminated manuscripts and books.

A massive square tower of gray stone blocks rises in front of the church. The archaeological museum across the piazza is still an important collection of Etruscan antiquities although more than 100 precious exhibits were stolen one night in 1971 and have never been recovered. What the thieves left behind is still impressive: bronzes, statuettes, sarcophagi, and terra-cotta vases, some with polychrome designs.

Chiusi's main attraction for lovers of Etruscan lore is the string of tombs on nearby hills. To visit them it is necessary to contact the guardian of the archaeological museum.

The most interesting of the burial sites is the so-called Tomb of the Monkey north of the town on the two-mile road to Lake Chiusi. Faded frescoes in the burial chambers from the fifth century B.C. show a monkey tied to a tree; a deceased woman under a parasol, watching funeral games enacted in her honor; clowns, flute players, dancers, athletes, and warriors; and chariot races. The underground site, hewn out of tufa rock, was discovered in 1846. Small Lake Chiusi, once considered unhealthy in summer, is now a popular spot for outings, picnics, and water sports.

Chianciano Terme is a spa 7.5 miles northwest of Chiusi, linked with the Chiusi railroad station by frequent bus runs. Its sulphur springs were already renowned in antiquity. King Porsena is said to have delighted in them, according to a Latin tablet that was put up in the Renaissance. Latin writers and poets like Varro, Horace, and Tibullus praised its healing waters.

Today many Italians still swear by the curative powers of the springs for all sorts of ills, and fill Chianciano's many hotels from April to October every year. The fortunate slogan that contributed to the enduring success of the place is *"Chianciano—fegato sano"* ("Chianciano—healthy liver").

AREZZO ▪

Some visitors get out of the train or leave their car at a parking lot, make a beeline for the Church of San Francesco to look at the world-famous frescoes by Piero della Francesca, and leave the city right afterward. Others come for the glorified flea market, grandiloquently called the Antiques Fair, held on the first weekend of every month, and perhaps pick up a couple of old candlesticks or a vintage telephone. Many more people arrive during the week for business at one of the modern workshops and factories that have sprung up around the old town during the last few decades to turn out shoes and apparel, building materials, and appliances.

Arezzo has become a thriving center of more than 90,000 people, with plenty of small and medium-sized industries, at the edge of a fertile plain. Yet the city's walled core, rising in tiers on a slope, has to a great extent kept its Renaissance character with the severe lines of its reddish-brown and gray buildings on narrow streets and dramatic piazzas.

There is a lot to see besides the Piero della Francesca murals: Etruscan bronzes, a Roman amphitheater, medieval walls, a Medici fortress with a view of the hills of Tuscany and the Arno Valley, and splendid churches, loggias, and palaces.

Arezzo is easy to reach because it lies on Italy's main north-south axis, the Florence-Rome railroad line and the Autostrada del Sole (Motorway of the Sun). A trip from Rome takes a couple of hours, from Florence about one hour.

The Aretines, as the city's inhabitants are called, have a reputation for cleverness, and they live well. Their restaurants excel in pasta dishes, like cannelloni with spinach-and-ricotta filling, tender steaks, and venison during the hunting season. It's advisable to try the dry red local wine.

The city's greatest treasure is the choir of the Church of San Francesco with the frescoes that Piero della Francesca painted between 1452 and 1466. The visitor who has seen reproductions may be shocked at first because the lighting is unfavorable most of the day and some of the murals are vastly damaged. Inserting coins into the slot of an apparatus on the wall will floodlight the paintings for a few minutes. The best time to view the frescoes is around noon and during summer evenings when there is enough light to reveal Piero's refined palette of pale blues, browns, and grays and his subtle contrasts of bright and dark. The noble realism and the plasticity of the paintings are striking even in their deteriorated state; experts debate constantly about what might be done to save what still can be saved.

Piero della Francesca's theme for decorating the friars' choir was the Legend of the True Cross by the Blessed Jacobus de Voragine, a medieval Italian churchman who wrote about biblical subjects and saints. Among the episodes illustrated by the frescoes are the death of Adam, the meeting of Solomon and the Queen of Sheba, the Annunciation, and the victory of Emperor Constantine under the sign of the Cross.

Other sights in Arezzo's higher parts are the 600-year-old Gothic cathedral and the even older Church of Santa Maria della Pieve. A Petrarch House near the medieval city hall stands on the site of an older building in which Francesco Petrarca (Petrarch), the poet and humanist, was born in 1304. Arezzo had then already been under the domination of Florence for twenty years. Another famous native son, Giorgio Vasari, the painter, architect, and author of *The Lives of the Most Eminent Painters, Sculptors, and Architects of Italy*, has his own museum in his graceful house at 55 Via Venti Settembre. It contains frescoes by Vasari and his archives, including letters from Michelangelo. On the same street, No. 19, is the house where Pietro Aretino, the adventurer, pamphleteer, and muckraking "Scourge of Princes," was born in 1492.

An archaeological museum near the ruined Roman amphitheater has a collection of coralline or Aretine ware, red clay pottery that was manufactured in Arezzo in the first century B.C. Medieval, Renaissance, and modern sculptures and ceramics as well as paintings by minor but interesting fifteenth-century artists may be found in another museum in the sixteenth-century Palazzo Bruni-Ciocchi, in the northwestern corner of the old city.

The Arezzo Antiques Fair has been a monthly event since 1969. Its setting, Piazza Grande, or Piazza Vasari, is an irregular sloping square behind the Church of Santa Maria della Pieve, with its airy "Campanile of the Hundred Holes," or windows, and its late-Romanesque façade with three tiers of columns. The piazza is lined with medieval houses with crenellated walls and, on the north side, a loggia that Vasari designed. During the fair, which spills into nearby streets, the vendors offer Roman coins and terra-cotta vases that have been taken from some Etruscan tomb or manufactured in one of the flourishing fakers' workshops, alabaster statuettes, Art Nouveau bronzes, and much bric-à-brac. Many of the objects on display will have already been exhibited in the flea markets of Rome, Gubbio, and Lucca. There is a regular Italian antiques circuit, with unsold merchandise being trucked from one market to the next.

However, the Arezzo fair does occasionally yield the odd little treasure—not necessarily the mythical Giorgione hidden under a darkened eighteenth-century portrait, but perhaps a shard of genuine Etruscan pottery or a 150-year-old chest of drawers that enchants the connoisseur. Competently restored old furniture and various objets d'art may be bought also between fairs at the antiques shops in and near Piazza Grande, but the prices are hardly lower than those in similar stores in Rome, Florence, or Milan.

Much older than the Arezzo Antiques Fair is a pageant enacted, also in the Piazza Grande, in the afternoon of the first Sunday in September. The event, known as the Joust of the Saracen, consists of a parade in thirteenth-century costumes and a charge by mounted lancers at the figure of a Moslem infidel. Superior horsemanship, still highly valued in Tuscany, is expected from the participants in the joust, a reminder of the Crusades and of the tournaments in the Age of Chivalry.

SANSEPOLCRO ▪

Because this little town near the border between Tuscany and Umbria is the birthplace of Piero della Francesca and guards one of his most powerful frescoes, it attracts a trickle of art lovers all year round. But even without the glory derived from the fifteenth-century painter who introduced innovations in perspective and the treatment of light, and who speaks so strongly to modern viewers, Sansepolcro would be a spot where one would like to stay for some time, or even to make one's home.

The valley of the young Tiber—the river rises twenty-five miles to the north—is already broad here. The town of 16,000 inhabitants snuggles on a slope overlooking the Tiber and green fields with rows of olive trees. New small industrial plants turning out food products, ceramics, building materials, and machinery have lately joined the big old Buitoni pasta factory, filling much space between farmhouses in the valley. Agriculture seems nevertheless to be making a comeback, with an accent on intensive techniques and high quality.

The core of Sansepolcro is a densely built-up rectangle with many ancient churches and palaces, enclosed by sixteenth-century walls that are still intact in long stretches. The newcomer is likely first to seek out the Civic Museum, one of Tuscany's most important art collections outside Florence, in a narrow street in the upper section of Sansepolcro. The museum is housed in the old town hall and is at most times mercifully uncrowded, permitting one to view its riches at leisure.

Room VIII is entirely devoted to Piero, with the *Resurrection* as its most precious treasure. The 6.5-by-7-foot fresco, in a marble frame, was painted in another hall of the same building around 1463 when Piero was at the height of his powers; it was transferred to the present site during the master's lifetime.

Whether or not you agree with the English writer Aldous Huxley that this is "the greatest picture in the world," you will be struck by the haunting quality of the work, showing Jesus rising from a sarcophagus, holding a banner in His right hand and gazing straight ahead like a visionary while four Roman soldiers at His feet sleep

175

in various poses of abandon. The background of hills and trees is an Umbrian landscape in the pale light of dawn.

The same room also contains a polyptych, *The Madonna della Misericordia*, an early work (started in 1445) in fifteen panels, representing the Virgin Mary sheltering the Christian faithful under her cloak, with four saints on her sides, surmounted by a Crucifixion, all on gold ground. On a side wall is a fragment of a fresco by Piero della Francesca discovered in the former Church of Santa Chiara in Sansepolcro in 1954; the rest of the work, which according to experts was painted around 1455, seems to have been lost forever. What has been recovered is the head of a young saint (maybe St. Julian) with a startled or angry expression. Another fragment of a fresco, representing St. Ludovic, in the Piero hall of the museum may actually have been executed by a disciple.

Also to be seen in the high-vaulted rooms of the Civic Museum are a *Crucifixion* by Luca Signorelli (1441–1523), works by local painters of the sixteenth and seventeenth centuries, terra-cottas, church vestments, reliquaries, and archaeological material.

On the same street as the Civic Museum is the house of Piero della Francesca, a fifteenth-century building probably designed by the master himself. The façade carries a large memorial plaque. A monument to Piero rises in the municipal park opposite.

The arcaded Palazzo delle Laudi, an imposing Renaissance structure close to the Civic Museum and the Piero della Francesca house, is now Sansepolcro's town hall. Next to it stands the cathedral, dating from the eleventh century.

The church's bright limestone façade, facing a narrow street (Via Giacomo Matteotti), is from the fourteenth century; its round arches and rose window show the transition from the late-Romanesque to the Gothic style. Inside, note in the choir a Resurrection polyptych by a fourteenth-century painter of the Sienese school, maybe Pietro Lorenzetti, that surely influenced the young Piero della Francesca.

The cathedral probably occupies the site of a medieval abbey that was said to treasure relics from the Holy Sepulcher in Jerusalem. According to legend, the venerated objects were brought from the Holy Land by two pilgrims, a Greek and a Spaniard, who built a chapel to hold them. The abbey and settlement that in the tenth century grew around the reliquary became known as Borgo di San Sepolcro (Town of the Holy Sepulcher).

A few steps south of the cathedral is Piazza Torre di Berta, which the local people call Piazza Quadrata (Square Piazza), the geometrical and social center of Sansepolcro. Groups of chatting men, some of them farmers who have come to town, stand in the square late in the morning and again toward evening. The Berta Tower, a medieval structure after which the square is named, rose in the middle of the square until retreating German troops blew it up in 1944; it has not been rebuilt. Another old tower, incorporated in a thirteenth-century building on the west side of the piazza, has survived. Opposite is an ornate sixteenth-century edifice with the Medici coat of arms, six red balls on a field of gold.

Via Venti Settembre, which bisects Sansepolcro from the Florentine Gate in the west to the Roman Gate in the east, skirting the north side of the central piazza, sees the traditional late-afternoon promenade of the townspeople; who walks with whom and who stops to talk to whom will provide tidbits for dinner-table conversations.

Admirers of Piero della Francesca should not miss the side trip to Monterchi, the birthplace of his mother, 12.5 miles south of Sansepolcro. The chapel of the village cemetery contains Piero's famous *Madonna del Parto*. The fresco represents the pregnant Virgin between two angels who draw aside the flaps of an Oriental tent; her long blue dress is open down the front, and she points at her bulging body with a delicate gesture of her right hand. Expectant women have for centuries come to pray in the chapel.

This is a breeding ground of genius: the birthplace of Michelangelo Buonarroti is only nineteen miles northwest of Sansepolcro; in a town whose official place name is now Caprese Michelangelo. The modest building in which one of the greatest artists came into the world on March 6, 1475, has become a museum with reproductions and photos of his works, period furniture in the room where according to tradition he was born, and a library. A Michelangelo monument, erected in 1911, is nearby. The austere little thirteenth-century church where Michelangelo was baptized is at the entrance to the restored castle of Caprese with an outdoor museum of sculptures by modern artists that was inaugurated in 1969.

*RIGHT: Volterra,
Palazzo dei Priori
(Town Hall)*

*BELOW: Portoferraio harbor,
Isle of Elba*

*OPPOSITE, TOP: Siena,
cathedral*

*OPPOSITE, BOTTOM:
Siena, flagbearers
at the Palio*

San Gimignano

Fortress at Chiusi

Montepulciano, cathedral and Town Hall

OPPOSITE: Arezzo, the Antiques Fair in Vasari's loggia

RIGHT: Sansepolcro, monument to Piero della Francesca

BELOW: Cortona, Etruscan ruins

CORTONA ▪

From the train, at a distance, it looks like the loveliest hilltown the traveler has seen, but Cortona, on a slope near the border between Umbria and Tuscany, has no railroad station of its own. Motorists who want to visit it must get off the Autostrada del Sole (Motorway of the Sun, A-1) and drive for half an hour or more on winding provincial roads.

One of Italy's oldest towns, Cortona is also one of its quietest. For painters, writers, or composers and for anyone who wants to rest among friendly people in a supremely civilized landscape, this is the ideal hideaway. Quite a few expatriates have bought properties in the area lately. From spring to autumn there is a trickle of tourists, including Britons, Germans, and Scandinavians, and a number of American students on summer programs.

Every August 14 and 15, Italian visitors crowd the town during its steak festival, when choice cuts are broiled and roasted in a giant barbecue. The meat of the steers bred in the wide Val di Chiana, which Cortona overlooks, is renowned all over the country. An antique-furniture fair is held in September, rivaling the monthly antiques fair in nearby Arezzo. Most of the year, however, and especially in winter, nothing much happens.

The prevailing character of Cortona is medieval, but traces of a much more remote past are all around. According to archaeologists, the town was founded by the Umbrians, a pre-Roman people, and conquered by the Etruscans in the seventh or sixth century B.C. As Corito, it became one of the twelve confederate cities of the Etruscan League, and like the other eleven was eventually subdued by the Romans. After a checkered history during the Middle Ages, Cortona lived under Florentine rule from 1411 to Italy's unification in the nineteenth century. Today the about 20,000 inhabitants of Cortona still talk a lot about cattle, olive oil, wine, and field crops, although many younger people commute to factory jobs in the plains. Scholars from abroad are a familiar sight in the town.

Etruscan antiquities abound. The medieval and Renaissance town walls, one and a quarter miles in circumference, follow closely the outline of the 2,500-year-old Etruscan fortifications. Stretches of

Etruscan walls, huge sandstone blocks piled on one another to a height of twelve feet and more, can be seen on the upper outskirts; traffic still moves through gates that Etruscan guards once manned.

Etruscan tombs, statues, bronzes, and diverse artifacts have been systematically dug up in and near Cortona since the eighteenth century. In 1726 a group of Italian enthusiasts founded an Etruscan Academy in Cortona. Enlightened Europe became interested; Montesquieu, Voltaire, Winckelmann, and other erudite foreigners joined as members. The institution held contests to encourage poetry in praise of the Etruscans, organized scholarly meetings, published learned papers, and opened a museum.

Reorganized after World War II after a long period of inactivity, the Etruscan Academy occupies a dozen halls of the Palazzo Casali behind Cortona's town hall. The stone-and-brickwork building from the fourteenth century, with a Renaissance façade, was the seat of the Casali family, lords of Cortona for more than a century until 1409. The palace courtyard, with two external stairways and a top-floor loggia, is a paragon of architectural elegance.

The showpiece of the Etruscan collection in the Palazzo Casali is a circular bronze chandelier weighing 125 pounds, found near Cortona in 1840. The lamp, from the fifth century B.C., has a central oil container with sixteen burners around it; they are decorated with the relief figures of eight satyrs in lustful poses and eight nymphs. Egyptian, Roman, and Renaissance objects are also on display in the museum.

The main façade of the thirteenth-century town hall, with a squat, crenellated bell tower, a broad outdoor flight of stairs, and a narrow balcony that was added only 100 years ago, is on Piazza della Repubblica (Republic Square), the heart of Cortona. A small rectangular square with an open loggia overlooking the piazza diagonally from the town hall is the Pescheria (Fish Market), where catches from the nearby Lake Trasimeno used to be sold.

Walk from the rear of the town hall, through Via Casali, to reach Cortona's cathedral. Displaying Gothic, Renaissance, and Baroque elements, it is noteworthy above all on account of frescoes in the choir and sacristy by Luca Signorelli (1441–1523). A native of Cortona, he was a disciple of Piero della Francesca and was to win fame for his decorations in the cathedral of Orvieto. A *Deposition*, a *Communion of the Apostles*, and other works by Signorelli and his assistants are to be seen in the diocesan museum in the former Church and Baptistery of Jesus, a Renaissance building opposite the cathedral. The museum treasures also an *Annunciation* painted by Fra Angelico da Fiesole around 1434, and a *Virgin with the Child* on gold ground attributed to the Sienese master Duccio di Buoninsegna (early fourteenth century).

The Via Nazionale and Via Roma, running almost straight in opposite directions from the town hall, are about the only two level streets in Cortona, dividing the town into two unequal parts. The upper half tends to be steeper than the lower town. Stairways and sloping passages lead into neighborhoods where the upper floors of some archaic houses overhang the narrow streets and are propped up by wooden supports. Archways frame unexpected views of the countryside below as if the town were floating in the air.

From the highest point of the spur on which Cortona sits, at 2,133 feet, the ruined Medici fortress—a symbol of Florentine domination—looks out on the towers, roofs, and walls of the town, on the Val di Chiana, and on Lake Trasimeno to the southeast.

A large revival Romanesque church below the fortress was built in the nineteenth century. It adjoins an old Franciscan convent and contains the tomb of St. Margaret of Cortona (1247–1297), the town's own saint.

4

THE HINTERLANDS OF ROME

Umbria, Latium, the Marches, and Abruzzo

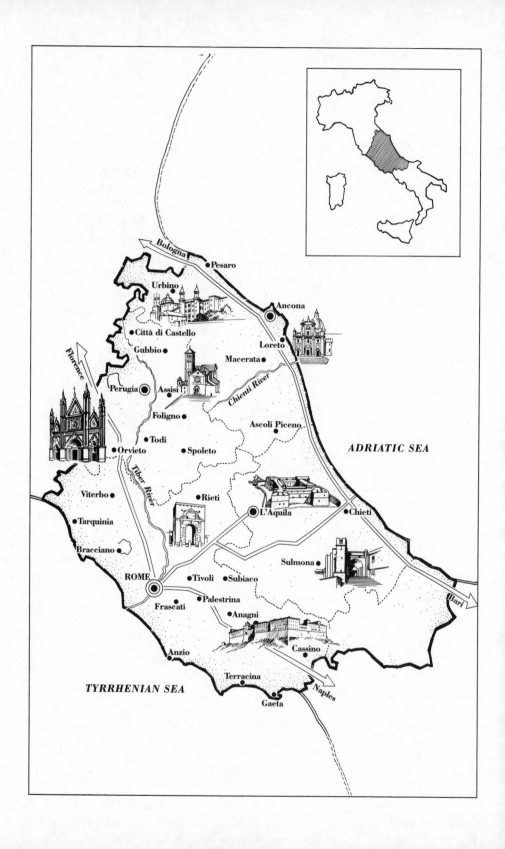

Bologna

Pesaro

Urbino

Ancona

Città di Castello

Loreto

Gubbio

Macerata

Florence

Perugia

Assisi

Chienti River

Foligno

Ascoli Piceno

Todi

ADRIATIC SEA

Orvieto

Spoleto

Tiber River

Viterbo

Rieti

L'Aquila

Chieti

Tarquinia

Sulmona

Bracciano

Bari

ROME

Tivoli

Subiaco

Frascati

Palestrina

Anagni

Anzio

Cassino

Terracina

Naples

TYRRHENIAN SEA

Gaeta

Traveling south from Tuscany you notice a change in the scenery after passing Chiusi or Siena. The countryside becomes solitary and looks unkempt in comparison with the tidy fields and vineyards you have just traversed. Distances between towns lengthen, and some villages with their old gray houses huddling on hills seem downright forbidding. Sheep graze in pastures that border on sandy or loamy patches. As you enter Latium, the province of Rome, the panorama may assume a certain sullenness.

However, turning eastward by leaving the main north-south route—the Autostrada del Sole or Motorway of the Sun (A-1)—at Chiusi, or by changing trains at Terontola-Cortona, you are rewarded by the soothing charm of green Umbria; it will be deepened by the mystical atmosphere of Assisi, the town of St. Francis. From there, Rome can be reached by way of Foligno and Spoleto.

Whatever approach to the capital travelers choose, they will cross the Campagna Romana, a belt of flatlands surrounding the metropolis from which the dome of St. Peter's can be glimpsed from afar when the weather is right. Until quite recently the Campagna was an unhealthy place to live because of the age-old scourge of malaria, finally vanquished thanks to vast drainage projects and efficient pest control. In some stretches, nevertheless, the plains around Rome retain their old mood of loneliness, with scattered Etruscan tombs, ruined Roman aqueducts, medieval strongholds, and vistas of distant hills that enchanted Goethe and Romantic artists.

On the horizon to the east rise peaks and ridges guarding the access to the Abruzzo, a region of high mountains that may remain snowcapped when the bathing beaches near Rome are crowded. Farther to the east, the fertile region of the Marches and the "Abruzzo Riviera" border the Adriatic Sea. An older name for the area is "the Abruzzi" or just "Abruzzi," but these terms now have archaic and even faintly derogatory overtones; the authorities and many local people prefer "Abruzzo."

The Tiber, winding down from the Tuscan Apennines across Umbria and Latium to the Tyrrhenian Sea, is Italy's second-largest river. One of history's most illustrious waterways, it usually looks quite peaceful and, in its lower reaches, lazy. Alas, it is thoroughly polluted. After rainstorms in central Italy, the Tiber may flood vast areas in Umbria and Latium and roar under the bridges of Rome, carrying shrubbery, entire trees, debris, and a few drowned sheep with it.

The City of the Seven Hills on either bank of the river, fifteen miles from its mouth, has for more than 2,000 years drawn food, energies, talent, and other resources from the land surrounding it—first as the center of the Roman Republic and the Roman Empire, then as the seat of the papacy, and eventually as the capital of modern Italy. With its universal outlook and interests, the metropolis on the Tiber overwhelmed, and neglected, its hinterlands for many centuries.

In the Middle Ages and long afterward, robbers used to waylay foreign pilgrims journeying to Rome; and in the wild Abruzzo gorges, banditry was still common into the late nineteenth century.

The roads that the Roman consuls—the chief magistrates of the ancient republic—had built converge on the capital, forming a web of communications that is still in use; the national highways in the area follow the general route of the ancient consular roads, and so do the main railway lines.

Roman emperors and senators first and pontiffs later, as well as their chief aides, favorites, and hangers-on, maintained estates, sumptuous villas, castles, and palaces throughout central Italy, and would spend long periods in bucolic spots not too distant from the crowded, and at times dangerous, capital.

After the fall of the Roman Empire much of central Italy came under the domination of the papacy. The pontiffs acted as temporal rulers of territories that stretched from Bologna to the Adriatic Sea and to the frontiers of the Kingdom of Naples. These States of the Church survived until their last remnant, the city of Rome, was incorporated into the unified Italian state in 1870.

A sojourn in Italy's capital today offers an opportunity for worthwhile side trips to fascinating cities and towns, most of them just a couple of hours or so from Rome. As one would expect, historical reminders abound in these places. There are plenty of vestiges also from pre-Roman civilizations, such as those of the Umbrians and the Etruscans.

The dialects spoken in Latium and the adjacent regions are earthier than the language one hears in Tuscany; people throughout central Italy tend to be informal, frank, and hospitable.

Expect to find hearty and substantial, rather than refined, food in the cities and towns mentioned in this section: stomach-filling no-nonsense pasta and tender lamb everywhere, pork and suckling pig in Abruzzo, delicate artichokes all over Latium, and fresh seafood in the Adriatic provinces. Desserts come rich with walnuts and almonds.

Frascati, which is white, and the other vintages from the hills south of Rome are usually lighter than the robust wines of the interior; the pale Verdicchio of the Marches is the perfect companion for fish. Serious native eaters will usually order an after-dinner *amaro* or *digestivo*, one of the bitter or syrupy local liquors that are supposed to help in the assimilation of a good meal; in some restaurants it's on the house.

The visitor to Rome who rents a car may tour Frascati and the other Castelli Romani—the wine-producing towns around extinct volcanoes—in one exhilarating day, or combine a trip to one of them with a foray to Palestrina, Anagni, or Tivoli, or, farther inland, to Subiaco.

To do justice to Umbria, at least two days should be set aside. Foligno with the picturesque hilltowns nearby, Spoleto, Assisi, Perugia, and Gubbio, are links of a splendid circuit that can be completed by way of Città di Castello, Orvieto, and Todi. A visit to Orvieto, where one might want to stay at length, can also be combined with a tour of other "Etruscan Places" (to borrow a phrase from D. H. Lawrence), namely Bracciano, Viterbo, Tarquinia, and Porto Santo Stefano. Administratively a part of the Region of Tuscany, Porto Santo Stefano looks to Rome rather than to Florence.

Another suggestion for a one-day excursion from Rome includes the mountain towns of the interior—Rieti, L'Aquila, and Sulmona. A side trip to Chieti, on a hill near the Adriatic coast, is advisable. If at all possible, don't miss Urbino. Ancona, the administrative capital of the Marches, as well as Pesaro to the north and Loreto,

Macerata, and Ascoli Piceno to the south, may be visited from there.

A day at the seaside south of Rome can be used also for visits to Anzio and Terracina (but keep away from either place on weekends).

FRASCATI ▪

When the Roman sun is especially fierce some summer afternoon, it is no small pleasure to laze in a terraced piazza a thousand feet above the sweltering Eternal City, enjoying the breeze from the sea and a glorious view, and eating *gelato* or sipping chilled white wine from grapes grown on the nearby volcanic slopes. Frascati, only fifteen miles from the center of the metropolis, has offered repose to un- counted generations of Romans. Today it represents the easiest ex- cursion from the Italian capital, a side trip that may not take more than three hours while fitting into the tightest sightseeing schedule. Yet Frascati, with 25,000 inhabitants, is no mere suburb; it is a real town. It gives hurried travelers an excellent idea of how the people in the smaller places of central Italy live.

The name evokes in many Italians and knowledgeable foreigners the medium-dry taste and robust bouquet of a white wine that Romans insist on calling "blond," although it now often comes pale to col- orless. Not every liquid labeled "Frascati" or poured out as such from an open straw flask is trustworthy. Refuse the sulphurous brew that quite a few Roman *trattorie* try to palm off as Frascati: A headache is sure to come with it. The chances for getting the real thing are better, though not approaching certainty, on and around that piazza above the vineyards.

Frascati is the most popular of the Castelli Romani, the wine- producing towns nestling on and below the ridges of the Alban Hills southeast of Rome. Rising to a 3,113-foot peak, Mount Cavo, the hills and their two circular lakes—Lake Albano and Lake Nemi— are the remnants of a system of volcanoes that were already extinct at the dawn of history. Vines were planted early in the lava soils, yielding plentiful, tasty, and cheap vintages year after year. Even Roman slaves got Alban wines with their daily food rations.

The main center in the Alban Hills was then Tusculum, on a slope some 1,000 feet above the site of present-day Frascati. After serving as a staunch ally of Rome in the early struggles for hegemony in central Italy, Tusculum was a smart resort in classical times. Cicero, Lucullus, Maecenas, and other rich and prominent Romans owned villas there. From the tenth to the twelfth centuries the bellicose counts of Tusculum tyrannized Rome from their hilltop castle and imposed their popes on the Church. Then the tide turned, and the Romans destroyed the castle and all of Tusculum. Nothing has remained of the proud ancient town but a Roman amphitheater that could hold 3,000 spectators, and a few other ruins. They can be reached over footpaths from Frascati, Tusculum's heir.

The slopes overlooking Rome with the cupola of St. Peter's and the sea on the horizon in the west became fashionable again in the late Renaissance. Wealthy families of Rome's papal nobility built villas in the neighborhood of the town that had sprung up on a brow of the hill of Tusculum after the latter's disastrous end. The name Frascati is derived from the Italian word for brushwood huts, an echo of the town's humble beginnings.

The most grandiose of the aristocratic mansions is the Villa Aldobrandini, which dominates Frascati's main square. Giacomo della Porta, the architect who completed the dome of St. Peter's after Michelangelo, designed the imposing hillside palace for Pietro Cardinal Aldobrandini, a nephew of Pope Clement VIII, around 1600. The park, rising on terraces on the steep slope on which the palace was built, is an outstanding example of the elaborate pleasure gardens that were laid out in and around Rome in the Baroque era. Stout oak trees and natural rocks are incorporated into a pattern of artificial grottoes and ruins, fountains and ponds, galleries and statues. A large section of the Villa Aldobrandini is now a public park; the entrance is from the mall on the right side of Frascati's main piazza.

The tourist office at the lower left side of the piazza will supply information on how to visit the other villas around Frascati and the remaining places of interest in the Alban Hills—the neighboring towns of Grottaferrata and Marino, ancient Albano, Castel Gandolfo with the pope's summer palace, Rocca di Papa on the rim of an extinct volcano, Mount Cavo above it, Ariccia, Genzano, Nemi, and Velletri. Each of the hilltowns has a distinctive flavor, although with their unregulated building activities some have grown into one another. Nemi is famous for its strawberries in season and its lake views, Genzano for its flower festival in the week of the feast of Corpus

195

Christi. The yearly event, in which religious devotion and folklore blend, was held even during the first several years after World War II, when the Communist Party wielded such power in the town that Genzano was then known as "Little Stalingrad."

It helps to have a car for visiting the Castelli Romani, but the main spots can be reached also by public transport. Buses for Marino, Albano, and other towns leave from Frascati's main piazza.

In Frascati itself most buildings in the narrow streets and small squares are new. The town, seat of the Nazi military high command in Italy in 1943, was a prime target of Allied air raids, and four-fifths of Frascati was bombed into rubble. The sumptuous villas around it were also heavily damaged. After the war Frascati was speedily rebuilt, and the aristocratic mansions were repaired.

Strolling to the left from the main piazza, the visitor sees after a few steps the exuberant Baroque façade of the cathedral, in shades of gray and light brown. Inside, on the left, is a plaque commemorating Charles Edward Stuart, the "Young Pretender," who after fighting unsuccessfully for the English throne lived in Rome and died in Frascati in 1788. Yellow street signs point the way toward a Jesuit church whose interior is curious because of a painted trompe-l'oeil cupola in the taste of the seventeenth century. Farther on stands the fifteenth-century Bishop's Palace, which looks like a fortress. Nearby is a small and airy Romanesque bell tower, the Campanile di San Rocco, which leans slightly.

Near a cliff that marks the eastern rim of Frascati a market is held every weekday in a hall and the piazza outside. Romans who happen to visit won't miss the chance of buying a loaf of country bread, for which the town is renowned, and some bottles or flasks of its wine.

Frascati and the other towns in the Alban Hills were well-liked summer resorts from the turn of the century until World War II. Now the Roman middle-class families who used to spend the hot months in the Castelli Romani fancy seaside vacations. Frascati today has few hotels, and they are modest.

Nevertheless, many Romans still like to come out to the town for a meal in one of its dozen or so restaurants. Several varieties of pasta are served, usually followed by lamb or pork. Suckling pig is a local specialty. After a heavy lunch with plenty of Frascati wine, patrons may, true to a time-honored Castelli Romani custom, ask the host whether there is some quiet room for a siesta, alone or in company. Such hospitality is often granted; it is one of the attractions that the hilltowns hold for practitioners of *la dolce vita*.

PALESTRINA ∎

One of the rare examples of war contributing to a better understanding of the past occurred in this town, which is several centuries older than Rome. Repeated heavy Allied air attacks in 1944, which reduced much of Palestrina to rubble, bared the imposing ruins of what scholars think was the largest sanctuary of ancient Italy. The huge temple complex was dedicated to Fortuna Primigenia, the goddess of Fate, represented as mother and nurse of all other divinities, and it was the seat of a widely renowned oracle whom Roman emperors, foreign potentates, and other illustrious personages would consult.

The rebuilt town, most picturesquely rising on a spur of the Apennine foothills twenty-four miles east of Rome, today has a population of about 12,000. It is a place for visitors who like fresh air and quiet and don't mind stairways. One street, all steps, in the multiterraced town is called Via Thomas Mann in honor of the German writer who together with Heinrich, his brother, spent part of the summer of 1897 here.

At an altitude of more than 1,600 feet there are fine views from the higher neighborhoods of Palestrina. The cathedral dedicated to St. Agapitus (a local teenage martyr of the third century) has a Romanesque bell tower, and is flanked by a modern statue of Giovanni Pierluigi da Palestrina. The sixteenth-century composer and conductor of Vatican choirs, a native of the town who pioneered polyphonic harmony in church, is praised as "Prince of Music" in an inscription on his monument.

Town life, such as it is, doesn't center on the cathedral square (Piazza Regina Margherita) but on the nearby Piazza della Liberazione. There are a couple of modest hotels and a few equally plain restaurants in Palestrina, nothing fancy. Only an hour by bus from the Italian capital, a rather tedious drive through Rome's seedy eastern outskirts, the place is strikingly provincial. Most people in the town seem to know one another, and they will start to nod at any foreigner who stays longer than a day.

Palestrina's historic grandeur is proved by its ruins and its National Archaeological Museum in the restored baronial palace of the Barberini family, situated at the highest point in town. Nearby, to the right, are the remains of prehistoric walls, large irregular stones put together without mortar, in the "cyclopean" manner. A fortified settlement existed at the site already in the seventh century B.C. Rounded little toilet boxes in beaten bronze (*cistae*) and other artifacts of an early, pre-Roman civilization were found in the tombs of a burial ground at the foot of the present town and are on display in the museum.

Praeneste, the ancient name of what is now Palestrina, fought long and hard against rising Rome, and later took sides in the Roman civil wars. Sulla, the dictator, razed the city to the ground in 82 B.C. because it had supported his adversary, Marius. Soon, however, Praeneste was restored, and the Temple of Fortuna, which Sulla had spared, was enlarged.

In the imperial era the shrine of Fortuna covered the entire area now occupied by Palestrina. Supported by enormous foundation walls, which can in part still be seen, the various sacred buildings were surrounded by stairways, porches, courtyards, arches, columns, and fountains. Scholars have worked up a scale-model reconstruction of the immense sanctuary, on view in the museum. Step out of the Barberini Palace, which incorporates remains of an ancient portico and staircase, and look down from a terrace on four lower levels of temple ruins.

In the courtyard of the former seminary adjoining the cathedral, a rounded chamber hewn out of living rock may have been the hall where the priests of the oracle examined petitions and gave their responses. A grotto with three niches, also in the seminary courtyard, is described as the "Cave of the Lots," the place where the—usually ambiguous—pronouncements of the oracle, written on small tablets, were to be picked up.

Praeneste was not only a famous cult center, but also a fashionable resort. Horace wrote of its bracing air; Augustus and later Hadrian had imperial villas here; wealthy and smart Romans came to rub elbows with the mighty.

The prize exhibit of the museum, in a top-floor hall all by itself, is a stunning mosaic that was found on the floor of one of the temple structures. The colors are so brilliant, the design is so vivid and realistic that the visitor at first thinks he is seeing a modern work. The large tableau, possibly from the first century B.C., is believed to be a copy of an earlier Greek original. It shows an Egyptian landscape with the flooded Nile, oarsmen in papyrus and basket boats, revelers and Roman legionnaires on the shores, archers, and many animals—ducks, ibises, snakes, rhinos, and crocodiles, some labeled with Greek lettering.

When Christianity triumphed in the Roman Empire, the Temple of Fortuna decayed and the local people made themselves at home in its ruins. Over the centuries Praeneste and later Palestrina were repeatedly destroyed and rebuilt. Three battlemented doorways which guarded the approaches to the medieval town are still in existence.

A road starting at the left side of the museum near the Baroque Church of Santa Rosalia winds up to the village of San Pietro Romano near the 2,467-foot top of Mount Ginestro, the hill on whose slope Palestrina is built. Ruins of a medieval castle on the site of a prehistoric fortress crown the summit. On clear days, especially toward evening, the vast panorama embraces the Roman plain, the dome of St. Peter's, and the Tyrrhenian Sea. Mornings are often foggy; standing above Palestrina one feels transposed to the dawn of history.

ANAGNI ▪

A tremendous curse that a pope hurled against this hilltown southeast of Rome and against its people nearly seven centuries ago must have worn off. Anagni appears to be doing quite nicely today, although the papal malediction is still remembered whenever frosts ruin the olive trees or hailstorms cause havoc in the vineyards.

A few of the 15,000 inhabitants of this attractive, neat town about an hour's car ride from the Italian capital still grow olives and wine on its slopes, but many more have jobs in the factories and workshops that since the end of the 1950s have been dotting the plains 900 feet below Anagni, and others commute to work in the nearby resort of Fiuggi.

The main reasons for a visit to quiet Anagni will be its stupendous

Romanesque-Gothic cathedral and its frowning medieval quarter at the highest elevation of the lengthy ridge that the town straddles. Like the much larger city of Viterbo northwest of Rome, Anagni too served as a refuge for various popes during the Middle Ages at times when they felt unsafe in the Vatican. One of them, Boniface VIII, will never be forgotten here.

Elected in 1294 as successor to Pope St. Celestine V, who had resigned, Boniface tried unsuccessfully to reassert papal authority. He found a powerful adversary in King Philip IV the Fair of France. When the pope opposed the French king's efforts to squeeze money out of the clergy, Philip IV in 1303 sent a delegation to Anagni where Boniface was then residing. The French king's chancellor, Guillaume de Nogaret, led the group, assisted by a Roman nobleman, Sciarra Colonna, from a clan who were rivals of the pope's family, the Caetani. Three hundred mercenary horsemen backed the king's representatives.

The cardinals and other members of the pontifical court vanished, and the townspeople, who had opened the gates to the delegation and its men-at-arms, remained passive. Boniface, abandoned by his entourage and the citizens of Anagni, seated himself on his throne in his palace to await the unwelcome visitors. De Nogaret told him bluntly that the French king wanted him to step down. Colonna went so far as to strike the pontiff in his face.

The ancient chroniclers report that Boniface was kept a prisoner in his own palace for three days, but stubbornly refused to resign despite ill-treatment, and that the townspeople eventually turned against the invaders and chased them out. The pope journeyed back to the Vatican and died soon afterward, but not before excommunicating King Philip and pronouncing a solemn imprecation against Anagni. The Romans said by way of an obituary that Boniface VIII had "entered like a fox, reigned like a lion, and died like a dog."

A yellow sign outside an old building near the cathedral now directs sightseers to the *Sala dello Schiaffo* (Hall of the Slap) in what is called the Palace of Boniface VIII. Actually, only a few arches of the papal residence have survived from the Middle Ages. The Boniface VIII Museum on the premises, with Cistercian nuns in charge, contains mainly material from an exhibition in the 1960s that was devoted to Anagni's history and territory.

The cathedral, dating from the eleventh century and featuring an imposing loggia, is remarkably well preserved. Statues of Boniface

VIII that were put up shortly after his election and years before his clash with the French king are outside the tower and the right aisle. In the interior and the crypt are fine mosaic pavements from the thirteenth century; the frescoes in the crypt are of the same period.

The dark-gray stone houses, massive arcades, and crooked streets at the approaches to the cathedral cannot have changed much since the grim days of Boniface VIII.

The long main street that leads up to the cathedral opens about halfway into a square, Piazza Cavour, with an airy view of the wide Sacco River Valley, the Lepini Mountains to the south, and the green hills of southern Latium all around. The town walls, in part an inheritance from antiquity, are best preserved on the opposite (north) side of Anagni.

Fiuggi, twelve miles to the northeast, is a spa that is popular above all with middle-class Romans. It has many hotels, well-kept gardens, chestnut woods in the vicinity, and a thriving mineral water–bottling business.

TIVOLI ▪

The name conjures visions of refined pleasures, but first-time visitors to the town 19.5 miles northeast of Rome may initially feel let down. Has the place been overadvertised? The forty-minute drive from the Italian capital to Tivoli on the ancient Via Tiburtina is uninspiring. The highway, clogged with commercial traffic, is flanked by chemical and pharmaceutical plants, machine shops, and other small industry. Farther on, vast quarries come into sight; much of Rome was built over the ages with the travertine blocks and the chalk from the flatlands below Tivoli. On the right are the sulphur springs of Bagni di Tivoli (Baths of Tivoli), which had many aficionados until they were found to have become tainted by infiltrations of sewage. Then the road rises amid olive groves and curves up to the old town.

The first impression is that of a teeming and rather scruffy suburb of Rome at the picturesque spot where the Aniene River, the Anio of the ancients, breaks out of the Sabine Mountains through a ravine to cascade into the Roman plain.

It may be a good idea to approach Tivoli by railroad for a start.

201

As the train climbs the hillside in a wide loop, after a few tunnels the traveler suddenly beholds the town spreading out, barren hills as a backdrop, the Aniene waterfalls close in front. Most of the time the cascades are thin now because much water is diverted upstream into a hydroèlectric plant that supplies Rome with power and light.

At the railroad station the visitor is welcomed by a modern sculpture of a falcon with, underneath, an old Latin motto: *"Tibur Superbum,"* "Proud Tivoli." In antiquity the town gloried in being much older than Rome and, later, in its sophistication as a resort where rich and prominent Romans, even emperors, had opulent villas. The place was famous for its cool summer nights, its fruits, its baths, and its fashionable religious cults.

The Piazza Garibaldi, a park at the point where the Via Tiburtina enters the town, is Tivoli's balcony overlooking the Campagna Romana, the plains around Rome; the skyline of the metropolis with its towers and cupolas is visible on the horizon to the west. Until the late nineteenth century the Campagna was a landscape of grazing sheep, ancient ruins, sweeping vistas, and melancholy loneliness that enchanted Romantic painters and bred malaria. Now, from the Piazza Garibaldi terrace, 760 feet above sea level, one beholds the metropolis reaching out toward Tivoli with tentacles of modern housing, industrial developments, heavy traffic on a network of roads, car parks and car cemeteries, and the military airport of Guidonia. Two small towns, Montecelio and Palombara Sabina, on top of twin hills northwest of Tivoli complete the panorama.

Tourists arriving by coach from Rome are herded past souvenir stands into the Villa d'Este gardens, now Tivoli's main attraction. The steeply sloping walled park with tall cypresses and other evergreens and flower beds is renowned for its waterworks on terrace after terrace, including an "Avenue of Hundred Fountains" and a "Water Organ," and for its glimpses of the Campagna below and the town above. Sound and Light spectacles take place in the Villa d'Este on summer nights. The park is closed on Mondays and can be visited on other days from morning to an hour before sunset; admission tickets must be bought at a window in the cloisterlike courtyard of a sixteenth-century building through which the gardens are reached.

The ornate complex at the site of a former Benedictine monastery was laid out, beginning in 1549, for Ippolito II Cardinal d'Este, a rich churchman belonging to the family then ruling the Duchy of

Ferrara. The park remained a property of the Este family and their heirs until Archduke Franz Ferdinand of Austria-Este, heir apparent to the Habsburg throne, was assassinated at Sarajevo in 1914 and World War I broke out.

Another park on the eastern fringe of Tivoli beyond the Aniene, the Villa Gregoriana, permits a close look at the cascades and encloses the remains of a circular Roman temple with ten well-preserved Corinthian columns. Popularly known as the Temple of the Sibyl, the shrine may really have been dedicated to Vesta, the goddess of the hearth. Near it is the ruin of another, rectangular temple that may actually have been a place where the mythical prophetess the Sibyl was venerated.

The best views of Tivoli and its waterfalls can be enjoyed from Via delle Cascatelle, a curving road that from a turnoff above the Villa Gregoriana leads to the Palombara Marcellina railroad station about five miles northwest. From its cascades downstream the Aniene becomes increasingly polluted, also because of the many industrial plants in what used to be the solitary Campagna; near where the river joins the Tiber in the north of the Italian capital it is, as present-day Romans say with a shudder, an open sewer. Plans for a water-clearing plant are far from realization.

Tivoli's citadel, with towers and battlements, near Piazza Garibaldi, was built under Pope Pius II in the fifteenth century. The remains of a Roman amphitheater are behind the stronghold. Tivoli, with about 50,000 inhabitants today, has a few palaces that have seen better days, and a vast medieval quarter that is a maze of narrow, sloping streets, stairways, and gloomy, dilapidated houses. The Baroque cathedral near the northern edge of this neighborhood looks musty, with weeds growing on its roof and walls.

On weekends many Romans drive out to Tivoli for a meal in one of the restaurants overlooking the Aniene ravine and the cascades; quite often there will be some wedding party going on in a separate room or at a long table on the terrace. The food is that of the average *trattoria* in Rome—solid, though undistinguished, as long as patrons stick to the standby pasta dishes, veal or pork, and vegetables that are in season.

A trip to Tivoli should include a visit to the Villa Adriana, Hadrian's Villa, three miles west of the town on a road from a turnoff on the Via Tiburtina. Although the 180-acre site has been plundered through the centuries it still gives some idea of the splendor and extravagance of Emperor Hadrian, who had these pleasure grounds created for himself toward the end of his life (he ruled from A.D. 117 to 138). Not content with a huge palace and lush gardens in a natural bowl in the hillside, the emperor also wanted to see around himself replicas of notable buildings and other landmarks that had caught his fancy during his incessant travels all over the Roman world. To please the emperor's whims the grounds were filled with amphitheaters, copies of Greek buildings, colonnades, baths, artificial lakes, a "naval theater" around a pond, and quarters for bodyguards and slaves.

A small museum in Hadrian's Villa contains statuary and other finds unearthed in new excavations that started in 1950. Many of the sculptures that were found earlier in the imperial villa are now displayed in the Vatican Museums or in other collections in Rome and elsewhere. Most visitors get tired after wandering around the imposing ruins for an hour or so, and repair to the restaurant outside for a drink or a snack. Whoever wants to learn more should hire a guide—licensed ones usually hang around—or buy one of the brochures or books that are available at the entrance. Sound and Light shows are offered in Hadrian's Villa in the warm season.

SUBIACO ▪

Barely an hour and a half from Rome by public bus or car, this quiet little town at an altitude of 1,340 feet near a gorge of the Aniene River is steeped in the past, and the pace of its present life is remarkably calm. Emperor Nero had a villa here, St. Benedict lived in a nearby cave as a hermit, and popes would at times take up residence in the eleventh-century castle on a steep hill that dominates Subiaco.

More recently, painters came here and to the nearby hilltown of Anticoli Corrado (at 1,680 feet) to re-create the romantic scenery on canvas, and to try to persuade some pretty local girl to pose for them or possibly follow them to Rome. The hill country around here has long been famed for the pulchritude of its women and as a supplier of professional painters' models; one of the film queens of Rome's *dolce vita* era, Gina Lollobrigida, came from Subiaco. The town has now some 9,000 inhabitants, and some of them commute to Rome every working day.

From the capital, the visitor travels up the valley of the Aniene. Here the stream is still almost limpid; it will be unspeakably polluted by the time it joins the Tiber in the north of Rome. One or the other of the rustic eating places along the Via Sublacense, the route to Subiaco, even advertises "river trout," although the fish are actually hatched in ponds.

As the Aniene Valley turns a little toward the left, Subiaco comes into view, climbing up a slope on the river's left bank. High above the town is the Borgia Rock, the ruined hilltop castle that is named after the family of the Spanish-born Pope Alexander VI (pope from 1492 to 1503). The name of another pope, Pius VI, is on a triumphal arch built in the classic Roman manner that rises at the entrance to Subiaco. It was erected as a memorial of a pontifical visit in 1789; nine years later the aged Pope Pius VI would be made a prisoner in Rome and deported to France on Napoleon's orders, and he would never see the Vatican or Italy again.

Pius VI's name is also on the façade of Subiaco's stately parish church on Piazza Sant'Andrea opposite the modern town hall. To the left of the church is a terrace with a monument to war victims and a fine view of the Aniene Valley deep below, with a paper mill in the foreground.

From the little square, Subiaco's forum for meeting and watching people, the main street descends again and, flanking the Aniene as Via dei Monasteri (Street of the Monasteries), leads to a turnoff. A narrow road, left, winds up to the site among rocks and evergreen oaks where the Benedictine idea of "pray and work" (*ora et labora*) was born. St. Benedict, a native of Nursia (now Norcia) near Spoleto, retired to this wilderness after studying in Rome at the beginning of the sixth century. Other ascetics gathered around him, and St. Benedict built a cluster of twelve small monasteries for them.

The local clergy did not look kindly at the new religious community. St. Gregory (pope from 590 to 604) would later write that a Subiaco priest, attempting to scandalize St. Benedict's first followers, egged on some loose women to dance nude in the courtyard of the saintly hermit's monastery. Whatever happened in the Aniene Gorge, St. Benedict moved on to Monte Cassino in 529 to found the first abbey of his nascent order there (*see* Cassino).

From Subiaco, the visitor reaches the Convent of St. Scholastica. One of the religious houses founded by St. Benedict, it was repeatedly destroyed and rebuilt, and was named after the saint's twin sister St. Scholastica, by Pope Benedict VII in 981. The main building of the convent with an imposing façade of soft beige stone is a modern reconstruction. In front of it, separated by a terrace, are a Roman-esque campanile from the eleventh century and an ancient church that was rebuilt in the eighteenth century.

A plaque on the wall facing the entrance to the Church of St. Scholastica records in Latin that during an air attack on Subiaco on May 23, 1944 (when the Allied forces were advancing to take Rome), a twenty-year-old seminarian, Antonio Pelliccia, was killed by bombs (*"igniferum globulorum iactu"*) at that spot. As I was looking at the inscription during my most recent sojourn in Subiaco, an elderly man came out of the church and told me: "Antonio was my brother-in-law. The frame of his eyeglasses was all that was ever found of him."

Behind the modern convent building are, in a row, three monastic buildings of ascending age: The First Monastery is from the late sixteenth century; the Second Monastery is in Gothic style; and the Third Monastery, with a Romanesque cloister and mosaics inspired by Byzantine models, goes back to the twelfth century. The various parts of the building complex are intercommunicating, and are supported on the south side by stout arches and walls above the access road.

Proceeding for twenty minutes on a footpath beyond the three monasteries, one sees the Church and Monastery of St. Benedict, built into an overhanging cliff. The site is known as the Sacro Speco (Sacred Cave). Stairs lead from the frescoed upper church to the lower church and the grotto where St. Benedict lived. A side chapel, dedicated to St. Gregory, contains a restored portrait of St. Francis, who was a guest of the monastery around 1218. His picture was painted by an anonymous artist, probably soon after the visit by the saint from Assisi and before his death in 1226 because St. Francis is represented without his stigmata and the customary halo. He reputedly worked a miracle during his stay near Subiaco: He transformed into roses the brambles into which St. Benedict would dive whenever he was distracted by the temptations of the flesh. Roses still grow in the monastery's romantic little garden.

Back at the Convent of St. Scholastica, look at the opposite side of the ravine. Terraces and ruined walls can be made out there; they are remains of one of Nero's many estates.

The emperor's villa on the Aniene was the scene of an incident that contemporaries viewed as a bad omen. It happened sometime after Nero had his mother, Agrippina, murdered in A.D. 59. He was relaxing in his villa at Sublaqueum (now Subiaco), named so after a nearby artificial lake. "While Nero was reclining at dinner," Tacitus reports, "the table with the banquet was struck and shattered" by a flash of lightning. The emperor was unhurt, but the awesome occurrence, coming at a time when a comet was blazing in the sky night after night, was taken as an added portent that his reign was coming to an end. Tacitus says that "people began to ask, as if Nero was already dethroned, who was to be elected" his successor. It would nevertheless take several more years before a military rebellion was to prompt Nero to take his own life in A.D. 68.

Today, rather few strangers come to Subiaco to see the Neronian ruins or, for that matter, the Benedictine monasteries, or to paint. Most of the town's scarce tourist business is represented by skiers who pass through on winter weekends to drive up to the snowy slopes of the 4,598-foot-high Mount Livata. A hotel near the summit is open also during the summer months for guests who like the pure air and the Apennine panorama.

SPOLETO ▪

For a few weeks every June and July the sloping archways and amiable piazzas of this hilltown in green Umbria stage a parade of cultural and often snobbish sophistication—"The Festival of Two Worlds"— that draws an arty crowd of foreigners, many of them from the United States. Afterward, much of the cosmopolitan makeup comes off, and Spoleto shows its true face again—the severe dignity of its Romanesque and Gothic churches; its medieval and Renaissance palaces; its stone-gray narrow streets with, perhaps, a gratifying view of the surrounding hill country around the next corner; its unassuming people. The few hotels again have room for those who want to stay as long as they like, which may be very long. Only two hours from Rome, off-season Spoleto, with around 35,000 inhabitants, is a little world full of provincial charm, a place for strollers to enjoy leisurely its quiet, harmonious beauty.

St. Francis of Assisi had a particular liking for Spoleto. It was in his day a leading city in the region, as it had been for centuries and would remain until the 1860s, when unified Italy designated nearby Perugia as the administrative center of Umbria. Talk to any native, and you will sense that plenty of rivalry with Perugia, forty miles to the northwest, lingers here, and not only because of the soccer championship.

Travelers on the Via Flaminia (National Route No. 3) between Rome and the Adriatic coast skirt Spoleto and pass a tunnel under its "Rock," and many just move on without taking the trouble of stopping and walking up to the old town. The road that Caius Flaminius built in 220 B.C. is still one of Italy's main highways; in the past the city's location on that important artery gave it power and brought frequent trouble. Hannibal tried to take Spoleto and failed; factions in the Roman civil war fought for its possession; barbarian invaders occupied it. In the sixth century Longobard dukes ensconced themselves in the palaces from which they had ousted the Romans. The Germanic duchy of Spoleto lasted for hundreds of years until, in the early thirteenth century, the city became a part of the Papal States. Spoleto has not forgotten its splendor under the Longobards: The dukes are recalled by place names and business signs. The city is the seat of an academic center for research into the High Middle Ages, and plays host to medievalists at periodic international symposia.

The visitor who arrives by railroad is greeted outside the station by a 55-foot-high abstract steel sculpture named after Spoleto's enterprising early-seventh-century Duke Theodolapus. The huge stabile, suggesting the skeleton of some prehistoric animal, is a work by Alexander Calder. Smaller steel sculptures by other artists are placed in some nooks of the old city, surprisingly blending in with the dark medieval walls; they were all gifts to Spoleto at the end of a modern art exhibition in 1962. More debatable are the mock-archaic wrought-iron street lamps with electric light bulbs that the city fathers thought fit to install in the oldest neighborhoods to prettify them. The

208

international festival has generated also a scattering of fashion boutiques, cutesy restaurants, and antiques stores with prices like those demanded in Rome and Milan. However, Spoleto is a priceless antique in itself.

Its prominence in Roman times is evidenced by vast ruins. The amphitheater, more than half as large as the Colosseum in Rome, was one of the biggest in the empire's provinces. Its remains, now enclosed by an army barracks complex, cannot be visited easily today and are not of particular interest anyway. Instead, the Roman theater, on a slope near the central Piazza della Libertà, is freely accessible and is used for open-air performances during the festival. Spectators have behind them the gentle contours of the Umbrian countryside. Farther up, on the way to the cathedral, the stroller walks through a Roman archway built in honor of Drusus when the adoptive son of Emperor Tiberius was an official guest in A.D. 23.

Many generations of local and guest artists have worked on the nearly thousand-year-old cathedral. It has mosaics of Byzantine inspiration; frescoes by the Florentine ex-monk Filippo Lippi (who is buried in the church), and by Pinturicchio; a Renaissance porch that was added later to its Romanesque-Gothic façade; and a rather chilly Baroque interior. To contemporary tastes the building looks more beautiful outside than inside. The main approach to the cathedral is by a broad stairway that dramatically sweeps down into a secluded square. On some evenings during the festival period the cathedral piazza becomes an auditorium for outdoor concerts. A plaque on the right wall of the square reads in moving terseness: "Here are guarded the ashes of Thomas Schippers (1930–1977)." The American conductor was closely associated with the Spoleto festival, promoted since 1958 by the composer Giancarlo Menotti.

Festival performances take place also in the 400-seat Teatro Caio Melisso (named after a Spoletan who was a friend of Maecenas in the Augustan age) in an old building to the left of the cathedral, and in the nineteenth-century Teatro Nuovo, which holds 600 spectators and has a stage curtain depicting the defeat of Hannibal under the walls of Spoleto. Opera and legitimate drama are from time to time produced in this municipal theater also in winter.

The Civic Museum on Cathedral Square contains Roman and medieval collections. Visitors shouldn't miss Piazza del Mercato, near the Roman archway, where a lively open-air market is held weekday mornings, and the stupendous Romanesque Church of St. Gregory on Piazza Garibaldi near the lowest portion of the old city walls.

"The Rock," at 1,486 feet crowning the hill on which Spoleto is built, has been fortified since Roman times. Alvarez Cardinal Albornoz, the fourteenth-century Spanish prelate and general who restored papal rule throughout central Italy after a long period of Church weakness, erected a large castle with six towers on the site. The grim structure served as a penitentiary from 1817 until a few years ago; the authorities have not yet decided what to do with the castle now, and whether it should eventually be opened to the public.

Piazza Campello, south of the cathedral, opens to a remarkable circular promenade around The Rock with changing views of the castle above olive trees and sheer cliffs. On the other side of the road, signs warn that unauthorized persons may not search for truffles on the steep slopes. Black truffles grow underground on the hills around Spoleto, usually sniffed out by trained dogs and dug up by their handlers. Truffled dishes, like pasta with paper-thin slices of the flavored delicacy, are often on the menu at local eating places.

An old viaduct and aqueduct, to local people simply "The Bridge," daringly spans the ravine of the Tessino River, which at times runs dry, east of The Rock. Although the airy structure, borne by ten arches, and 230 feet high at some points, looks in need of repairs, one is still permitted to walk the 700 feet across to the towers that guard access at the opposite side. The wooded slope of Mount Luco to which the viaduct leads affords a lovely view of Spoleto and its castle. The Bridge, built some 600 years ago to create a link between the hilltop fortress and its outworks on the east side of the ravine, probably replaced a much older viaduct.

Tourist agents in Spoleto will suggest side trips by coach, public bus, or car to several interesting places nearby. Among them are the Fonti del Clitunno (Sources of the Clitumnus River), a sightseeing spot already in antiquity, as classical authors attest. The springs of the small river fill a pond surrounded by weeping willows, poplars, and other trees in a setting of great serenity seven miles to the north (National Route No. 3).

Norcia, a town of 5,000 at an altitude of 1,982 feet, thirty miles northeast of Spoleto (National Routes Nos. 395 and 396), is distinguished by its monumental piazza with a thirteenth-century town hall and a Gothic cathedral. A modern statue of St. Benedict, the founder of the Benedictine Order who was born near Norcia, stands in the center of the square. A few modest *trattorie* in town offer inexpensive, solid fare, garnished with truffles.

FOLIGNO ▪

Travelers on the Via Flaminia (National Route No. 3) who bypass this modern-looking town in a fertile plain roughly halfway between Rome and the Adriatic coast miss an essential piece of Umbria. Welcoming, well-to-do Foligno is a place where one may savor the region's placid everyday life without having to climb medieval stairways to get a meal or a cup of cappuccino. In the espresso bars and in the historical piazza at the center, farmers from the countryside, traders, and the town's renowned craftsmen discuss politics and sports. The national soccer championship and the pool lottery tied to it dominate Sunday afternoons.

The railroad and highway to Assisi and Perugia branch off the Rome-Ancona line and the Via Flaminia at Foligno. This role as a traffic hub—which made the town a target of Allied bombers during World War II—brings a good deal of business to it today.

Stroll into Foligno's center and have a look at the twelfth-century cathedral, which takes up one side of the main square. An arch links the church with the rebuilt Palazzo del Governo (Government Palace), the power seat of the Trinci family when they ruled Foligno in the fourteenth and fifteenth centuries. Works by Niccolò Alunno and other minor masters of the Foligno School of Umbrian painting may be seen at the municipal museum. On a side street off Corso Mazzini, the town's main artery, is a disused fifteenth-century chapel, the Oratorio della Nunziatella, with the fresco *The Baptism of Jesus* by Perugino.

Foligno has a population of more than 50,000, many of them workers in its small and medium-sized industrial plants on the outskirts, and not counting students commuting from nearby places. The town is surrounded by a garland of appealing smaller communities, each with its own distinctive character and none farther than eight miles away. To visit them it helps to have a car, although two are reachable from Foligno by railroad and all by public bus.

Palestrina: town in foreground, ruins of the ancient Roman sanctuary across center, Barberini Palace (housing National Museum) at top

Palestrina, view from Barberini Palace

Tivoli, Hadrian's Villa

Frascati, Fountain of Apollo

Frascati, ruins of ancient Tusculum

*OPPOSITE, TOP: Subiaco,
Bridge of St. Francis*

*OPPOSITE, BOTTOM: Subiaco,
Convent of St. Scholastica*

*RIGHT: Foligno,
cathedral*

BELOW: Spoleto

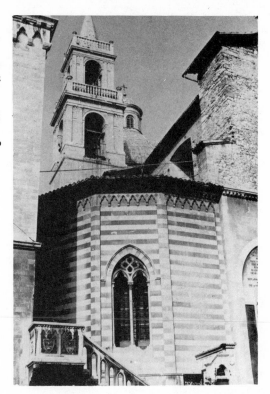

OPPOSITE:
Spoleto, cathedral

LEFT: Perugia, fountain
and Palazzo dei Priori

BELOW: Perugia, choir stall
of the Basilica of St. Peter

On a steep, conical hill eight miles southeast of Foligno, on the Rome-Ancona railroad line, *Trevi* overlooks the Clitunno River valley. At the approaches to the town with population 7,000 lies the Church of St. Martin with a fresco of the Virgin Mary surrounded by four saints, painted in 1512 by Lo Spagna (the nickname of Giovanni di Pietro, who was of Spanish descent), one of the greats of the Umbrian school. Other works by Lo Spagna can be seen in the small art gallery in the town hall.

Montefalco ("Falcon's Mountain"), 1,550 feet high and seven miles southwest of Foligno, is a walled town of some 5,000 inhabitants that is known as the "Balcony of Umbria" because it overlooks almost the entire region. The panorama is most impressive from the top of the municipal tower (Torre Municipale) to which visitors are admitted by a caretaker at their request. In good weather all the green hills, valleys, towns, and cities from Spoleto in the southeast to Perugia in the northwest can be seen. The town's coat of arms shows a falcon on a heraldic hill. Its fortified nest was repeatedly fought over by warring factions in the Middle Ages and the Renaissance because it represented a natural observation post. The town walls and ramparts above olive groves are still redoubtable.

The people in the calm and picturesque little town appear glad today to see strangers, and are intensely proud of its history and local traditions. It has its own saint, a St. Clare who was unrelated to the spiritual companion of St. Francis of Assisi; she died in 1309 and is buried in a church outside the town walls. A native Renaissance artist, Francesco Melanzio, was reputedly a bizarre character. Paintings and frescoes by him may be viewed in a small chapel in the town square and in the no longer used Church of St. Francis in Via Ringhiera Umbra (Umbrian Balustrade Street) a little off the piazza. Now a museum, the former church houses also a rich collection of frescoes and paintings by Umbrian masters from Benozzo Gozzoli to Melozzo da Forlì. While Montefalco is important to students of Umbrian art, no visitor to the region who passes through Foligno should miss this delightful place.

Bevagna, a town of 5,000 in the Clitunno Valley seven miles southwest of Foligno, is notable for its medieval piazza and its walls, which incorporate ancient Roman fortifications.

Spello, three miles west of Foligno, off the railroad and highway to Perugia, climbs in terraces up Mount Subasio (on whose northwestern spur Assisi nestles). With its huddled mass of bright stone buildings Spello looks like the quintessential Umbrian hilltown. There is an ancient Roman doorway near the railroad station. Arches span some of the stairways and narrow alleys, and Roman ruins dot other spots. A side chapel in the cathedral was frescoed by Pinturicchio in 1501. In a panel representing the Annunciation the artist fitted a self-portrait into a picture on the wall of the Virgin's room.

In all four towns near Foligno mentioned above, visitors will find unassuming eating places, some with rooms for anyone wanting to stay over. Not a bad idea.

ASSISI ∎

One of the miracles of St. Francis, and not the least, is that his birthplace has been spared the embraces by concrete that threaten to suffocate all too much of Italy's natural and artistic beauty. Assisi, with the delicate grays, pinks, and violets of its old houses and churches, is still serenely spread out beneath the hump of its hill, surrounded by olive groves, rows of cypresses and pines, wheatfields, and vineyards.

From the ruined medieval citadel, the Rocca Maggiore, on top of Mount Subasio and from vantage points that unexpectedly open in the streets of the town on its slopes, the eye rests on a wide valley with shades of green dotted with the bright spots of distant hamlets and towns. Even the railroad station down in the plain is delightfully old-fashioned, with cast-iron supports and antiquated lettering, "ASSISI."

In the slow trains from Foligno and Terontola, and in the buses that park outside the town gates, streams of visitors arrive all year around. They are priests, friars, and nuns from throughout the world; groups on pilgrimages or on package tours; a great many young people with sleeping bags; students and art lovers who want to see the Cimabue and Giotto frescoes; and honeymooning couples.

Souvenir shops and stands clutter the town, unsurprisingly, but they are less offensive in their unabashed vulgarity than shoddy or pretentious architecture would be. Tourists can buy, among other kitsch, ceramics with views of Assisi, sweatshirts, and bottles of a dark "San Francesco" liquor supposedly distilled from walnuts and black truffles.

Before starting their obligatory religious devotions or sightseeing, as the case may be, visitors will do well to stroll up and down Assisi's long, irregular streets at random and let the solemnity and mysticism of the place sink in, that is, when no noisy travel hordes are around. Early mornings and evenings are best.

It is also a good idea to read up on the lives of St. Francis and of his spiritual associate, St. Clare, to get a better grasp of Assisi's atmosphere. However, coming upon the well-preserved façade of a Roman temple that honored Minerva, now a church, with six tall, fluted columns in the narrow Piazza del Comune, the visitor will realize that the town (which today counts about 25,000 inhabitants) had some importance long before St. Francis was born there in 1182. He was the son of a wealthy and well-traveled cloth merchant and his French wife in what must have been a thriving community.

Like nearby Perugia, long a rival, Assisi was an Etruscan settlement before being conquered by the Romans. The lyric poet Propertius, a contemporary of Emperor Augustus, was a native son. The remains of a small Roman amphitheater near a wooded slope in the town's northeast also attest to a certain status of the town in ancient times.

What will impress the stroller at once is the great number of churches and convents. Each branch of the vast family of Franciscan orders for friars and sisters has its own establishment here. Mount Subasio, on whose western spur Assisi sits, supplied the marble for the town's ancient and medieval builders. Franciscan architecture is characterized by transition from Romanesque sturdiness to a Gothic elegance clearly influenced by French models, with lacework rose windows as its signet. All over town geraniums and other flowers abound on windowsills, balconies, and terraces, and in enchanting little gardens.

Assisi's principal shrine, the Basilica of St. Francis, is also its main attraction for devotees of the arts. The edifice is really two large churches, one above the other, surmounted by a square tower and flanked by a huge convent resting on walls and arches that become taller as the hillside descends. The extraordinary complex of bright stones, jutting out of the town's northwestern end like a bulwark or the bow of an enormous boat, is visible from far away.

The remains of St. Francis are venerated in a crypt that is approached from the Lower Church over a double staircase. The saint's rough stone coffin was secreted by his followers in a vault hewn from the living rock for fear it might be stolen, and was rediscovered only in 1818. The crypt was dug between 1818 and 1822.

The dim, low-vaulted Lower Church, more Romanesque in character than the church above, was built a few years after St. Francis's death in 1226. Cimabue, Giotto, and, above all, their assistants and pupils decorated it. For viewing their work, the light must be turned on. The Upper Church, linked with the Lower Church by a double flight of outside stairs on the side of the tower, is sufficiently lit through its Gothic stained-glass windows. Walls, pillars, and vaults of the soaring interior are covered with paintings and painted ornaments.

The dramatic *Crucifixion* by Cimabue today looks like a film negative because originally bright colors have blackened as a result of oxidation. Even in its present sad state, the greatness of Cimabue's achievement is nevertheless evident. His work and a row of twenty-eight frescoes by Giotto and his assistants in the Upper Church are considered milestones of Italian art. The frescoes, painted around 1320, depict episodes from the life of St. Francis and the legends surrounding it. Panels show the youthful saint who has renounced all worldly possessions returning his fine clothes to his angry father; St. Francis expelling demons from Arezzo; his sermon to the birds; and other scenes. The backgrounds, with their contemporary townscapes and rural scenery, their trees and animals, are as fascinating as the human figures in the wall paintings.

Conservationists worry about the dangers of further deterioration. Art officials recently requested that the Italian air force stop exercises in the airspace near Assisi, fearing that the sonic booms of jet aircraft might crack the Cimabue and Giotto masterworks.

A Renaissance cloister, built behind the Basilica of St. Francis more than 200 years after its completion, is a fugue in mellow stone dominated by the majestic apse of the two churches, one superimposed on the other, with its high windows, flanked by two stern towers.

From Assisi's main sanctuary, Via San Francesco leads up to the central piazza with the Temple of Minerva and the fourteenth-century town hall. Farther east is the medieval cathedral with a font where St. Francis and St. Clare were presumably baptized. On a lower ledge of the slope is the Church of St. Clare with a façade of alternating stripes of pink-white and reddish marble and with stout flying buttresses.

St. Clare, who founded the nuns' order of the Poor Clares, is buried in a crypt beneath the main altar. The apse is decorated with frescoes by disciples of Giotto. Through a grating the visitor may glimpse an ancient Byzantine crucifix in yellow and red colors that, according to legend, spoke to St. Francis. A veiled nun behind the window will tell the story of that relic. Poor Clares live in strict seclusion behind the forbidding walls of the adjacent convent.

A steep road leads from the eastern end of Assisi to a small wood at a height of 2,560 feet to which St. Francis liked to retreat for prayer and solitude amid the oak trees. Tiny chapels for him and his friars, a rock bed on which he slept, and an old tree at which he is said to have preached to the birds are shown at this hermitage (the Eremo).

A small chapel, the Porziuncola ("little section"), in which the first followers of St. Francis used to meet, can be seen under the dome of the pompous Baroque Church of Santa Maria degli Angeli; the church, situated in the plain on the other side of the railroad tracks near the Assisi station, 2.5 miles from the town, was built around the chapel in the late sixteenth century.

The crowds of pilgrims in Assisi are largest on October 4, the feast day of St. Francis, and on August 12, the feast of St. Clare. The otherworldliness of the unique town speaks most persuasively on days in late autumn or early spring when the setting sun transforms the rocks, the olive trees, the churches, and the Umbrian valley below into a magic landscape.

PERUGIA ▪

If you had visions of a quaint old place steeped in the tender mysticism of Perugino and the other painters of the Umbrian school, you will feel disappointed on approaching the city and seeing the modern housing, business districts, and industrial plants around it. There are nevertheless many art treasures and traces from a long history in Perugia, but one has to look for them. A two-hour stop in the tour operators' standard "Hilltowns of Umbria" trip may give visitors a chance of glimpsing some of the principal sights, but they will miss the city's atmosphere.

Since the end of World War II Perugia has more than doubled its population, and now numbers almost 150,000 inhabitants. Around its historical core on the four spurs of an X-shaped hill 1,000 feet above the valley of the young Tiber River, a great deal of building has been going on during the last few decades. Perugia, the administrative capital of the Region of Umbria, is today also a dynamic center of food, apparel, and other "soft" industries. It has a strong Communist Party and a floating presence of thousands of young people from abroad, mainly from Third World countries.

These guests are students of the Italian State University for Foreigners, which was opened in 1926; many of them are in Perugia on scholarships or grants. They take classes in Italian language and culture before being admitted to regular courses at the University of Perugia or an institution of higher learning elsewhere in the country. Americans who have chosen to attend medical school in Italy also learn the language in Perugia.

The foreign students are conspicuous in the streets, taverns, and movie houses of the city; letting rooms to them is a local cottage industry. A few Arabs, Iranians, or Africans will be found on almost any railroad train between Perugia and Rome.

Perugia's cultural activities today—concerts, recitals, lectures, art shows—appeal to a cosmopolitan public. The Italian security services keep a watchful eye on the many young foreigners in the city on the assumption that some of them may be involved in their home country's politics or even in international skulduggery.

Perugia looks out at spectacular vistas on all sides. From the prefecture building on Piazza Italia and the terraces near it, officials can see almost the entire province they administer. Many street corners, squares, loggias, and buildings in the city center and on the slopes also command views of the Tiber Valley, Assisi, and the main range of the Apennines.

The steep roads that lead from the railroad station and the national highways nearby up to the heart of Perugia are often clogged with traffic. Visitors arriving by railroad by way of Foligno and Assisi may get out of their train at Ponte San Giovanni, a business town straddling the Tiber, and board a railcar that will take them in ten minutes to the Stazione Sant'Anna, a terminal below Piazza Italia, and proceed to that square by escalator.

The prevailing color of Perugia's old town is the gray of the stones that have been the favored local building material since the Etruscans flourished in a walled city, Perusia, on top of the hill 2,500 years ago. A massive Etruscan arch, built with huge stone blocks, on the small Piazza Fortebraccio in the north of the historical quarters is a landmark. To the west of it the remains of Etruscan town walls are visible. The arch bears a Latin inscription (*"Augusta Perusia"*) from the Roman imperial age; a loggia was added in the Renaissance. Nearby is the center of the University for Foreigners, the dignified eighteenth-century Palazzo Gallenga.

A wealth of Etruscan and Roman sarcophagi, vases, bronzes, inscriptions, household articles, and other finds are on view in the National Archaeological Museum in the former Convent of St. Dominic in the city's southeast. The adjacent Church of St. Dominic, built in the Gothic style in the early fourteenth century and thoroughly changed in the Renaissance, is also worth a visit.

The fifteenth-century cathedral of Perugia, in the middle of the old town, has lately been undergoing extensive repairs. A graceful Renaissance doorway on the left side of the large, externally unfinished church leads to a cloistered courtyard and to the Cathedral Museum, with a *Madonna* by Luca Signorelli.

Piazza Quattro Novembre, formerly known as Piazza del Municipio, outside the cathedral is one of Italy's great public squares. A sinister reputation lingers because the piazza was the scene of savage fights between the aristocratic clans who contended for supremacy in the city for a long period, the Baglioni and the Oddi. After the Oddi were at last forced to abandon Perugia the city became a beleaguered fortress of the Baglioni, who used even the cathedral as a barracks. Jacob Burckhardt, the historian of the Italian Renaissance, wrote: "Plots and surprises were met with cruel vengeance; after 130 conspirators who had forced their way into the city were killed and hung up at the Municipal Palace in the year 1491 thirty-five altars were erected in the square, and for three days masses were said and processions held to remove the curse from the city. A nephew of Pope Innocent VIII was stabbed in broad daylight."

The fountain (Fontana Maggiore) at the center of the square, consisting of three basins, with many bas-reliefs by Nicolò Pisano and his son Giovanni, famous sculptors from Pisa, is a thirteenth-century work praised as one of the most accomplished compositions of its kind anywhere.

A vaulted, sloping gateway leads from the northwest corner of the piazza, behind the cathedral, to the small Church of the Maestà delle Volte, named after a thirteenth-century fresco showing the Virgin Mary in her "majesty" with angels.

The south side of Piazza Quattro Novembre is taken up by a façade of the Palazzo dei Priori, an imposing edifice built in the thirteenth century and enlarged later. It is a reminder of Perugia's power and pride when the city dominated large parts of Umbria, virtually independent, or only reluctantly acknowledging the pope in Rome as its sovereign.

A griffin and a lion, medieval heraldic symbols of Perugia and of the papal faction (the Guelphs), surmount the portal on the square. Below are bars of gates and chains that used to close the streets of Siena, trophies of a Perugian victory over the Sienese in a battle in 1358. An outside flight of stairs, added later to the façade, leads to a marble pulpit from which the municipal leaders, the priors, used to address the citizenry.

The main entrance to the palace around the corner on Corso Vannucci, the old town's main street, admits visitors to the frescoed halls of the former city government and to the National Gallery of Umbria on the top floor. This important collection contains paintings by Perugino, Raphael's teacher, whose real name was Pietro Vannucci, as well as by Pinturicchio (Barnardino Betti), Piero della Francesca, Fra Angelico da Fiesole, and other Umbrian and Tuscan masters. It is advisable to get the gallery's catalog; supplementary literature is also available at the entrance.

Next to the priors' palace on Corso Vannucci is a narrow fifteenth-century building, the former money exchange (Collegio del Cambio), with a hall and a chapel in which frescoes by Perugino and his pupils, probably including the young Raphael, can be admired. The wall paintings represent classical, biblical, and allegorical figures—Socrates and Scipio; Jehovah, and the Magi adoring the Infant Jesus; the Prophets and the Sibyls; Fortitude and Temperance; and so on—in the all-embracing spirit of Renaissance humanism.

227

Those who stay in Perugia longer will make other discoveries—an Etruscan gate, the Porta Marzia, close to an underground Renaissance passage; an Etruscan wall near the cathedral; a delightful Renaissance church, the Oratorio of San Bernardo, in the city's northwest; and many corners and stairways in the old town that seem not to have changed in centuries.

GUBBIO ▪

This somber town at the mouth of a gorge between steep cliffs in an out-of-the-way corner of Umbria shakes itself out of its customary quiet every May 15. Notables and members of its historic guilds don medieval costumes and parade Gubbio's three "candles" around the narrow streets and severe squares.

The "candles" are wax figures of saints on hourglass-shaped wooden contraptions, twenty-five feet tall, that are borne by athletic young men in white trousers and in shirts of various colors with red sashes. The *ceraioli* (candle-bearers) of the guild of masons, in yellow shirts, are in charge of Gubbio's patron in Heaven, St. Ubaldus. The men of the merchants' guild, in blue shirts, carry St. George, and those of the peasants' guild, in dark shirts, St. Anthony.

When the procession approaches the Gate of St. Ubaldus in the town walls in the upper part of Gubbio, the carriers start running while balancing the candles of their saints, and proceed as fast as they can on the road that winds up the slope of Mount Ingino until they breathlessly reach the Church and Convent of Sant'Ubaldo more than 900 feet above the town. The uphill race over nearly one and a half miles, which requires stout hearts, usually takes less than a quarter of an hour.

Inevitably, though unofficially, bets are taken on the outcome of the bizarre contest—will St. Ubaldus win again, or will St. George or St. Anthony be first?

Gubbio's Festival of the Candles on the eve of the Church feast of St. Ubaldus (May 16) celebrates the town's signal victory over a coalition of no fewer than eleven hostile neighbor communities in a battle in 1151. Ubaldus, a native of Gubbio, was then its bishop, and members of his flock were convinced that he had won supernatural support for their military forces.

The saintly bishop died in 1168, and in 1192, after various miracles had been attributed to him, was canonized by Pope Celestine III. To this day some Gubbian couples call their firstborn son Ubaldo.

The Race of the Candles may be one of the reasons why other Umbrians will tell you with condescending smiles that the inhabitants of Gubbio, all 30,000 of them, are *tutti pazzi* ("all crazy"). This old reputation for weirdness may, however, also spring from the forbidding character of the town, whose ocher-colored buildings and medieval towers huddle beneath the steep Mount Ingino, on which the sanctuary of St. Ubaldus stands, and beneath Mount Calvo across the canyon of the Camignano torrent.

With Apennine hills as a harsh backdrop, and without much greenery to rest one's eyes on, Gubbio may seem oppressive. Its historic core is formed by five streets, each on a different level, linked by sloping alleys. Some of the old houses have a narrow opening beside the doorway—the "gate of the dead" through which the coffin passes whenever someone in the building has died. Gubbio, off the region's main routes of communication, has thus preserved medieval architecture and features like few other places in Italy. Today's Gubbians nevertheless strike the visitor as genial and welcoming.

One Gubbio theme recurs in religious art throughout Italy, the legend of St. Francis and the wolf. The huge and greedy animal, so the pious tale goes, had long been terrorizing the countryside when the ascetic from Assisi (1182–1226) came to town. St. Francis sought out the wolf of Gubbio in its lair, gently upbraided it for its ferocity, and soon had the brute at his feet. The wolf promised in tears never again to harm anyone, and proferred its paw to the saint to seal its vow, a scene on which painters would later feast. According to the edifying story, the people of Gubbio grew fond of their former tormentor, fed the reformed wolf until it died of old age, and gave it a Christian burial.

The heart of Gubbio is the dour Piazza della Signoria, dominated by the battlemented Palace of the Consuls and its tower. When the Gothic building went up in the first half of the fourteenth century, it was meant as the government headquarters of the independent city-state of Gubbio. Independence, however, was soon to end; the Montefeltro rulers of nearby Urbino took control of the town, and, like Urbino, Gubbio would later become a part of the Papal States.

Today the Palace of the Consuls houses a Civic Museum and Municipal Picture Gallery. The Iguvine Tablets are the most famous exhibit, seven bronze tablets that were found in Gubbio (the Iguvium of the ancient Romans) in 1444. Measuring 16 by 12 inches to 33 by 22 inches in size, the tablets are engraved on both sides. The texts, written variously between 400 and 90 B.C., concern the rituals of a priestly brotherhood and contain much information about pagan religious practices. More important, the inscriptions are in part in ancient Umbrian and represent the main source for the study of that dialect, which with Latin belongs to the Italic branch of the Indo-European family of languages.

In the Palace of the Consuls there are also other antiquities, paintings from the fourteenth to the eighteenth centuries, and old furniture. Note especially the majolicas by Maestro Giorgio (Giorgio Andreoli), a Renaissance master potter who invented a technique for giving ceramics a much-envied reddish sheen, suggesting metal. Pottery is at present still a local industry, and its products fill Gubbio's souvenir shops.

The town hall is opposite the Palace of the Consuls. A steep street leads up to the cathedral, built in the twelfth and thirteenth centuries, whose foundations are dug deep into the sloping ground. Opposite the church stands the Ducal Palace, a medieval building that toward the end of the fifteenth century was enlarged and altered to resemble the palace of Federico of Montefeltro in Urbino.

In the plain below Gubbio—the basin of a prehistoric lake—lie the ruins of a Roman theater of the Republican era, which was repaired under Emperor Augustus. Farther south, close to the national highway leading to Perugia, is a stark memorial for the "Forty Martyrs," local hostages whom the Nazis executed in 1944 in retaliation for attacks by Italian partisans.

The Church and Convent of Sant'Ubaldo, overlooking Gubbio from a height of 2,690 feet, can be reached over the road on which the Race of the Candles is run, or by a funicular from a terminal in the east of the town beyond the Vavarello torrent. The three candles with the figures of the saints are always kept in the Church of Sant'Ubaldo except on May 15, when they are taken down to Gubbio.

CITTÀ DI CASTELLO ▪

This walled market town in the upper Tiber Valley northwest of Perugia is a monument to the building craze that in the Renaissance even minor nobles shared with the era's great popes and princes. The Vitelli family were then the lords of Città di Castello, and they filled it in the fifteenth and sixteenth centuries with their palaces.

Some of the Vitelli hired out to one or the other of the epoch's major powers as leaders of mercenary troops. One member of the family, Vitellozzo, was a notorious cutthroat who was strangled in the harbor town of Senigallia in 1502 on orders from his commander in chief, the sinister Cesare Borgia. Before dying, Vitellozzo Vitelli asked to be absolved from his sins by the father of his executioner, Pope Alexander VI.

The lively city of the Vitelli, with at present a population of 40,000, has long spilled beyond the long rectangle of its Renaissance fortifications. Its historic core is dotted with churches for which the young Raphael painted the first works commissioned to him (the pictures are now all elsewhere). Between the several Vitelli edifices there are narrow alleys and a large central piazza that have not changed much, architecturally, in 500 years.

The traveler who arrives by car is advised to leave it in the vast parking lot outside the western ramparts: The cramped maze of one-way streets within the walls can be confusing to the newcomer. Obligingly, the town fathers have recently had escalators installed that take visitors from the parking lot up to the municipal gardens behind the huge cathedral. The spot, with a monument to Garibaldi, commands a pleasant view of the Tiber Valley and green hills beyond it.

The cathedral is a Renaissance structure with a Baroque façade built between 1482 and 1540 above and around the remains of an eleventh-century church with the tombs of the town's patron saints, St. Floridus and St. Amantius. An archaic round tower soaring above the cathedral is a survivor from the medieval construction.

The square municipal tower, now leaning slightly, stands opposite the cathedral. Market stalls offering ceramics, clothing, and many other items are lined up in the piazza between the church and the town hall.

One of the Vitelli buildings that are scattered around Città di Castello, the Palazzo Vitelli della Cannoniera, houses the civic picture gallery. The collection includes a *Madonna* that may be a work by the Sienese master Duccio di Buoninsegna (1255–1319), a *Martyrdom of St. Sebastian* and a church banner painted by Luca Signorelli (1441–1523), and many frescoes and paintings on wood or canvas by Umbrians and other artists from the fourteenth through nineteenth centuries. The palace, which overlooks the town's southern bulwarks, got its name from the gun emplacements that the Vitelli officers had positioned there. Città di Castello strategists realized early the advantages of artillery, but did not want their adversaries to make use of the newfangled firearms; one of the Vitelli condottieri, Paolo, had the eyes of captured enemy arquebusiers gouged out and their hands cut off.

The largest architectural complex in town consists of a Vitelli palazzo and a palazzina (little palace) across a park in the eastern salient of the walls; the railroad station is now outside.

A paleontological and historical museum, set up by the Association of the Upper Tiber Valley in a building near the cathedral, contains prehistoric material and Etruscan and Roman antiquities. The site of what is today Città di Castello was occupied by a town known in Roman times as Tifernum Tiberinum; it was destroyed by the Ostrogoths in the sixth century. Today, whenever officials or notables of Città di Castello resort to high-flown oratory, they call the citizenry Tifernians.

ORVIETO ▪

A grandiose Gothic cathedral, medieval towers and palaces, and a celebrated white wine that doesn't travel well and is best drunk on the spot are attractions of this Umbrian hilltown seventy-six miles northwest of Rome. Some neighborhoods with dark, severe stone houses don't seem to have changed much since the Middle Ages.

Travelers on the Rome-Florence highway or railway line suddenly glimpse the town, high up on a 600-foot tufa plateau, huddled around its majestic cathedral. The vision is particularly impressive after nightfall when the sheer brown walls of Orvieto's isolated rock pedestal are floodlit and friendly lights twinkle from above.

On Sundays many Romans flock to Orvieto to breathe its fresh air and have a look at its cathedral before a meal of *agnolotti*, the plump local pasta specialty, and lamb or venison, washed down with the slightly fizzy local wine. The visitor arrives at Orvieto Scalo, a modern jumble of hotels, restaurants, service stations, workshops, and residential housing around the railroad station in the wide, wine-producing valley of the Paglia River, a tributary of the Tiber. The cable cars that used to whisk people up to the old town no longer function. Instead, orange municipal buses link the railroad station with Cathedral Square near Orvieto's highest point (1,066 feet). There is also a steep footpath.

Long before the ancient Romans extended their power over central Italy, Orvieto was one of the twelve federated cities, and a religious center, of the Etruscan League. The ruins of an Etruscan temple and an Etruscan necropolis, or cemetery, flank the 2.5-mile highway (National Route No. 71) that winds from Orvieto's railroad station amid olive groves up to the historical city. Also visible, in some stretches, are the ravages from continual erosion of the porous rock on which Orvieto sits. Geologists fear that the tufa walls, nearly perpendicular in some sections, may give way further, but the long-projected works to consolidate them are slow.

On the plateau where over 20,000 people live today, the prevailing colors are the dark grays and browns of the buildings constructed with blocks of the local tufa. Often it is hard to figure where the rock base ends and manmade walls start.

The polychrome façade of the cathedral provides a happy contrast to the pervasive somberness. The red, green, blue, ivory, and gold of its mosaics are particularly resplendent in bright sunshine and mellow at sunset. The soaring, gabled front of the church, with a rose window and rich bas-reliefs in addition to the mosaics, was designed by an artist from Siena, Lorenzo Maitani. The three bronze doors are modern.

The tall church, with alternate horizontal layers of dark basalt and grayish-yellow limestone, is one of the foremost examples of the Italian Gothic style. Pope Urban IV, a Frenchman, ordered its construction as a memorial to a miracle that was said to have occurred in the nearby lakeside town of Bolsena in 1263.

A priest from Bohemia who was plagued by doubts as to whether the consecrated bread was really transformed into the body of Jesus during mass was officiating at the Church of Santa Cristina in Bolsena when the host began bleeding. Pope Urban IV instituted the Church festival of Corpus Christi, or Corpus Domini, as an annual commemoration of the miracle, and had the bloodstained linen cloth that the doubting priest had been using at mass in Bolsena brought to Orvieto, where the pontiff was then residing. The relic is kept in a tabernacle in a frescoed chapel at the left side of the cathedral. The gem-studded, gilt reliquary, a four-and-a-half-foot-high replica of the Maitani façade, is shown to the faithful at Easter and at Corpus Christi, which is celebrated with special solemnity in Orvieto every year.

The "New Chapel" at the right of the transept is decorated with wall and ceiling paintings by Fra Angelico, Luca Signorelli, and other masters. The famous frescoes, completed after 1500, powerfully illustrate such apocalyptic themes as the punishment of the damned at the end of the world. Michelangelo is said to have borrowed from Signorelli's Orvieto panels when he painted his *Last Judgment* in the Vatican's Sistine Chapel. Taped explanations of the sights in the cathedral can be heard in various languages at coin-operated machines affixed to its inside walls.

Off the right side of the cathedral façade rises the medieval Palace of the Popes. The massive battlemented building served as a refuge for several popes whenever they didn't feel safe in Rome. Today it is a museum with Etruscan and Roman antiquities, splendid church vestments, sculptures, and paintings (including detached frescoes) by Signorelli and other artists. More antiquities, especially ceramics, can be viewed in another, small museum (Museo Claudio Faina) in the Gothic palace opposite the front of the cathedral. The stores on and near Cathedral Square sell painted and glazed earthenware, a local product.

Have a look at the twelfth-century city hall off Corso Cavour, Orvieto's narrow main street, and the equally old Palazzo del Capitano, a Gothic headquarters of medieval city rulers, on a nearby square.

The Well of St. Patrick on the city's northwestern end is a curious reminder of Orvieto's old role as a papal fortress. Pope Clement VII, the Medici pontiff who had just escaped mortal danger in the Sack of Rome by the soldiery of Emperor Charles V in 1527, ordered his engineers to build a deep well that would assure enough water for Orvieto even during a prolonged siege. The result was a circular shaft, in part cut into the rock, in part enclosed by masonry, more than 200 feet deep and 16.5 feet wide.

Two spiral staircases with 248 steps each wind around the walls; mules carrying water buckets were driven down on one and up on the other so they wouldn't bump into one another. Well-traveled churchmen soon found a similarity with the Holy Wells at Struell, Northern Ireland, near St. Patrick's presumed grave, whence the popular name of the Orvieto pit. In idiomatic Italian the phrase *pozzo di San Patrizio* ("St. Patrick's well") means to this day something unfathomable.

The shaft, lit by seventy-two windows, can be visited. Admission is through the round red-brick wellhead in a little park with a fine view of the valley below. A plaque outside notes, in Latin, that "what nature grudged the defense, [human] diligence supplied"—namely water.

It is advisable to negotiate the winding stairs *before* sampling the Orvieto wine, which seems light but has been known to be treacherous.

TODI ▪

For someone who needs a luminous place to paint or a quiet place in which to write the great novel, this might be perfect. A small town that has almost no local industry, and to which the farmers of the surrounding Umbrian countryside are still important, Todi is full of quaint and noble sights, and from an altitude of 1,348 feet it looks out on green fields in the valleys and on hills with soft contours. The air is clean and the light strong, the food wholesome and the wine cheap; the townspeople—about 16,000—aren't jaded by too many tourists. Except for an annual antiques fair and some outdoor concerts in summer, little ever happens in Todi. The place seems lonesome, though Rome is only a ninety-minute drive away.

Todi's dominant hues are brown and gray. Outside and below its medieval walls a few clusters of bright houses and workshops have lately sprung up, but the town has not grown much in recent times and it has been spared the excrescences marring the outskirts of Umbrian cities like Orvieto and Perugia.

The arriving traveler ascends the hill of Todi on steep roads, and enters the town through one of three gates that bear the names of Rome (at the southwest), Perugia (north), and Orvieto (southeast). The walls linking the three gates form a triangle. They are the latest, and widest, of three different systems of fortifications that were built at various times in history. Penetrating into the town through the Rome Gate, which dates from the Middle Ages, after about 500 yards the visitor passes the Gate of the Chain, which the ancient Romans built; nearby, the remains of Roman town walls are visible. Another 120 yards behind it is the Porta Marzia, erected by the Etruscans around the fourth century B.C. as part of what is the town's oldest and narrowest defense belt that is still discernible.

Before the Etruscans conquered the settlement on the hill, Umbrians lived here, but little is known about these early inhabitants of the region. The Etruscan place-name, Tutere, which under the Romans became Tuder, was borrowed from the Umbrian language. Excavations in and around Todi during the last two centuries have brought to light a wealth of Etruscan artifacts. The so-called Mars of Todi, a third-century-B.C. bronze statue of a warrior with an Umbrian inscription, probably a votive offering, is in the Vatican's Etruscan Museum. Other finds from the Todi area are on display in the town's Etruscan-Roman Museum in the Palazzo del Popolo (People's Palace).

This massive, severe thirteenth-century building occupies the southeast of Piazza del Popolo, the heart of Todi and one of Italy's most impressive squares. The arcaded, battlemented palace—the town hall—in Lombard Gothic style with a sturdy corner tower comprises two distinct structures that were eventually linked by a stairway.

The south side of the piazza is taken up by another frowning, crenellated building, the Priors' Palace, which was the seat of the town's medieval rulers, and later of the papal governors after Todi had become a part of the Papal States. A tower with a trapezoidal base rises on the palace's left. Stone eagles—the proud bird is Todi's heraldic emblem—glower from the façades of both the People's Palace and the Priors' Palace.

The cathedral's rectangular façade, in white marble, closes the north side of the square. The church was started at the beginning of the twelfth century on a site where a Temple of Apollo is said to have stood. A broad stairway leads up to the cathedral front, with three portals and three rose windows, the middle one particularly elaborate. The short Gothic campanile on the right side of the façade looks as if funds had run out while it was being built. A patched-up roof was slapped on it in the nineteenth century.

Piazza Garibaldi, in a right angle to Piazza del Popolo and bordering on the south façade of the town hall, ends with a parapet that commands a sweeping vista of farmland and hills, characteristic Umbrian scenery.

Walk through winding streets from Piazza del Popolo southwest to Piazza della Repubblica below the fine portal in the unfinished façade of the Church of San Fortunato. The Gothic church encloses the tomb of the town's greatest son, Fra Jacopone da Todi (Jacopo Benedetti). Born around 1230, he became a Franciscan friar and won fame as a poet in Latin and in the Italian vernacular; the hymn "Stabat Mater Dolorosa" on the sorrows of the Virgin Mary by the Cross is attributed to him. An inscription in the church's crypt indicates the year of Jacopo's death as 1296, but according to the chronicles he died in 1306. Epigraphs can be wrong.

From the Church of San Fortunato proceed southeast to the few remnants of a medieval fortress, La Rocca (The Rock), in a park. The view from the site encompasses green ridges and hills to the left, and the Tiber Valley with farms and rows of poplars to the right.

In the left foreground below the former citadel is the pilgrimage church Santa Maria della Consolazione (Our Lady of Consolation), a large, harmonious edifice in the Renaissance style on a vast, open platform outside the medieval walls, half a mile southwest of the town center. It took ninety-nine years, from 1508 to 1607, and generations of architects to build the church on a base in the form of a Greek cross.

The cool elegance of the domed structure in pastel gray stone has led experts to speculate that Bramante, the architect who drew up the original plans for St. Peter's in Rome, contributed designs or advice to the Todi project. The cupola of Santa Maria della Consolazione, a detached curve on Todi's skyline, is visible for miles.

BRACCIANO ∎

A haughty fortress on a hill overlooking a large circular lake with Mount Soracte of classical fame as a backdrop, a medieval town crouching, as if seeking protection, beneath a flank of the mighty stronghold—the setting is dramatic. Only twenty-five miles northwest of the Italian capital, and renowned for its mild climate all year around, Bracciano has long been a place to which Romans like to go on a Sunday outing or to spend summer vacations. Lately the town of 15,000 has become somewhat unfashionable, and this may be the reason why its inhabitants are particularly cordial toward visitors, clearly eager to make them feel welcome.

Bracciano means above all the castle that Napoleone Orsini, then the chief of a princely family that for centuries was a dreaded force in papal Rome, had built between 1470 and 1481. The huge, menacing structure, with five towers over battlements, terraces, and ramparts, has the gray-brown color of the volcanic tufa that abounds in the region, which provided the main material for Napoleone's architects.

Guided half-hour tours of the castle start from the doorway in Piazza Mazzini at various times daily except Mondays. Visitors see splendid halls with beamed and stuccoed ceilings, frescoes and paintings by minor masters of the fifteenth and sixteenth centuries, and Renaissance furniture. The panorama from the windows and battlements is spectacular. On the horizon, northeast, is the isolated ridge of the 2,267-foot-high Mount Soracte, praised by Virgil and Horace.

The castle's Hall VI on the main floor, known as Isabella's Hall, is a reminder of a murky Renaissance tragedy in which four much-discussed personages died. Isabella de' Medici, a daughter of Grand Duke Cosimo I of Tuscany, became the wife of Prince Paolo Giordano Orsini, then the head of his powerful clan, and lived for some time in the Bracciano castle. Famed for her beauty, learning, and wit, Isabella "captivated every heart but her husband's," as a Florentine chronicler put it. She also had a reputation as a devourer of lovers. Bracciano rumormongers whispered that she would ask local youths to spend the night with her in the castle, and in the morning have them disappear forever by springing the trap door of a dungeon, an oubliette.

The story sounds like a posthumous slander floated by the Orsini faction after Prince Paolo Giordano strangled his wife in a villa near Florence in 1576. The prince then had the husband of his mistress, Vittoria Peretti, assassinated, and married her. Pope Sixtus V outlawed the murderer, and the prince died as an exile in Venice. Vittoria was stabbed to death at the orders of another Orsini. The chain of crimes heralded the ruin of the Orsini family. At the end of the seventeenth century the castle of Bracciano was bought for 386,300 scudi by another Roman aristocratic family, the Odescalchi, who are still its owners today.

Bracciano's *borgo medioevale*, the medieval part of town, nestles on a slope descending from what was once the castle's drawbridge, now a bridge in masonry over a moat, to an outer wall at the foot of the castle hill. A rather humdrum collegiate church in Baroque style occupies the highest point of the old town; nearby is "The Sentry," a lookout with a sweeping vista of the lake.

A walled private park with tall palms occupies the north side of the castle hill. A road leads down to the lakeshore with a few cafés, hotels, and a bathing beach. An outdoor market is held every morning in what was a moat, and a weekly fair takes over Piazza Mazzini on Wednesdays. The modern neighborhoods of Bracciano, pleasant and unassuming, spread between the old town and the railroad station, also on a slope.

Bracciano is a good base from which to explore the lake that is named after it, and the smaller shore communities. Lake Bracciano, 19 miles in circumference and 525 feet deep at the center, is the crater of a prehistoric volcano. Once celebrated for its succulent eel and other fish, pollution in the lake has recently caused alarm among environmentalists.

The ancient Romans had no such worries. Emperor Trajan built an aqueduct to bring water from the lake to the metropolis, and Pope Paul V had the old conduits restored in 1612. The water of his Acqua Paola system still feeds fountains on the Janiculum Hill and in the Vatican. Stories that eels from the lake that had slipped through damaged filters ended up in the pipes and clogged the fountains in St. Peter's Square at one time or another are probably apocryphal.

Trevignano, hugging the lake's northern shore for a mile, seven miles from Bracciano, is dominated by a hill with a ruined castle; the fortress was destroyed by Cesare Borgia, the son of Pope Alexander VI, in 1496. The recent discovery of an Etruscan cemetery in Trevignano seems to support the theory that the town is on the site of the lost Etruscan settlement of Sabate, which according to tradition was swallowed by the flooded lake. On the opposite side of the lake, 8.5 miles from Bracciano, the old village of Anguillara—the name is similar to the Italian word for "eel," *anguilla*—rises picturesquely on a promontory with a fine view. Filmmakers who need medieval scenery often choose Anguillara as a location.

VITERBO ▪

When Franco Zeffirelli needed a medieval location for his 1968 film *Romeo and Juliet*, he took his troupe to this city, fifty miles northwest of Rome, rather than to faraway Verona where Shakespeare had his young lovers meet their fate. Viterbo's San Pellegrino quarter in the south of the walled city is indeed a maze of narrow, cobblestoned streets around a picturesque piazza that doesn't seem to have changed much in centuries. Many houses are of gray volcanic *peperino* stone, have external staircases, and are linked with each other by archways. Artisans turn out handmade earthenware, polish furniture, or hammer metal in their workshops.

However, quite a number of people living in the ancient neighborhood, like many others among today's 60,000 or so Viterbans, commute every working day to jobs in Rome. On weekends, conversely, entire Roman families enjoy their second homes in Viterbo while hundreds of visitors from the capital crowd the city's eating places.

Viterbo's robust cuisine is a blend of Roman and Tuscan cooking, but its own specialty is believed to go back to Etruscan times. Called *acqua cotta* ("cooked water"), it is a thick soup of greens, codfish, eggs, bread, and spices. Viterbans drink white Colli Etruschi wines and sweet red Cannaiolo from the nearby hills.

The architecture of the city's churches and palaces reflects Viterbo's role as temporary residence and occasional refuge of popes during the Middle Ages; it claims to be the "third papal city" after Rome and Avignon. No fewer than seven pontiffs were elected here in the thirteenth century before Avignon in southern France became the seat of the papacy for sixty-seven years.

The longest interregnum between the death of a pontiff and the election of his successor saw the cardinals assembled in Viterbo for two years, nine months, and two days, from 1268 to 1271. The princes of the church had gathered in the city's Papal Palace, then brand-new, after the death of Pope Clement IV, and with their aides and retainers kept wining and dining at the expense of the townspeople between unsuccessful efforts at overcoming their deep divisions and agreeing on the person of a new pontiff. At last the exasperated Viterbans took matters into their own hands to end the costly reunion. When the cardinals were once again assembled in the large hall of their palace for another vote that would probably be as futile as all the innumerable preceding ones were, the citizenry locked them in, rationed their food and wine, and uncovered the roof.

The cardinals came quickly to a decision. The stalemate was broken, and they designated Teobaldo Visconti, who became Pope Gregory X. In 1274 the new head of the church issued an apostolic constitution, or ecclesiastical law, laying down procedures for the papal election that are essentially still in force. Clearly remembering the Viterbo impasse, Gregory X ruled that after the death of a pope the college of cardinals must be locked in "by key" (in Latin, *cum clave*) for the election of a successor; the term *conclave* is derived from the medieval Latin phrase.

In Viterbo's Papal Palace, on the right side of the cathedral, holes in the flooring of the great hall are shown, said to have been driven into the ground for the supports of makeshift awnings when the cardinals found themselves without a roof over their heads. Gregory X and the six other popes who were chosen in Viterbo blessed the townspeople from the palace's Gothic loggia.

The adjoining Cathedral of San Lorenzo was built in the twelfth and thirteenth centuries on top of the ruins of an Etruscan stronghold and sanctuary. The church and its Gothic campanile were modified in the sixteenth and seventeenth centuries; the Renaissance façade is in sharp contrast with the severe medieval architecture of the other buildings in Cathedral Square. The cathedral contains the tomb of Pope John XXI (pope from 1276 to 1277). Two other thirteenth-century pontiffs, Clement IV and Adrian V, are buried in the Church of San Francesco near the former castle of the popes (La Rocca, The Rock) in Viterbo's north.

Viterbo's main square in the middle of the city, northeast of the cathedral, is Piazza del Plebiscito, with the thirteenth-century Municipal Palace, a fifteenth-century bell tower, and other medieval and Renaissance buildings. The small Church of Sant'Angelo in the northeast corner of the piazza, whose original Romanesque architecture has been entirely altered, displays on its façade a Roman sarcophagus. According to popular belief, the stone coffin once contained the body of a maiden, the "Beautiful Galiana," who was murdered by a nobleman after she had spurned him; the legendary crime is said to have touched off a twelfth-century feud between aristocratic factions in Rome and Viterbo, which the Viterbans won.

From Piazza del Plebiscito the city's main street, Corso Italia, runs straight to the northeast, lined with stores and cafés. Local people still observe the rite of the evening promenade up and down the street. Another straight major street, Via Cavour, links the main square, from its south side, with Piazza Fontana Grande. That square is named after the largest fountain in Viterbo, erected in the Gothic style in the thirteenth century and fed by an aqueduct that the ancient Romans had built. Farther to the southeast is a Baroque gateway, the Porta Romana, through which the highway from Rome (Via Cassia) enters the old town. Parts of the walls and towers encircling the historical core go back to the Longobards in the early Middle Ages.

The Porta Romana is the starting point of a procession every year when Viterbo celebrates the feast day of the local saint, St. Rosa. She died in 1252, only seventeen years old, and her mummified body rests in a side chapel of the old Church of Santa Rosa in the city's northwest, rebuilt in the nineteenth century.

Still a child, St. Rosa became a member of the Third Order of St. Francis of Assisi, experienced mystical visions, and incited the Viterbans to resist the troops of Emperor Frederick II who were besieging their town in 1243. In the evening of each September 3 the image of the saint on top of an elaborate sixty-foot-high wooden tower (*macchina di Santa Rosa*) is carried in a torchlight parade from the Porta Romana to her church by sixty-two young men, dressed up in medieval garb with sashes as Cavaliers of St. Rosa.

Outside another gate in the town walls, the Porta della Verità, north of the Porta Romana, are a former thirteenth-century convent and church, Santa Maria della Verità (St. Mary of Truth), the seat of the Civic Museum. The church is remarkable for a *Marriage of the Virgin* and other frescoes by Lorenzo da Viterbo, a pupil of Piero della Francesca. The museum contains prehistoric, Etruscan, and Roman objects and a picture gallery with works by minor painters of various schools.

Many Viterbans and Romans swear by the curative powers of hot sulphur springs forming a bubbling pond, Il Bulicame, on a hill two miles southwest of the city. The road to these thermal waters passes the cathedral and leaves the old town through the Porta Faul. Roman ruins near the springs prove that the ancients maintained a bathing establishment there; Dante mentioned them, and Montaigne praised them for having relieved him of his kidney stones.

Other side trips from Viterbo include:

Madonna della Quercia (Our Lady of the Oak), a pilgrimage church at a 1,300-foot altitude two miles east of Viterbo, with a fine Renaissance portal and a Dominican convent with two cloisters. A good restaurant is nearby.

Bagnaia, a village beyond the Madonna della Quercia sanctuary, dominated by the Villa Lante, a Renaissance building with a pleasure garden, once the summer residence of a Roman aristocratic family.

Bomarzo, thirteen miles northeast of Viterbo, is a place for camera-happy tourists because of its Monster Garden in the Villa Orsini, another mansion of Roman nobility. Grotesque larger-than-life sculptures carved from *peperino* stone—mean-looking dogs, a whale, a sphinx, a mermaid, among others—emerge from weeds and bushes in a deep, narrow valley. A member of the Orsini family commissioned the extravaganza from an unknown landscape architect at the end of the sixteenth century. An enormous mask with a cavernous mouth carries the message: "You who travel the world to see its marvels, come here where horrid faces, elephants, lions, bears, ogres, and dragons await you!"

TARQUINIA ▪

The traveler on the Tyrrhenian coast from Rome to Pisa or Genoa sees the dark, jagged skyline of this town from afar. Tarquinia, sitting on a limestone plateau with cliffs facing north and west, 480 feet above the lonesome Maremma plain, still has eighteen towers dating from the Middle Ages. The foundations of twenty more such tall strongholds exist in scattered places; the town must have looked like a big, grim hedgehog on its hill in old times.

Most of today's visitors, however, don't come for the towers but for the intriguing people who lived here 2,500 years ago, the Etruscans, for their stupendous painted tombs, winged horses, and imported Greek pottery. Yet even without all these archaeological treasures Tarquinia would be worth the brief trip from Rome because it is one of the best-preserved medieval towns in central Italy.

Pigeons and other birds nest in the moss-covered tops of the ruined towers; the ground floors of some of these structures have been converted into cozy small apartments. A large portion of the 13,000 residents of Tarquinia live in dark-gray stone houses hundreds of years old that often have external stairways to the upper floors. The Via degli Archi (Street of the Archways) and the Via delle Torri (Street of the Towers) lead to a ruined castle that Countess Matilda of Tuscany is said to have built in the eleventh century. The domains of that redoubtable noblewoman once included also Tarquinia. (It was outside another of Matilda's castles, Canossa near Reggio nell' Emilia, that Emperor Henry IV humbly waited barefoot in the snow for three days in January 1077 before Pope Gregory VII, then the countess's guest, lifted his excommunication.)

In the Middle Ages Tarquinia, then called Corneto, counted more than fifty churches, of which a few can still be seen: Santa Maria in Castello, a soberly Romanesque edifice near the castle ruins, and the Romanesque-Gothic churches of Santa Maria Annunziata and San Pancrazio. The town's cathedral, modernized in the Baroque style, is remarkable only for the archaic little piazza in which it stands.

Tarquinia's sloping, irregular main square, with a fountain in front of the town hall, permits a glimpse of the sea down the straight, narrow main street, Il Corso. The view is much better from Piazza

Cavour at the lower end of the street; from terraces on either side one sees the coast with the Argentario promontory and the islands of Giglio and Giannutri.

Turning around, the visitor beholds, on the left, Tarquinia's pride, the Palazzo Vitelleschi, seat of the National Etruscan Museum. Named after a fifteenth-century cardinal who had the building enlarged, it has flamboyant tracery windows and an elegant top-floor loggia, showing the transition from the late Gothic to the early Renaissance style.

Prehistoric, Etruscan, and Greek antiquities fill the courtyard and the showrooms on three floors of the palazzo. There are sarcophagi with hunting and battle scenes in relief, tombstones, bronze helmets, earthenware, jewelry, and other artifacts. The exhibits that attract the most attention are a pair of winged horses in terra-cotta, found in 1938 at the nearby ruins of an Etruscan temple; many black-figured and red-figured Greek vases and an Egyptian vase of the eighth century B.C.; and several frescoes that were detached from the walls of tombs in the area to save them from dampness. The lively paintings show dancers, players of the double flute, wrestlers, mariners, and banqueters.

The museum will provide a guide for a visit to the painted tombs, which may take up to two hours. Tourists in cars may drive to the necropolis, or burial ground, on a ridge stretching from the eastern tip of the town toward the southeast for two miles. The 500-foot-high hillside, known as Monterozzi, is honeycombed with thousands of tombs and is indeed one of the main areas for studying the civilization of the Etruscans. The early Romans learned from that skilled people how to build a solid arch, how to grow grapes for wine, how to foretell the future from the entrails of animals, among other things.

Frescoes are conserved in a fairly good state in about sixty underground burial chambers, but only a few of them are shown to ordinary visitors; scholars may apply for a permit to see other tombs. The paintings that the Etruscans wanted their dead to have around them depict robust life on earth—feasting and dancing, hunting and fishing—as well as mythological scenes. The Etruscan painters were, the experts say, strongly influenced by Greek art. They were exuberant in the use of vivid colors: their leopards are yellow and spotted, their panthers blue, their horses sometimes green, and their dolphins pink.

The human figures in the tomb paintings aren't idealized, but represent well-nourished, sensual-looking women and dark-haired, paunchy men. Curiously, quite a few present-day Tarquinians bear a resemblance to the characters in the frescoes. The tomb art proves that, much though the Etruscans appear to have been preoccupied with the nether regions, they thoroughly enjoyed the pleasures of this world.

The utensils, vessels, helmets, coins, and jewelry that dead Etruscans were buried with for their journey to the underworld are no longer in the tombs. Much of this material was looted over many generations. What the tomb robbers (an age-old profession in this part of Italy) didn't spirit away is on display in the Palazzo Vitelleschi and in museums in Rome and elsewhere.

Etruscan Tarquinia occupied a 554-foot-high rocky hill that is separated from the necropolis by a valley and rises two miles northwest of the present town. Today little is to be seen on the barren site. Archaeologists have concluded from scattered remains that the ancient city's walls measured five miles in circumference, and have identified a rectangle of stone blocks on a terrace as the foundations of a 120-by-80-foot Etruscan temple. The winged horses in the museum were unearthed at this spot.

Tarquinia was surely one of the oldest Etruscan settlements, and probably the head of the Etruscan League of twelve city-states. Ruling long over a vast area, ancient Tarquinia wielded much influence in fledgling Rome, and gave the struggling shepherds' village on the Tiber two of its semi-mythical kings, or at least their names, Tarquinius Priscus and Tarquinius Superbus (they may have been one and the same person). After the Romans overthrew Tarquinius Superbus, according to tradition in 510 B.C., the Roman Republic was repeatedly at war with Tarquinia.

At the height of Tarquinia's power in the sixth and early fifth centuries B.C. its ships sailed from its seaport, six miles to the west, to Greece and Egypt, and brought back merchandise and strangers. Greek craftsmen and traders visited Tarquinia; vestiges of a Greek shrine with many votive offerings have recently been dug up at the nearby coast.

Rome eventually subdued Tarquinia along with all the other Etruscan cities. Goths, Longobards, and Saracens raided and destroyed Roman Tarquinia, and its survivors settled on the northwestern end of the necropolis ridge, the site of the present town. The walls of medieval Tarquinia, of which long stretches are still standing, were built in the ninth and tenth centuries. Modern neighborhoods have lately developed outside the walls and at the foot of the hill.

All over present-day Tarquinia there are business signs in mock-Etruscan lettering (the Etruscans borrowed their characters from the Greek alphabet): "Etruscan Bar," "Etruscan Tavern," and so forth. "Etruscan Ceramics" means modern earthenware, made locally.

Archaeologists and Etruscan buffs who want to spend some time in Tarquinia during the warm months may interrupt their scholarly pursuits and commute to Lido di Tarquinia. This is an unassuming beach strip with bathing concessions, hotels, second homes, and modest restaurants less than four miles from the hilltown and linked with it by public bus service.

PORTO SANTO STEFANO ▪

If you have a Roman friend who owns or has chartered a yacht, don't pass up an invitation for a maritime weekend. Chances are, the craft will be moored in Porto Santo Stefano or Port'Ercole on the promontory of Mount Argentario about 100 miles northwest of Rome. You will not only enjoy the delights of a cruise in the Tyrrhenian Sea but also become acquainted with the southernmost tip of Tuscany, an isolated corner of cliffs, ruined watchtowers and citadels, vines and olive trees on terraced slopes, pine groves, snug little harbors, lagoons teeming with fish, rocky islands, and the remnants of ancient civilizations.

Even without yachting, a trip to Mount Argentario may provide a welcome interlude between museum visits and other strenuous sight-seeing in Rome or Florence. Nature may have set Mount Argentario apart from the mainland, but it is now crowded during the hot months. Porto Santo Stefano has 14,000 year-round inhabitants; in July and August the population more than doubles.

Mount Argentario has become increasingly fashionable since the 1950s. Many well-to-do Romans have bought or built second homes here, and will make the two-hour trip to the promontory also on sunny winter weekends. From the twin bays of Porto Santo Stefano, row after row of new villas and condominiums climb up the hillsides.

Every summer, clumps of pine trees and large patches of underbrush go up in smoke, and there is almost always a suspicion that the fires are the work of arsonists in cahoots with real estate developers who crave more land for their bulldozers, cranes, and concrete mixers, and who hope to evade the zoning laws by destroying the vegetation.

In the late 1970s a conservationist majority elected Susanna (Suni) Agnelli, a sister of the president of the mighty Fiat motor company, mayor of Porto Santo Stefano; an ex-governor of the Bank of Italy, Guido Carli, became finance commissioner of the town. The mayor, a member of one of the wealthiest and most influential families in Italy, and the former chief of the nation's credit system were relative newcomers who had taken a liking to the town. While this elitist administration lasted, it strove to curb real estate speculation and to make Porto Santo Stefano a model community. By the mid-1980s a new coalition that was more responsive to local business interests had taken control of the Porto Santo Stefano town hall, and ex-Mayor Agnelli wrote a book about her experiences and frustrations as first citizen of the scenic place.

Despite its present role as a playground and marina for the rich, Porto Santo Stefano has not entirely lost its old flavor as a little Tyrrhenian outpost and port town. Local fishermen still sail their battered craft, although they may hire out to amateur skippers during the yachting season. Inhabitants of Giglio Island, off Mount Argentario, arrive on the daily boat to do their shopping. There is always something going on along the waterfront that hugs Porto Santo Stefano's double harbor.

The view embraces a wide bay at the right, with the Talamone peninsula eight miles to the north and a row of hills on the horizon, and Cape Lividonia, a rib of Mount Argentario, to the left. Proceeding on the waterfront in the direction of that cape one reaches a steep panoramic road that at various points and from little terraces on its shoulder affords enchanting vistas. The sea is hundreds of feet below, the road turns, and the tall granite mass of Giglio Island, ten miles to the southeast, comes into sight. The low-slung island of Giannutri can be made out farther to the south.

The motorist or hiker reaches a crossroads from which one may either descend by way of a saddle to return to Porto Santo Stefano or proceed to Port'Ercole on the east side of the promontory. Smaller than Porto Santo Stefano and with fewer permanent residents, Port'Ercole is built around a bay that is now essentially a marina, and it boasts an intimate deluxe hotel on the panoramic road.

Port'Ercole is much older than Porto Santo Stefano; it was the Portus Herculis (Hercules' harbor) of the ancient Romans, a convenient cove to put in to when the sea was rough. Porto Santo Stefano, instead, was founded in the seventeenth century by a Spanish governor of Mount Argentario. The promontory was for long periods a Spanish military base (*presidio*), and Spaniards built the fortresses whose ruins hulk above Porto Santo Stefano and Port'Ercole.

Access to the promontory from the mainland is over three roads on strips of land that look like causeways. Mount Argentario was actually an island in prehistoric times; the connections with the Maremma plain were formed naturally. According to scientists, tides and currents raised the three ribs of sand and earth in the shallow neck between Mount Argentario and what had been the former coast, and thus created a double lagoon with an average depth of five feet.

The traveler from Rome or Florence traverses the sparsely populated flatlands of the Maremma, once swampy and malarial, and in order to reach Porto Santo Stefano or Port'Ercole by the most convenient way crosses the middle of the lagoon. On this isthmus, first a third of a mile wide and then narrowing, one passes a walled town, Orbetello, that on its north and south looks out on the lagoon. The site has been inhabited for thousands of years and was once an Etruscan settlement. Orbetello's fortifications are from the Middle Ages and its cathedral is from the sixteenth century. Quite a few Italian families spend some weeks in Orbetello every summer.

It is much more prestigious, however, to own or rent a villa at Ansedonia, a cluster of mostly new constructions on a 374-foot conical hill from which the south tongue to Mount Argentario (Tombolo di Feniglia) stretches out. The hill commands a fine view of the sea and the promontory, but Ansedonia is a collection of fancy second residences rather than a permanent community, and it looks abandoned in winter. It was a bustling Etruscan town, Cosa, 2,500 years ago, as impressive ruins prove.

The Cosa of the Etruscans near where present-day Ansedonia occupies the hill was the seaport of the big and wealthy city of Vulci, now an expanse of ancient cemeteries and other archaeological remains in the Maremma plain twenty miles to the east. Stretches of Cosa's town walls, at some points thirty-six feet high, and ruins of houses can still be seen. Of particular interest is a system of canals, hewn deep into the rock, whereby the Etruscan engineers regulated the level of water in the Orbetello lagoon and in another body of water near the coast, six miles to the northeast, the Lagoon of Burano. This Tagliata Etrusca ("Etruscan cut") channel functions to this day.

Giglio Island, a one-hour boat ride from Porto Santo Stefano, is a nearly treeless rock, 8.5 square miles in area, luminous and wind-swept. Fewer than 2,000 people live on the island all year round, most of them near the harbor, Giglio Porto, while only a few still hold out in the old houses of Giglio Castello, a depopulated hamlet near a ruined citadel at an altitude of 1,634 feet. The islanders grow grapes for wine, tend their kitchen gardens, sail their fishing boats, and rent rooms to vacationers.

When I first visited Giglio Island in July 1950, there were only a handful of summer guests there who liked the solitude, the limpid sea, and the grand panorama, and didn't mind that the water taps ran dry and that electric light was more off than on. The composer Goffredo Petrassi was among them.

Islanders told me then that the fear of hostile incursions was in their bones. Dim memories of the many raids by Saracens and Barbary pirates that Giglio endured in centuries past linger on; in 1544 the redoubtable Algerian corsair Khair ad-Din, known as Barbarossa, paid the island an unwelcome visit, and his crews of ruffians carried 700 inhabitants off into slavery. Now the Gigliesi, as the islanders are called, dread the invasion of cars, for which there is no parking space. In July and August autos with Italian license plates are barred from coming ashore at Giglio Porto.

The island of Giannutri is a crescent-shaped rock about 200 feet above the sea, 1.5 square miles long. During the summer months, vacationers live in a tourist village, and the island's bay is a favorite with the yachting set, as it was already with ancient Greek mariners who found a refuge there during storms. Because of the island's outline the Greeks called it Artemisia, the abode of the moon goddess. The Greek goddess Artemis became Diana in ancient Rome, and her island was called Dianium. A family of Roman generals and officials, the Domitii Ahenobarbi, owned a villa there in the first century A.D.; its remains are still visible.

RIETI ∎

The story of the womanless men of Romulus banding together and snatching the wives and daughters of their rustic Sabine neighbors is probably a myth. However, if the Rape of the Sabine Women, that inspiration of voluptuous paintings, happened at all, it might have taken place in Rieti. The city, which the ancient Romans called Reate, was the capital of the Sabine people, and probably would have afforded the widest choice of desirable females.

Today's Romans still like to visit Rieti, although they usually bring their womenfolk with them now. Many Roman families own a *podere*, a little house with a few acres of land, near the Sabine city, and drive out to their property every weekend to see how the vines and the olive trees, usually tended by local help, are coming along. Thousands of skiers pass through Rieti in winter on their way to and from Terminillo, the 7,260-foot "house mountain of Rome," with its hotels, co-ops, and snowy slopes. The ski runs are only half an hour by car from Rieti, which itself can be reached from the Italian capital in an hour the way Roman motorists drive.

There is almost no trace of the old Sabines in present-day Rieti, if not in the bluff and cordial manner of the natives. There are no outstanding sights or celebrated art treasures either. Yet the Romans love the place, which means roots to many of them.

The foreign visitor too will be struck by Rieti's unaffected ways, its hearty food, simple wine, and the rural charms of its countryside, and may be secretly relieved that no frescoes in musty churches or archaeological finds in museums have to be inspected.

It's enough to linger awhile in Rieti's main square, Piazza Cesare Battisti, before or after a meal that may be a bit on the heavy side—say, fettuccine with mushrooms followed by roast pork and a rich cake.

The airy piazza is one of the more attractive public spaces in Italy, with a rhythm of its own. At an altitude of 1,319 feet it looks out on the hills circling the city, on a sloping municipal park, and deeper down, on the verdant valley of the Velino River, whose waters eventually flow into the Tiber.

The east side of the piazza is taken up by the huge cathedral with a Renaissance porch, a Romanesque campanile (whose bells seem particularly loud), and to the rear of its right side, a thirteenth-century bishop's palace resting on massive vaults.

Free-standing in the piazza are a hotel with a famous ground-floor café, espresso bar, confectioner's shop, and *gelateria*. The provincial administration is also housed in the square, in a building with a loggia overlooking the luxuriant municipal gardens.

Rieti is a city for leisurely strolling in its medieval streets. Many of the old patrician buildings are dilapidated and uninhabited; their owners have moved to Rome or into modern homes in Rieti's bucolic countryside. What may appeal to some visitors as romantic atmosphere, especially in some neighborhoods in the eastern part of this city of barely 40,000, may shock others as urban neglect. The old city walls are well preserved in long stretches on Rieti's north side and near the battlemented gate, the Porta d'Arce (Citadel Gate), in its east.

L'AQUILA ▪

The loftiest peak in the Apennines, the 9,581-foot-high Gran Sasso d'Italia (Great Rock of Italy), is visible from many points in this city in the heart of the rugged Abruzzo region. Other high mountains are all around. Many of the sloping streets in L'Aquila end with vistas of ridges and steep hillsides just a few miles away.

People from Rome and from lowlands elsewhere in central Italy once used to flock here in summer because L'Aquila, at an altitude between 2,000 and 2,300 feet, is airy and has pleasantly cool nights, but the rage now is beach vacations during the hot months. Here, the visitors arrive now mainly in winter to set out for the chair lifts and ski runs of Campo Imperatore in the Gran Sasso group.

The name L'Aquila means "The Eagle." Emperor Frederick II, whose father was a German and whose mother was a Norman, chose the bird of prey as the heraldic symbol of the city when he founded it around 1240 as an outpost to challenge the political ambitions of the papacy. The Latin motto underneath the eagle of L'Aquila reads: "*Immota manet,*" ("Steadfast it stays.")

It is a stern city. There is a streak of natural dignity in many Aquilans, even those of modest condition. Round faces, black hair, dark eyes—typical features of the Abruzzesi—prevail in the city's population of close to 70,000. Many Aquilans have moved to Rome lately, but they come back on weekends and in summer.

Legend ignores Frederick II and his antipapal moves, and has L'Aquila suddenly coming into existence with ninety-nine castles, ninety-nine fountains, ninety-nine churches, and ninety-nine squares. It is true that the emperor didn't create L'Aquila out of nothing, but as a union of several existing villages, hamlets, and castles. There may not have been exactly ninety-nine churches, but some sixty old church buildings can be counted in and around the city even today, some of them no longer used for religious services but occasionally for theatrical and ballet performances or as concert halls.

The magic number of ninety-nine—thirty-three times the number in the Trinity—occurs also in a much-photographed landmark near the railroad station and the small Church of San Vito on the southwestern outskirts of the city. The Fountain of Ninety-nine Spouts is a large trapezoidal trough of pink and white marble on a slope that is overgrown with shrubbery. Cool water, which is abundant in L'Aquila, flows from the mouths of ninety-nine marble masks and animal heads, each different, into a U-shaped trench. A plaque dates the fountain to 1272, but much of it appears to be Renaissance work, and some of the masks are from the seventeenth century.

In many other old buildings in L'Aquila it is equally hard to tell which wall or arch was erected at what time. The reason is that earthquakes are frequent in the geologically unsettled mountains of Abruzzo, and many structures have been repeatedly damaged, destroyed, repaired, and rebuilt over the centuries.

The old city walls are nevertheless still largely intact. They were built by the Spaniards, then ruling in Naples, after they had conquered L'Aquila in 1529. To defend their new possession, the Spaniards also constructed an imposing castle with four corner bastions as a northeastern salient of the city walls. The fortress, surrounded by a moat, commands a splendid view of the Gran Sasso, and is the seat of the National Museum of the Abruzzo. On display in the halls where the Spanish governors once lived are prehistoric and archaeological collections, paintings from various epochs, wood-carvings, and examples of jewelry and other local handicrafts. A fossil section includes the skeleton of an elephant that was dug up west of L'Aquila in 1954.

Strolling from the castle southward one reaches the arcaded Corso Federico II, the modern center of city life, with espresso bars and shops. The street leads to the vast, rectangular Cathedral Square, where an outdoor market is held on weekday mornings. L'Aquila was once a hub of the wool trade when the region's economy depended largely on its innumerable sheep. Today sheep-breeding no longer has the importance in the Abruzzo it used to have through the ages, and plenty of light industry has moved into the valleys. Many of the foodstuffs and textiles on sale in the markets and stores of L'Aquila are imported from other parts of Italy or from abroad.

L'Aquila's cathedral, which has been repaired several times after earthquakes, is undistinguished. Walk north from the cathedral, past the narrow and fashionable Via Tre Marie, to Piazza del Palazzo. A graceful yellow Renaissance building, flanked at its left by a gray bell tower, was the residence of Margaret of Parma, the illegitimate daughter of Emperor Charles V, after she had resigned as ruler of the Netherlands in 1576. The palace now houses public offices. The bronze statue that stands in front of it but looks to the side represents Sallust, the Roman historian who was born in what was Amiternum, now the village of San Vittorino, five miles northwest of L'Aquila, in 86 B.C.

From Piazza del Palazzo walk back to Corso and beyond it to the Church of San Bernardino of Siena. The saint, a zealous Franciscan preacher, died in L'Aquila in 1440, and is buried in the church. Architecturally, the edifice is remarkable above all for its façade, which was added to it in 1527; almost square, of mellow-hued stone, it has three tiers of columns separated by cornices.

Another noteworthy church, the Basilica of Santa Maria di Collemaggio, rises near a mental institution amid gardens on the southeastern outskirts of L'Aquila, beyond the old city walls. The building, with a Romanesque façade of white and pink marble and three rose windows, was started around 1280 at the urging of Pietro da Morrone, a hermit in the Abruzzo mountains who had a reputation for holiness. In 1294 the cardinals in Rome, to break a long deadlock after the death of Pope Nicholas IV, sent for the Abruzzo ascetic, then eighty years old, and forced the papal crown on him. The hermit styled himself Celestine V, but saintliness on the pontifical throne was no success. The unworldly old man felt unable to cope with political pressures and resigned after five months. He died, virtually a prisoner, in 1296. Dante, in a famous passage of *The Divine Comedy*, condemned Celestine V's "cowardice," but the Church canonized the hermit-pope in 1313.

The remains of St. Celestine are in a Renaissance tomb in a chapel off the right aisle of the church. The medieval precedent of St. Celestine's resignation, Dante's aspersion notwithstanding, is today cited as proof that a pontiff of the Roman Catholic Church may step down.

CHIETI ▪

It is up and down most of the time in this bustling provincial capital on a hill near the Adriatic coast. Maybe the exertion that over the ages has been a part of living in Chieti is one of the reasons for the proverbial drive of its inhabitants. While the city is not exactly overrun by foreign tourists, people whose roots are in Chieti can be found in many parts of the world, and they have usually made good.

Today it is so hard to find parking space in Chieti proper that travelers arriving by car will do well to leave the car at the foot of the hill—in Chieti Scalo (also known as Chieti Stazione), the suburb around the railroad station. Proceed by public bus on the tree-lined winding road that leads up to the city center.

You will find a few old buildings, façades and portals, and some ruins from antiquity that attest to Chieti's long history. However, the city's aspect and atmosphere are thoroughly modern. Its special attractions are its views from airy vantage points.

From a park near the cathedral and the city hall you can look, in the foreground, at the olive trees on the slopes of the hill on which Chieti sits and, deeper down, at the widening valley of the Pescara River with vineyards and rows of fruit trees between the neat fields. The sea, at the crowded city of Pescara, is only twelve miles to the east.

The vast public gardens at the opposite end of Chieti, the Villa Comunale, command a superb panorama of the Maiella Mountains, rising higher than 9,000 feet some twenty miles due south. These vistas alone would make a visit worthwhile, but there is more to Chieti.

The city's main street, along the crest of its 1,082-foot-high hill, is the lively Corso Marrucino. The name refers to the pre-Roman inhabitants who belonged to the tribe of the Marrucines, about whom scholars know little. The Romans called the hilltown Teate Marrucinorum (Teate of the Marrucines).

The National Museum of Antiquities in two buildings in the Villa Comunale gardens, one of the most important archaeological collections in the region, provides tantalizing glimpses of Marrucine life. Bronze and iron tools and other artifacts found in various grottoes in the area are on display, together with a statuette from the sixth century B.C. called the Warrior of Capistrano; it is named after the town between Chieti and L'Aquila where it was found. The museum contains also Greek and Roman statuary, inscriptions, coins, and marble fragments.

The remains of three small Roman temples, found in 1935 beneath two old chapels and a house, are visible north of the post office, near Corso Marrucino. An ancient Roman cistern can be seen on the hillside south of the city. This rainwater tank, 180 feet long and 43 feet wide and comprising several units, was cut out of the tufa slope in the first century A.D.

Chieti's cathedral, in a dominant position overlooking Piazza Vittorio Emanuele, dates from the early Middle Ages but has undergone extensive restoration work in various later epochs. The bell tower, built in the fourteenth and fifteenth centuries, was damaged by an earthquake in 1706, and restored only in 1935.

The city, its cathedral, and the episcopal residence played a part in Roman Catholic Church history when Gian Pietro Caraffa (or Carafa), a Neapolitan ascetic, was the stern archbishop of Chieti before becoming Pope Paul IV in 1555. He founded a religious order to curb moral laxity in Roman Catholicism and combat the Lutheran reform movement; from the Latin name of Chieti the priests of the new pugnacious church society became known as the Theatines.

No longer the fountainhead of religious rigorism, Chieti seems today on its way to becoming a center of higher learning. The city, with its population of 60,000, prides itself on its young university and has ambitious plans for expanding it.

SULMONA •

The earth shakes often in this part of the Abruzzo region, and several catastrophic quakes have been recorded here through the centuries. Each time the indomitable people of Sulmona have repaired the damages and rebuilt what has been destroyed. Today this resilient town of 25,000 inhabitants in a fertile trough surrounded by high mountains is ringed with factories and workshops that have brought new well-being but also made the approaches to Sulmona look scruffy. Penetrate into the historic center and you will be agreeably surprised.

The four letters in the town's coat of arms that the visitor sees on public buildings and on banners during festivities, SMPE, aren't the initials of one of the business firms that have installed themselves here lately. They stand for *"Sulmo mihi patria est"* ("Sulmona is my hometown"), a line from Ovid. The elegant poet of the Augustan age was indeed born here in 43 B.C., and would always praise his cool, well-watered native place while spending delicious years in Rome. He would die around A.D. 17 in faraway Tomis, a frontier fortress in what today is Rumania. Augustus had exiled him there because of an undisclosed "error," presumably an indiscretion involving a member of the imperial family, and Ovid would never again see his hometown, or his beloved Rome for that matter, despite all his sad pleas for pardon.

Many people in Sulmona today may have never read or heard a verse of Ovid, but nobody is allowed to ignore that he was the town's most illustrious son. The slightly curving main street that bisects the old neighborhoods is called Corso Ovidio; it opens midway into a square, Piazza Venti Settembre, with a modern bronze monument of Ovid. A high school named for Ovid and a fifteenth-century terracotta statue of the poet in the Civic Museum are other reminders that the author of the sophisticated *Ars Amatoria* (*The Art of Love*), which amused the ladies of the imperial court in Rome, had come from a one-horse town in the mountains of the rough interior.

Corso Ovidio, running from north to south, leads to Piazza Garibaldi, a vast square on a slightly lower level, beyond the arches of a medieval aqueduct with a great view toward east. The aqueduct feeds a graceful fifteenth-century waterworks, known as the Fountain

257

of the Old Man (Fontana del Vecchio), because the stone sculpture of a bearded head tops it. Another fountain is at the center of Piazza Garibaldi.

A teeming outdoor market is held in the panoramic square every Wednesday and Friday when villagers and mountaineers from the surroundings—some of the older ones still wearing the somber clothes of the Abruzzo region—come to town. On Easter Monday every year the piazza is the setting of a religious pageant in which the Resurrection of Jesus is reenacted.

A church overlooking Corso Ovidio from its west side, opposite the market square, is a compendium in stone of Sulmona's history of disasters. The church, called San Francesco della Scarpa (St. Francis of the Shoe) dates from the end of the thirteenth century; it suffered heavy damages in earthquakes in 1456, 1706, 1905, and 1933, and needed repairs also after countless minor tremors. It still stands, and its Romanesque portal, a remnant of the original structure, has withstood all shocks.

The quaint name of the church is due to a privilege enjoyed by the Franciscan friars who once lived in the adjacent convent: They were allowed to wear shoes, whereas other members of their order who hadn't gone soft continued clopping around in wooden pattens.

The most noteworthy building in Sulmona is the Palazzo dell'Annunziata in a central square that is named after it (Piazza dell'Annunziata). The complex, including a church, was started in 1320 by a religious brotherhood, the Confraternity of Penitents, and has long housed a hospital. Elements of Romanesque, Gothic, Renaissance, and Baroque styles blend happily in the monumental façade with three doorways. Sculptures adorning the front represent the Virgin Mary, to whom the building is dedicated, as well as angels, saints, and doctors of the Church. Four halls of the palace serve as the Civic Museum, which contains pre-Roman and Roman material, detached frescoes by painters of the Abruzzo region from the fourteenth through sixteenth centuries, and samples of local handicraft.

The cathedral in the north of the town's center was founded in the early Middle Ages, and also has been damaged repeatedly by earthquakes and fires. A modern sports stadium and a public park adjoin the church.

At the opposite, or southern, end of the old town the Porta Napoli (Naples Gate), from the fourteenth century, gives an idea of Sulmona's medieval fortifications. The massive Gothic doorway is said to have been the largest of the town's twelve gates. Sulmona belonged for centuries to the Kingdom of Naples.

From the east side of the market square and from many other points in Sulmona, which is for the most part level, the highest peaks of the Apennines can be seen: the Gran Sasso d'Italia (9,581 feet) to the north, the Maiella group with the 9,170-foot-high Mount Amaro (Bitter Mountain) to the east, and the Mount Morrone, 6,755 feet high, a little to the left of Mount Amaro.

At about 1,700 feet in altitude on the rocky slope of Mount Morrone is a chapel marking the spot where Pietro da Morrone, whose real name was Pietro Angeleri, was living when the cardinals forced the papacy on the saintly hermit, and had him crowned supreme pontiff of the church in L'Aquila. (About his short reign and his abdication, see L'Aquila.) Nearby are the remains of a Roman building that is popularly known as "Ovid's Villa," although there is no evidence that the poet ever lived in it.

Whether visitors choose Sulmona as their base for excursions to the wild mountains, or prefer to look at them from the market square, they will appreciate robust Abruzzo cuisine and wines. A potent local brew is *vino cotto* (cooked wine), a mixture of some Abruzzo vintage with boiled grape juice. Another Sulmona specialty, *confetti*, is marketed all over Italy. *Confetti* are almonds coated in sugar—white or in pastel pinks, blues, or greens—to be presented in fancy confections to friends at weddings, christenings, or first communions. Anyone receiving a box of *confetti* is supposed to reciprocate with a gift.

URBINO ▪

Here is Italy at its best. Raphael's birthplace, encircled by its old walls, is a time capsule tucked away in the hills near the upper Adriatic coast. It gives a clearer idea of how life in the Renaissance must have been than do all the monuments and museums in Florence and Rome.

A city of 17,000, Urbino is off the country's main lines of communication. To get there, the rail traveler from Rome, Florence, or Milan has to change trains at least once; the daily direct bus from

Rome takes four hours; the motorist on the old Via Flaminia (National Route No. 3) must watch out for the turnoff to Urbino near the picturesque Passo del Furlo (Furlo Gorge). Such relative remoteness accounts to some extent for the architectural integrity of Urbino's core and its snug atmosphere.

It is by no means a museum city, though. It is a thriving agricultural center—its olive oil is renowned—and the home of outstanding craftsmen. Urbino is also the seat of a small university. Young people troop to lecture halls or to the academic cafeteria near the cathedral, sit on the steps overlooking the central square (Piazza della Repubblica) in the afternoon to watch what's going on and to debate and flirt, and fill the taverns at night. Alas, they also ride noisy motor scooters until late at night, which didn't happen in the Renaissance.

In other respects the city is charmingly old-fashioned. Weather permitting, cabinetmakers and coppersmiths ply their trades outside their shops in narrow, sloping streets. The façades of many buildings haven't changed in centuries. The outdoor market at the center of town is lively with a lot of haggling, but there is little noise or confusion; one imagines that a produce market in the same place five centuries ago looked and sounded very much the same.

Watch the crowd there or at the fair that is held near the east wall every Saturday morning when many people from the outlying villages come to town: You will notice quite a number of young women whose features seem quotations from Raphael Madonnas—the round faces, the dark eyes, the sweetness. The master, painting in Rome, habitually reproduced the looks that had been familiar to him in early youth.

Raffaello Santi, or Sanzio, left Urbino, where he was born on April 6, 1483, when he was fourteen years old, but he never forgot the city and always spoke and wrote about it as *la patria*, the fatherland. Today all of his major works are elsewhere, as far away as Washington and Leningrad. The only undisputed Raphael in Urbino is *La Muta* ("the mute woman"), the portrait of an enigmatic-looking gentlewoman with an uncharacteristically elongated face, probably Giovanna della Rovere; it was painted in 1507 when Pope Julius II, formerly Giuliano della Rovere, was reigning in Rome. *La Muta* vanished in a sensational art theft in 1975 and was retrieved two years later; she is now a prisoner in a plexiglass cage in the Ducal Palace.

That irregular, massive yet graceful palace was built on uneven ground in the fifteenth century. It dominated the entire city and can be seen from far away; its western façade is particularly impressive. The structure, praised for the classical perfection of its architecture, is one of the finest Renaissance buildings in all of Italy. Over the doorways, under the windows, and on the heroic-size fireplaces in giant halls the inscription "FE DUX" recurs. It stands for the latinized name and title of the singular personage who had the palace built, Duke Federico of Montefeltro.

The duke, who died a year before Raphael was born, was a leader of troops for hire, a condottiere. As such, "he shared the political morality" of those who commanded mercenary bands in foreign wars, wrote Jacob Burckhardt, meaning that the duke was no stranger to the cynicism and frequent treachery of his class.

As ruler of his little city-state, Federico spent at home the money he earned abroad, and taxed his subjects as lightly as possible. In Urbino he had 500 people in his service; Giovanni Santi, Raphael's father, was the duke's court painter and poet. The ducal court functioned also as a military academy for the sons of other princely houses, and their education was a matter of honor for Federico. Urbino was then one of the most civilized places in Europe, rivaling in sophistication Florence, Ferrara, and Mantua.

The duke, a passionate collector, assembled a splendid library, treasuring manuscripts of classical texts. Visit the Ducal Palace with its library, the picture gallery (with paintings by Paolo Uccello, Piero della Francesca, and Luca Signorelli, in addition to *La Muta*), Federico's study with its admirable woodwork, the graceful main courtyard, and the huge staircases.

Another must is the house where Raphael was born, into a family of clearly comfortable means. In its beautiful patio the future darling of pontifical Rome is said to have mixed colors as a boy. The old brick building at 57 Via Raffaello Sanzio was restored in 1958.

Wander around Urbino's historic core with its palaces, churches, and graceful houses, and walk up one of the nearby hills for a look at the ramparts, the palace, and the town. A new quarter with modern housing, some hotels, a university hostel, and business buildings spreads beyond the walls to the north but is less jarring than the young suburban sprawl of many other historic Italian cities.

Urbino boasts no deluxe hotel or top restaurant, but visitors are nevertheless well taken care of. The eating places in town and in nearby villages feature the solid fare of the Marches region, with suckling pig a specialty, and its wines, mostly whites like the slightly sparkling Verdicchio.

If you want to stay longer, as well you might, inquire about lodgings in some private home. Urbino is geared to letting furnished quarters to members of the university faculty and students. Room and board with an Urbino family provides a chance for watching Italian provincial life from a special vantage point and picking up the language. There may be no better way.

ANCONA ∎

Travelers arriving from Rome or the north pass a disheveled stretch on the Adriatic coast where recent earth tremors that persisted over long periods have caused landslides and damaged or destroyed old buildings. The route then skirts a vast industrial park with oil tanks and clusters of shipping containers. After such unpromising sights, one finally gets a good look at Ancona, rising on two promontories and spreading in the low saddle between them. The best seaport on Italy's Adriatic coast between Venice and Bari, Ancona, a city of around 110,000, appears crowded and busy, with many new constructions amid gray nineteenth-century neighborhoods. It takes some time before the visitor discovers the city's ancient hillside core. Traffic is intense, and the motorist who ventures downtown has trouble finding parking space.

From the center of Ancona's mile-long, curving waterfront, passengers board the big car ferries that link Italy with Greece and Yugoslavia. In the southern section of the harbor hundreds of tightly packed fishing boats ride at anchor side by side when the sea is rough; they sail out again as soon as the Adriatic calms down.

The restaurants and taverns near the harbor are renowned for their fresh seafood. "Ancona soles" are much in demand throughout Italy, but nowhere are they as tasty as in the port city. Another local specialty is *brodetto*, a composition of various kinds of fish on toast, with vegetables, spices, and a white-wine sauce. Most of the catches that the Ancona fishing fleet brings in come from the waters near the Dalmation offshore islands across the Adriatic; every now and then

Yugoslavian authorities charge that the Italians are poaching on their fishing grounds, or even detain some vessel from Ancona and its crew until a fine is paid or diplomacy settles the incident.

Ancona's waterfront district is as salty as one might expect, but not as tough as are the corresponding sections of, say, Genoa or Naples. At its northern extremity rises a triumphal arch that the "Senate and People of Rome" erected in A.D. 115 to thank Emperor Trajan for having had the harbor repaired. The Latin inscription expresses gratitude also to the emperor's wife, the modest and popular Plotina, and to his sister Marciana. The Ancona monument is not as magnificent as Trajan's Arch in Benevento; the bronze statues of Trajan and his womenfolk that crowned it in antiquity have long vanished.

The harbor's northern breakwater, built by the ancient Romans, was extended on orders from Pope Clement XII (pope from 1730 to 1740), who has his own triumphal arch, designed by the architect Luigi Vanvitelli. Facing the sea, this Arco Clementino stands on the pier about 500 feet west of Trajan's Arch.

Up from the center of the waterfront and the landing place for the ferryboats is a little church, Santa Maria della Piazza, dating from the tenth century with a graceful façade from the early thirteenth century. South of it stands a late-Gothic building that wouldn't be out of place in Venice, the Loggia dei Mercanti, with a sculptured façade from the fifteenth century; it served as a meeting place for shipowners and traders.

Follow the streets that climb Mount Guasco in the north of the city to the cathedral, more than 200 feet above the sea. The domed edifice, begun in the twelfth century, combines Byzantine and Romanesque elements; its impressive front porch, with red stone lions supporting columns, is from the thirteenth century. The church occupies the site of an ancient temple of Venus, and a stone fragment from the pagan shrine can be seen in the courtyard of the Archbishop's Palace adjoining the cathedral. A great Renaissance pope, Pius II (see Pienza), died in the palace in 1464, disillusioned because the Christian powers would not heed his calls for a crusade against the Turks, who eleven years earlier had conquered Constantinople, a crusade that he himself had intended to lead.

Points near the cathedral command a vast panorama of the harbor and the sea. One understands why the Doric Greeks from Syracuse who settled here around the end of the fourth century B.C. called the promontory *ankon*, "the elbow": It juts out of the coast in such a way that the Adriatic is northeast and southwest of the city. Some residents of Ancona see the sun rising from and setting into the sea.

Romans and then Byzantines succeeded the Greeks as rulers of Ancona, and in the Middle Ages the harbor city was an independent maritime republic, rivaling Venice in the Levantine trade. The papacy took control under Clement VII in 1532.

A little below the cathedral, the sixteenth-century Palazzo Ferretti on Piazza del Senato is the seat of the National Museum of the Marches. The collection is noteworthy for its war chariots, helmets, shields, and other artifacts from the Bronze Age and Iron Age that were unearthed in the region; there are also Greek and Roman antiquities. The Municipal Picture Gallery in the nearby Palazzo Bosdari, dating from the thirteenth century, boasts Madonnas by Titian and Lorenzo Lotto, and various works by masters from Venetia, the Marches, and other Italian regions.

An old Jewish cemetery can be found near the sea below the eastern slope of Mount Guasco. For centuries Ancona has harbored a sizable Jewish community. The city's central districts, between Mount Guasco and the southern promontory, Mount Astagno, with an old fortress, developed in the nineteenth century and expanded eastward after World War I. New suburbs have clustered on the hilly outskirts since World War II. As capital of the Marches since the early 1970s, Ancona has taken on new administrative tasks and keeps growing.

PESARO ▪

To many Italians and foreigners this Adriatic seaport means just two and a half miles of broad, sandy beaches. Quite a few guests never leave the waterfront district with its regular streets, its hotels, bathing concessions, neon-festooned pizza and *gelato* havens, and discos. Yet Pesaro, which has 90,000 inhabitants in winter and a summer population of far more than 100,000, isn't only a part of the Adriatic Riviera, the fifty-five-mile strip from the south of Ravenna to Fano that earns several hundred million dollars every year and provides inexpensive seaside vacations for multitudes of Europeans.

The real Pesaro (the accent is on the first syllable), starting beyond the traffic-congested Viale della Vittoria a quarter of a mile from the seafront, deserves more than a cursory visit. It is an ancient city with narrow streets, artisans' workshops, many houses whose doors seem never to open, a Romanesque cathedral, a ducal palace and a fortress, and interesting museums. Majolica-making has been an important industry here since the Renaissance. Another local industry is cultivating the memory of Gioacchino Rossini.

The simple house where the composer was born in 1792 is on the street that leads from the city's heart, Piazza del Popolo, to the center of the beach quarter, Piazzale della Libertà; it is of course named Via Rossini. The city boasts also two Rossini monuments, a Rossini conservatory, and a Rossini theater.

The conservatory, or Liceo Rossini, occupies a vast old building, the Palazzo Macchirelli, in the city's south. A seated figure of the composer in the garden of the institution was commissioned in 1864 when Rossini was still alive and at the peak of his fame. After he died in Paris in 1868, his native city received a substantial bequest, which it used to build an auditorium for the conservatory.

The Teatro Rossini, farther south, is the setting of an annual Rossini Opera Festival in August and September, one of Italy's major seasonal music events. The elegant theater, with four tiers of red-and-gold boxes around the intimate main floor, was known as the Teatro del Sole (Theater of the Sun) until 1854, when it changed its name in honor of Pesaro's great native son.

A marble statue of Rossini adorns the side wall of the former Church of San Domenico, now the entrance to the post office, in the central Piazza del Popolo. The west side of the square is taken up by the low, arcaded Ducal Palace, now the headquarters of the Pesaro-Urbino provincial administration. The palace was built in the second half of the fifteenth century for the Sforza family who, after seizing power in Milan, were for a short time also lords of Pesaro.

In 1512 the city passed under the domination of the dukes of the della Rovere family after they had won possession of nearby Urbino. During some years toward the end of the sixteenth century Pesaro was a center of art and learning when Lucrezia d'Este, the accomplished wife of Duke Francesco Maria II della Rovere, held court in the Ducal Palace. In 1631 Pesaro was incorporated into the Pontifical State the way Urbino had been a little earlier.

The Ducal Palace was thoroughly restored in the 1920s. Medieval styles were then the architectural vogue in Fascist Italy, and the Pesaro palace was made to look archaic with forbidding battlements that it didn't originally have.

The Civic Museums, until 1936 in the Ducal Palace, are now housed in the eighteenth-century Palazzo Mosca, one block away. The collections consist of a picture gallery and a pottery section. The Pesaro Retable (Pala di Pesaro), painted in 1475 by the Venetian Giovanni Bellini, has pride of place. It is a vast altar shelf with a panel picturing the coronation of the Virgin Mary, and with representations of St. Terentius, the heavenly patron of Pesaro, St. Francis of Assisi, and other saints.

The majolicas in the museum include hundreds of objects from famous workshops in Pesaro, Urbino, Gubbio, Faenza, and other ceramics centers. Pesaro's archaeological museum, southeast of the Ducal Palace, contains material from a burial site of the eighth century B.C. discovered near Pesaro in 1892, as well as Etruscan, Greek, and Roman antiquities, and early-Christian reliefs.

The old cathedral, dating from the early Middle Ages and repeatedly rebuilt, stands on the right side of Via Rossini. To the east of it is the Rocca Costanza, a fifteenth-century fortress named after Costanzo Sforza, which more recently was used as a penitentiary.

For a gratifying side trip by car, cross the Foglia River in the east of the city and take the Panoramic Road, a seventeen-mile corniche, to the seaside resort of Gabicce Mare. From Monte San Bartolo, a 646-foot-high hill northwest of Pesaro, fine views of the city, its harbor, the Adriatic Sea with many fishing craft, and the vineyards and orchards of the green Foglia Valley can be enjoyed. The road passes near a castlelike country mansion on the western slope of the hill, the Villa Imperiale. It owes its name to the circumstance that Emperor Frederick III laid the cornerstone of the main building during a journey to Italy in 1469 as a favor to Alessandro Sforza.

The route, amid brushes and clumps of pine and cypress trees, passes the old hilltowns of Fiorenzuola di Focara and Castel di Mezzo before reaching Gabicce Monte, on another hill, and eventually Gabicce Mare at sea level. Another wooded height, Monte Ardizio, southeast of Pesaro, commands a vast panorama; a good road leads up to it from the city.

LORETO ∎

This pretty and curious town looking out on the Adriatic Sea from its hill was for centuries Europe's foremost shrine of the Virgin Mary. Popes, sovereigns, and millions of other Roman Catholics have made pilgrimages to Loreto. The Marian cult found new centers in Lourdes in the south of France during the nineteenth century and in Fatima, Portugal, during World War I, and these are now outshining Loreto; yet the Adriatic sanctuary still draws crowds of devotees all year round. Many Church-sponsored conventions and conferences are held here.

With some 10,000 permanent residents, Loreto lives almost entirely on the pilgrimage business. If you aren't particularly interested in religion, you may nevertheless want to visit the place because, unlike Lourdes or Fatima, it offers magnificent views, boasts remarkable Renaissance architecture and art, and possesses the charm of other small towns in the honest-to-goodness Marches region.

The fortunes of Loreto rest on a few chunks of medieval masonry and on a legend that Church authorities now say the faithful are not bound to believe because it is "no part of the patrimony of Revelation." According to the pious tale, the house in Nazareth where the Virgin Mary lived was miraculously transferred to what is now Loreto after the last Christian stronghold in the Holy Land, Acre, fell to the infidel in 1291: Flights of angels carried Mary's humble dwelling first to a hill near Fiume, now Rijeka, in Yugoslavia, then, in 1294, across the Adriatic to a laurel forest near the town of Recanati southeast of here, and eventually to the hill that is now the site of the shrine. The town that soon sprang up around the Holy House was first known as Villa Santa Maria, and later was called Loreto, the Italian form of the Latin lauretum, "laurel grove."

Some Roman Catholic scholars have lately advanced the theory that when the Crusaders were ousted from Palestine they took stones from the revered home of the Virgin in Nazareth with them, and that the relics somehow ended up on the Adriatic coast. A Greek or Byzantine family whom the Latins called Angelo or De Angelis are supposed to have been involved in shipping the stones to Italy, whence the story of the "angels." Whatever the origin of the legend, records show that pilgrims have flocked to the hillside shrine of the Virgin Mary since the beginning of the fourteenth century.

The Holy House stands today, enclosed by a richly decorated marble screen, beneath the dome of the basilica of Loreto in a noble building complex that suggests a little Vatican. In the heart of the sanctuary visitors see the remains of a one-room building, 12.5 by 28 feet, with walls of stones and, higher up, of bricks; patches of fourteenth-century frescoes representing Our Lady and the Apostles are visible on the inside. The vault in masonry that covers the ruin, 13.5 feet above the floor, is from the fifteenth century. Gilt oil lamps hang from the side walls. The marble altar is surmounted by a crowned statue of the Virgin Mary and the Infant Jesus in black cedar wood, clad in a long, gold-embroidered dalmatic. The sculpture is a modern replica of a very old one, which was destroyed in a fire in 1921.

Bramante, on orders from Pope Julius II (pope from 1502 to 1513), designed the marble structure around the Holy House, and such renowned artists as Andrea Sansovino and Antonio Sangallo the Younger executed it. With its half-columns, friezes, statues, and high reliefs the big white marble box containing the Holy House recalls ancient Roman triumphal arches. Its reliefs represent scenes from the Bible and the legends surrounding the Virgin Mary, from the creation of Adam to the arrival of the angels with the former dwelling of the mother of Jesus in Loreto. Some pilgrims move on their knees around the four sculptured outer walls of the marble chamber before entering the Holy House itself.

No fewer than thirteen sacristies and chapels open in a semicircle around the Holy House. They are all adorned with works of art, including frescoes by Melozzo da Forlì (1477) and Luca Signorelli (1479) and modern paintings. There is an American Chapel, decorated with contributions from the Western Hemisphere; other ones are known as the French, German, Swiss, Polish, and Spanish chapels. The basilica is so spacious also because it incorporates a fourteenth-century castle; from the outside its battlemented apse looks like a fortress. The church was started in 1468 in the late-Gothic style, and famous architects during the following centuries made additions and changes. Giuliano da Sangallo, who worked with Raphael on St. Peter's in Rome, completed the dome of the Loreto church in 1500. The Baroque campanile with its bulbous cupola on the left side of the Renaissance façade (1583) was designed by Luigi Vanvitelli in 1751.

Two big clocks on the basilica's façade indicate, on the left, the astronomical time and, on the right, the hours for the canonical prayers (matins, prime, terce, and so on). In front of the church, to the left of the main portal, is a bronze statue of Pope Sixtus V (pope from 1585 to 1590), the zealous Franciscan who raised Loreto to the rank of a town. The seated pontiff imperiously looks out on Loreto's main square, Piazza della Madonna, which has some of the majesty of the great public spaces in Rome or Venice. The square is enclosed on the east by the façade of the basilica, on the south by a former Jesuit college known as the Illyrian Palace, and on the north and west by the Apostolic Palace. The latter, L-shaped with two tiers of arcades, was built in the sixteenth century by Andrea Sansovino and Antonio Sangallo the Younger. A part of the building is occupied by a museum with Flemish tapestries after Raphael, Renaissance ceramics, and paintings by Lorenzo Lotto, the Venetian master who died in Loreto in 1556, and by other artists. A monumental fountain in the piazza is the work of seventeenth-century sculptors from nearby Recanati.

Ecclesiastically, Loreto is supervised directly by the Holy See through a resident apostolic delegate with the rank of an archbishop. Parts of the Apostolic and Illyrian palaces have lately become a convention center with a modern auditorium for 1,000 persons and accommodations for 500 overnight guests.

To reach Piazza della Madonna, the basilica, and the Holy House, visitors ascend the sloping streets of the town, which are lined with hotels, hostels, rooming houses, and shops offering religious articles. Forbidding ramparts surround the sanctuary hill. In front of the stately doorway that leads through the west wing of the Apostolic Palace into the main square is a large bronze statue of Pope John XXIII, who made a pilgrimage to Loreto in 1962. After that pontiff's death his longtime secretary, Monsignor Loris Capovilla, became apostolic delegate at the shrine, and in that capacity was able to welcome Pope John Paul II during two visits.

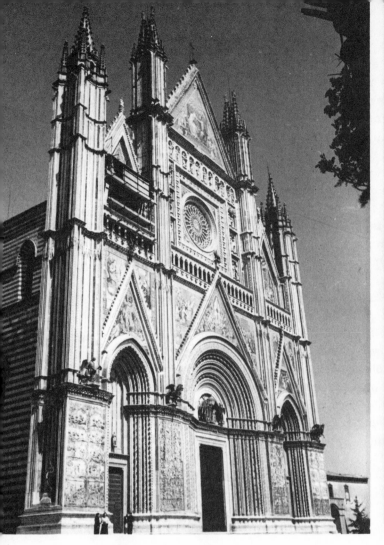

ABOVE: *Orvieto, cathedral*

OPPOSITE, TOP: *Assisi*

OPPOSITE, BOTTOM: *Todi, cathedral*

LEFT: Tarquinia

BELOW: Viterbo

OPPOSITE, TOP:
Cathedral at Macerata

BOTTOM: Beach
at Pesaro

Ascoli Piceno, Piazza del Popolo

No small asset of Loreto is its panorama: From some spots along the ramparts one sees the Adriatic Sea, the coastline, and the Apennines.

MACERATA ▪

An outdoor *Aida* in a tranquil hillside city in a remote corner of the Marches region, thirty miles south of the Adriatic seaport of Ancona, seems a hopeless, maybe even comical, provincial affair. Yet summer after summer Macerata, hardly ever in the news during the rest of the year, manages to compete with the open-air galas in the Baths of Caracalla in Rome and the Arena of Verona, luring opera fans from far away to listen to big-name singers who didn't mind the long trip either.

Money from ambitious local sponsors and skillful promotion have helped make the operatic season in Macerata, a few weeks in July and August, a recurrent success. However, the basic reason the city is able to tackle Verdi and Donizetti and sign up ballet dancers from La Scala in Milan is that it possesses the perfect setting for al fresco opera and shows. It is the Sferisterio, or ball court, a huge amphitheater originally built for a game related to jai alai and pelota.

Long before soccer fever started gripping Italy toward the end of the nineteenth century, a different kind of ball-playing was the rage, and game courts dotted the country. Macerata, spurred by small-town pride or boredom, must have decided it wanted the biggest ball court of them all.

The Napoleonic wars had ended, Europe was under the stifling guardianship of the Holy Alliance of sovereigns, and Macerata—which for a few heady years had belonged to the French-ruled Kingdom of Italy—was again a part of the Papal States. Ennui was reigning supreme, and ball-playing was one of the few permitted evasions from the all-enveloping torpor. A hundred wealthy citizens of Macerata banded together to finance the construction of a game court that would cause envy far and wide.

Selected by the hundred citizens, the architect Ireneo Aleandri built the Sferisterio between 1821 and 1829. Whatever else may be said about the stone structure, which is 270 feet long and 105 feet

276

wide, it is solid. Aleandri's eclectic style owes a little to the Colosseum in Rome, to Palladio, and to the Bernini of St. Peter's Square. The construction is composed of a high, straight wall facing a colonnade with two tiers of boxes for spectators and a top gallery, and two similar, though shorter, colonnades on either side.

After court games had slipped out of fashion and soccer had become Italy's national ritual, the Sferisterio of Macerata was occasionally used for track-and-field contests, fairs, political rallies, and religious ceremonies. One promoter even tried to bring bullfights to the Marches, but the corrida in the former ballpark didn't catch on. Italy isn't matador country.

About a century after the Sferisterio was built, a local devotee of bel canto, Count Pieralberto Conti, had the idea of staging grand opera in the game court. Since then the Macerata performances have become an institution, drawing audiences above all from the seaside resorts along the Adriatic coast, but also from more distant places.

Out-of-town spectators who arrive—as most of them do—on the road from Civitanova Marche on the Adriatic coast, seventeen miles to the east, find the Sferisterio at their right immediately after entering the inner city at the Porta Picena (Picene Gate). Like Ascoli Piceno, nearly sixty miles to the south, and other centers in the area, Macerata cultivates the dim memories of the Picenes, the pre-Roman forefathers of the Marchigiani.

Even during other times of the year when Macerata offers no opera, a visit can be recommended to anyone who could use a little rest and would like to savor the old-fashioned placidity of Italian provincial life.

At an altitude of 1,020 feet on the heights between the valleys of the Potenza and Chienti rivers, the city looks out on pleasant scenery of green hills and nearby mountains. Fresh breezes are frequent. With a population of 45,000, Macerata is the administrative capital of a largely rural province, and boasts one of the lowest crime rates in Italy. Pretty girls walk up and down the tree-lined streets along the old town walls during the daily promenade before dinnertime. Young people are conspicuous in the city, the seat of a small law school.

A 180-foot-high bell tower, built in 1558, rises in Macerata's central square, Piazza della Libertà, with the city hall and the provincial administration headquarters. The nearby Loggia dei Mercanti

(Merchants' Loggia) from the beginning of the sixteenth century provides a touch of Tuscan Renaissance sophistication.

The Civic Museum in the Piazza Vittorio Veneto, linked with the central square by the lively Corso della Repubblica, contains a musical and theatrical section illustrating Macerata's artistic dreams. Next door is a curious collection of twenty-two coaches from the seventeenth to the early nineteenth centuries. The cathedral, near the northeastern town gate, is unremarkable, and there are no other interesting sights except a few palazzi.

However, the air is clean, the panorama charming, and the cuisine generous in the way of the Marches region. Above all, the local people go out of their way to make strangers feel welcome.

ASCOLI PICENO ■

A massive double gate from the first century B.C. greets the traveler who arrives from Rome on the Via Salaria, the ancient road of the salt trade; the next sight is a neighborhood of huddling gray-brown houses with many square towers from the Middle Ages. If, instead, you come on the motorway from the Adriatic coast, you pass, at some distance, a modern high-security prison, then an industrial park, and eventually a bright new suburb with high-rises, supermarkets, schools, and a Viale Kennedy.

Between the twin gateway (Porta Gemina) and the high-rises is ensconced one of the most genuinely Italian cities. The Tronto and Castellano rivers hug old Ascoli Piceno, and join in the space between it and the new satellite town on its east. Hills and mountains surround the city like a green amphitheater open to the sea, twenty-two miles away.

"We are really well-off here," the saleslady at the pet shop in the main piazza told me with a smile when I complimented her on her city after buying some birdseed. "We are so fortunate; I wouldn't live anywhere else." One can hear similar remarks quite often in Ascoli Piceno. Contentedness is a rare plant, but it seems to be thriving here. The city is an attractive place with lively squares, old monuments, and fine—though not world-famous—works of art.

The Ascolani, as its inhabitants are called, have a reputation for being fun-loving, cordial, and straightforward; they are reliable and skilled workers, but they won't think twice about taking off a couple of hours or more to do honor to their wholesome food, excellent wine, and locally distilled anisette, and they like a chat in the piazza.

Ascoli Piceno, with a population of 60,000, has achieved unostentatious prosperity through a healthy balance of farm-based activities and small to medium-sized industries all around. The city has a well-equipped hillside recreation area, and the Adriatic beaches can be reached in half an hour.

The irregularly oblong main square, Piazza dell'Arringo (Assembly Square) has through the ages been the city's political and religious center. Its east side is taken up by the cathedral and, to its left, a free-standing baptistery. The cathedral is dedicated to St. Emidius (Emidio) of Trier, the first bishop of Ascoli Piceno, who, according to tradition, was beheaded in 309; his remains are believed to rest in the Roman sarcophagus in the church's crypt. The martyr is revered throughout the Marches as a protector from the scourge of earthquakes. If an Italian has Emidio (as distinct from Emilio) as his first name, you may be pretty sure he is from Ascoli Piceno or some other place in the Marches.

Work on the cathedral went on for centuries. Begun in Romanesque style in the Middle Ages, it has a Gothic nave and a Renaissance façade that was never completed. The interior was thoroughly redecorated at the end of the nineteenth century. One of Ascoli Piceno's main treasures is in a chapel in the right aisle: an altarpiece in various panels (a polyptych), painted by Carlo Crivelli, a Venetian, in 1473.

The baptistery, probably built on the remains of a much older structure, has retained its twelfth-century Romanesque sternness, with a square base and an octagonal upper part.

The bishop's palace and the city hall, side by side, are in a right angle to the cathedral in the piazza's south. The two buildings went up during the Middle Ages, and were extensively altered later. In the twelfth century the arcaded ground floor of the city hall was the Loggia of the Assembly, where the guilds of Ascoli Piceno held their meetings.

The picture gallery on the second and third floors of the city hall comprises 400 items. Among them are many works by Cola dell'Amatrice, a sixteenth-century artist from the mountains of the interior who did much of his work in Ascoli Piceno and probably designed the façade of its cathedral. There are also two triptychs by Crivelli, a damaged *Vision of St. Francis* by Titian, and paintings by Canaletto, Reni, Van Dyck, and Rubens. Another exhibit, an embroidered cope made in England in the thirteenth century, has a curious history: It was presented to the local cathedral by Pope Nicholas IV in 1288, was stolen in 1902, was acquired by John Pierpont Morgan and eventually returned by him to Ascoli Piceno.

The archaeological museum in the Palazzo Panichi, also in Piazza dell'Arringo, displays Iron Age artifacts linked to the Picenes, a warlike people—perhaps of Dalmation or Balkan origin—who inhabited the Marches long before the Roman conquest. The memory of the Picenes is perpetuated in the name of the city, Ascoli Piceno. The other material in the museum includes Roman mosaic floors unearthed during construction work in the city center.

From the Piazza dell'Arringo it is a short walk northwest to the city's ever-pulsating heart, Piazza del Popolo (People's Square). Motor traffic is banned from this spacious rectangular square full of character, crowded with strollers, gossiping groups, and many youngsters late in the morning and again early in the evening. Elegant Renaissance arcades and battlemented edifices line much of the piazza. The prevailing hue is the honey color of travertine, the porous stone used in many old buildings in Ascoli Piceno, the "City of Travertine."

The sturdy thirteenth-century Palazzo dei Capitani del Popolo (Palace of the People's Leaders), with a clock tower, rises at the south side of the piazza. Facing the palace across the square is the Gothic Church of San Francesco, which was started in the thirteenth century and completed, with a cupola, 200 years later. Note a large crucifix in multicolored, sculpted wood at the left side of the interior. A crenellated Merchants' Loggia was added to the austere church in the Renaissance.

Behind the Church of San Francesco, on Via del Trivio, is an old convent with two cloisters. Vegetables and fruits from the countryside are arrayed on stands in the open-air market that is held in the larger one of the two arcaded courtyards every weekday morning.

The merchants' center of medieval Ascoli Piceno was in Piazza Ventidio Basso, a little to the northwest of the Church of San Francesco. The campanile of the church on the square's northeast side, which is dedicated to Saints Vincent and Anastasius, is from the tenth century. The building's geometric façade, carrying sixty-four square stone panels with traces of long-faded frescoes, was built in the fifteenth century. The water from a little well in the church's crypt was said to heal leprosy. Another church, San Pietro Martire (St. Peter Martyr), from the thirteenth century, stands across the piazza.

Northwest of the two churches is a gate in the old city walls, the Porta Solestà, leading to a stone bridge from the time of Emperor Augustus that is still in use; it spans the Tronto eighty feet above the water.

The Baroque façade of a chapel built into a cave under a precipice on the northern outskirts of the city, beyond the Tronto, is said to mark catacombs where the first Christians buried their dead. The sanctuary is known as Sant'Emidio alle Grotte (St. Emidius at the Grottoes).

The Colle di San Marco, a 2,250-foot hill in the city's south, owes its name to another little old church wedged into living rock, San Marco. From a distance the flat church, above chestnut trees, blends into the cliff as if it were a natural outgrowth.

An eight-mile-long road with many bends leads up to the hill with its villas, hotels, tennis courts, children's playground, swimming pool, and plenty of space for other outdoor activities or plain loafing. Pine, chestnut, and oak trees abound, and many points command good views of the Adriatic Sea.

Soccer is the overriding passion of many Ascolani, and a home game of the local team is a big event in the city. Carnival time sees a lot of revelry in the historic neighborhoods, and the entire city seems to participate in its folklore festival in summer. The four-day affair culminates on the first Sunday in August with a pageant that brings visitors from all over the Marches. Nearly 1,000 people in medieval costumes—civic dignitaries, representatives of the city districts, riders in armor, flag bearers, and pretty damsels—parade through the old streets and in the squares. Eventually, horsemanship is displayed in the stadium in the city's east, near a ruined medieval fortress on the Castellano River, when riders in turn attack with their long lances a dummy on a pole, "the Moor." Ascoli Piceno's Quintana pageant is, like Arezzo's Joust of the Saracen in September, a remote echo of the Crusades.

ANZIO ▪

Many middle-class Roman families spend summers in this old seaside town, but it is far less fashionable now than it used to be in classical times, when Antium was an elegant resort renowned for its marble temples and sumptuous villas. Cicero liked the place, and so did several Roman emperors who lived later. Caligula and Nero were born here. Today little of the ancient splendor is left. Anzio has grown with Nettuno, a former occasional lair of Saracen pirates a few miles to the northeast, into one continuous strip of modern, often garish, housing with several hotels and pensions and many seafood restaurants.

Yet Anzio is not just another of the concrete-and-neon sprawls that at present disfigure all too many stretches of Italy's coastlines. Some authentic maritime atmosphere lingers in its little harbor; the decaying old estates on the level pine-green hillside overlooking the bay speak of the past grandeur of the princely houses of the Albani, Aldobrandini, and Borghese; and behind the coastal shelf are the military cemeteries with white-marked graves of many thousands of United States, British, and German soldiers who died during World War II battles around the Anzio beachhead.

Anzio is the seaport closest to Rome, only thirty-five miles south-east of the city. (Small boats can put in at Fiumicino, where one of the arms of the Tiber River empties into the sea near Leonardo da Vinci International Airport; though only seventeen miles from the center of Rome, it's a landing place rather than a real harbor.) It takes less than an hour to reach Anzio by railroad or car from the capital. Many Romans have second homes here, and some come to sail their boats or yachts. The restaurants are filled on fair-weather weekends also in winter. Anzio's permanent population is close to 30,000.

The present seaport, built under Pope Innocent XII toward the end of the seventeenth century, is protected by the spur of a prom-ontory and a mole extending it farther out into the sea. An old papal stronghold with dark gray battlements secured the harbor entrance; it is a relic today.

A small fleet of fishing boats still uses Anzio as its home port, but catches are poor. The Tyrrhenian Sea is notoriously polluted; many species of fish have disappeared from it. Much of the seafood offered in the local stores, markets, and restaurants comes by refrigerator truck from the Adriatic coast, from Sicily, or from even farther away.

Anzio harbor has a small marina, and provides docking for the hydrofoil services to the offshore islands of Ponza (travel time seventy minutes), Ventotene (two hours), and Ischia (three hours), and to Naples (four hours).

In ancient times Anzio's harbor was west of the spur that juts out into the sea. Remains of a circular breakwater that Emperor Nero had built can still be seen, especially when the sea is choppy. Ancient Roman brickwork is visible below the cliff on which a lighthouse rises and in other places. Caves below the lighthouse, known as the Grottoes of Nero, were the approaches to an imperial villa. A narrow, sandy strip along what was the waterfront of Nero's harbor is now Anzio's bathing beach, very crowded in summer; there is bathing also farther east, toward Nettuno. A scowling fortress hovering over Nettuno was built at the orders of Alexander VI, the Borgia pope. During the nineteenth century another pope, Pius IX, spent several vacations in Anzio, as a waterfront plaque recalls. The coast beyond Nettuno becomes lonesome. The panorama, toward southeast, embraces the promontory of Monte Circeo, rising from the sea like a rocky island.

The Anzio-Nettuno area saw heavy fighting during winter and spring 1944. A large British-American force landed here on January 22, 1944, in an attempt at hastening the liberation of Nazi-occupied Rome. Complete surprise of the enemy was achieved, but the German divisions in central Italy regrouped quickly and counterattacked. The Germans managed to contain the beachhead until the Allied units that had advanced from southern Italy broke through near Cassino and linked up with the Anzio troops in May. Rome fell to the Allies soon afterward, on June 4, 1944.

Today the stillness of the war cemeteries with their rows after rows of graves poignantly contrasts with the bustle of the nearby seashore. The parks in the higher parts of Anzio and Nettuno, and the ridge above the twin towns with its solemn pine groves and palms have retained some of the lush charm that Cicero praised. So close to Rome, Anzio seems much more southern and Mediterranean than the capital.

TERRACINA ▪

Coming from Rome you cross a fertile plain, the former Pontine Marshes, for more than thirty miles. You approach a promontory on your left and see to your right what looks like a rocky island but is actually another promontory, Monte Circeo, the mountain of the enchantress Circe, abruptly rising from a flat tip of the mainland.

The two masses of rock—Monte Circeo dark on the horizon and the limestone cliffs above Terracina bright in the sun—on either side of a wide bay mark the gateway to the *Mezzagiorno*, Italy's land of the hot noonday. Fig and orange trees, palms, oleanders, and prickly pears proclaim: This is the south. You are almost halfway between Rome and Naples.

There are two sharply distinct Terracinas. One is a medieval town on the hillside, built smack into the ruins of a place where in antiquity well-to-do Romans had their houses and temples. At the foot of the promontory a modern town and beach resort spread out, with an elegant shore promenade reaching out for more than a mile toward Monte Circeo.

Many Italian families spend summer vacations here. Other guests stay for longer periods in rest homes in the modern neighborhoods and on the hillside. There is plenty of sunshine all year; the frequent breezes are welcome in summer but feel sharp in the cold season.

Ancient town walls with massive gateways survive on the slope; their foundations go back to the Volscians who were fierce enemies of Rome before they were subdued and Romanized in the fourth century B.C. Terracina is proud of its pugnacious forbears, as a Via dei Volsci (Street of the Volscians) attests. The Volscians called Anxur what was to become Tarracina in Roman times and Terracina later.

Steep paths lead from the new and old towns to the 748-foot summit of the promontory, which is topped by a horizontal structure with many arches. Looking from afar like a fortress half dug into the rock, the flat, arcaded ruin was a platform from which a temple rose, 110 feet long and 65 feet wide. With its tall marble columns it must have been a magnificent sight, especially from the sea. Scholars still debate whether Venus or Jupiter was venerated in the sanctuary.

The panorama from the old temple site is well worth the climb, which may take thirty to forty minutes. From right to left, one sees the Alban Hills and the Pontine plain, three-peaked Monte Circeo, farther out the offshore islands of the Ponza archipelago, the bay of Terracina, the town of Sperlonga, the promontory of Gaeta, the island of Ventotene, and on the horizon, isle of Ischia.

The slope of the hill is stony, with patches of low grass and just one solitary pine tree. Old Terracina below has a smug charm, with cats sunning on patches of Roman mosaic, stairways over ancient brickwork, and narrow alleys opening into Piazza del Municipio, the marketplace (*forum*) of the Roman settlement. The pavement in the pretty square is in large part the same as that on which the ancient Romans trod.

The cathedral in the piazza is an amalgam of substantial remains of a temple dedicated to the deified Emperor Augustus, and medieval architecture. A twelfth-century mosaic on the architrave of the vestibule, resting on eleven ancient columns, seems of Byzantine or even Egyptian inspiration; Kandinsky or Klee might have designed it, so modern does it seem now.

Terracina's city hall, at a right angle to the cathedral, is a building in sand-colored limestone that went up in 1950 in an eclectic style that satisfactorily blends into the ancient piazza. The vestibule commands a view of modern Terracina and the bay below. It contains a marble copy of a statue of Sophocles, the Greek tragic poet, that was found in Terracina in 1839 and is now treasured by the Lateran Museum in Rome. Even the copy justifies the sculpture's fame as one of the most accomplished ancient portrait statues. A plaque on the left wall of the city hall lobby was put up in 1962 to mark the 175th anniversary of Goethe's passage through Terracina during his Italian journey; he liked the town.

By far the larger part of Terracina's present population of 38,000 lives today in the modern districts in the lowlands. The new town is bisected by a canal in which scores of fishing boats are moored when they aren't out in the bay. Some of the day's catch is on sale in the outdoor market held along the canal every weekday.

Terracina's main drag and shopping street, always with much traffic, is Via Roma. It's really just another name for the ancient Via Appia, the road from Rome to Capua that Appius Claudius Caecus, as censor, built in 312 B.C. The highway was later extended to what is now Brindisi and became a lifeline of the Roman empire, *Regina Viarum*, Queen of the Roads. It is still serviceable after more than 2,000 years.

On leaving Rome, the Via Appia, now National Route No. 7, climbs the Alban Hills and descends into what for centuries was malarial swampland and is now good farm soil. The Pontine Marshes between the Alban Hills and Terracina were repeatedly reclaimed in history by Roman emperors and various popes. Again and again the swamps and the fever came back until, in the 1920s, an elaborate drainage system transformed the former marshland into the present expanse of truck farms, olive groves, and vineyards, an undeniable achievement of the Mussolini dictatorship. Terracina restaurants are good places to sample the succulent artichokes and other produce now growing in the former swamps.

The highway that Appius Claudius built rose from the plains to cross the promontory; many traces of the ancient road are still visible on the slopes above Terracina. Later, a level road variant skirting the bay was constructed. The needed space was gained by cutting a part of the promontory where it plunged into the sea, thereby creating a shoreside corridor. Rocks by the thousands of tons had to be removed for the purpose.

At the eastern end of Terracina, where Via Roma becomes Route No. 7 again, it passes a smooth perpendicular cliff. Just below eye level the eighteen-inch-high letters CXX—meaning the numeral 120—are engraved in the rock face. Other numbers in imperious Latin characters can be read higher up. The ancient contractors marked the depth of the hillside their slaves had cut away at intervals of ten Roman feet, starting from the top; the wall they thus created is 115 feet high. (The Roman foot, 296 millimeters, was slightly smaller than our standard foot, 304.8 millimeters.)

The rock face at the exit of Terracina is an eloquent testimonial to ancient engineering skill and to the backbreaking labor of the Roman slaves.

5
THE
MEZZOGIORNO

Southern Italy

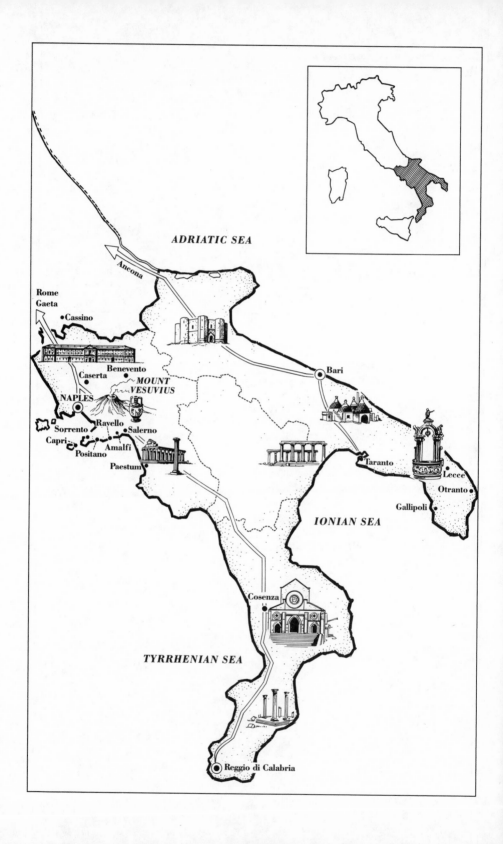

ADRIATIC SEA

Ancona

Rome
Gaeta
• Cassino

Benevento
Caserta
NAPLES
Sorrento   Ravello
Capri   Salerno
Positano   Amalfi
Paestum

MOUNT
VESUVIUS

Bari

Taranto
Lecce
Otranto
Gallipoli

IONIAN SEA

Cosenza

TYRRHENIAN SEA

Reggio di Calabria

■

The lower part of the Apennine peninsula, everything south of an imaginary line between Gaeta on the Tyrrhenian Sea and Vasto on the Adriatic, is called by Italians the *Mezzogiorno*. The word translates literally as "midday," conjuring up images of a landscape torpidly lazing in the noontime sun. Actually, parts of Italy's deep south are quite lively, and it is not always hot there either—during the winter months the mountain villages of Calabria, the toe of the peninsular boot, may be cut off from the outside world for days and even weeks by snowdrifts.

The *Mezzogiorno*, however, does keep the promise of its radiant name most of the time along its shores and on the plains of Apulia (Puglia or le Puglie), Italy's heel. The spectacular Gulf of Naples is often blessed with cloudless skies and balmy weather when the north of the country is tormented by storms or shrouded in fog. The traveler who follows the craggy coastline south of Naples is enchanted by the bays and coves following one another, with palms, oleander, and other subtropical vegetation crowning the cliffs, grapevines growing on ledges hewn out of the rock, and white houses looking out on the picture-postcard blue of the sea.

On the other hand, the Sila massif in the interior of Calabria is almost Alpine in character. Apulia with its olive groves, vast vineyards, cotton and tobacco plantations, and cornfields is an important agricultural area, as are the truck farms around Naples.

Naples, the main center of the deep south, is the nation's third largest city (after Rome and Milan). Today it is so crowded, disheveled, and overwhelmed by traffic that visitors to the region may prefer to make a smaller city or town their headquarters. This section suggests several options.

Legacies from a 2,500-year history are numerous in the south. The well-preserved Doric temples of luminous Paestum, south of Salerno, and the dead Greek-Roman city of Pompeii near Naples are

289

foremost among them. The Greeks had colonized vast territories in southern Italy long before the Romans conquered all of the peninsula. Later, Visigoths, Ostrogoths, Byzantines, Longobards, Arabs, Normans, Frenchmen, Germans, Turks, and Spaniards invaded chunks of the *Mezzogiorno* at various times. The Kingdom of Naples, under various dynasties, governed most of southern Italy for centuries until the kingdom collapsed like a decayed building when Giuseppe Garibaldi, the national hero, attacked it with a force of only about 1,000 men in 1860.

Up to this day the *Mezzogiorno* remains in many respects different from the rest of the nation. The traveler will notice new roads, bridges, industrial plants, hotels, and housing developments, yet the average incomes in the south are lower than those in the industrial north, and patches of the *Mezzogiorno* are among Europe's underdeveloped areas. Despite the overgrown urban centers in southern Italy, its economy is still predominantly farm-based. The southern way of life, especially in the interior, is as archaic as the black kerchiefs of the women. Southern society is to a degree still patriarchal. The economic, social, and cultural differences between north and south— between Parma and Cosenza, for instance—are summed up by the catch phrase "the two Italys." Government efforts to close the gap between the unequal halves of the nation have been going on for well over a century, but much remains to be done.

The socioeconomic backwardness of the deep south is not necessarily all negative. The foreigner will, for instance, find great courtesy everywhere, coupled with remarkable dignity. Life seems calmer in a southern town than in the northern cities with their hordes of commuters, and many southerners appear to enjoy their leisure.

The dialects of the *Mezzogiorno* may be impenetrable even to one who reads and understands Italian. There will, however, often be somebody around who speaks English—maybe an elderly man who after many years in the United States has come back to the old country to live on his Social Security check. (Since the late nineteenth century millions of southern Italians have emigrated to the Western Hemisphere and elsewhere around the world; rare is the inhabitant of the *Mezzogiorno* who does not have a relative in Brooklyn, Hoboken, Chicago, or San Francisco.)

Emigrants from this region took their cuisine with them, so that much of what is known and appreciated as Italian food around the world comes from the *Mezzogiorno*. Expect to find spaghetti in its many familiar variations on every restaurant menu in southern Italy; mozzarella and pizza too are ubiquitous. Fresh salads and other vegetables, grown locally in abundance, are served all year around. There is usually a rich choice of seafood; all cooking is done preferably with olive oil. The espresso coffee of the Naples area is praised as the best in all of Italy. Recommended wines are red Gragnano from the slopes of Mount Vesuvius, and the whites and reds from the isles of Capri and Ischia.

Of the places described in this section, Gaeta and Cassino (including the Abbey of Monte Cassino) can be visited in a one-day trip from either Rome or Naples. Caserta may be reached from the center of Naples in less than an hour. Add another hour to proceed to Benevento. The isle of Capri, the lovely coastal towns of Sorrento, Positano, Amalfi, and Ravello, and the city of Salerno form a circuit that no visitor should miss; side trips to Pompeii and Paestum are musts. Cosenza in Calabria and, especially, Lecce in Apulia are more remote (from Cosenza one can proceed readily to Messina in Sicily), but either city represents a distinctive facet of the *Mezzogiorno*.

GAETA ▪

This old fortress town on a tumulus-shaped promontory, often besieged through the centuries, guards one of the finest natural harbors in Italy, now a base of the United States Sixth Fleet. American warships assigned to duty in the Mediterranean, occasionally even giant aircraft carriers, ride at anchor in the bay that sweeps majestically from Gaeta toward Formia, a town some five miles to the northeast. United States Navy personnel on shore leave and their relatives are usually among the guests of the hotels in the radiant, scenic area. During the bathing season many Italian families spend vacations here, attracted by the fine sand of Serapo, south of the Gaeta promontory where salt flats once extended, or by the wide beaches of Formia, which is less expensive than Serapo.

The naval activities off Gaeta and Formia, as well as the presence of tankers that sail regularly into the bay to supply a big oil refinery near Formia with crude, may enliven the maritime scene, but they also contribute to the pollution of the offshore waters.

The 548-foot-high promontory of Gaeta and the mountain range that rises abruptly north of Formia combine into a natural amphitheater hugging the bay. Vineyards, olive plantations, and orange trees on the slopes close to the seashore complete the thoroughly Mediterranean setting. The waterfront restaurants serve seafood (that comes from anywhere but the picturesque bay they face), Neapolitan pasta and pizza, and the generous wines of the Campania region. Small wonder that the seamen of the Sixth Fleet like Gaeta.

For hundreds of years Italy's deep south officially started here. Gaeta's fortifications were meant to defend the northern frontier of the Kingdom of Naples first, and the Kingdom of the Two Sicilies, which was ruled from Naples, later. When Pope Pius IX was driven out of Rome by a rebellion in 1848 he took refuge in Gaeta, a guest of the king in Naples, and remained here until 1850. The conquest of Gaeta by Piedmontese troops in 1861 marked the end of the Bourbon kings' reign in southern Italy, and led to the proclamation of the unified Kingdom of Italy under the House of Savoy, which was to last until 1946 when King Umberto II was ousted by a plebiscite and Italy became a republic.

That Gaeta and Formia were popular already in antiquity is proved by the remains of several Roman villas, some of which must have been sumptuous places built out into the sea. Cicero is believed to have owned a house near what was then Formiae. It may have been there or thereabout that henchmen of Mark Anthony slew the statesman and writer in 43 B.C., although the Roman ruins that are pointed out locally as those of the villa or the tomb of Cicero date from later, imperial times.

A weather-beaten ruin on top of the promontory of Gaeta, popularly called the Torre d'Orlando (Roland's Tower) is really the tomb of a Roman consul, L. Munatius Plancus, a friend of Caesar and founder of the northern colonies that were to become Lyons in France and Basel in Switzerland. After Caesar's assassination he first sided with Mark Anthony but after a quarrel with Cleopatra wisely went over to Octavian's side. It was Munatius Plancus who formally proposed the title Augustus for the winner, Octavian. The associate of the first Roman emperor is said to have chosen his burial site himself; while he was alive, he must have particularly liked the panorama from the hill, which on clear days embraces Cape Misenum near Naples and the isle of Ischia. Remains of a Roman amphitheater and a theater at the foot of the promontory prove that Gaeta was a town of some importance in ancient times.

Normans in the Middle Ages and Spaniards later fortified Gaeta, and the Bourbon kings of Naples strengthened its ramparts and walls. After Italy's unification the old fortress served for a long time as a military prison. After World War II a pair of Nazi war criminals, SS Lieutenant Colonel Herbert Kappler and SS Major Walter Reder, who had been sentenced to life imprisonment for atrocities committed in Italy, were held in the Gaeta citadel for many years until their sentences were commuted.

Today some of Gaeta's 25,000 inhabitants still live in the medieval houses close to the fortifications, but entire new neighborhoods have sprung up along the road skirting the bay. The cathedral in the old town is remarkable for its campanile from the twelfth century; the tower's Norman-Sicilian style, with porcelain ornaments, betrays Arab influences. A 700-year-old candlestick (the learned term is *paschal candelabrum*) in the church, resting on four stone lions, is unusual for its size and for the bas-reliefs on it, which picture scenes from the lives of Jesus and of St. Erasmus, the martyr and patron saint of seamen who is believed to have been buried in Formia.

The bay of Gaeta sees a religious procession on boats every August 15, the Roman Catholic feast of the Assumption of the Virgin Mary. Hotels and restaurants are particularly crowded that time of the year, the height of Italy's holiday season. In the winter months there is always a chance of some day with warm sunshine in Gaeta and Formia.

CASSINO ▪

This entirely modern town in the wide valley of the Rapido River between Rome and Naples, hospitable though it is, would hardly be worth a visit by a traveler who doesn't have all that much time were it not for its fate during World War II and its proximity to the Benedictine abbey of Monte Cassino, a historic landmark of Christianity.

What through the centuries used to be Cassino, slightly to the north of the present town of 10,000, was completely destroyed in a chain of fierce battles between the German divisions that were holding their Gustav Line across central Italy and the Allied forces that had been advancing from the south. Building after building in old Cassino was pulverized as the attackers encountered stubborn Nazi resistance from fall 1943 to May 1944.

A somber climax in the struggle occurred on February 15, 1944, when Allied air squadrons bombed the ancient monastery on the dominant hill east of Cassino, reducing it to rubble. The action was prompted by information that German troops were using the abbey for military purposes. This has since then been proved untrue. The contention by the Benedictine Order that only the abbot with twelve monks and hundreds of refugees from nearby towns and villages were in the vast building at the time has found general acceptance. The bombing was a tragic mistake.

A pamphlet now available at the souvenir stand of the rebuilt abbey quotes Professor Herbert Bloch, a historian of Harvard University, as terming the 1944 air attack "forever a disgrace to our time and civilization."

The bombing of Monte Cassino did not resolve anything, for that matter. Another three months of bitter fighting were to pass before Allied troops, mainly Polish and Moroccan units, opened the road to Rome and made the liberation of the Italian capital from Nazi occupation possible.

The visitor who arrives in Cassino today will lose little time in the new town, and proceed on a road winding up to the 1,703-foot-high Monte Cassino hill. Military cemeteries all around are reminders of the toll, in many thousands of lives, that the fighting in 1943 and 1944 took. Cassino itself has long been rebuilt and has become a minor industrial center, assembling Fiat cars and turning out other products. Although the town has remained in the valley, new houses dot the lower slopes.

The abbey of Monte Cassino, founded by St. Benedict of Nursia (today's town of Norcia, near Spoleto) in 529, had been destroyed three times before World War II—in 581 by Longobard invaders, in 883 by Saracen raiders, and in 1349 by an earthquake. As it did after the earlier disasters, it has risen again also after the 1944 bombing, and is visible, over sheer rock, for many miles. According to the monks, 900,000 cubic yards of debris had to be carted away before reconstruction could start.

The cost was borne mainly by the Italian state. The Benedictines say that during World War II President Roosevelt promised an American contribution for the rebuilding of their monastery, but that no reparation funds ever came from the United States government.

The massive new abbey with its sober architecture houses now only a few monks because the number of novices who enroll in the Benedictine Order has fallen off, as have vocations to the Roman Catholic priesthood generally. The historic treasure of Monte Cassino—its many thousand priceless manuscripts, books, and documents that make up one of the greatest medieval collections in the world—is almost intact. The abbey's library had been removed to Rome for safekeeping before the bombing of February 1944.

Today the monks show visitors some of the library's illuminated parchments and early prints. A beacon of scholarship in the Dark Ages, the monastery that St. Benedict founded is credited with having preserved some texts from antiquity, such as portions of writings by Tacitus, that otherwise would have been lost forever.

The monk who serves as a guide for visitors to the abbey will tell them that the tomb with the urn containing the remains of St. Benedict and his sister, St. Scholastica, was not harmed in the 1944 bombing. The windows of the castlelike monastery command panoramic views of the mountains and valleys all around, the setting of one of the major battles of World War II.

CASERTA ■

This city of 70,000 people wouldn't stand out from among the scruffy suburbs, townships, and slums in the crowded plains around Naples if it were not for its astonishing monument to royal extravagance. The 1,200-room castle and huge park of Caserta are a little older than the United States, having been created, at enormous cost, between 1752 and 1774. The Bourbon king of Naples, Charles III, whose backward, impoverished, and bandit-ridden domains included southern Italy and Sicily, wanted a new residence that could compare with the Château of Versailles belonging to his royal cousins in France. He was never to live in the castle of Caserta because in 1759, long before it was completed, he became King of Spain and moved to Madrid.

Later Bourbon kings of Naples held court in Caserta, and so did Joachim Murat, Napoleon's brother-in-law, when he ruled over southern Italy from 1808 to 1815. After Italy's unification the castle of Caserta, one of the largest buildings in the nation, became a white elephant. It housed military units, and during the last stages of World War II in Italy was taken over by the Allied High Command. At present, parts of the castle are used by a government school for civil servants and for scientific and cultural gatherings. The former royal apartments are a museum, and the park is open to the public; both charge admission fees except on certain days.

The visitor arriving by railroad sees the castle across a vast open square in front of the station. Left and right are two lower, curving buildings, former military barracks. The main façade of the former royal residence, in an unsmiling version of the Baroque style, has thirty-seven windows on each of its five floors and three large doorways; there are four big courtyards and thirty-four staircases in the edifice.

To build his Neapolitan Versailles, King Charles III called a famous architect, Luigi Vanvitelli, from Rome. The labor force placed at Vanvitelli's disposal included convicts and Moslem slaves whom Neapolitan warships had brought home from their actions against Barbary pirates.

The heraldic fleur-de-lys pattern of French royalty recurs inside the castle's main floor. A grandiose throne room with a frescoed, vaulted ceiling and eight huge doors conveys an idea of the splendor with which the Bourbons surrounded themselves. In the many halls and rooms that may also be visited there are inlaid marble floors, massive gilt chandeliers, many eighteenth- and nineteenth-century paintings, vases, mirrors, canopied beds, and other period furniture.

The gardens are so vast that some visitors hire a horse-drawn cab or rent bicycles at the entrance. From the rear of the castle one looks out across the park at an artificial cascade, fed by an aqueduct, and mythological statuary on a slope almost two miles distant. Well-kept lawns, shady side alleys, cypresses, fountains, fishponds, sculptures, and false ruins combine into a theatrical landscape where highborn Rococo ladies disguised as shepherdesses might frolic. The immense vistas are particularly gratifying in a region of Italy where uncluttered spaces are rare.

On leaving the castle and turning left you find yourself back in a typically cramped southern Italian city with many new buildings on traffic-choked streets in a grid. Soldiers abound in the evening hours because Caserta has various barracks. The storefront premises of a "social club" in the circular Piazza Dante in the middle of the city are populated with men only.

What today is Caserta used to be a village, La Torre, before the castle was built. The royal residence brought new people and money, and the rapidly growing community took the name of a medieval town 1,310 feet high on a hill five miles to the northeast. Caserta Vecchia (Old Caserta), as it is now called, seems well on its way to becoming a ghost town. Many decrepit houses are abandoned. A ruined eleventh-century castle and tower and an isolated Romanesque cathedral show that the original Caserta once had some importance.

History buffs may want to take a side trip to the Capua of the ancients, a city that was famous for its luxury, pride, and political fickleness, and which has given its name to the entire region, Campania. It was in the pleasurable winter quarters of Capua that Hannibal's troops after their victory at Cannae in 216 B.C. lost their former discipline and mettle, a turning point in the Second Punic War. Capua saw also the start of an uprising in 72 B.C. when a Thracian, Spartacus, escaped from the local gladiators' school and gathered many runaway slaves around him. The rebels soon held sway over much of southern Italy, but the Roman legions eventually smashed the revolt and crucified thousands of slaves.

The site of classical *dolce vita* and of a Servile War is now called Santa Maria Capua Vetere, a market town in the fertile plain 3.5 miles northwest of Caserta. It can be reached by train or by the public buses that frequently leave from the square in front of the former royal castle. An amphitheater now in ruins on the outskirts of Santa Maria Capua Vetere, 618 by 459 feet, was the largest structure of its kind anywhere before the Colosseum was built in Rome in the first century of our era.

Many archaeological finds can be seen, together with examples of medieval art, in the Campanian Museum in modern Capua, another 3.5 miles northwest of Santa Maria Capua Vetere, also a railroad and bus stop. The small town was founded by refugees from ancient Capua after Saracen raiders destroyed it in the ninth century. Modern Capua lies on the Volturno, southern Italy's longest river. United States forces crossed the Volturno in heavy fighting in October 1943.

BENEVENTO ▪

Visitors may have left Naples only an hour earlier, but will feel they have traveled a long distance. True, there are plenty of men of all ages who don't seem to have anything to do in the narrow, crowded streets of Benevento too, as there are in Naples, but the mood is different; the Neapolitan drama—often comedy, at times sudden tragedy—and Neapolitan volubility are missing here. Beneventans are made of sterner stuff than Neapolitans.

Benevento, unlike Naples, looks thoroughly landlocked. The city sits on a plateau between two rivers, the Calore and the Sabato, in the middle of a fertile plain with Apennine ranges, covered with snow in winter, all around. One mountain to the southwest, the 4,095-foot Taburno, has suggested the shape of a sleeping beauty (*la bella dormiente*) to romantic souls.

Many Beneventans have relatives in the United States, Canada, and other parts of the world; thousands emigrated from the city and its surroundings during the last decades of the nineteenth century and the first half of the twentieth. At present, Benevento is still one of Italy's poorer cities, but there are some signs of well-being too— traffic jams, a few fashion boutiques in the historical center, and much new housing in the modern district in the eastern part of the city.

With a population of 65,000, Benevento today depends to a large extent on the farms and orchards that surround it and on its food and light manufacturing industries. *Torrone* (literally, "big tower"), the crunchy nougat sticks, and especially the yellow, anisette-flavored Strega liqueur are Benevento specialties, popular all over Italy. The liqueur's distillers sponsor one of Italy's major literary prizes, the Premio Strega, which is prestigious and provides good publicity. *Strega* means "witch," a reminder that sorcery is a recurrent theme in old Benevento folktales. The local belief in witchcraft goes back to antiquity; even though ingrained superstitions may now be on the wane, traces of a remote past can still be found in many places in the city, and Beneventans are proud of them.

Their best-loved monument is a triumphal arch that might well stand in Rome. It is one of the most perfectly preserved ancient structures of its kind anywhere. The Appian Way once passed through it, the Roman Empire's lifeline from the city of the Caesars to Brundisium (Brindisi), where travelers would take the boat for Greece or Asia Minor. The Benevento Arch, marking a crossroads where other imperial roads joined the Appian Way, was also known as the Porta Aurea (Golden Gate). It was erected in marble on orders from the authorities in Rome, "the Senate and the People," in A.D. 114 in honor of Emperor Trajan. The emperor was at that time expected back from his wars in the east, where he had annexed Armenia to the empire and where his legions were still battling the Parthians.

The fifty-foot arch rises in what is now a little piazza with a patch of greenery on the northeastern outskirts of old Benevento, commanding a fine view of the fertile plain and the mountains on the horizon. A plaque on a nearby house wall records repair work on the monument carried out during various periods.

The arch is covered with reliefs showing allegorical representations of episodes from Trajan's career—the emperor receiving a barbarian ambassador, the emperor being crowned by the goddess of victory, the emperor granting land to Roman veterans, and so forth. Trajan, who was Spanish-born, ruled from A.D. 98 to 117 and is ranked by historians among the most humane of the "good" emperors. Benevento considers him one of its own. A modern bronze statue of Trajan, an imitation of ancient sculptures, stands in front of Benevento's castle, and the Latin inscription underneath gives one of his official Roman titles, *optimus* ("the best").

Benevento's other principal remnant from antiquity is the Roman theater in the city's southeast. The ruin, a semicircle 270 feet in diameter with nineteen rows of stone seats, was dug up from under condemned slum houses between 1930 and the first years after World War II. The theater, built under Trajan's successor, Hadrian (emperor A.D. 117–138), is evidence that Benevento was then a flourishing center.

Its apparent loyalty, signaled by Trajan's Arch, must have gratified Roman patriots, for the city had been a stronghold of the backward and warlike Samnites during that people's long and fierce struggle to defend its independence. In 321 B.C. Samnite warriors trapped and captured a Roman army in the Caudine Forks, a defile less than twenty miles west of Benevento. The Roman soldiers were forced to prove their submission by passing under a yoke; this day of shame was never forgotten. A few decades after this humiliation the Roman legions had subdued the Samnites, but it took quite a while before the people of Beneventum, as the city was then called, were thoroughly Romanized.

Benevento still glories in its ancient Samnite traditions. The name Sannio (Samnium) is used in the names of local businesses and in other contexts to establish regional identity. Benevento's collection of antiquities, containing prehistoric, archaeological, and historical material, is officially known as the Museum of Samnium. Its seat is the Church of Santa Sofia, a circular building that dates back to the eighth century, and an adjoining Benedictine abbey with an elegant cloister whose slender columns and horseshoe arches betray Arab influences. Santa Sofia was founded when Benevento was the center of a Longobard duchy, a powerful outpost of Germanic overlords in southern Italy. Longobard rule in Benevento lasted from the fifth to the eleventh century, when the papacy succeeded in establishing control of the city and its surroundings.

The cathedral, at the heart of old Benevento, not quite halfway between Trajan's Arch and the Roman theater, is massive like a fortress. It was started under the Longobards in the ninth century, and was rebuilt by the papal government around 1200. The broad façade is in Romanesque style, with a bronze door decorated with reliefs of biblical scenes. The church's interior was redecorated in the Baroque era.

Benevento remained an outlying possession of the States of the Church and an enclave in the Kingdom of Naples almost uninterruptedly until Italy's unification in the nineteenth century. The only intermezzo was from 1806 to 1815, when Talleyrand, Napoleon's brilliant foreign minister, was the area's absentee ruler as duke of Benevento.

The apostolic delegates who represented the pontifical government resided for centuries in Benevento's medieval castle in the eastern part of the city. The oldest part of this citadel, a grim towerlike building with small turrets on top, is from the fourteenth century. Today the castle faces the modern government palace, which houses the provincial authorities, on the west side and large public gardens to the east. A medieval stone sculpture of a heraldic lion stands near the statue of Trajan. Remains of Longobardic and papal city walls can be seen at various points along the bluffs surrounding the Benevento plateau.

The city's railroad station is two-thirds of a mile to the northwest of the historical center. The station district was bombed heavily during World War II, because Benevento was, and is, a railroad hub with lines converging from Rome and Naples by way of Caserta, from Avellino, from Campobasso, and from Bari and Foggia. Today the straight, broad Via Principe di Napoli, linking the rebuilt station and the city center with a bridge across the Calore River is lined with characterless new buildings. Arriving in Benevento by train, discount the first impression and suspend judgment until you are out of the station area.

CAPRI ▪

The latest idea for squeezing even more money out of one of the world's top resorts calls for covering its *piazzetta* with a plastic or rubber dome from November to March so that tourists may, during this cold season, still sit in the celebrated little square and talk from table to table, or just stare at one another. The proposal, endorsed by Capri's mayor, drew immediate protests from environmentalists. Whether or not the theatrical 4,000-square-foot *piazzetta* will eventually be winterized with a circus tent, the suggestion is indicative of what has become of the isle of Capri.

Snobbishness, vulgarity, and greed are unsavory ingredients in a brew that all too often poisons enjoyment of one of the most beautiful spots on the globe. If this book nevertheless lists Capri among Italy's appealing Hundred Towns, it is with reservations.

First, never set foot on the island during a summer weekend when an armada of motorboats, hydrofoils, and helicopters disgorges thousands of day-trippers from Naples and Sorrento together with other tourists who will noisily swarm over Capri, munch pizza on the run, and pack the *piazzetta* to conquer a table or just gape at the extravagantly dressed people who are sipping their *aperitivo*, the gigolos

301

with shirts wide open to display their bronzed chests, the girls in the tightest of Capri pants, the mature women with facelifts under bizarre sunglasses, and the gay couples.

Second, during the week, stay overnight to savor the sunsets and breezy evenings and the mornings with their spectacular views of the aquamarine sea, the Gulf of Naples, and the three famous cliffs—the Faraglioni—that rise from the water east of the Marina Piccola; the fragrance of millions of flowers on the island; the sky that seems always to be cloudless; and the glorious early light. Most of the hit-and-run tourists leave around six in the evening, and the next invasion won't start before ten the following morning. Don't go to Capri around Easter or from July to September; May and October are best, but there are also sunny days in January when the island is delightful even without a geodesic dome over the *piazzetta*.

Consider staying in Anacapri, the second town of the island, at 940 feet almost 500 feet higher than Capri town, and airier and much more tranquil than the latter. Axel Munthe (1857–1949), the Swedish physician and writer whose novel *The Story of San Michele* contributed much to Capri's international renown, lived for many years in Anacapri; his Villa of San Michele with its park and magnificent views can be visited. Anacapri, on its high plateau beneath the 1,930-foot-high Mount Solaro, has a little piazza of its own, flat-roofed white houses that evoke the Orient, and vistas from some points surpassing those from Capri town.

Some Capresi and well-heeled guests who don't care for the honkytonk atmosphere on weekends simply stay in their white villas in pseudo-Moorish, -Catalan, or -Oriental styles or on their yachts until Monday morning. Lacking such refuges, the visitor who wants to get away from the crowds may choose one of several footpaths, most of them steep, it is true, that lead to isolated spots with remarkable scenery.

On a sunny off-season day Capri's *piazzetta*, officially Piazza Umberto I, won't fail to exercise its vaunted charm. Most of the square is taken up by the tables and umbrellas of its four cafés—Caso, Piccolo Bar, Tiberio, and Vuotto. A stagey flight of stairs leads up to the multidomed Church of Santo Stefano opposite the town hall.

The *piazzetta* is a good observation post to spot newcomers because the cableway from the Marina Grande, the main landing place on the north coast, ends here. Visitors may, however, reach the center of town also by cab, in one of the few horse-drawn carriages that are still in service (the horses wear straw hats with feathers on their nodding heads), or on foot in about half an hour.

Hotels, restaurants, and boutiques cluster around the *piazzetta*. On the south side of town is the Certosa of San Giacomo, an abandoned Carthusian monastery from the fourteenth century with an ornate campanile and a cloister; it now houses a private gallery with nineteenth-century paintings.

Via Tiberio runs from the town center eastward to Lo Capo, a promontory with the extensive remains of one of the twelve palaces and villas that Emperor Tiberius (42 B.C.–A.D. 37) had built for himself on the island. The panorama from the site, and from an old lighthouse nearby, is grandiose.

Tiberius, the diffident successor of Augustus, spent the last eleven years of his reign on Capri. He communicated with the Senate and imperial officers by letter and messenger, and never returned to Rome before his murky death. Ancient authors, especially Tacitus and Suetonius, depict the aging emperor's cruelty and debaucheries in lurid colors. Visitors to the Villa Jovis (Jupiter's Villa), Tiberius's residence on Lo Capo, are shown a rock 974 feet above the sea from which, according to local tradition, the emperor had his victims hurled to their deaths by athletic executioners. The spot is called the Salto di Tiberio (Jump of Tiberius). Ruins of other ancient Roman buildings, not all of them erected for Tiberius, can be found in other parts of the island.

For a different Capri panorama, stroll from the *piazzetta* southward on Via Vittorio Emanuele and Viale Matteotti to the Gardens of Augustus, a public park with a terrace overlooking the cliffs on the south coast. To the left is the promontory of Tragara with the Faraglioni, on the right the Marina Piccola with its narrow beach and its crowded bathing concessions, the bay teeming in summer with yachts and boats. A footpath, Via Krupp, descends past the Gardens of Augustus. The broad walkway, hewn out of the rock, is named after Fritz Krupp, a turn-of-the-century German steel magnate and Capri habitué who paid for the construction of the scenic shortcut to the Marina Piccola.

Another, more recent devotee of Capri, the popular British singer and comedienne Gracie Fields, created a fancy restaurant with a swimming pool and an enviable view of the Marina Piccola, the

Canzone del Mare (Song of the Sea). Miss Fields, who had entertained Allied troops during World War II, settled on Capri later and became the wife of a resident, Boris Alperovic, a Bulgarian expatriate.

At the Marina Grande, on the opposite side of the island, there are also cramped bathing concessions. Boatsmen tout trips to the Blue Grotto, the best-known of several natural caves along the coast (there are also a Green Grotto, a Red Grotto, and a White Grotto). Only small craft can enter the Blue Grotto, and only when the sea is calm, because the entrance is barely three feet high and visitors must duck. When the sun is shining outside—the best time is between 11:00 A.M. and 1:00 P.M.—its glare is reflected inside the large cave with a magic blue.

One of Capri's pleasures is leisurely al fresco dining amid the ubiquitous bougainvillea and with vistas of the sea. Neapolitan cuisine with plenty of pasta and seafood prevails in Capri eating spots. A specialty is chewy *insalata caprese*, or Capri-style salad—slices of mozzarella cheese and not-too-ripe tomatoes in olive oil, spiced with basil, marjoram, and other herbs. Capri wines are mostly white and are headier than one would think at the first cool sip.

The genuine Capresi, people who live on the island all year round, now number 15,000. The island has its own museum, created by a local turn-of-the-century doctor, Ignazio Cerio. The prehistoric and archaeological finds that he collected may be viewed and his library consulted in the Palazzo Cerio adjacent to Piazza Umberto I.

The building is the restored castle of Queen Joanna I of Anjou (1326–1382), a ruler of Naples who presumably was an accomplice in the murder of her husband, Andrew of Hungary, in 1345. If there is a lot of gossip on the isle of Capri every season now, it is hardly as juicy as it must have been in the days of Emperor Tiberius or Queen Joanna.

SORRENTO ▪

A marble plaque on the musty façade of the eighteenth-century Palazzo Correale lists famous guests of the town, from Goethe and Byron to Nietzsche and Tolstoy. An old song, still heard in Italian restaurants

all over the world, urges: *"Torna a Surriento!"* ("Return to Sorrento";
Surriento is local dialect). It's not an unmixed pleasure, though.

Revisiting the much-praised town in the south of the Gulf of Naples
after a few years' absence may cause a shock. Sorrento is sadly
overbuilt, and huge coaches with Italian and, above all, foreign tourists bottle up its streets. A new 400-room convention hotel with three
restaurants and six swimming pools linked by artificial waterfalls
dominates the hillside with its Miami-monumental bulk.

On weekends from May to November the town crawls with large
families from nearby Naples in addition to its seasonal contingent of
visitors from abroad. Like Capri—geologically a prolongation of the
Peninsula of Sorrento—the town is swamped by mass tourism. Shun
Sorrento, then?

On some sunny day in the trough between the end of November
and Easter, the old charm of the place may still work. At the end of
January, for instance, spring will already be in the air, oranges and
lemons may be glowing on the trees, and the gardens will be lusher
than during the dry summers. From the few unobstructed lookouts
along Sorrento's coast the gulf will shimmer in deep azure, and in
the evening a million lights are seen twinkling across the water in
Naples on the right and on Capri to the left.

Linked with Naples by the frequent trains of the Circum-Vesuvian
Railway and close to the Naples-Salerno motorway, Sorrento has
virtually turned into a suburb of the southern metropolis. Though
afflicted with some of its chronic congestion, Sorrento is nevertheless
much cleaner than most Neapolitan neighborhoods. Some people who
want to see the sights of the big city or do business in it prefer to
put up at a hotel in Sorrento and commute. Many of the town's nearly
20,000 permanent inhabitants take the train to Naples every morning.

One of Sorrento's assets through the ages has been its panorama.
To get a look at the gulf, with Mount Vesuvius to the north, visitors
will, however, have to find the way to one of two belvederes—one in
the public gardens behind the Church of San Francesco, the other
behind the Palazzo Correale—unless they have access to one of the
many hotels and villas that border the coast for a mile and a half.
Sorrento is built on a tufa plateau rising almost vertically from the
sea to a height of 150 feet and more; the seaside edge of this huge
rock shelf is private property almost throughout.

A breakwater divides the Bay of Sorrento, a part of the Gulf of Naples, into the Marina Grande in the west and the Marina Piccola in the east, two curved walls of cliffs with a few buildings and cramped bathing concessions near sea level. Boats from Naples and Capri put in at the tiny harbor in the middle. A winding street leads from the port up a ravine into the town.

Sorrento's bustling center is Piazza Tasso, about halfway on the straight main street, Corso Italia. The harbor and the sea aren't visible from it. The square is named after the town's most famous son, Torquato Tasso (1544–1595), the author of the epic *Jerusalem Delivered*, a sacred cow of Italian literature. The moody, tortured poet spent most of his adult life at the Este court in Ferrara and in Rome. A marble statue in the piazza represents him gazing heavenward rather than at his home town.

An overpass behind Piazza Tasso spans the ravine. Children in Sorrento are told by their elders that gnomes dwell in the deep, murky trench that leads to the harbor.

The oldest part of the town is to the west of the ravine. Sorrento's fifteenth-century cathedral, with a modern façade, is on Corso Italia, and is not particularly remarkable. The Church of St. Francis stands closer to the sea; the adjacent former convent, now the seat of a permanent arts and crafts show, encloses an elegant Gothic cloister, an enchanting garden with palms, flowers, and climbing plants. On a square not far from it is the Basilica of St. Antoninus with the tomb of Sorrento's patron saint, an abbot who lived around the year 600. The small streets of the neighborhood are cluttered with outdoor stands selling seafood, fruits, clothing, and other items.

Archways behind the cathedral and near the Marina Grande are remains of town gates from antiquity. Sorrento was probably founded by Greek colonists in the fifth century B.C.; a questionable interpretation would have the town's name derived from the Sirens of Greek mythology whose song lured mariners to their doom. In the imperial age, rich Romans had villas in what was then Surrentum, and some traces of such luxurious buildings are still visible in various spots.

A collection of antiquities found in the area is on view in the fine museum in the Palazzo Correale near the coast in the eastern part of Sorrento. The institution, closed at times for lengthy periods, contains also paintings of the Neapolitan school of the fifteenth through seventeenth centuries, antique furniture, porcelain and majolica, and samples of the inlaid woodwork in which Sorrento craftsmen have long excelled.

POSITANO ▪

It is hard to get to, and once there, you must climb stairways all day; the beach is small and always thronged during the bathing season; and there is really only one short street for strolling. Yet Positano has its flock of devotees who feel at home here more than they do in their city apartments and perhaps more than anywhere else in the world. They will travel to the former fishing village in the south of the Peninsula of Sorrento to spend a few days whenever they have a chance, even in the cool months or during rainy spells when the summer crowds have long gone, most hotels and restaurants are closed, and the cute boutiques are shuttered.

What nurtures such fierce loyalty has long ceased to be a village, and none of its 3,500 permanent residents lives by fishing anymore. Even when catches were still abundant in the Tyrrhenian Sea long ago, the fishermen of Positano were poor, and many of them emigrated overseas. Thousands of their descendants live in the United States today, especially in Brooklyn, New York.

Present-day Positano is a tightly packed cluster of little cubic houses, most of them white and quite a few with loggias toward the sea, built on terraces and rock ledges that rise from a small bay to the Amalfi Drive (*see* Amalfi) and beyond it, close to perpendicular cliffs. From afar the town looks like a North African casbah. It is a sophisticated, if chatty, casbah: Everybody knows everybody, and some of the stories that are told sound like soap operas; the newcomer is quickly drawn into Positano gossip.

The lanes and stairways have names like "Oleander Street," but addresses mean little in Positano. If you are invited to somebody's house, you will be told: "Ask for Nicola, the locksmith. We live next door, you can't miss it."

The Amalfi Drive is linked with the lower levels of Positano by two steep, winding one-way roads—one down from a turnoff on the western approaches to the town, the other up to a point at its eastern fringe. At the height of summer or at Easter the two roads are lined with parked cars, and the few parking lots are full. Many would-be visitors who arrive too late drive down into Positano proper and, finding no corner to wedge their car into, must drive right up again to find themselves anew on the Amalfi Drive.

The little space where the two one-way roads, one down, the other up, meet is called Piazza dei Molini (Mills Square), after an old mill that has long ceased grinding wheat. It's not a real piazza, but the post office and the pharmacy give the little area the character of a community center of sorts.

From Piazza dei Molini, Via Murat descends to the beach. It is named after Joachim Murat, Napoleon's brother-in-law, who was king of Naples from 1808 to 1815. Murat was supposed to use as his summer residence a Rococo palazzo that had been built a few decades earlier on the street, but he never got around to moving in. (He was shot in Calabria in 1815 in an attempt to regain his kingdom after Napoleon's defeat at Waterloo.) Palazzo Murat, in which the king never lived, is noteworthy for its elegant courtyard; it is now a hotel.

The place where one may be sure to meet everyone sooner or later is Lo Stradone (The Big Street), a fifty-yard strip paved with square stones that runs parallel to the beach from a flight of stairs to an archway. The people seated at the outdoor tables of the café-restaurants along Lo Stradone watch the strollers, and vice versa; who is being seen with whom will provide new food for the incessant talk of the town.

Steps lead from the strip up to the Chiesa Madre (Mother Church), Positano's parish church. Its majolica dome stands out from among the cramped buildings all around. The church dates from the Middle Ages, and was rebuilt in the eighteenth century. The most interesting object in the interior is a Byzantine icon over the main altar, representing the Virgin Mary with the Infant Jesus. How the ancient painting on cedarwood reached Positano is unknown.

The town's origins are controversial. Stone weapons and tools found in a nearby grotto recently proved to scientists that the area was inhabited already 15,000 years ago. Local tradition, not supported by any historical evidence, has it that Positano was founded in the tenth century by refugees from Paestum in the south of the Gulf of

Salerno who had fled when Saracen pirates were devastating their city. The name of the settlement may indeed have been derived from the name of Poseidon, the god of the sea who was worshipped in antiquity in Paestum, the Greek Poseidonia (*see* Salerno).

Positano became a part of the Republic of Amalfi and, later, of the Kingdom of Naples. Although it lacks a harbor, for centuries the town played a minor role in Mediterranean trade. It suffered often from Moorish and Turkish incursions, and like the other coastal communities along the peninsula Positano built several watchtowers. Two of these old lookouts, one round and the other square, rise close to the shoreline east of the town; they are now private homes.

The remains of another old tower can be seen on the largest of three small offshore islands southwest of Positano. The three islets, which are close together, are called Li Galli (The Roosters) because, seen from ashore, they suggest the crest of a rooster. Easily reached by rowboats when the sea is calm, the group of uninhabited islands served as the state prison of the Republic of Amalfi.

AMALFI ▪

The easy way to reach this singularly scenic town at the opening of a ravine in the rocky Peninsula of Sorrento is by boat from Naples, Capri, or Salerno during the warm season. But a case can be made for some suspense, or even toil, before enjoyment; the land route provides plenty of both.

The road is the Amalfi Drive, a corniche that in narrow bends skirts the cliffs and slopes of the dramatic coast, hugging inlets and fjords, crossing gullies on daring viaducts, and diving into tunnels pierced through mountain ribs. It may take the prudent driver a couple of hours to negotiate the entire twenty-eight miles of the famous highway along the south of the Peninsula of Sorrento, with Amalfi thirteen miles from its eastern end. The road, between 100 and 500 feet above the azure sea, is essentially the same that was built in the second half of the nineteenth century, although it has been broadened in various stretches since then.

It is not particularly difficult or dangerous to travel by car to Amalfi as long as the driver doesn't even glimpse at the stupendous scenery but keeps looking at the road, which inevitably will again curve within the next 150 yards. A manual gearshift helps. One quickly learns to stop and pull aside, or even back up a little, to permit an oncoming coach to maneuver around a tricky bend.

The Amalfi Drive and Amalfi are crowded from June to mid-October, especially on weekends. The coast, however, is blessed with a mild and sunny winter climate, and it may be a good idea to spend some off-season time in Amalfi, where most hotels stay open all year. When the Amalfitani, as the local people are known, woke up one day in January 1985 and found two fingers of snow on their window sills and terraces, only the oldest of them could remember anything like that having ever happened before.

The town is protected from the cold northern winds by the Lattari Mountains, a chain of ridges and peaks rising to almost 4,000 feet. The name of the peninsula's rocky spine is derived from the Italian word for "milk" (*latte*) and refers to the many cows and sheep that once grazed on its pastures. A few flocks of sheep can still be seen today. Chestnut trees, beeches, and oaks dot the slopes; closer to the sea, farmers tend their lemon and olive trees and grow grapes for wine, often on narrow rock ledges.

Only a few elderly fishermen still sail out from the villages near Amalfi now and then, but catches are meager. The Bay of Salerno is almost as badly polluted as the Bay of Naples northwest of the Peninsula of Sorrento. Amalfi now thrives on the tourist business, with a few paper and ceramics workshops surviving. The narrow streets and stairways of the town, under little arches linking the old houses, look like a permanent bazaar displaying souvenirs, earthenware, shoes, sweatshirts, and other merchandise that visitors might pick up.

Amalfi's permanent residents number today around 6,000—about one-tenth of its population at the height of its mercantile fortunes 900 years ago. The city was then a wealthy, independent republic whose ships sailed all over the Mediterranean. Amalfi traded with the Byzantine Christians and the Moslem states. Exotic wares were unloaded in its harbor, then one of the most important transshipping centers in the west. "Arabs, Indians, Sicilians, and Africans" had dealings with Amalfi, which piled up "silver, precious garments, and gold," according to a medieval chronicler, William the Apulian.

Mediterranean politics and the forces of nature conspired to ruin the small city-state. Pisa and Genoa emerged as aggressive rivals, the Normans took control of the area, Venice eventually rose as the foremost maritime power, and in 1343 catastrophic tidal waves following a seaquake destroyed Amalfi's harbor and swallowed at least one-third of the city.

A few remnants of ancient grandeur are still recognizable. Two halls with pointed arches near the waterfront are all that has survived of the arsenal where merchant vessels and warships, reputed to have been among the largest and best at sea in that epoch, were built. The Civic Museum treasures a fifteenth-century copy of the Amalfi Tables, a collection of rules governing relations among shipowners, sailors, and merchants from the early Middle Ages—a maritime code that was adopted by most seafaring nations. Amalfi claims also that the mariner's compass had its origins here in 1302. A statue of the presumed inventor, Flavio Gioia, was put up exactly 600 years later in front of the town gate facing the sea.

Amalfi's main monument is its Orientalizing cathedral, to which a high stairway leads up from the town's little central piazza a few steps behind the gate and the statue of Flavio Gioia. The campanile, on the left side of the church, dates from the twelfth century. The square tower is crowned with a round top surrounded by four smaller cylinders, all covered with strips of green and yellow majolica tiles in patterns borrowed from Arabic art.

The church itself was rebuilt several times. The glittering façade is a nineteenth-century reconstruction of the medieval original; some material that had been recovered when a part of the church collapsed in 1861 was reused. A gable mosaic, over statues of the twelve apostles in a row, represents Jesus on His throne.

The façade and portico of the cathedral are in black and white marble; an inscription on the bronze doors indicates that they were executed in Constantinople around 1066. The interior was completely redecorated in the Baroque period.

The crypt contains the body of St. Andrew, the apostle, brought here from Constantinople at the end of the Fourth Crusade in the early thirteenth century. (The apostle's head was guarded in the Vatican for several centuries and has recently been transferred to the Eastern Orthodox Patriarchate in Istanbul.) The relics in the Amalfi

311

cathedral are said to ooze an oily substance, popularly called the "manna of St. Andrew," that is believed to have miraculous properties. The apostle's feast day on November 30 is observed with special pomp in Amalfi.

A chapel on the left side of the portico leads into the small, graceful Cloister of Paradise, which might well be the patio of a mosque. Roman sarcophagi, other antiquities, and fragments of the cathedral's original façade are on view in the courtyard.

A huge statue of St. Andrew is carried from the cathedral to the beach in solemn procession every June 27 to commemorate a victory over the redoubtable Algerian corsair Khair ad-Din, known as Barbarossa, in the sixteenth century. Sailors carrying the statue back into the church decorate it with metal and plastic fish, following an old custom to remind the apostle that his help at sea is still needed.

The narrow pebble beach of Amalfi, adjoining today's small harbor, is packed in summer, as is the parking lot along the breakwater. Every four years galleys with eight oarsmen each, representing Italy's former maritime republics—Amalfi, Genoa, Pisa, and Venice—compete in a regatta in the bay here. The annual event rotates among the four historic rivals, which in the Middle Ages were all too often at one another's throats. Amalfi, in particular, was mercilessly sacked by the Pisans in the twelfth century. The modern regattas, usually preceded by pageants on land and followed by fireworks, were dreamed up by tourist industry promoters in the 1950s.

The best view of Amalfi is from the sea. The little old houses, most of them whitewashed under brown roofs, surge up the steep slopes of the cove in which the town snuggles. A round tower on a rocky promontory at the eastern entrance to Amalfi was built in the Renaissance as a lookout to spot Moslem raiders. Above it is a thirteenth-century Franciscan convent, now the Luna Hotel. A plaque on it recalls that Henrik Ibsen was a longtime lodger.

High above the left edge of Amalfi proper is another thirteenth-century monastery with a large, flowered terrace; Cistercian monks, and Capuchins after them, lived in the enviable spot before it became the Cappuccini Hotel in the nineteenth century.

A monumental arcade halfway up the hill that overlooks the town belongs to its cemetery. (Prominent dead were in earlier times buried in the Cloister of Paradise.) A truncated tower on top of the 550-foot-high hill, rising from the ruins of the medieval Castle of Pontone, rounds out the unique view.

RAVELLO ∎

In an international poll to determine the world's most picturesque spot, quite a few connoisseurs would nominate this serene town 1,200 feet above Amalfi, another likely favorite. Compared with the old seaport below it, Ravello has the advantage of its vistas of a more generous expanse of blue sea and its greater tranquillity.

Artists, writers, other famous people—Greta Garbo with Leopold Stokowski among them—and aesthetes have for generations flocked to Ravello for brief or long stays. During a visit here in 1880 Richard Wagner found in the Villa Rufolo the inspiration for the enchanted garden of Klingsor the sorcerer in his opera *Parsifal*. A platform in another luxuriant park that seems to hang over the sea like a lofty balcony is called the "Terrace of the Infinite."

Besides the two celebrated vantage points, Ravello charms visitors with an ancient cathedral, lovely little lanes and the stairways under arches, and subtropical vegetation in well-tended gardens. It has good hotels and many opulent villas. More than a resort, it is a beautiful place where one would dream to live forever. Some 2,000 permanent residents do.

Ravello's blessings include frequent cool breezes during the hot season and plenty of sun in winter, paths for pleasant walks in the surroundings, quiet, and the product of the nearby vineyards—one of the few genuine rosé wines in Italy. (What is served as rosé in other parts of the country is usually a mixture of red and white wines.)

On the Amalfi Drive (*see* Amalfi) the turnoff for Ravello is a little east of the village of Atrani, which has virtually become a suburb of Amalfi. A 3.5-mile-long panoramic road passes orange and lemon groves and rises in wide turns to the spur of the Lattari Mountains on which Ravello is built. One enters the stretched-out town at its northern end near Ravello's piazza with its graceful old fountain and its magnificent views.

Caserta, the Fountain of Venus and Adonis in the park of the Royal Castle

OPPOSITE: *Caserta, the Royal Castle*

Capri, Marina Piccola

OPPOSITE: Positano

Amalfi

LEFT: *Ravello, from Villa Rufolo*

BELOW: *Salerno*

Lecce, Basilica of the Holy Cross

OPPOSITE: *Lecce, Portal of the Basilica*

Many of the houses and villas are reconverted old buildings, or incorporate ancient structures. The town dates back to the early Middle Ages, and from the ninth century onward it was subject to the Republic of Amalfi and shared its fortunes. Between the eleventh and the early nineteenth centuries Ravello's relative importance was underlined by the fact that it had a bishop of its own. At the peak of its prosperity in the thirteenth century it may have numbered as many as 35,000 inhabitants.

The cathedral is dedicated to St. Pantaleo, a physician who, according to tradition, suffered martyrdom in Nicomedia, Asia Minor, in 305. A phial containing what is believed to be the saint's dried blood is kept in the chapel at the right of the main altar. St. Pantaleo's blood is expected to liquefy every July 27, the feast day of Ravello's patron saint, which is observed here with much solemnity. (Ravello's periodic miracle is similar to that of the more famous liquefaction of the presumed blood of St. Januarius [San Gennaro] in the cathedral of Naples at least twice every year.)

Ravello's cathedral was first built in 1086 and rebuilt in the Baroque period. The restored campanile at the back of the church, crowned by Arab-style interlacing arches, is from the thirteenth century. The cathedral's bronze doors, with a Byzantine-influenced representation of the Passion of Christ and figures of saints, are the work of the twelfth-century master Barisano da Trani. The marble pulpit in the interior, covered with mosaics and supported by six columns carried by lions, dates from the thirteenth century.

Moorish and Norman styles blend in various other buildings in Ravello. A prime example is the Villa Rufolo, or Palace of the Rufoli, south of the cathedral, a mansion built in the eleventh and twelfth centuries for a wealthy local family. Popes and royalty resided here on various occasions long before Richard Wagner became the most famous guest in recent times. Of the original two towers, one has survived and has been restored. The colonnaded courtyard seems out of a fairy tale, and the gardens are entrancing.

Farther south, past the small churches dedicated to St. Francis and St. Clare, is the Villa Cimbrone, in 1938 Greta Garbo and Maestro Stokowski's hideaway, and now a hotel. A long garden alley lined with statues leads to the Cimbrone Belvedere, the "Terrace of the Infinite," commanding a panorama that embraces the Bay of Salerno with Paestum far to the south.

SALERNO ■

Visitors to the balmy, fertile Campania region who would rather shun Naples with its chaotic traffic and other big-city ills might consider Salerno as an alternative. This uncluttered old city, spreading for miles along its magnificent gulf, has since the opening of Motorway A-3 (Naples–Reggio di Calabria) in the 1960s become a favorite of knowledgeable people who want to move around in this part of southern Italy. Naples is less than an hour away; Pompeii to the northwest and the stupendous Greek temples of Paestum to the southeast can be reached in half an hour or so; the scenic Amalfi drive from Sorrento leads, after some of Europe's most picturesque vistas and innumerable dangerous road bends, to relatively easy motoring on level ground just outside Salerno.

The city's Lungomare Trieste is an extended seafront promenade with palms and oleander trees, flower beds and modern buildings. Behind them is a straight shopping street, Via Roma. Where Salerno's business and residential neighborhoods end, its Lido with bathing concessions, eating places, and a broad sandy beach continues for another couple of miles. Unmistakably southern, this city of 170,000 doesn't seem as crowded as Naples, and it is comparatively neat.

The 900-year-old cathedral of Salerno is one of the more important monuments in Campania, a reminder of Norman dominance in the area during the Middle Ages. The large church, originally built in the eclectic style that the Normans developed in southern Italy, is dedicated to St. Matthew, and a reliquary in its crypt treasures what is said to be an arm and a tooth of the evangelist. The relics were reportedly brought to Salerno from Paestum by a Longobard prince, Gisulf I, in 954. Robert Guiscard, the heroic and cunning Norman who conquered large parts of southern Italy, ordered that the cathedral be built; and his architects used nearby Paestum as a handy quarry, removing several columns and marble blocks from the decayed temples to incorporate them in their Salerno church.

A chapel to the right of the high altar contains the tomb of Pope St. Gregory VII, the former Benedictine monk Hildebrand, one of the great pontiffs of the Church of Rome. For years he was locked in a historic Church-state conflict with Emperor Henry IV, and he

323

died in Salerno in 1085 after his ally Robert Guiscard had rescued him from the imperial troops in a raid on Rome. A Latin inscription in the chapel quotes St. Gregory VII's reputed last words: "I have loved justice and hated iniquity, therefore I die in exile."

When the Normans were holding sway in Salerno in the eleventh century the city was at the height of its fame as the medical center of the Western world. Students from all over Europe flocked to the classes of doctors who derived their knowledge from Greek, Roman, Arab, and Jewish learning. The city where the art of healing was taught was also an enviable place to live. A contemporary poet, William the Apulian, praised it in Latin verses as a paradise blessed with an abundance of trees, fruits, and wine, beautiful women and honest men. By the fourteenth century the glory was over, but the medical school survived until 1817. Today Salerno is the seat of a state university.

From the cathedral a series of steep streets and stairways, and eventually a footpath, lead up to a 900-foot-high hill with a ruined fort from which the Longobards scanned the horizon for approaching Saracen raiders. Robert Guiscard took the castle after a long siege.

A ride to Paestum, thirty miles away, takes the traveler along the flat beach where United States and British forces landed in September 1943 after Italy had signed its armistice with the Allied powers. Fierce fighting with the German troops who were retreating from Italy's deep south to Naples raged here, as the military cemeteries attest.

The honey-colored Doric temples of Paestum are among the best-preserved examples of ancient Greek architecture anywhere. On a limestone plateau an average of seventy feet above the nearby sea, the three sanctuaries, built in the sixth and fifth centuries B.C., were the center of a flourishing Greek colony, Poseidonia, which was famous for its pottery and its roses. The largest of the three structures, 197 by 80 feet, is known as the Temple of Neptune (Greek Poseidon), the god of the sea, but scholars have determined that it was really dedicated to Hera (Juno).

The best time to visit is late afternoon when the tourist coaches have left and the setting sun lights up the temples with a golden glow. The National Archaeological Museum near the temple site contains fragments and bronze vases from a recently discovered shrine of Hera (fifth century B.C.) and a wealth of friezes, statuary, bronzes, ceramics, and other artifacts dug up in the area.

The wide beach of Paestum is still uncrowded, although it attracts an increasing number of vacationists during its long bathing season. Hotels and motels, some of which stay open all year, as well as service stations, other businesses, and new housing threaten to encroach on the temple area. Yet with its noble Greek ruins, its cypresses and oleander trees, and its quiet before and after the daily tourist invasion, this is still a magic spot.

COSENZA ▪

Travelers familiar with the route between the Italian mainland and Sicily like to stop over in this Calabrian city because it lies on the *autostrada* at a convenient 332 miles from Rome and 272 miles from Palermo, and it offers good accommodations and a few adequate restaurants. But Cosenza deserves more than just an overnight stay.

The city, which counts about 100,000 inhabitants, has three sharply defined sections: the old town with a Norman hilltop castle overlooking the confluence of two mountain streams, the Busento and the Crati; an extended modern district in a plain stretching to the north; and, farther north, the suburb of Rende with the University of Calabria.

This institution, founded in the 1960s, was meant as a college with most of the students living on campus. The ambitious plans didn't quite come off, but the university does possess modern on-campus dormitories, which are rare in Italy. University students and faculty members, many of either group commuters, are conspicuous in Cosenza, now the intellectual center of rugged Calabria, one of Italy's least developed regions. Significantly, it was at the local university that the first-ever academic research into the activities of the Sicilian Mafia and its Calabrian offshoot, the *'ndrangheta*, was undertaken.

Cosenza, at an altitude of 787 feet, is a little cooler in summer than the coastal town of Paola, twenty-two miles to the northwest, where travelers on southern Italy's principal railway line change trains for the university city. A couple of hours is sufficient for a cursory visit of Cosenza's old-town district. From the bridge spanning the Busento the narrow, winding main street, Corso Telesio, leads up to the cathedral. Begun toward the end of the twelfth century, the church is essentially Gothic with a few earlier Romanesque elements in the interior, all of it rather gloomy. An elaborate tomb of Isabel of Aragon, wife of King Philip III the Bold of France, who died in Cosenza on her way back from a journey to Tunis in 1271, is in the left transept. She died after being spilled by her horse in wild Calabria.

Farther up in the old town the visitor finds a few public buildings, including a small museum with prehistoric and Roman artifacts (lately closed for reorganization) and a terraced park with a fine view. The ruined castle, at 1,263 feet, can be reached over a footpath; it was built by the Norman overlords of Calabria in the eleventh century.

Every now and then archaeological prospectors arrive in Cosenza in the hope of locating at last the secret spot where Alaric, king of the Visigoths, was buried with his fabled treasure. The barbarian leader had piled up immense riches when his warriors conquered and sacked Rome in A.D. 410. The Visigoths, with their spoils and slaves, then marched southward to the tip of the Italian peninsula and attempted to cross the Strait of Messina, but a storm caused them to give up their project of invading Sicily. Alaric died in or near Cosenza after a short illness in 412.

The Visigoths, according to their chronicler Jornandes, forced a multitude of their prisoners to divert the Busento and dig a royal sepulcher in the dry riverbed; the barbarians buried their king with his Roman gold and trophies, restored the original course of the stream, and massacred all the captives who had carried out the work.

The somber tale of Alaric's nighttime funeral, the theme of a celebrated ballad by the early-nineteenth-century poet August von Platen (translated into Italian by Giosuè Carducci, a poet in his own right), has excited generations of romantic Germans. During the Nazi era, Heinrich Himmler, the chief of the SS, sent a German scientific team to Cosenza for another effort to recover the Visigoth hoard. The unpublicized search was futile, and so were more recent diggings at and near the spot where the Busento joins the Crati. But the treasure hunters keep coming.

Cosenza is a convenient base for exploring the huge, sparsely populated Sila massif. Driving from the city eastward on National Route No. 107, travelers are within an hour amid an Alpine setting with chestnut and fir woods, jade-colored mountain lakes and high pastures where millions of flowers bloom in spring and summer, and skiers schuss in winter. For those who want to breathe the sharp Sila air longer, look at or climb the jagged ranges all around with peaks up to 6,300 feet high, get acquainted with one of the remotest parts of Italy, and study the archaic folkways of the untalkative mountaineers, the best place to stay is San Giovanni in Fiore, a 3,445-foot-high town thirty-eight miles from Cosenza. It has a few plain hotels. The Sila is southern Italy's "Little Switzerland," but Cosenza is no Zurich or Geneva.

LECCE ∎

Time hasn't exactly stopped in this Baroque city in the heel of the Italian boot, but life here has retained some of the civility of a bygone era. Lecce has vigorously grown lately and has achieved a measure of well-being through unhurried industrial development, yet has managed to avoid the dreariness of the new neighborhoods that have sprung up in the other centers of the flat region of Apulia—Bari, Taranto, Foggia, and Brindisi. Its very remoteness may have favored Lecce.

After traversing miles and miles of vineyards, tobacco fields, and expanses with rows of olive trees, the visitor is astounded by the city's mellow grace and indeed beauty, by the luxuriant limestone façades of its palaces and churches, and by the mood of its languorous evenings when the sultry sirocco wind from Africa is caught in its palms. The Leccesi treat strangers with ceremonious courtesy, and they like to speak about their city, their university, their intelligentsia (provincial though it may appear to the outsider), and their soccer team and huge new soccer stadium. Because of its grand architecture dating from the sixteenth through eighteenth centuries, Lecce is called the "Florence of the Baroque Period." Another sobriquet is "Athens of Apulia," an allusion to the prestige that learning and culture have always enjoyed here.

Wine, olive oil, and to some extent tobacco still play a big role in the city's economy, but many of Lecce's 90,000 or so inhabitants now have jobs in factories that produce shoes, apparel, chemicals, and machinery, while thousands of others do piecework at home for the new industries. That there is more money around now than until recently can be deduced from the amount of restoration work in the historic city center. The smart thing today is to live in a readapted apartment in one of the old palaces with their extravagant façades—all fruits, flowers, caryatids, grotesque masks, and snaky ribbons carved from the region's soft yet compact golden stone. Some of the buildings still bear the coats of arms of the Spanish noble families who had commissioned them.

All the former masters of Lecce—Greeks, Romans, Byzantines, Normans, and the various dynasties of the Kingdom of Naples—left traces in ruins, archaeological remains, buildings, dialect expressions, and the way of life; the influence of the Spaniards who were for centuries entrenched in southern Italy is particularly conspicuous. Spanish is the grave politeness of many people here; some faces seem familiar from Valázquez paintings; and Spanish is the way the Leccesi value family honor and religion.

Piazza del Duomo (Cathedral Square) is the showcase of the Lecce Baroque style. The cathedral, built between 1658 and 1670, takes up the south of the square with an elaborate side facade and showy portals. On the left is the 229-foot campanile, which can be seen from far away; on clear days one can glimpse the mountains of Albania across the Adriatic Sea from its top. The elegant tower is divided into five segments of diminishing bulk, four square ones and the octagonal crown, with balustrades as dividers. To the right of the cathedral are the bishop's palace and the seminary, both with upper-floor loggias. The four ecclesiastical structures, although erected decades apart, form an architectural composition of remarkable unity.

East of the cathedral is Piazza Sant'Oronzo with the city hall and a statue of the city's patron saint, which was erected during a plague in 1656. Vast remains of an ancient Roman amphitheater for 25,000 spectators extend in the south of the square; discovered at the beginning of the century, the ruins were almost completely dug up recently. A smaller Roman theater was unearthed southeast of the cathedral in the 1920s.

From the city hall walk a few steps to the northeast where the most famous of Lecce's Baroque churches, Santa Croce (Holy Cross), stands. When I was last visiting, the basilica with its richly decorated façade was still trussed in with scaffolding for repair work that had started several years earlier. The church adjoins the rambling building of a former convent of the Celestine Order, now the headquarters of the provincial authorities, or prefecture. East of Santa Croce are the public gardens.

A sixty-foot-high triumphal arch with the coat of arms of Emperor Charles V rises in the northwest of the old town, a remnant of fortifications built in 1548 on orders from the Habsburg ruler on whose domains, including the Kingdom of Naples, "the sun never set." Farther to the northwest, near the cemetery, is the Church of Santi Nicola e Cataldo, noteworthy for its blend of Norman and Baroque styles. A large fortress south of the public gardens was also built on Charles V's behest; it has long been used as an Italian army barracks.

Old Lecce is girded by broad avenues and surrounded by modern districts. A seaside village with good bathing beaches 7.5 miles northeast of Lecce, San Cataldo, has lately grown and almost become a suburb of the city. Visitors to Lecce should not miss side trips to two captivating towns in the Salento Peninsula, as this extreme part of Italy is called, namely Gallipoli and Otranto.

Gallipoli (stress the second syllable), a seaport and bathing resort twenty-three miles southwest of Lecce, owes its name to the Greek eye for scenery: its settlers from Taras (now Taranto), the center of *Magna Graecia* ("Greater Greece"), called it Kallipolis, the beautiful city. The old town, on an island about a mile in circumference, is a warren of white houses that give it an Oriental character. Its sixteenth-century walls have been razed, making space for a circular coastal boulevard, the Riviera, with magnificent vistas of the Gulf of Taranto, the offshore island of Sant'Andrea, and the sweeping coastline with a bay on either side of the town. From an old castle in the east of old Gallipoli a bridge links the island with a promontory and the town's modern section, Borgo, with streets in a chessboard pattern. Hotels, restaurants, and bathing concessions line the coastal road north and southeast of Borgo. Gallipoli has about 20,000 permanent residents and thousands of summer guests.

Otranto (stress the first syllable) has given its name to the 46.5-mile strait connecting the Adriatic with the Ionian Sea. It is a harbor town twenty-six miles southeast of Lecce, with barely 5,000 people. It too attracts holidaymakers during the hot months, and is dominated by a castle. This fifteenth-century stronghold, from which the Albanian coast can be seen, was chosen by Hugh Walpole as the—anachronistic—setting for his famous *The Castle of Otranto, a Gothic Story*

(1765), the tale of thirteenth-century terror that started an enduring literary genre. Real terror swooped on Otranto, then a flourishing seaport, in 1480 when a Turkish fleet captured and destroyed it. Otranto never regained its former prosperity. Its severe cathedral, dating from the eleventh century, attests to the town's importance in the Middle Ages; note especially its well-preserved twelfth-century mosaic floor. On a weekday in the off-season you will probably be alone in the church that once was looted by the marines of Sultan Mohammed II the Conqueror.

6

THE ISLANDS

Sicily and Sardinia

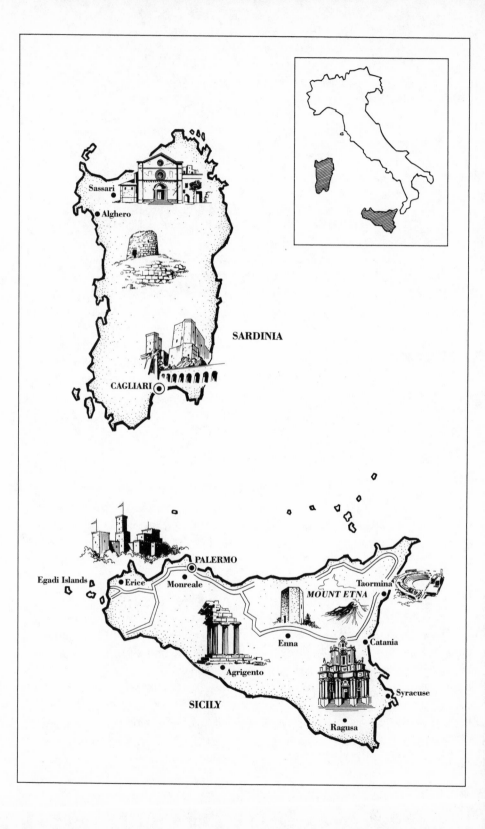

SARDINIA

Sassari

Alghero

CAGLIARI

PALERMO

Egadi Islands

Erice

Monreale

Taormina

MOUNT ETNA

Enna

Catania

Agrigento

Syracuse

SICILY

Ragusa

The two largest islands in the Mediterranean Sea are grouped together by Italian geographers, statisticians, and sociologists as *Italia Insulare*, or Insular Italy. Sicily and Sardinia, separated by nearly 200 miles of sea, are nevertheless quite unlike each other, while the more than 6.5 million people who live on them consider themselves different from the Italians of the "Continent," their name for the mainland. Since World War II each island has won a degree of political and administrative autonomy from the central government in Rome.

Sicilians will tell you that "several Sicilies" coexist on their island. The tourist who, for instance, visits only Palermo or Taormina misses important aspects of this complex land of 10,000 square miles—about the size of Vermont—and five million people at the center of the Mediterranean. This section selects half a dozen places to see in the various "Sicilies."

The island, which the ancient Greeks called Trinakria ("triangle") because of its shape, gets more sun than the rest of Italy. It is subtropical along its coasts, and mountainous, even harsh, in the interior. Snow still caps its highest peak, the 10,730-foot Mount Etna, while vacationers bathe in the nearby sea. Europe's biggest active volcano, Etna often grumbles, and its periodic eruptions can be seen even from the tip of the Italian mainland.

Oranges and lemons, grown in vast plantations, are Sicily's chief exports; the traveler will also see vegetable farms, olive and almond trees, cotton fields, and vineyards. Industry—including petrochemical plants—is concentrated between Catania and Syracuse and at the approaches to Palermo.

Traveling through Sicily is like reading a 3,000-year history of the Mediterranean. Trinakria was to the ancient Greeks the alluring west, where a man could make his fortune, their "America." When the first Greek settlers arrived in Sicily in the eighth century B.C. they apparently had little trouble with the native inhabitants, but found that Phoenician colonists had already been there and that a related Semitic people, the Carthaginians, were entrenched in the island's west.

The Greeks founded cities, built sanctuaries, seaports, and fortifications, and between wars traded profitably with Carthage and the Etruscans. The most powerful Greek-Sicilian city-state, Syracuse, was a rival of Athens and defeated its expeditionary force during the Peloponnesian War in the fifth century B.C. Temples and other vestiges of the long Greek presence survive in many parts of Sicily.

All of the island fell to Rome during the Punic Wars of the third and second centuries B.C., and Sicily remained Roman for more than 600 years as one of the granaries of the empire. Then, from the sixth century A.D., a succession of foreigners ruled all or parts of Sicily— Byzantines, Arabs, Normans, Germans, Frenchmen, and Spaniards. Between 1735 and 1860 the island was governed from Naples. Garibaldi, the northern patriot, began his lightning invasion of southern Italy from the western tip of Sicily, and eventually the island was incorporated into the unified Kingdom of Italy. During World War II, in July 1943, Italy's liberation from Fascist and Nazi dominance started with the Allied landings on the Sicilian shores.

Hostility toward the many foreign masters the Sicilians had to put up with during their checkered history is usually adduced as a reason why the islanders have always sought to settle their affairs among themselves—through underground networks that eventually developed into the Mafia subculture.

Novels and films about the Mafia should not keep anyone from visiting Sicily and enjoying its scenic beauty, soft climate, and cultural treasures. I have traveled in Sicily many times over three decades, visited every corner of the island, and everywhere found only courtesy. True, the "honored society" still survives, and has lately reaped enormous profits in international drug traffic, but as a rule the mafiosi leave foreigners alone.

The usual round-Sicily tour starts from Messina (occasionally from Catania) and proceeds to Taormina, and then clockwise to Syracuse, Agrigento, and Palermo, taking in some of the sights to be found along the coasts. This section recommends side trips to Enna in the island's geographical center, and to lofty Erice. Every visitor to Palermo, the island's capital, should spare at least half a day for nearby

Monreale. A week is hardly enough for getting an idea of what Sicily has to offer.

The accent of the Sicilian cuisine is on rich pasta—often garnished with olives and eggplant—and on seafood. Swordfish (*pesce spada*) is a favorite dish. The Sicilians have a sweet tooth, probably inherited from the Arabs. Cakes and nougats are crunchy with almonds; the supreme triumph of Sicilian desserts is *cassata*, a composition of frozen cake, ice cream, candied fruit, and, often, chocolate and cream. Sicilian wines are high in alcohol content; whites and reds from the lava soils of Mount Etna and the sweet Marsala vintages are the best-known.

The once-pristine shores of Sardinia, Italy's other big island, have lately become highly fashionable with the international yachting set and, beyond its sophisticated enclaves, attract also multitudes of less affluent vacationers from mainland Italy and all over Europe.

The deluxe hotels, condominiums, and country clubs on the Costa Smeralda (Emerald Coast) in the island's northwest and more modest vacation havens along its shores don't belong in this book, and few foreigners ever venture into Sardinia's interior, which may look cheerless and even rough. Dotting the countryside are *nuraghi*, tall ruined fortress homes of the headmen of a prehistoric population about whom scholars know little.

Carthaginians and Etruscans vied for control of Sardinia before Rome took over, but even the Romans never succeeded in pacifying the island's interior completely. Later, Genoa and Pisa fought over Sardinia, which eventually became a Spanish dependency. At the end of the eighteenth century the European powers awarded the island to the dukes of Savoy, who styled themselves kings of Sardinia while ruling also over Piedmont and, later, Liguria. Italy was unified under the Savoy dynasty between 1859 and 1870.

While the interior of Sardinia will impress the visitor as still somewhat archaic, in striking contrast with the building boom and economic development in its capital, Cagliari, and along its coasts, this section does suggest a visit to an inland city, Sassari, with side trips to such fascinating coastal places as Catalan-speaking Alghero. If you fly to Sardinia from Rome or Milan, you will need at least three days to get an adequate impression of Sardinia from Sassari and its surroundings.

TAORMINA ▪

Sicily's most famous resort is today overbuilt, crowded on weekends, expensive, and occasionally presumptuous. Observations in this book about Agrigento, Capri, Portofino, Positano, and Sorrento are to a large extent true also of Taormina. The visitor will nevertheless be enchanted by the mild climate and the lush gardens, the stupendous Greek theater and other vestiges from antiquity, and above all by the incomparable views: Taormina is perched 750 feet above the blue Ionian Sea and an inviting coast; the cyclopean pyramid of Mount Etna rises in the south with snow on the upper slopes and a crown of clouds and fumes, with fiery flashes at night, during its frequent sputterings; to the northeast the mountain ranges of Calabria are visible, suggesting another island rather than the extreme tip of the European continent.

Late winter and early spring are Taormina's deluxe tourist season, when well-heeled guests from colder climes, many Americans, Britons, and Scandinavians among them, loll in the sun. They may, however, also be disappointed by rainy spells, or by days filled with icy gusts of the *grecale* wind, which sweeps across the sea from the Balkans. The town numbers some 10,000 permanent residents.

Taormina's busy, narrow main street, Corso Umberto, cuts through the elongated town for about a mile from the Messina Gate to the Catania Gate. Short alleys and stairways branch off on either side; little squares encourage lingering at some café table. Strolling up and down Corso Umberto is a ritual in Taormina; motor vehicles are barred from the street during certain hours. Stores and boutiques display fashion articles, jewelry, antiques, English-language books, Sicilian lace and embroidery, paintings, prints, and crockery.

The back streets are much quieter than Corso Umberto. Geraniums and other flowers in vivid colors brighten windows and terraces throughout the town. Some of the buildings lining the street have Gothic doorways and gables. Façades with Renaissance and Baroque lines carry decorations in black lava and in the different kinds of marble quarried in the nearby hills. Lingering Moorish influences in Taormina's architecture are unmistakable; the town was under Arab domination from 902 to 1078, when Norman knights conquered it.

336

As early as March some of the guests from the north will go down to the pebbly beaches below the town—for the Swedes the water here never seems too cold. Italians will with never-ending amazement watch the early bathers from the waterfront restaurants. Later in the year, from June to September, the bathing concessions between Mazzarò and Naxos on the coast near Taormina will teem with local people and Italians from what Sicilians call "the Continent."

Throughout the year the top hotels in town, particularly the San Domenico, cater to wedding parties from Messina, Catania, Syracuse, and other places in eastern Sicily. The father of the bride, who traditionally foots the bill, may have to go into debt, but status is asserted and prestige won through such a Taormina affair.

The San Domenico Palace Hotel was a Dominican convent from the fifteenth century to 1896; its wainscoted bar is the former refectory. The complex includes two cloisters, a new wing that once was a separate hotel, a swimming pool, and terraced gardens. The opulent establishment, which commands some of Taormina's finest views, rests on one of four spurs of Mount Tauro on which the town is built. The hill, about 1,200 feet high, gave Taormina its name: The modern form is derived from the Greek Tauromenion, meaning "Home of the Mount Tauros Dwellers."

It is controversial whether the Greek colonists were thinking of Mount Tauros in Asia Minor when they sighted the hill on Sicily's east coast, or whether the pre-Greek native inhabitants of the area, the Sicels, already had called it by a name that sounded similarly.

Taormina, at any rate, is very old. Excavations have proved that Sicels were living on Mount Tauro when the first Greeks landed at Cape Schisò to its south in the eighth century B.C., and called that site Naxos, after the largest and most fertile island in the Cyclades. It was the oldest Greek settlement in Sicily. In the fourth century B.C. Tauromenion too became Greek, a small city-state that most of the time was a protectorate of Syracuse, then the foremost power in the region.

We know a great deal about the government of Greek Tauromenion—the names of its officials, its elections, its finances—from inscriptions on pilasters and stone tablets that have come to light since the eighteenth century. The ancient city was an oligarchy run by elected members of a few property-owning families. Tauromenion had around 20,000 inhabitants, double the figure of the permanent population in present-day Taormina. Greek continued to be spoken in the ancient city long after it had submitted to the Romans during the Second Punic War at the end of the third century B.C.

Taormina's most impressive legacy from the ancients is its Greek theater. It was built, probably on the site of an older structure for public entertainment, during the second or first century B.C. when the city was already officially Roman; much of what is seen today is Roman reconstruction work from the second century A.D. The semi-circular auditorium was hewn out of a brow of Mount Tauro; it has been calculated that more than a million cubic yards of rock were removed. Some of the granite columns and brickwork arches of the two-story stage building together with dressing and storage rooms are preserved, whereas most of the marble decorations were pillaged over the centuries.

The theater could accommodate more than 5,000 spectators, including some 600 women who were allowed to sit on a terrace. Even today, with much of the original structures missing, the acoustics astonish: A word spoken on the stage is clearly heard on the highest seats. Among Greek remains of the kind on Italian soil only the theater of Syracuse is larger than the Taormina ruin, but the view is more magnificent here. From the top of the auditorium, looking southeast, one sees the massive stage building in the foreground, and behind it Mount Etna to the right, the valley of the Alcantara River, and the coastline with its promontories and bays to the left. The scenery is most admirable at sunrise and sunset.

Classical drama is performed in the Greek theater in summer; from time to time the ruin is also used for concerts and film shows. The Antiquarium, a small archaeological museum next to the theater, contains statuary, inscriptions, and architectural fragments. The remains of a small Roman theater, dug up at the end of the nineteenth century, can be seen close to the Church of Santa Caterina and the battlemented medieval Corvaia Palace near the Messina Gate in the town's north.

A panorama of Mount Etna and the coast can also be enjoyed from Piazza Nove Aprile, about halfway on Corso Umberto, with an arched clock tower. Other spots with remarkable vistas are the well-tended public gardens southeast of the Greek theater, and a terrace (Belvedere) off the three-mile-long road that winds steeply past cliffs up from the coastal highway at Giardini, entering the town at the Messina Gate.

Taormina's cathedral, in the southwestern part of town, is a sturdy edifice with a fourteenth-century Gothic portal. A graceful Baroque fountain in Cathedral Square faces the main entrance.

Those who love grandiose views should climb the hills near Taormina, which can be done by car or, if you don't mind steep paths, on foot in about three hours up and down. The ruined Castle of Taormina sits at 1,305 feet, overlooking the town. Separated from it by a saddle, the village of Castel Mola, a cluster of houses on a 1,476-foot-high rock ledge, is farther northwest, surmounted by the remains of another old castle.

SYRACUSE (SIRACUSA) ■

No visitor to Sicily should miss this luminous city in the island's southeast. It is full of reminiscences from antiquity and enjoys a mild and sunny climate—an attractive seaside place in which to spend a few restful days any time in the year.

Syracuse is also an illustrious name in ancient history. Older than Rome, the city was for centuries a beacon and outpost of Greek civilization in the western world, second only to Athens in its cultural radiance. Aeschylus, Pindar, and Plato journeyed to Syracuse much in the same way that European creative talent seeks success in New York today. Archimedes, the greatest mathematician of the ancient world, and Theocritus, the poet of idyls, were natives. The apostle Paul preached here.

Modern Syracuse, *Siracusa* in Italian, has during the last few decades greatly expanded, spawning undistinguished business and residential neighborhoods. It now has a population exceeding 100,000, yet it still numbers only one-third of the ancient city's inhabitants at the height of its power and splendor some 2,400 years ago.

Today, Italians who have painfully become accustomed to frequent reports about organized crime in other parts of Sicily almost never hear of Syracuse. "We have no Mafia here," local people will boast. The atmosphere is indeed remarkably serene. The stranger will encounter grave politeness and dignity almost everywhere, coupled with pride in the city's Hellenic heritage. Perhaps it is more than just an illusion of one finds quite a few present-day Syracusans having profiles with straight noses that seem "Greek," like the figures on the vase paintings in the archaeological museum. Bloodlines over the millennia?

Until World War I Syracuse was essentially an old town crammed into a club-shaped island, the Ortygia of the Greeks, separated from the Sicilian mainland and many ancient ruins by a narrow canal, and accessible over a bridge. Since then new city districts with long, straight streets have sprung up, enveloping the remains of the vast ancient mainland quarters. A map will help to find the principal sites, some of them now hidden by modern Syracuse.

When colonizers from the Greek isthmus city of Corinth first settled in Ortygia during the eighth century B.C., the island was already inhabited by an indigenous population. Traces of pre-Greek dwellings have been found here. A neolithic village existed on the mainland a few miles to the north, and Bronze Age tombs have been dug up nearby, all within the area that would eventually be taken up by the walled Greater Syracuse of the Greeks.

Today Ortygia island, with long, narrow and curving streets, little squares, quiet seaside promenades, old churches, and medieval and Renaissance buildings, seems a pocket compendium of a long history. The Doric columns of a temple of Athena, erected in the fifth century B.C. and praised by Cicero a few hundred years later, can still be seen in the cathedral, which was built into the ruins of the pagan shrine in the seventh century.

The National Archaeological Museum opposite the cathedral is one of the best-organized in Italy. In a room all by itself the *Venus Anadyomene*, the headless Roman copy of a Hellenistic statue of a girl emerging from her bath, charms the visitor. The museum holds many other treasures, including a vast collection of prehistoric artifacts found in various places in eastern Sicily.

Stroll from the museum southward to the Fountain of Arethusa in a basin with papyrus plants. Syracuse and its surroundings are among the few areas in Europe where the papyrus, brought by the Arabs to Sicily from the Nile Valley, grows spontaneously. The spring, named after a nymph, was in ancient times believed to spout water from a

Greek river that reached Sicily through a channel below the Ionian Sea. Farther south, the tip of the island of Ortygia is secured by Maniace Castle, a fortress built by the Swabian kings of Sicily in the thirteenth century. Ruins of Greek temples, Roman baths, and other structures are scattered in various points of the old town.

The most important sights on the mainland are the Greek theater and the celebrated quarries. The semicircular open-air theater, larger than the Theater of Dionysus in Athens, is well preserved and from its upper tiers offers a magnificent view of Syracuse and its Great Harbor west of Ortygia (the Little Harbor is east of the island). The panorama is particularly impressive in the afternoon.

Aeschylus in person supervised here what may be called the world premiere of his play, *The Aetnae*, in 472 B.C. A large Roman amphitheater, built under Emperor Augustus for races and the brutal gladiatorial shows that the Greeks abhorred, is in the same area, together with several other Greek and Roman ruins.

The *latomíe*, typical of Syracuse, are the quarries where local contractors found the chalk and stones for temples, fortifications, and other projects. The deep excavations were worked by slaves and by criminals sentenced to forced labor, and were sometimes used to hold prisoners of war. Seven thousand Athenian soldiers and marines ended up in the quarries after the disaster of their expeditionary force in the campaign against Syracuse during the Peloponnesian War in 413 B.C. Many died, Thucydides reports, and others were sold as slaves after seven months' captivity. A few were set free because they knew by heart verses of the much-admired Euripides that had not yet reached Syracuse—a life-saving declamatory skill.

Today the *latomíe*, to be found in various spots in mainland Syracuse, are lushly overgrown with many species of southern trees and plants. The protection and constant warmth offered by the old quarries account for an almost tropical luxuriance of their manifold vegetation.

The most famous of the quarries is the Latomía of Paradise, more than 100 feet deep, between the Greek theater and the Roman amphitheater. An oval grotto in it is known as "The Ear of Dionysius." Dionysius I, the tyrant, or absolute ruler, of Syracuse from 406 to 367 B.C. is said to have been able to monitor here what his prisoners were saying thanks to extraordinary acoustics in the quarry. Today

341

guides will whisper a few words in a far corner, and the visitors will hear them. The vast excavations include also a lengthy grotto where ropemakers used to ply their trade. The extended Latomía of the Capuchins (named after an old convent) near the eastern shore is probably the quarry where the Athenians were detained. Sir Winston Churchill painted here when he was spending a vacation at the nearby Villa Politi Hotel after World War II.

History and military buffs may go by car or tourist coach to the Castle of Euryalus, a fort built under the rule of Dionysius I at the point where the north and south walls of Greater Syracuse met on a plateau four miles from the shore. If the weather is clear, as it usually is in Syracuse, the visitor who has climbed one of the strongholds of the vast ancient fortifications may see Mount Etna to the north and the mountain ranges of Calabria beyond the Strait of Messina on the horizon.

There is also a Christian Syracuse. Converted by St. Paul, the Syracusans adopted St. Lucy (Lucia), who was said to have been martyred in the year 304, as their patron saint. A life-size silver statue of the saint, made in the seventeenth century, is kept in her chapel in the cathedral. Every year on December 13, the feast day of the saint, the statue is carried in solemn procession to the 700-year-old Church of Santa Lucia on a square in the east of the mainland city that marks the spot where the saintly maid is said to have died for her faith. Eight days later the statue is returned to the cathedral, again with a procession, and a fireworks display ends "St. Lucy Week." For the popular celebration in December, guests from Sweden, where the saint is particularly venerated, usually arrive in Syracuse. A Caravaggio painting, *The Funeral of St. Lucy*, that used to adorn her church has recently been restored (it was badly deteriorated), and was shown in the National Museum in the Palazzo Bellomo.

A large new church of questionable architecture on the northern outskirts of Syracuse, known as the Sanctuary of Our Lady of the Tears, treasures a statuette of the Virgin Mary that is said to have been observed weeping on various occasions in recent years. The presumed miraculous events attracted, and still attract, many believers from all over Sicily and from nearby regions of the Italian mainland.

Syracuse, Italy's southernmost major city, and one of its oldest, has much to offer to a variety of interests.

ENNA ■

Of all the ninety-five provincial capitals of Italy, this is, at 3,271 feet altitude, the loftiest. The traveler who traverses the often harsh interior of Sicily on the Palermo-Catania motorway sees the citadel of Enna with its towers from afar. Drive up the steep, winding road to the town: It has character. Enna looks stern; the lushness of Taormina and the languor of Agrigento seem much farther away than just a couple of hours by car.

Enna is Sicily's geographical center, and it looks out from its hill on an immense panorama, with the cone of Mount Etna to the east and the forbidding Madonie range to the northwest. In the foreground, almost at the same height as Enna but separated from it by the deep valley of the Morello River, is the little town of Calascibetta; the two neighbors face each other like two Sicilian families who live on either side of an alley, each with a balcony, one on the sixth and the other on the fifth floor.

The Hellenistic poet Callimachus, and Cicero after him, called Enna the "navel of Sicily," and Livy described the town as "*inexpugnabilis*" ("impregnable"). In fact, when rebelling slaves entrenched themselves in Enna in 135 B.C., it took the besieging Roman troops two years to retake it.

Today Enna seems stagnant: It has around 30,000 inhabitants, nearly the same number as in 1930. The town would be much bigger if all the natives who during the last few decades have migrated to Sicily's coastal cities, to the Italian mainland, and to Switzerland, West Germany, and America were to come back; few do because jobs are scarce here.

In contrast to the bustle and occasional seediness in the cities on the island's coasts, Enna is calm and tidy. Its people conduct themselves with great dignity and are proud to speak about their town. "This is the most Swabian place on the entire island," a student told me, repeating a phrase that I had heard over and over again during earlier visits here. History-conscious Sicilians regard Emperor Frederick II (1194–1250), a descendant of the dukes of Swabia, as one of their own. He had a special liking for Enna and stayed here often. One of the most fascinating figures of the High Middle Ages, Frederick, *"Stupor Mundi"* ("The Amazement of the World"), was the son of a Hohenstaufen emperor and a Norman princess. He was born in southern Italy, brought up among Saracens amid dangers and intrigues, and reputedly felt like a Sicilian. (He is buried in the cathedral of Palermo.)

It was Frederick who had the fortress on the highest point of Enna built. It stands grimly at the eastern tip of the town, patches of moss growing on its gray-brown stones. Six of the original twenty turrets have survived; the best view is from the battlemented Pisan Tower in the north of the stronghold. Open-air opera is occasionally performed in the agreeably cool summer evenings in one of the three large courtyards, with room for an audience of 8,000.

The citadel is known as the Castello Lombardo, probably because it was built near a neighborhood that was once inhabited by northern Italians (Lombards), maybe stonemasons from Como or Campione among them. A spur jutting out toward northeast from the site of the fortress is called the Rocca di Cerere (Rock of Ceres), a reminder of Enna's role as a cult center in antiquity.

A famous temple of Demeter (the Ceres of the Romans) with a giant statue of the goddess of agriculture that has long vanished stood here in Greek times; images of the goddess appear on coins struck in the ancient town, then called Henna. (Some scholars assume that a fertility goddess was worshipped here already by the pre-Greek inhabitants of the place.) The daughter of Demeter, Persephone (Proserpina to the Romans) is supposed to have also had a shrine in the town, but its site has not been located.

According to one theory, the temple to Persephone occupied the site where the cathedral now stands. This edifice, Our Lady of the Visitation, faces Piazza Mazzini, a square at the northern edge of the town, 500 yards west of the fortress. The church dates from the thirteenth century and was thoroughly remodeled later. Its Baroque façade is surmounted by a stout, square tower; the interior is lavishly decorated with spiral columns, sculptured marble, and gilt stuccoes. A small museum behind the apse of the cathedral contains fossils and archaeological items unearthed in the area, coins from various epochs, ceramics, and bronzes.

Enna's main street, Via Roma, leads to the town center, Piazza Vittorio Emanuele, with a Franciscan church and convent and a terrace looking out on the valley with the river, the railroad tracks, and the highways, and on Calascibetta, more than a mile away as the crow flies.

A little beyond the main piazza, Via Roma takes a sharp turn southward to the public gardens, which surround the octagonal Tower of Frederick II. The medieval structure is said to mark the exact center of Sicily.

Enna was until 1927 Castrogiovanni, a corruption of its Arab name, Kasr Janni, in the early Middle Ages. Mussolini restored the town's ancient appellation the way he had done for other places in the nation.

A highway descends from Enna's southern outskirts to Lake Pergusa, 6.5 miles away. This is an oval body of greenish water about three miles in circumference at an altitude of 2,210 feet. It is surrounded by slopes with eucalyptus trees and other greenery, a few hotels and restaurants, and the bungalows of a tourist village. Motor races are occasionally held on the road around the lake.

According to one of the Greek myths, Pluto, or Hades, the god of the underworld, abducted Persephone while she was gathering flowers near Lake Pergusa; a grotto on its south side is supposed to be the passage through which he carried his victim (and future wife) to his shadowy realm. A bronze replica of Bernini's *Rape of Proserpina* adorns a fountain in Enna's Piazza Francesco Crispi. (The original sculpture, dating from 1620 or thereabout, is in the Galleria Borghese in Rome.)

A recommended side trip is to the ruins of a vast Roman villa from the third or fourth century A.D. south of the hilltown of Piazza Armerina, a little more than 20 miles southeast of Enna. Magnificent mosaic floors, among the best examples of Roman art in the imperial age, came to light there during excavations after World War II, and have become one of Sicily's major sights. When I first visited the place in 1949, a pavement showing young women in a gymnasium had just been dug up, causing a stir because the mosaic figures were clad in what looked like two-piece bathing suits. The word *bikini* was then still a novelty, as was the bare-midriff fashion. The world's tabloids suddenly became interested in archaeology, splashing pictures of the "Bikini Girls of Ancient Rome."

The villa near Piazza Armerina, in an area now known as Casale ("farmhouse"), surely belonged to a high Roman official, maybe even to Subemperor Maximianus, co-ruler with Emperor Diocletian from A.D. 286 to 305, or to Emperor Maxentius, who reigned from 306 until his defeat by Constantine the Great at the doors of Rome in 312.

AGRIGENTO ∎

The Doric columns of the ancient shrines amid acacias and, in February and March, expanses of white almond blossoms in the Valley of the Temples with the dark blue sea farther down strike the visitor today no less than they must have amazed Pindar 2,500 years ago when he proclaimed Akragas, now Agrigento, "the most beautiful city of mortals." But turn around and you behold a modern hotel much too close to the sanctuaries of Greek divinities and above them the garish high-rises and other constructions that have recently gone up in total disregard of zoning laws.

Abusivismo, the widespread flouting of building codes, has plagued Italy, and especially Sicily, for at least a generation; environmentalists denounce Agrigento as one of the most blatant cases. The city has been paying a price for its anything-goes building spree. Landslides have occurred, damaging an aqueduct and impairing the water supply.

The paradox is that despite all the concrete that has been poured during three decades, Agrigento's population has remained at around 50,000. The city has hardly any industry, and is essentially still an agricultural center and a tourist attraction. Some money comes from abroad, sent home by workers from the Agrigento region who have emigrated to France, Switzerland, or West Germany. Other funds are believed to have illegal origins. Agrigento's real estate fever seems to be feeding on itself.

Even though developers may threaten to engulf the vestiges of Greek civilization, the Valley of the Temples is still a place of timeless beauty, the reason why no trip to Sicily is complete without a visit to Agrigento. The most favorable light in the archaeological area is early in the morning and just before sunset when the limestone of the ruins takes on an amber color. A panoramic road (Strada Panoramica) that branches off National Route No. 118 below the most modern neighborhoods of Agrigento and rejoins it before its junction

346

with National Route No. 115 (the coastal highway), permits rewarding views of the ancient sanctuaries.

Least decayed among them is the so-called Temple of Concord, 138 by 65 feet, with thirty-four columns. Next to the Temple of Theseus in Athens, it is the best-preserved Greek cult building anywhere. Agrigento's zealous early Christians did not destroy it the way they wrecked other pagan shrines because the structure was used as a church dedicated to St. Gregory.

To the east, in a dominant position on a cliff, is the so-called Temple of Juno, with twenty-five fluted columns still standing, some badly eroded. To the west are the ruins of a shrine to Zeus; it was, at a length of 331 feet, one of the biggest temples in the Greek world, much larger than the Parthenon in Athens. The remains of temples dedicated to Hercules, to Aesculapius, and to the Dioscuri, Castor and Pollux, are nearby. All attributions are tentative, based on inscriptions found in the area, other archaeological evidence, or mere tradition; different gods of the Greek pantheon may actually have been venerated in the temples, which date from the late sixth century and the fifth century B.C.

Akragas was then a rich, combative city-state, deriving much of its wealth from trade with Carthage, in what is now Tunisia, across the channel of the Mediterranean that is called the African Sea. Fruitful commercial exchanges alternated with wars, and at the end of the fifth century B.C. the Carthaginians conquered and pillaged Akragas. The city was rebuilt but never recovered its earlier splendor. In Roman times it was, as Agrigentum, a provincial center where many inhabitants kept speaking Greek. A "Hellenistic-Roman District" with houses and streets in a grid pattern has recently been dug up north of the temples. In the Middle Ages Agrigento was ruled by Arabs, Normans, and Sicily's other alien masters.

In 1964 a modern archaeological museum was opened near the little Romanesque-Gothic Church of San Nicola, which in the Middle Ages was built with stones from the nearby Greek ruins. The museum covers Agrigento's prehistory and history from the Stone Age to Greek colonization to Roman, Arab, and Norman dominance. Explanatory panels help the visitor understand the exhibits. Of particular interest is a collection of votive offerings from the fifth and fourth centuries B.C. that were dug up in and near the temples. The Civic Museum in the old town contains art from the Middle Ages to our era.

OPPOSITE, TOP: *Taormina,*
Greek Theater

OPPOSITE, BOTTOM: *Taormina*

LEFT: *Syracuse,*
"The Ear of Dionysus"

BELOW: *Monreale,*
interior of the cathedral

LEFT: *Sassari, provincial
headquarters*

BELOW: *Sassari, Church of
St. Mary of Bethlehem*

In classical times Akragas consisted of districts in and around the Valley of the Temples with perhaps five times as many inhabitants as modern Agrigento has. An acropolis, or fortified area with a temple, overlooked the Greek city from the ridge above what is now the main archaeological zone. The exact location of that citadel and its shrine is controversial. According to one theory the fourteenth-century cathedral of Agrigento, near the highest point of the 1,069-foot hill on which the medieval city was built, rises on the site of the ancient acropolis; some scholars hold, however, that the fortress-and-sanctuary was on top of the 1,150-foot hill southeast of the old city, which is known as the Rock of Athena. Walls, in part still traceable, enclosed the twin hills and the Valley of the Temples. The hills descend abruptly on their north side, and a terrace above a cliff near the cathedral looks out on the high mountains of Sicily's interior toward the north.

The broad, tree-lined Viale della Vittoria at the foot of the Rock of Athena is the main boulevard of modern Agrigento, a developer's dream and an urban planner's nightmare. A short stroll farther southeast, past a cemetery, leads to the Church of San Biagio, which in Norman times was built on a platform that had been cut out of the rock in the early fifth century B.C. for a temple, believed to have been dedicated to Demeter, the goddess of agriculture, and her daughter, Persephone. The spot commands a celebrated panorama of the Valley of the Temples, the coastline, and the sea.

Demeter is no longer honored in Agrigento, but agriculture still plays a part in the city's religious life. In a thanksgiving rite on the first Sunday in July, carts drawn by oxen and mules and loaded with grain and other farming produce move in a procession to the Church of San Calogero between the twin hills.

Four miles southwest of Agrigento is the city's harbor, Porto Empedocle, built in the seventeenth century. Boats for the island of Lampedusa leave from the small artificial port, which is guarded by a watchtower. The town of 18,000, with straight streets, is named after the philosopher, statesman, and healer Empedocles, who belonged to the aristocracy of Akragas in the fifth century B.C. East of the harbor is Agrigento's bathing beach, San Leone, with seaside eating places.

About halfway between Porto Empedocle and Agrigento is the borough of Villaseta, the birthplace of Luigi Pirandello (1867–1936).

Manuscripts, books, and other memorabilia illustrating the career of the dramatist and author who won the 1934 Nobel Prize in Literature can be viewed in the house where he was born.

ERICE ▪

This unusual town, sometimes called the "Switzerland of Sicily," is an aerie perched on an isolated rock that rises in the island's north-western tip, looking out on a luminous Mediterranean panorama with spectacular sunsets. Erice (pronounced EH-ree-cheh) has the seaport of Trapani at its feet, with straight, long streets in the city's modern district and glittering salt flats along the shore. Farther southwest, the Egadi, the three islands of the Aegadian archipelago—Favignana, Levanzo, and Marettimo—with their hills and tuna fisheries, seem to float in the azure sea. The northernmost part of Africa, with Tunisia's Cape Bon 109 miles to the southwest, can be glimpsed on some winter days. South of Erice, the verdant coastal plains stretch to the vineyards of Marsala. Turn east and you can see the peaks of Sicily's rugged interior and, on clear days, even Mount Etna, Europe's largest volcano, 130 miles away.

At 2,450 feet, Erice is like an airship serenely gazing at immense horizons. The town is much cooler than Trapani and the coast below. The refreshing breezes turn quite often into biting winds; at times the mountain and buildings are wrapped in cold fog. Even at the height of summer it is advisable to pack woolens for a trip up to Erice.

The bracing climate is not the only reason why the town of 25,000 has a "Swiss" cachet. Erice's neatness and quiet strike the visitors who on their way up have passed through bustling, noisy, and often scruffy Sicilian cities. "Cleanliness and silence are signs of civilization" is the somewhat polemical message that can be read on one of Erice's town gates. If you notice an empty cigarette pack on the dainty, hexagonal-patterned stone pavement in the town's narrow streets you may be sure it was dropped by a careless tourist and will soon be picked up.

The old gray stone houses huddling within the town walls are well kept, many of their wooden doors freshly polished, and their courtyards uncluttered and often brightened up with flowers. Cars don't have much space to move around the town, whose several levels are linked by broad stairways, so there isn't much traffic noise. The inhabitants themselves aren't given to boisterousness. The older men still wear the black Sicilian hoods whenever it gets chilly, and the women too are often in black. They all move and speak in a dignified way; they seem a breed apart in a spot that has seen plenty of history.

When the Phoenicians, Greeks, and Carthaginians invaded and colonized Sicily in successive waves before 1000 B.C., they probably found already existing a sanctuary and a town on the rock that carries today's Erice, and which may have been a sea mark for mariners since prehistoric times. The early mountaintop settlement was inhabited by Elymians, one of Sicily's pre-Greek tribes that was perhaps of Ligurian origin. In the Elymian sanctuary, a goddess—possibly transplanted from Minoan Crete—was venerated; she became Astarte, Aphrodite, and Venus as Carthaginians, Greeks, and Romans in turn captured the strategic site.

Remains of the temple of Astarte-Aphrodite-Venus have been identified among the foundations of the castle that the Norman overlords of Sicily built on the highest point of the mountain in the eleventh or twelfth century. Today the castle is surrounded by a public park, which commands the finest views in town.

Phoenician masons' marks have been found on some of the stone blocks of Erice's cyclopean walls underneath long stretches of the town's medieval fortifications. In and near the town, archaeologists have dug up Punic, Greek, and Roman coins, fragments of statuary, and other ancient artifacts; some of these finds can be viewed in the small museum adjoining the library in the town hall.

A bell tower near the Trapani Gate in the west of Erice's walls is from the thirteenth century, and the oldest portion of the nearby cathedral dates from the fifteenth century; the church was thoroughly restored in 1865. From the days of the Normans the town was known for eight centuries as Monte San Giuliano. Erice, the Italian form of its name in antiquity, Eryx, became official in the 1930s.

The town is a place to rest in simple, quiet surroundings, to linger at an outdoor table in Piazza Umberto I, to take walks in the nearby pine groves, and to read or maybe do some creative work. Evenings are uneventful. For some years an Italian scientific foundation has organized international seminars of physicists in Erice in summer.

The town can be reached by car or public bus over two steep roads with many bends from Trapani or from the Palermo-Trapani highway. A cableway that used to link Erice with Trapani in ten minutes had suspended its service when I last visited the area. Hikers climb to Erice over footpaths from the eastern outskirts of Trapani in two to three hours.

MONREALE ∎

This town on a 1,150-foot hill five miles southwest of Palermo, with its incomparable cathedral and cloister and its views of the lush orange and lemon groves deep below perpetuates the brief Norman dream in Sicily. Stroll through the crowded streets of Monreale, and every now and then you will notice someone who speaks and acts like a native but—with blond or reddish hair, a lanky frame, a lengthy face—won't fit at all the cliché of the swarthy, squat southerner. Here perhaps more than anywhere else in Italy the Normans have left a genetic heritage in addition to a cultural legacy.

The knights and mariners who were descendants of the Norse raiders of the Dark Ages moved into the Mediterranean from their base at the mouth of the Seine in France as mercenaries and fortune-seekers at the beginning of the eleventh century. By 1101 one of them, Roger I, was lord of all of Sicily after his men had defeated the Saracen princes who had been ruling the island.

Monreale is the creation of a great-grandson of Roger I, King William II the Good (son of William I the Bad), who reigned from 1166 to 1189. "From the manhood to the premature death of that amiable prince," wrote Gibbon, "Sicily enjoyed a short season of peace, justice and happiness, whose value was enhanced by the remembrance of the past and the dread of futurity." The Norman adventure in Sicily was indeed soon to end.

The Normans, whose forefathers had come from rougher climates, must have been enchanted by the luxuriant vegetation of the Conca d'Oro, the "Golden Shell" near their capital, Palermo, and below Monreale. The ancient Romans and later the Arabs had tapped the springs and developed an intricate network of shafts and canals, increasing the natural fertility of the plain that is shaped like an

355

arena hugged by an amphitheater of hills and mountains. The irrigation system that fascinated the seafaring Normans still functions today, allegedly run to a large extent by a "Mafia of the Waters." From the hill above the Conca d'Oro one sees only the deep green of the trees and the gold of their fruit, not the wells.

Monreale means "royal mountain." William II founded an archbishopric here, close to the much older archiepiscopal see of Palermo, and had a cathedral and an adjoining Benedictine monastery built. It didn't take long for a town to grow around the new ecclesiastical establishment on the hillside. Today many of the 27,000 residents of Monreale commute to jobs in Palermo, but they will invariably stress that they are not Palermitans. "I am from Monreale," the typical explanation is. "Our family has Norman blood." True or imaginary, descent from the twelfth-century overlords is highly valued in Sicily.

Monreale's cathedral is the outstanding example of Norman architecture and art in the Mediterranean, incorporating Byzantine-Greek and Arab elements. Pointed arches of the kind the Saracens introduced in Sicily make the choir on the outside of the large church particularly remarkable. The two squat towers flanking the entrance are a characteristic feature of the Norman style. The bronze doors of the portal are the work of Bonanno da Pisa, who had been called to Sicily. His reliefs depict biblical episodes with inscriptions that show the transition from medieval Latin to the emergent Italian vernacular. This is a matter for specialists, but the interior of the cathedral with its grandiose mosaics speaks to everyone.

The 130 mosaic panels, covering more than 70,000 square feet on all the walls, contain scenes, on a golden background, from the Old and New Testaments and from the lives of the apostles. There are also images of saints, a tableau above the royal throne showing Jesus bestowing the crown on William II, and opposite, above the archbishop's throne, a mosaic depicting the king offering a model of the cathedral to the Virgin Mary. A giant representation of Christ in the solemn Byzantine pose as ruler of the universe (*Pantokrator*) rises in the apse. Inscriptions on the mosaics are mostly in Latin, some in Greek. The tombs of the "bad" William and the "good" William are in the right transept.

The Romanesque cloister, also with Arab pointed arches, adjacent to the cathedral is all that has remained of the monastery that William II had built. Arcades in mellow hues of gray, brown, and yellow surround subtropical plants in the courtyard, with a thoroughly Oriental wellhead in one corner. There are 216 columns in pairs, each with a capital of a different design. Their carvings represent human figures, animals, and imaginary beings in a mixture of realistic and fantastic elements. One might spend an entire day merely studying the sculptures, and would want to come back to that unique cloister.

SASSARI ▪

Hardly to be compared with some of the more illustrious places on the Italian mainland and in Sicily described in this book, this city in the north of Sardinia prides itself on having provided the Italian Republic, born in 1946 from the ashes of Fascism and the ruins of World War II, with two of its presidents, Antonio Segni and Francesco Cossiga. Another son of Sassari, Enrico Berlinguer, headed the Italian Communist Party, the strongest Marxist movement in the West, as its secretary general from 1972 to his death in 1984. The remarkable role that politicians from Sardinia's second city (after Cagliari on the southern coast) have played in modern Italy may in part be due to the importance that its upper class has attached to education since the centuries of Spanish rule. Sassari's university, long controlled by the Jesuit Order, is more than 400 years old; it has turned out generations of lawyers and physicians, quite a few of whom entered public life.

Since 1948 Sardinia has been a semiautonomous region of the Italian state. The visitor to the island may have a better chance in Sassari of coming to know its inhabitants, who have a reputation for reserve and clannishness, than in the somewhat ramshackle administrative capital, Cagliari (population about 250,000). Sassari is in the interior, but close to fashionable beaches; the city is also surrounded by *nuraghi*, Sardinia's prehistoric towers of hewn and unhewn stones that rise in the shape of a truncated cone to a height of forty to sixty feet; these served as fortress dwellings of chieftains in the third and second millennia B.C.

With its 120,000 inhabitants Sassari is an essentially modern city on a plateau that declines toward the northwestern coastal plain; the sea is visible on the horizon. Vast new districts with rectilinear streets

357

and a few high-rise buildings enclose the old town, a maze of narrow, irregular lanes, on three sides. The straight, busy Corso Vittorio Emanuele cuts through Sassari's core, ascending from the railroad station toward the modern section in the city's southeast.

The cathedral, on a square south of Corso Vittorio Emanuele, was built between 1480 and about 1530 in the Aragonese Gothic style; it has a Spanish Baroque façade from the beginning of the eighteenth century. Town walls built by the Genoese and an Aragonese castle have long been razed. By Italian standards, Sassari is a relatively young city, having been founded in the Middle Ages as a refuge for the people of Porto Torres in the northwest, which was a harbor already in antiquity, and for residents of other coastal towns and villages that were then continually harassed by Saracen raiders. Pisans and Genoese were rivals for control of Sassari until the town was absorbed, with the rest of Sardinia, by the empire of Aragon-Catalonia in the fourteenth century. Eventually all Sardinia was ruled by Spanish viceroys. The House of Savoy, already in possession of Piedmont on the mainland, acquired Sardinia in 1720 (in exchange for Sicily), and its heads styled themselves kings of Sardinia until they became the sovereigns of unified Italy in the nineteenth century. The oldest neighborhoods of Sassari, around the cathedral, still have a distinct Spanish flavor.

Today the business center of Sassari is Piazza Cavallino, once the site of the Aragonese castle. The rectangular square with its office buildings and rows of palm trees marks the conjunction of the old town and the modern districts. A few steps from it is the spacious Piazza d'Italia with a monument of King Victor Emmanuel II and the massive prefecture building, the seat of the provincial bureaucracy. The Sassaresi come to this square and to the broad Via Roma, which leads from it to the southeastern outskirts, for their customary evening promenade.

About halfway on Via Roma is a park with the National Museum, named after a wealthy nineteenth-century collector, Giovanni Antonio Sanna. It contains archaeological material from Sardinia's intriguing prehistory until Roman times, and a picture gallery with paintings by minor Italian, Spanish, and Flemish artists that somehow found their way to Sassari, as well as a few works by anonymous Sardinians. Costumes, weapons, and other products of Sardinian craftsmen and folk art can be viewed in a separate building in the park.

The main buildings of Sassari University, the city's pride, cluster in the south of the historic center near the public gardens, where students hang out when the weather is balmy. Farther south are the graceful sixteenth-century Church of Sant'Agostino and, beyond the teaching clinics on Viale San Pietro, an airy square with a vast panorama and a little church, San Pietro di Silki, with a thirteenth-century campanile. Another noteworthy church, close to the railroad station, is Santa Maria di Betlemme (St. Mary of Bethlehem), with a dome and a thirteenth-century Gothic façade that in its ornaments betrays Arabic influences. A torchlight parade is held here in the evening of every August 14 to commemorate the cessation of a plague in the sixteenth century; on that occasion representatives of the old craft guilds, now purely traditional groupings, don old Spanish costumes.

The visitor to Sassari has a choice of side trips either to the *nuraghi* and the wild mountains of Sardinia's interior, or to the beaches and towns on the nearby coast. One of the gloomiest of the prehistoric strongholds is the Nuraghe Nieddu (*nieddu* means "black" in Sardinian) in the hills near the town of Ploaghe ten miles southeast of Sassari. It contains several chambers, one above another, and was built with chunks of lava from a long-spent volcano, 1,597-foot Mount San Matteo. A broad, hardened lava stream from an eruption thousands of years ago can be seen in the vicinity.

The beach nearest to Sassari is Lido di Platamone, nine miles northwest of the city, with a lagoon, pine groves, and a few hotels. Porto Torres, twelve miles northwest of Sassari, is its harbor and the landing place for the car ferry from Genoa. Probably used already by the Carthaginians and certainly by the ancient Romans, Porto Torres was chosen as one of the focal points for Sardinia's industrial development after World War II. A petrochemical complex was built, but at least initially the project was not a success.

Stintino, a fishing village in a picturesque fjord in the northwest tip of Sardinia, thirty miles from Sassari, has become a resort where many well-to-do families from Sassari own second homes.

The most appealing coastal town near Sassari is Alghero, twenty-two miles to its southwest, on a promontory with remains of Spanish ramparts, a small harbor, and new hotels. Many local people still speak a form of Catalan, the language of their ancestors whom the kings of Aragon settled here in the fourteenth century. Residents will inform the stranger that Emperor Charles V, during a stopover on his way to Tunis in 1541, addressed the townspeople from a still existing Gothic corner-window of the former Palazzo d'Albis near the waterfront where he was staying: "All of you shall be knights." Every native of Alghero may thus lay claim to imperial nobility. New fancy resort developments in the magnificent bays northwest of Alghero include Fertilia and Porto Conte.

APPENDIX ∎
Practical Travel Information

The following pages contain practical information for the hundred cities and towns of Italy, which are listed in alphabetic order and followed occasionally by other nearby places for suggested side trips.

I use the American term "ZIP code," although the official Italian abbreviation for the system is "CAP" (*codice di avviamento postale*). As for the telephone area codes, omit the initial zero if you call from abroad, using instead the country code for Italy, 39. Telephone numbers, given in parentheses after addresses, are in various areas of Italy in the process of being changed, usually with the addition of one digit or two. For operator assistance in Italy, dial 175.

Travel information for most places indicates the duration of the railroad trip from Rome or some other major city on the assumption that the most convenient trains are used; highway distances in miles refer to recommended routes. It should also be kept in mind that Italy's domestic air services offer flights to many destinations throughout the peninsula and the islands.

The code initials after the names of hotels and restaurants mean: (T) top category; (M) medium range; and (P) plain. When no hotel or restaurant is listed, it is because I felt unable to make a recommendation from personal experience, but visitors should almost always be able to find a place to get a meal or a snack, or to spend the night.

Museums and collections are listed with their telephone numbers so that would-be visitors may inquire about opening times and admission fees.

The information offices listed are operated by municipal, provincial, or regional authorities; whenever there are more than one of such agencies in a city or town, the most convenient one is emphasized. Some of the towns described lack any public information office, and therefore there is no listing.

A brief pronunciation guide may be in order: Most Italian words and names carry the stress on their penultimate syllable, as in Treviso (treh-VEE-zoh); exceptions are sometimes marked by a grave accent, as in Forlì (for-LEE), and sometimes aren't, as in Modena (MOH-deh-nah) or Sassari (SASS-ah-ree). The letter groups *ce* and *ci* become in Italian "cheh" and "chee"; *ge* and *gi* are pronounced "jeh" and "jee"; *che* and *chi* become "keh" and "kee." The hard *g* sound in the English "get" is in Italian expressed, before the vowels *e* or *i*, by the letters *gh*. The letter groups *gn* and *gl* before a vowel are pronounced as the following examples show: Anagni (ah-NAN-yee); Puglia (POOL-yah).

ADRIA ▪ ZIP code 45011; telephone area code 0426. By rail from Rome, with change of trains in Rovigo, 6 hours; from Venice, with change of trains in Rovigo, 1 hour 40 minutes. By car from Rome, 299 miles on Motorway A-1 to Bologna, Motorway A-13 to Rovigo, and National Route No. 443; from Venice, 40 miles on Motorway A-4 to Padua, Motorway A-13 to Rovigo, and National Route No. 443. ▪ *Hotel*: Stella d'Italia (P), 4 Viale Maddalena (21062). ▪ *Restaurant*: Laguna (P), 2 Via San Francesco (22431). ▪ *Museum*: National Archaeological Museum, 1 Piazza degli Etruschi (21612).

ROVIGO ▪ ZIP code 45100; telephone area code 0425. ▪ *Information*: 101 Corso del Popolo (22835). ▪ *Hotels*: Europa Palace (M), 92 Viale Porta Po (29504), on southern outskirts; Cristallo (M), 1 Viale Porta Adige (30701), near railroad station. ▪ *Restaurant*: Belvedere (M), 33 Viale Regina Margherita (31332), near railroad station. ▪ *Museum*: Picture Gallery of the Accademia dei Concordi, 14 Piazza Vittorio Emanuele II (21654).

AGRIGENTO ▪ ZIP code 92100; telephone area code 0922. By rail from Palermo in 3 hours; from Catania in 3½ hours; from Naples in about 15 hours; from Rome in about 17½ hours. By car from Palermo, 80 miles on National Routes Nos. 121 and 189; from Messina 168 miles on Motorway A-18 to Catania, and on Motorway A-19 and National Route No. 122. (The distance from Catania to Agrigento by road is 108 miles.) ▪ *Information*: 255 Viale della Vittoria (26926). ▪ *Hotel*: Villa Athena (T), Via dei Templi (23833), overlooking the temples. ▪ *Museums*: Regional Archaeological Museum, Contrada San Nicola (26323); Civic Museum, 283 Piazza Municipio (20722); Pirandello Museum, Frazione Villaseta, Contrada Cos.

AMALFI ▪ ZIP code 84011; telephone area code 089. By rail from Rome to Salerno in 3½ hours, from Naples to Salerno in 1 hour; from Salerno to Amalfi, 16 miles by bus or cab. Seasonal boat services from Naples, Capri, Sorrento, and Salerno. By car from Rome, 170 miles on Motorway A-2 to Naples, Motorway A-3 to Vietri a Mare, and National Route No. 163; from Naples, 39 miles on Motorway A-3 to Vietri a Mare, and National Route No. 163. ▪ *Information*: 25/27 Corso delle Repubbliche Marinare (871107). ▪ *Hotels*: Cappuccini (T) (871008); Luna (T) (871002); Miramalfi (M) (871247); all three with views of the sea. ▪ *Restaurant*: La Caravella (M) (871029). ▪ *Museums*: Civic Museum, Piazza Municipio (871241); Museum of Paper,

Valle dei Mulini (872615), a collection of prints, books, posters, and equipment for paper manufacture in an old paper mill.

ANAGNI ▪ ZIP code 03012; telephone area code 0775. By rail from Rome in 45 minutes to Anagni station; bus to town center, 5 miles. Public coach service from Rome, Castro Pretorio bus terminal, to Anagni in about 1 hour. By car from Rome, 41 miles on Motorway A-2, or National Route No. 6 (Via Casilina). ▪ *Hotels*: Santoro (P), 38 Via San Magno (725355); Coccinella (M), near motorway exit, 1.5 miles outside town (78133), with garden and swimming pool. ▪ *Museums*: Boniface VIII Museum, Piazza Innocenzo III (727053); Cathedral Treasury, Duomo (727228).

ANCONA ▪ ZIP code 60100; telephone area code 071. By rail from Rome in 3½ hours. By car from Rome, 179 miles on Motorway A-1 to Orte, National Route No. 204 to Narni, National Route No. 3 (Via Flaminia) to Fossato di Vico, National Route No. 76 to Falconara, and National Route No. 16; or 230 miles on Motorway A-25 to Pescara and Motorway A-14. ▪ *Information*: Stazione FF.SS. (Ferrovie dello Stato railroad station, phone 43221). ▪ *Hotels*: Palace (M), 24 Lungomare Vanvitelli (201813); Jolly (M), 14 Via Ventinove Settembre (201171); Roma & Pace (M), 1 Via Leopardi (202007). ▪ *Restaurants*: Passetto (M), Piazza Quattro Novembre (33214); Miscia (M), Molo Sud (201376), on the waterfront. ▪ *Museums*: National Museum of the Marches, 2 Piazza del Senato (22669); Municipal Picture Gallery, 17 Via Pizzicolli (23632).

ANZIO ▪ ZIP code 00042; telephone area code 06. By rail from Rome in 55 minutes. By car 35–38 miles on National Routes No. 7 (Via Appia) or No. 148, and National Route No. 207. ▪ *Information*: 3 Via Pollastrini (9846119). ▪ *Hotels*: Hotels and pensions tend to be crowded and noisy in summer; many of them are closed from October to Easter. It may be preferable to spend the night in Rome. ▪ *Restaurant*: Turcotto (M), 44 Riviera Mallozzi (9846340), below the lighthouse, good seafood.

AOSTA/AOSTE ▪ ZIP code 11100; telephone area code 0165. By rail from Turin in 2 hours 10 minutes; from Milan, with change of trains in Chivasso, in 3 hours 20 minutes. By car from Turin, 71 miles on Motorway A-5; from Milan, 115 miles on Motorway A-4 to Santhià, and Motorway A-5 to Aosta. ▪ *Information*: 8 Piazza E. Chanoux (35655 or 40526). ▪ *Hotels*: Valle d'Aosta (M), 174 Corso Ivrea (41845), on eastern outskirts; Turin (M), 14 Via Torino (44593), near Praetorian Gate. ▪ *Restaurants*: Cavallo Bianco (T), 15 Via Aubert (2214), central; Piemonte (M), 13 Via Porte Pretoriane

(40111), near central square. ▪ *Museum*: Regional Archaeological Museum, 10 Via Sant'Orso (41421).

L'AQUILA ▪ ZIP code 67100; telephone area code 0862. By rail from Rome in 3½ hours with change of trains in Terni; or 4 hours with change of trains in Sulmona. By car from Rome, 75 miles on Motorway A-24. Bus service from Piazza della Repubblica in Rome. ▪ *Information*: 8 Via Venti Settembre (22306). ▪ *Hotels*: Grand Hotel (M), Viale Crispi (20240); Duca degli Abruzzi (M), 10 Via Duca degli Abruzzi (28341). ▪ *Restaurant*: Tre Marie (M), 3 Via Tre Marie (20191). ▪ *Museum*: National Museum of the Abruzzo, Castello (26029).

AREZZO ▪ ZIP code 52100; telephone area code 0575. By rail from Rome in 2 hours; from Florence in 1 hour 10 minutes. By car from Rome, 136 miles on Motorway A-1; from Florence, 50 miles on Motorway A-1. ▪ *Information*: 116 Piazza Risorgimento (20839). ▪ *Hotels*: Minerva (M), 6 Via Fiorentina (27891), outside the town walls; Europa (P), 43 Via Spinello (32701), near railroad station. ▪ *Restaurants*: Buca di San Francesco (M), 1 Piazza di San Francesco (23271); Spiedo d'Oro (M), 12 Via Crispi (22873). ▪ *Museums*: Vasari House, 55 Via Venti Settembre (20295); Archaeological Museum, 10 Via Margaritone (20882); Medieval and Modern Museum, 8 Via San Lorentino (23868).

ASCOLI PICENO ▪ ZIP code 63100; telephone area code 0736. By rail from Rome, with change of trains in Pescara and San Benedetto del Tronto, in 5 hours. By motor coach from Rome in 3 hours; coaches are lined up in and near the Via Castro Pretorio, close to Rome's central rail terminal, Stazione Termini, and depart from there rather than from a permanent bus terminal. By car from Rome, 120 miles on Motorway A-25 to Pescara, Motorway A-14 to San Benedetto del Tronto, and motorway to Ascoli Piceno. ▪ *Information*: Piazza dell'Arringo (53045). ▪ *Hotels*: Marche (M), 34 Viale Kennedy (50035), in modern district on the eastern outskirts; Roxy Miravalle (P), Colle San Marco (52452), on hill 8 miles from the city center, with garden and swimming pool (open May to October). ▪ *Restaurants*: Gallo d'Oro (M), 13 Corso Vittorio Emanuele (53520); Kursaal Grill (M), 221 Corso Mazzini (53140); Tornasacco (M), 29 Via Tornasacco (54151); Il Cacciatore (M), Colle San Marco (62462), on hill south of the city. ▪ *Museums*: Civic Picture Gallery, Piazza dell'Arringo (53063); Archaeological Museum, Palazzo Panichi, Piazza dell'Arringo (53562).

ASOLO ▪ ZIP code 31011; telephone area code 0423. By rail from Rome, with change of trains in Padua, to Montebelluna in 7 hours, then from

Montebelluna to Asolo, 10 miles by public bus; from Venice to Montebelluna in 1 hour, then bus. By car from Rome, 560 miles on Motorway A-1 to Bologna, Motorway A-13 to Padua, and National Route No. 307 to Castelfranco Veneto and Asolo; from Venice, 42 miles on National Route No. 348 to Montebelluna, and National Route No. 248 to Asolo. ▪ *Information*: Via Regina Cornaro (55045). ▪ *Hotels*: Villa Cipriani (T), Contrada Canova (52166), with garden; Duse (P), Via Robert Browning (55241), near parish church. ▪ *Restaurant*: Villa Cipriani (T), Contrada Canova (52166). ▪ *Museum*: Civic Museum, Via Regina Cornaro (52011).

ASSISI ▪ ZIP code 06081; telephone area code 075. By rail from Rome, with change of trains in Foligno, in 2 hours 50 minutes; from Florence, with change of trains in Terontola–Cortona, in about 3 hours. By car from Rome 110 miles on Motorway A-1 to Orte, National Route No. 3 *bis* to Perugia, and National Route No. 75 eastward; from Florence 112 miles on Motorway A-1 to Chiusi–Chianciano Terme and National Routes Nos. 75 *bis* and 75. ▪ *Information*: 12 Piazza del Comune (812534). ▪ Hotel: Subasio (M), 2 Via Frate Elia (812206), near Basilica of St. Francis.

BASSANO DEL GRAPPA ▪ ZIP code 36061; telephone area code 0424. By rail from Rome, with change of trains in Venezia-Mestre, in 8½ hours; from Venice in 1 hour 20 minutes. By car from Rome, 340 miles on Motorway A-1 to Bologna, Motorway A-13 to Padua, and National Route No. 47; from Venice, 48 miles on Motorway A-4 to Padua, and National Route No. 47. ▪ *Information*: 9 Via delle Fosse (24351). ▪ *Hotel*: Belvedere (M), 14 Piazza Generale Giardino (29845). ▪ *Restaurants*: Al Sole (M), 42 Via Vittorelli (23206); Al Ponte (M), 60 Via Volpeto (26703), with garden and panorama. ▪ *Museums*: Civic Museum, 4 Via del Museo (2235); Canova Museum, Via Canova, 31054 Possagno (0423-54323).

BENEVENTO ▪ ZIP code 82100; telephone area code 0824. By rail from Rome in 2 hours 50 minutes; from Naples in 1 hour 50 minutes. By car from Rome, 145 miles on Motorway A-2 to Caserta, and National Route No. 7. ▪ *Information*: Via Nicola Sala (21960). ▪ *Hotel*: President (M), 1 Via Perasso (21000), near castle; with restaurant. ▪ *Museum*: Museum of Samnium, Piazza Santa Sofia (21818).

BERGAMO ▪ ZIP code 24100; telephone area code 035. By rail from Milan in 45 minutes; from Venice, with change of trains in Brescia, in 3½ hours. By car from Milan, 30 miles on Motorway A-4; from Venice, 145 miles on Motorway A-4. ▪ *Information*: 2 Via Torquato Tasso (210204). ▪ *Hotels*: Excelsior San Marco (M), 6 Piazza della Repubblica (232132); Moderno

(M), 106 Viale Papa Giovanni XXIII (233033); both in Lower Bergamo. ▪ *Restaurants*: Da Vittorio (M), 21 Viale Papa Giovanni XXIII (218060) in Lower Bergamo; Taverna del Colleoni (T), 7 Piazza Vecchia (232596) in Upper Bergamo; Gourmet (M), 1 Via San Vigilio (242523), near Funicular of San Vigilio, with rooms. ▪ *Museums*: Picture Gallery of Carrara Academy, 81 Piazza Carrara (242409); Archaeological Museum, Piazza Cittadella (233513); Donizetti Museum, 9 Via Arena (737474); Risorgimento Museum, 12 Piazza della Rocca (247116).

BOLZANO/BOZEN ▪ ZIP code 39100; telephone area code 0471. By rail from Rome in 8 hours; from Milan in 3–4 hours; from Venice in 3 hours 45 minutes. By car from Rome, 401 miles on Motorway A-1 to Modena North, and Motorway A-22; from Milan, 185 miles on Motorway A-4 to Verona, and Motorway A-22; from Venice, 166 miles on Motorway A-4 to Verona, and Motorway A-22. ▪ *Information*: 8 Piazza Walther (21867). ▪ *Hotels*: Park-Laurin (T), 4 Via Laurino (47500), with garden; Grifone-Greif (T), 7 Piazza Walther (27057); Scala-Stiegl (M), 11 Via Brennero (41111), with garden. ▪ *Restaurant*: Città-Stadthotel, 21 Piazza Walther (25221). ▪ *Museum*: Civic Museum, Via Museo (39212).

BRACCIANO ▪ ZIP code 00062; telephone area code 06. By rail from Rome (central Termini Station or San Pietro Station), with many intermediate stops, in 1 hour 15 minutes. By car from Rome, 25 miles on National Route No. 2 (Via Cassia) to the suburb of La Storta, and from there on National Route No. 493. ▪ *Information*: 58 Via Claudia (9024451). ▪ *Hotel*: Casina del Lago (P), 11 Lungolago Argenti (9024025), on the lakeshore 1 mile from the town center. ▪ *Restaurant*: Grotta del Castello (P), 1 Piazza Mazzini.

BRESCIA ▪ ZIP code 25100; telephone area code 030. By rail from Rome, with change of trains in Verona, in 7 hours; from Milan in 50 minutes; from Venice in 2 hours 10 minutes. By car, 348 miles on Motorway A-1 to Modena North, Motorway A-22 to Verona, and Motorway A-4; from Milan, 58 miles on Motorway A-4; from Venice, 115 miles on Motorway A-4. ▪ *Information*: 34 Corso Zanardelli (43418). ▪ *Hotels*: Vittoria (M), 20 Via delle Dieci Giornate (52122); Ambasciatori (M), 90 Via Santa Maria Crocifissa (308461). ▪ *Restaurants*: La Sosta (T), 20 Via San Martino della Battaglia (295603), in a seventeenth-century building in the south of the inner city; Augustus (M), 8 Via Laura Cereto (292130), central. ▪ *Museums*: Roman Museum, 57 Via dei Musei (46031); Civic Picture Gallery, 1 Via Martinengo da Barco (59120); Risorgimento Museum, 9 Via del Castello (44176).

BRESSANONE/BRIXEN ▪ ZIP code 39042; telephone area code 0472. By rail from Rome in 9 hours, 45 minutes; from Milan in 4½ hours. By car from Rome, 426 miles on Motorway A-1 to Modena North, and Motorway A-22; from Milan, 212 miles on Motorway A-4 to Verona, and Motorway A-22. ▪ *Information*: 9 Viale Stazione (22401). ▪ *Hotels*: Elefante-Elephant (T), 4 Via Rio Bianco (22288); Jarolim (M), Piazza Stazione (22230), opposite railroad station, with garden and swimming pool. ▪ *Restaurant*: Elefante-Elephant (T), 4 Via Rio Bianco (22288). ▪ *Museum*: Diocesan Museum, Palazzo Vescovile.

CAMPIONE D'ITALIA ▪ ZIP code 22060; telephone area code via the 091 Swiss telephone network (international code 41). By rail from Milan to Lugano, Switzerland, in 1 hour; from Lugano by cab or public bus in 10 minutes, by lake boat in 20 minutes. By car from Milan, 45 miles on Motorway A-9 to Como, Chiasso, and Bissone near Lugano, and local lakeshore road to Campione. ▪ *Information*: Lugano Tourist Office, 5 Riva Albertolli, CH-6901 Lugano, Switzerland (091-214664). ▪ *Restaurant*: Sporting Club Campione (686131).

CAPRI ▪ ZIP code 80073; telephone area code 081. From Naples by boat in 1½ hours, by hydrofoil (*aliscafo*) in 30 minutes. ▪ *Information*: Piazza Umberto I (8370686). ▪ *Hotels*: Quisisana (T), 2 Via Camerelle (8370788); Scalinatella (T), 8 Via Tragara (8370633); La Pineta (M), 6 Via Tragara (8370644). ▪ *Restaurants*: La Pigna (T), 30 Via Lo Palazzo (8370280); Canzone del Mare (T), Marina Piccola (8370498). ▪ *Museum*: Capri Museum, 8a Piazzetta Cerio (8370858).

ANACAPRI ▪ ZIP code 80071; telephone area code 081. ▪ *Information*: 19a Via Orlandi (8371524). ▪ *Hotels*: Europa Palace (T), 2 Via Capodimonte (8370955); Bella Vista (M), 10 Via Orlandi (8371463).

CASERTA ▪ ZIP code 81100; telephone area code 0823. By rail from Naples in 30–40 minutes; from Rome in 2 hours 20 minutes. By car from Naples, 20 miles on Motorway A-2; from Rome, 120 miles on Motorway A-2. ▪ *Information*: 39 Corso Trieste (321234). ▪ *Hotel*: Jolly (M), 7 Via Vittorio Veneto (325222), near the castle. ▪ *Museums*: Historical Apartments in the Royal Castle (321127); Campanian Provincial Museum, 85 Via Roma, Capua (0823-961402).

CASSINO ▪ ZIP code 03043; telephone area code 0776. By rail from Rome in 1 hour 50 minutes. By car from Rome, 82 miles on Motorway A-2 or National Route No. 6 (Via Casilina). ▪ *Information*: Via Leopardi (21292). ▪ Benedictine Abbey of Monte Cassino, 03043 Monte Cassino, Frosinone (0776-21397).

CHIETI ▪ ZIP code 66100; telephone area code 0871. By rail from Rome in 3 hours 20 minutes. By car from Rome, 125 miles on Motorways A-24 and A-25. ▪ *Information:* 29 Via Spaventa (65231). ▪ *Hotels:* Sole (P), 1 Via dei Domenicani (66681), central; Nuovo (P), Chieti Scalo (52109), 3 miles from city center. ▪ *Restaurant:* Venturini (M), 10 Via De Lollis (65863), central. ▪ *Museums:* National Museum of Antiquities, Villa Comunale (65704); Provincial Picture Gallery, 10 Via de Lollis (67554).

CHIOGGIA ▪ ZIP code 30015; telephone area code 041. By boat from Venice 1½ hours. By rail from Venice, with change of trains in Rovigo, 2 hours; from Rome, with change of trains in Rovigo, in 6½ hours. By car from Venice, 34 miles on National Route No. 309; from Rome, 320 miles on Motorway A-1 to Orte, National Route No. 204 to Narni, National Route No. 3 to Fano, Motorway A-14 to Rimini, National Route No. 16 to Ravenna, and National Route No. 309. ▪ *Hotels:* Grande Italia (P), Piazza Vigo (400515); hotels at Lido di Sottomarina during the summer months: Ritz (M), Largo Europa (401900). ▪ *Restaurant:* El Gato (M), 653 Campo Sant'Andrea (401806).

CHIUSI ▪ ZIP code 53043; telephone area code 0578. By rail from Rome in 2 hours 10 minutes; from Florence in 1 hour 50 minutes. By car from Rome, 100 miles on Motorway A-1; from Florence, 78 miles on Motorway A-1. ▪ *Hotel:* Longobardi (P), 59 Via Leonardo da Vinci (20157), near railroad station. ▪ *Restaurant:* Zaira (M), 12 Via Arunte (20260) in the old city; restaurant at Lake Chiusi: Hotel-Restaurant La Fattoria (M), 2 miles from the city (21407). ▪ *Museum:* National Archaeological Museum, Via Porsena (20177); Museum of Sacred Art, Piazza del Duomo (20240).

CITTÀ DI CASTELLO ▪ ZIP code 06062; telephone area code 075. By rail from Rome, with change of trains in Terni and Perugia–Ponte San Giovanni, in 4 hours. By car from Rome, 161 miles on Motorway A-1 to Orte, National Route No. 204, and Superhighway 3 *bis*. ▪ *Information:* 2 Piazza Garibaldi (853417). ▪ *Hotel:* Tiferno (P), 13 Piazza Raffaello Sanzio (8550331), with restaurant. ▪ *Restaurant:* Didon (P), 5 Via Roma (8555729), outside the town walls. ▪ *Museums:* Pinacoteca Comunale (Civic Picture Gallery), Palazzo Vitelli, Via V. E. Orlando (852680); Historical-Paleolontological Collection, 2 Piazza Garibaldi (853417).

CIVIDALE DEL FRIULI ▪ ZIP code 33043; telephone area code 0432. By rail from Rome, with change of trains in Udine, in 7 hours 20 minutes to 8 hours 20 minutes; from Venice in 2 hours. By car from Rome, 410 miles on Motorway A-1 to Bologna, Motorway A-13 to Padua, Motorway A-4 to

Palmanova, Motorway A-23 to Udine, and National Route No. 54. ▪ *Hotel*: Roma (P) (731871). ▪ *Restaurant*: Al Fortino (M), 46 Via Carlo Alberto (731217). ▪ *Museum*: National Archaeological Museum, Piazza del Duomo (71119).

COMO ▪ ZIP code 22100; telephone area code 031. By rail from Milan (Central Station) in 40 minutes; from Milan (Nord, North Station) to Como Nord on the lakefront in 1 hour. By car from Milan, 30 miles on Motorway A-9. ▪ *Information*: 16 Piazza Cavour (269491). ▪ *Hotels*: Excelsior (M), 1 Piazza Cavour (266531); Villa Fiori (M), 12 Strada per Cernobbio (557642), on the northwestern outskirts, with magnificent views and garden; Park Hotel (M), 20 Via Rosselli (556782). ▪ *Restaurant*: Da Celestino (M), 3/7 Lungo Lario Trento (263470), on the lakefront. ▪ *Museums*: Archaeological Museum, 1 Piazza Medaglie d'Oro (271343); Civic Museum (regional history, folk art, biology), 1 Piazza Medaglie d'Oro (268053); Volta Temple, Viale Marconi (559976).

CORTINA D'AMPEZZO ▪ ZIP code 32043; telephone area code 0436. By rail from Venice to Calalzo–Pieve di Cadore in 2½ hours; from Calalzo station to Cortina d'Ampezzo by state railroad bus in 1 hour. By car from Venice, 111 miles on Motorways A-4 and A-27 to Vittorio Veneto, and National Route No. 51 to Cortina d'Ampezzo. ▪ *Information*: 8 Piazzetta San Francesco (2711). ▪ *Hotels*: Miramonti Majestic (T), 104 Pezziè (4201), 1.25 miles south of town, with vast gardens and nine-hole golf course; Cristallo (T), 42 Via Menardi (4281); De la Poste (T), 14 Piazza Roma (4271), central; Concordia Park Hotel (M), 28 Corso Italia (4251), with garden; Trieste (M), 28 Via Majon (2245). ▪ *Restaurants*: El Toulà (T), 123 Via Ronco (3339); Bellavista (M), Località Gillardon (61043), on western outskirts of town; Cinque Torri (P), 15 Largo della Posta, central. ▪ *Museum*: Museum of Ra Regoles (history, folklore, art, handicrafts), 17 Corso Italia (66222).

CORTONA ▪ ZIP code 52044; telephone area code 0575. By rail from Rome to Terontola-Cortona in 2 hours 10 minutes; from Florence in 1 hour 40 minutes; from Terontola-Cortona by bus to Cortona in 10–15 minutes. Local trains from Orte or Chiusi–Chianciano Terme (northbound), and Florence (southbound) stop in Camucia-Cortona; from there by bus to Cortona in 5 minutes. By car from Rome, 125 miles on Motorway A-1 to the Val di Chiana exit, and provincial road to Camucia; from Florence, 73 miles on Motorway A-1 to the Monte San Savino exit, provincial road eastward, and National Route No. 71. *Information*: 10 Piazza Signorelli (603056) ▪ *Hotels*: Oasi (M), 1 Via Contesse (603188), in a park on the southeastern outskirts, with fine panorama; San Luca (M), Piazza Garibaldi (603787), near town walls, with panorama ▪ *Restaurants*: Tonino (M), Piazza Garibaldi (603100), in the Hotel SanLuca; la Loggetta (M), 3 Piazza Pescheria (603777), central. ▪ *Museums*: Museum of the Etruscan Academy, Piazza Signorelli (603677); Diocesan Museum, Piazza del Duomo (62850).

COSENZA ▪ ZIP code 87100; telephone area code 0984. By rail from Rome, with change of trains in Paola, in 8 hours; from Naples, with change of trains in Paola, in about 5 hours. By car from Rome, 332 miles on Motorway A-2 to Naples, and Motorway A-3; from Naples, 196 miles on Motorway A-3. ▪ *Information*: Via Pasquale Rossi (30595). ▪ *Hotels*: Europa (M), at Rende, 2.5 miles north of Cosenza (36531); Jolly (P), 2 *bis* Lungo Crati di Seta (74481).

CREMONA ▪ ZIP code 26100; telephone area code 0372. By rail from Rome, with change of trains in Piacenza, in 7 hours; from Milan, by way of Treviglio (direct train), in 2 hours. By car from Rome, 326 miles on Motorway A-1 to Piacenza South, and Motorway A-21; from Milan, 58 miles on Motorway A-1 to Piacenza South, and Motorway A-21. ▪ *Information*: 2 Galleria del Corso (23233). ▪ *Hotel*: San Giorgio (P), 20 Via Dante (20462), near railroad station. ▪ *Restaurant*: Antica Trattoria del Cigno (M), 7 Via del Cigno (21361), near cathedral. ▪ *Museums*: Civic Museum, 4 Via Ugolani Dati (29349); Stradivarius Museum, 5 Piazza Marconi (23766); Museum of Peasant Civilization in the Po Valley, Cascina Cambonino, Via Castelleone (22138). ▪ International Professional Institute for Violin-Making Crafts, 5 Piazza Marconi (27129).

ENNA ▪ ZIP code 94100; telephone area code 0935. By rail from Palermo in 3 hours 15 minutes; from Catania in 1½ hours. By car from Palermo, 84 miles on Motorway A-19; from Catania, 52 miles on Motorway A-19. ▪ *Information*: 1 Piazza Garibaldi (24007). ▪ *Hotels*: Sicilia (M), Piazza Colajanni (21127); Belvedere (P), Piazza Francesco Crispi (21020), fine view. ▪ *Restaurants*: Centrale (M), 6 Via Ree Pentite (21025); Ariston (M), 365 Via Roma (26038). ▪ *Museum*: Archaeological Museum, Piazza Mazzini (24720).

ERICE ▪ ZIP code 91016; telephone area code 0923. By car from Palermo, 63–70 miles on National Routes Nos. 186, 113, and 187, and turnoff for Erice on right side of No. 187; or Motorway A-29 to Trapani, and 9 miles on provincial road from Trapani to Erice (or cableway if it operates). ▪ *Information*: Viale Conte Pepoli (869173). ▪ *Hotels*: Moderno, Via Vittorio Emanuele (869300); Ermione, Pineta Comunale (869138). ▪ *Restaurant*: Taverna di Re Aceste, Viale Conte Pepoli (869084). ▪ *Museum*: Civic Museum, Piazza Municipio (869258).

FAENZA ▪ ZIP code 48018; telephone area code 0546. By rail from Rome, with change of trains in Florence, in 5 hours 10 minutes; from Florence in 2 hours. By car from Rome, 230 miles on Motorway A-1 to Orte, National Route No. 204 to Narni, National Route No. 3 to Fano, and National A-14; from Florence, 65 miles on National Route No. 302. ▪ *Hotel*: Vittoria (M), 23 Corso Garibaldi (21508), central, with restaurant. ▪ *Museums*: International Ceramics Museum, 2 Via Campidori (21240); Civic Picture Gallery, 1 Via Santa Maria dell'Angelo (29453); Museum of the Neoclassical Era, 15 Via Tonducci (26493).

BRISIGHELLA ▪ ZIP code 48013; telephone area code 0546. By rail from Faenza in 15 minutes. By car from Faenza, 8 miles on National Route No. 302. ▪ *Hotels*: Terme (M) (81144), with garden and restaurant; Gigiole (P) (81209), with good restaurant (M).

FERRARA ▪ ZIP code 44100; telephone area code 0532. By rail from Rome in 5 hours; from Florence in 2 hours; from Venice in 1 hour 45 minutes. By car from Rome, 264 miles on Motorway A-1 to Bologna, and Motorway A-13; from Florence, 96 miles on Motorways A-1 and A-13; from Venice, 69 miles on Motorway A-13. ▪ *Information*: 22 Largo Castello (35017). ▪ *Hotels*: De la Ville (M), 11 Piazza Stazione (53101), near railroad station, with pleasant restaurant; Astra (M), 55 Viale Cavour (26234); Ferrara (M), 4 Piazza della Repubblica (33015), near castle, with good restaurant. ▪ *Museums*: National Picture Gallery, 21 Corso Ercole I d'Este (21831); Cathedral Museum, Piazza Cattedrale (32969); Schifanoia Museum, 23 Via Scandiana (36468); National Archaeological Museum (Spina Collection), 124 Via Venti Settembre (33869); Ariosto House, 67 Via Ariosto (32303).

FIESOLE ▪ ZIP code 50014; telephone area code 055. From Florence (railroad terminal, cathedral, or Piazza San Marco) with No. 7 bus in 15–20 minutes, depending on traffic. By car from Florence, 5 miles on Viale Alessandro Volta, Via San Domenico, and Via Vecchia Fiesolana. ▪ *Information*: 45 Piazza Mino da Fiesole (598720). ▪ *Hotels*: Villa San Michele (T), 4 Via Doccia (59451), on eastern outskirts, with park and view; Aurora (M), 39 Piazza Mino da Fiesole (59100), on main square, with small garden and view; restaurant. ▪ *Museums*: Archaeological Museum, 1 Via Marini (59477); Bandini Museum, 1 Via Dupré (59061); Ethnographic-Missionary Museum, Colle di San Francesco (59175).

SETTIGNANO ▪ By car from Fiesole, 4 miles on Via dei Bosconi. From Florence (Piazza San Marco) with No. 10 bus in 15 minutes. By car from Florence, 4 miles from Viale Edmondo de Amicis.

371

FOLIGNO ▪ ZIP code 06034; telephone area code 0742. By rail from Rome in 1½–2 hours; from Florence, with change of trains in Terontola-Cortona, in 3 hours 10 minutes. By car from Rome, 99 miles on Motorway A-1 to Orte and National Routes Nos. 3 *bis* and 3 via Terni and Spoleto; from Florence, 118 miles on Motorway A-1 to Chiusi–Chianciano Terme and National Routes Nos. 75 *bis* and 75 via Perugia and Assisi. ▪ *Information*: 126 Porta Romana (50493). ▪ *Museum*: Civic Museum, Palazzo Trinci, Piazza della Repubblica (53440).

FORLÌ ▪ ZIP code 47100; telephone area code 0543. By rail from Rome, with change of trains in Bologna, in 5 hours 40 minutes; from Bologna in 35 minutes. By car from Rome, 276 miles on Motorway A-1 to Bologna, and Motorway A-14; from Bologna, 40 miles on Motorway A-14. ▪ *Information*: 23 Corso della Repubblica (25545). ▪ *Hotels*: Della Città (M), 8 Via Fortis (28297), central; Principe (M), Via Emilia (29362), 1.5 miles west of city center, good restaurant; Astoria (P), Piazza Ordelaffi (26220), central. ▪ *Restaurants*: Da Pirin (M), 15 Via Mameli (25447); Amarcord (M), 1–3 Via Solferino (27349). ▪ *Museums*: Municipal Picture Gallery (Pinacoteca), Archaeological Museum, and Ethnological Museum, all 72 Corso della Repubblica (32771).

CESENA ▪ ZIP code 47023; telephone area code 0547. By rail from Forlì in 20 minutes. By car from Forlì, 12 miles on National Route No. 9. ▪ *Hotel*: Leon d'Oro (M), Piazza del Popolo (21103). ▪ *Restaurant*: Da Gianni (M), 9 Via dell'Amore (21328). ▪ *Museums*: Municipal Picture Gallery (Pinacoteca), 10 Corso Garibaldi (21142); Museum of Antiquities, 1 Piazza Bufalini (21297).

FRASCATI ▪ ZIP code 00044; telephone area code 06. By rail from Rome's central Termini Station in 30 minutes (frequent trains). By bus from Rome's Cinecittà subway station in 20 minutes. By car from Rome, 15 miles on Via Appia Nuova and Via Tuscolana (National Route No. 215). ▪ *Information*: 1 Via Marconi (9420331), off the main square. ▪ *Restaurant*: Spartaco (M), 1 Viale Letizia Bonaparte (9420431), near main square, with terrace.

GAETA ▪ ZIP code 04024; telephone area code 0771. By rail from Rome to Formia in 1 hour 20 minutes; from Naples to Formia in 1 hour 10 minutes; bus service from Formia to Gaeta. By car from Rome, 88 miles on National Route No. 7 (Via Appia) to Terracina, and National Route No. 213; from Naples, 59 miles on National Route No. 7 *quater*. ▪ *Information*: Piazza Diciannove Maggio (461165). ▪ *Hotel*: Flamingo (P), Corso Italia (461738). ▪ *Museum*: Diocesan Museum, Piazza Duomo (461225).

GUBBIO • ZIP code 06024; telephone area code 075. By rail from Rome to Fossato di Vico–Gubbio in 2 hours 25 minutes; bus from Fossato di Vico to Gubbio, 12.5 miles. By car from Rome, 136 miles on Motorway A-1 to Orte, and National Routes Nos. 3 *bis* and 298. • *Information*: 6 Piazza Oderisi (9273693). • *Hotels*: San Marco (M), 5 Via Perugina (9272349), near the town walls; Bosone (M), 22 Via Venti Settembre (9272008), near Piazza della Signoria. • *Restaurant*: Taverna del Lupo (M), 21a Via Ansidei (9274368), near town hall • *Museums*: Civic Museum and Municipal Picture Gallery, Piazza della Signoria; Cathedral Museum, Via Ducale.

LECCE • ZIP code 73100; telephone area code 0832. By rail from Rome in 9–11 hours; from Naples in 7 hours. By car from Rome, 376 miles on Motorway A-2 to Caserta, Motorway A-30 to Nola, Motorway A-16 to Canosa, Motorway A-14 to Bari, National Routes No. 16 and No. 379 to Brindisi, and Motorway Brindisi-Lecce; from Naples, 258 miles on Motorway A-16 to Canosa, Motorway A-14 to Bari, National Routes No. 16 and No. 379 to Brindisi, and Motorway Brindisi-Lecce. • *Information*: Piazza Sant'Oronzo (24443). • *Hotels*: President (M), 6 Via Salandra (51881), in the city's east; Risorgimento (M), 19 Via Imperatore Augusto (42125), central. • *Restaurant*: Plaza (M), 16 Via 140° Fanteria (25093). • *Museum*: Provincial Archaeological Museum, Viale Gallipoli (47025).

GALLIPOLI • ZIP code 73014; telephone area code 0833. By rail from Lecce in 1 hour 5 minutes. By car from Lecce, 25 miles on National Route No. 101. • *Hotel*: Joli Park (P), Piazza Salento (476129). • *Restaurant*: Marechiaro (P), Lungomare Marconi.

OTRANTO • ZIP code 73028; telephone area code 0836. By rail from Lecce, with change of trains in Maglie, in 40–60 minutes. By car from Lecce, 26 miles on National Route No. 16. • *Information*: Via Garibaldi (81436). • *Hotel*: Miramare (P) (81023). • *Restaurant*: Il Gabbiano (P) (81251).

LERICI • ZIP code 19032; telephone area code 0187. By rail from Rome to Sarzana in 5 hours 10 minutes; from Genoa to Sarzana in 2 hours; from Sarzana to Lerici by bus or cab in 10–15 minutes. By car from Rome, 260–270 miles either on Motorway A-12 to Civitavecchia, National Route No. 1 to Livorno, and Motorway A-12 to Sarzana, or on Motorway A-1 to Florence and Motorways A-11 and A-12 to Sarzana via Lucca; from Sarzana to Lerici on National Route No. 331. From Genoa, 66 miles on Motorway A-12 to Sarzana, and National Route No. 331. • *Information*: 47 Via Roma (967346). • *Hotels*: Shelley & Delle Palme (M), 5 Lungomare Biaggini (968204); Byron (M), 13a Via S. Biaggini (967104); Florida (P), 35 Lungomare Biaggini (967344). • *Restaurants*: Da Paolino (M), 15 Via San Francesco (967801), near parish church; Il Parma (M), 12 Piazza Battisti (967394), near shore walk.

LORETO ▪ ZIP code 60025; telephone area code 071. By rail from Rome, with change of trains in Ancona, in 4 hours. By car from Rome, 212 miles on Motorway A-25 to Pescara and Motorway A-14. ▪ *Information*: 3 Via Solari (977139). ▪ *Hotel*: Giardinetto (M), 10 Corso Boccalini (977135). ▪ *Restaurant*: Girarrosto (P), 7 Via Solari (970173).

LUCCA ▪ ZIP code 55100; telephone area code 0583. By rail from Florence in 1 hour 5 minutes to 1 hour 50 minutes, depending on the train. By car from Florence, 46 miles on Motorway A-11. ▪ *Information*: 40 Via Vittorio Veneto (46915). ▪ *Hotels*: Villa La Principessa (T), on National Route No. 12 *raddoppiata*, 3 miles south of Lucca proper (379112), with park; Napoleon (M), 1 Viale Europa (53141), outside the walls near the westernmost gate. ▪ *Restaurants*: Antico Caffè delle Mura (M), 2 Baluardo Santa Maria (47962), with garden; Buca di Sant'Antonio (M), 1/5 Via della Cervia (55881), central. ▪ *Museums*: National Museum, Villa Guinigi, Via della Quarquonia (46033); National Picture Gallery, 43 Via Galli Tassi (55570). ▪ Botanical Garden, 1 via del Giardino Botanico (46665).

MACERATA ▪ ZIP code 62100; telephone area code 0733. By rail from Rome, with change of trains in Fabriano, in 4 hours 10 minutes. By car from Rome, 160 miles on Motorway A-25 to Pescara, Motorway A-14 to Civitanova Marche, and National Route No. 485. ▪ *Information*: 12 Piazza della Libertà (45807). ▪ *Hotels*: Centrale (M), 98 Via Armaroli (47276), near main square; MotelAgip (M), 149 Via Roma (34248). ▪ *Restaurant*: Da Secondon (M), 26 Via Pescheria Vecchia (44912). ▪ *Museums*: Civic Museum and Picture Gallery, 2 Piazza Vittorio Veneto (49942); Coach Museum, 4 Piazza Vittorio Veneto (49942). ▪ *Opera* (Ente Lirico): information, 40576; ticket reservation, 40735.

MANTUA (Italian: *Mantova*) ▪ ZIP code 46100; telephone area code 0376. By rail from Rome, with change of trains in Modena, in 6–7 hours; from Milan, with change of trains in Modena, in 3½ hours. By car from Rome, 294 miles on Motorway A-1 to Modena North, and Motorway A-22; from Milan, 99 miles on Motorway A-4 to Verona, and Motorway A-22. ▪ *Information*: 6 Piazza Mantegna (350681). ▪ *Hotels*: San Lorenzo (M), 14 Piazza Concordia (27044); Broletto (P), 1 Via Accademia (326784). ▪ *Restaurants*: Il Cigno–Da Tano (M), 1 Piazza d'Arco (27101); Ai Garibaldini, 7 Via San Longino (29237). ▪ *Museums*: Ducal Palace, 40 Piazza Sordello (320283); Palazzo del Te (365886); Mantegna House, 3 Via G. Acerbi (360506).

MERANO/MERAN ▪ ZIP code 39012; telephone area code 0473. By rail from Rome, with change of trains in Bolzano/Bozen, in 9 hours; from Milan in 5 hours. By car from Rome, 417 miles on Motorway A-1 to Modena North, Motorway A-22 to Bolzano-South, and National Route No. 38; from Milan, 204 miles on Motorway A-4 to Verona, Motorway A-22 to Bolzano South, and National Route No. 38. ▪ *Information*: 45 Corso della Libertà (35223). ▪ *Hotels*: Palace (T), 2 Via Cavour (34734), with park and health club; Meranerhof (M), 1 Via Manzoni (30230), on river enbankment. ▪ *Restaurants*: Andrea (T), 16 Via Galilei (24400); Birreria Forst (M), Corso della Libertà (30308), popular brasserie. ▪ *Museum*: Civic Museum, 43 Via Galilei (26724). ▪ Health Spa Center, 9 Via Piave (37724), a thermal bath complex.

MODENA ▪ ZIP code 41100; telephone area code 059. By rail from Rome in 6 hours; from Milan in 2 hours 10 minutes. By car from Rome, 252 miles on Motorway A-1; from Milan, 106 miles on Motorway A-1. ▪ *Information*: 3 Corso Canalgrande (222482). ▪ *Hotels*: Canalgrande (M), 6 Corso Canal Grande (217160); Palace (M), 27 Via Emilia Est (236091). ▪ *Restaurants*: Fini (T), Largo San Francesco (223314); Oreste (M), 31 Piazza Roma (243342), near Ducal Palace. ▪ *Museums*: Este Gallery, 309 Piazza Sant'Agostino (222145); Civic Archaeological and Ethnological Museum, 309 Piazza Sant'Agostino (243263); Civic Museum of Medieval and Modern History and Art, 309 Piazza Sant'Agostino (223892); Este Numismatic Collection, 309 Piazza Sant'Agostino (222145); Cathedral Museum, 6 Via Lanfranco; Mirandola Civic Museum, 12 Via Verdi, 41037 Mirandola (0535-51987). ▪ Botanical Garden and Herbarium, 127 Viale Caduti Guerra (236132). ▪ Maserati Motor Works, 322 Via C. Menotti (219577). ▪ Ferrari Motor Works and Racing Organization, 2 Via Abetone Inferiore, 41053 Maranello (0536-941161).

MONREALE ▪ ZIP code 90046; telephone area code 091. From Palermo with No. 9 bus from Via Roma in 15 minutes. By car, 5 miles on National Route No. 186. ▪ *Information*: 35 Piazza Castelnuovo, 90100 Palermo (091-90141).

MONTEPULCIANO ▪ ZIP code 53045; telephone area code 0578. By rail from Rome to Montepulciano Stazione, with change of trains in Chiusi–Chianciano Terme, in 2 hours 20 minutes; from Florence to Montepulciano Stazione, with change of trains in Chiusi–Chianciano Terme, 1 hour 50 minutes; from Montepulciano Stazione to the center of Montepulciano, 7 miles by public bus or cab. By car from Rome, 110 miles on Motorway A-1 to Chiusi–Chianciano Terme, and National Route No. 146; from Florence, 75 miles on Motorway A-1 to Val di Chiana, provincial road to Torrita di Siena,

National Route No. 326 to Bottola, and provincial road to Montepulciano. ▪ *Hotel*: Il Marzocco (P), 25 Piazza Savonarola (75762), near northern town gate. ▪ *Restaurant*: Il Cantuccio (P), 1/3 Via della Cantine (757870). ▪ *Museum*: 15 Via Ricci (757049).

Ortisei (German: *St. Ulrich*; Ladin: *Urtijëi*) ▪ ZIP code 39046; telephone area code 0471. By rail from Rome to Bolzano/Bozen in 9 hours; from Milan to Bolzano in 4 hours; from Bolzano bus terminal, near the railroad station, public bus to Ortisei in 1 hour (several runs daily). By car from Rome, 435 miles on Motorway A-1 to Modena North, Motorway A-22 to Bolzano North, National Route No. 12 to Ponte Gardena, and National Route No. 242; from Milan, 208 miles on Motorway A-4 to Verona, Motorway A-22 to Bolzano North, and National Routes No. 12 and No. 242. ▪ *Information*: Piazza Stetteneck (76328). ▪ *Hotels*: Aquila-Adler (M), (76203); Rainell (M), (76145); Arnaria (P), Roncadizza, 1 mile east of Ortisei (76649). ▪ *Museum*: Museum of the Val Gardena, Cësa di Ladins, 83 Via Rezia.

Orvieto ▪ ZIP code 05018; telephone area code 0763. By rail from Rome in 1 hour 10 minutes. By car from Rome, 76 miles on Motorway A-1. ▪ *Information*: 24 Piazza del Duomo (5172). ▪ *Hotels*: Maitani (M), 5 Via Maitani (33001) near the cathedral; Virgilio (M), 5/6 Piazza del Duomo (5252), with view of the cathedral; La Badia (M), on National Route No. 71, 2 miles south of Orvieto (90359), in a restored abbey dating from the eleventh century, comfortable. ▪ *Restaurants*: Maurizio (M), 78 Via del Duomo (33212); Morino (T), 37/45 Via Garibaldi (5152).

Padua (Italian: *Padova*) ▪ ZIP code 35100; telephone area code 049. By rail from Rome in 5½–6 hours; from Florence in 2½–3 hours; from Venice in 40 minutes. By car from Rome, 307 miles on Motorway A-1 to Bologna and Motorway A-13; from Florence, 140 miles on Motorway A-1 and Motorway A-13; from Venice, 23 miles on Motorway A-4. ▪ *Information*: 24 Riviera Mugnai (651856). ▪ *Hotels*: Plaza (M), 42 Corso Milano (656822); Donatello (M), Piazza del Santo (664895), near Basilica of St. Anthony, with restaurant. ▪ *Museums*: Civic Museum, 10 Piazza del Santo (23713); Antonian Museum, Piazza del Santo (25063). ▪ *Botanical Garden*, 15 Via Orto Botanico (656614).

Palestrina ▪ ZIP code 00036; telephone area code 06. By public (blue) bus from Piazza dei Cinquecento in front of Rome's Termini Railroad Station in 1 hour. By car from Rome, 24 miles on the Via Prenestina (the provincial highway starting at the Porta Maggiore), or National Highway No. 6 (Via Casilina) and National Highway No. 155. ▪ *Information*: Piazza Regina

Margherita (955250). ▪ *Hotel*: Stella (P), Piazza della Liberazione (9558172), with restaurant. ▪ *Museum*: National Archaeological Museum, Palazzo Barberini, Piazza della Cortina (9558100).

PARMA ▪ ZIP code 43100; telephone area code 0521. By rail from Rome in 6 hours; from Florence in 2 hours 40 minutes; from Milan in 1 hour 40 minutes. By car from Rome, 287 miles; from Florence, 126 miles; from Milan, 76 miles, all on Motorway A-1, ▪ *Information*: 5 Piazza Duomo (34735). ▪ *Hotels*: Maria Luigia (T), 140 Vial Mentana (21032); Stendhal (M), 3 Piazzetta Bodoni (36653). ▪ *Restaurant*: La Filoma (M), 15 Via Venti, Marzo (34269), near the cathedral. ▪ *Museums*: National Gallery, Palazzo della Pilotta (33309); Bodoni Museum, Palazzo della Pilotta (22217); National Museum of Antiquities, Palazzo della Pilotta (33718); Glauco Lombardi Museum (Marie-Louise and her time), 15 Via Garibaldi (33726); Arturo Toscanini's birthplace, 13 Via Tanzi (35964).

PAVIA ▪ ZIP code 27100; telephone area code 0382. By rail from Milan in 16–30 minutes. By car, 24 miles on National Route No. 35. ▪ *Information*: 1 Corso Garibaldi (26788). ▪ *Hotel*: Ariston (M), 10 Via Scopoli (34334). ▪ *Restaurant*: Bixio (M), 81 Strada Nuova (25343), near Visconti Castle. ▪ *Museum*: Civic Museum, Visconti Castle (33853).

CERTOSA DI PAVIA ▪ By rail from Milan in 34 minutes (local train); from Pavia in 7 minutes. By car from Milan, 17 miles on National Route No. 35; from Pavia, 7 miles on National Route No. 35. ▪ *Information*: Carthusian Fathers, 27012 Certosa di Pavia (0382-925613).

PERUGIA ▪ ZIP code 06100; telephone area code 075. By rail from Rome, with change of trains at Foligno, in 3 hours; from Florence, with change of trains in Terontola-Cortona, in 2 hours 40 minutes. By car from Rome, 108 miles on Motorway A-1 to Orte and on National Route No. 3 *bis*; from Florence, 97 miles on Motorway A-1 to Chiusi–Chianciano Terme and National Route No. 75 *bis*. ▪ *Information*: 96 Corso Vannucci (23327). ▪ *Hotel and restaurant*: La Rosetta (M), 19 Piazza Italia (20841). ▪ *Museums*: National Gallery of Umbria, Corso Vannucci (23385); National Archaeological Museum of Umbria, Piazza Giordano Bruno (21398).

PESARO ▪ ZIP code 61100; telephone area code 0721. By rail from Rome, with change of trains in Falconara Marittima, in 4 hours. By car from Rome, 190 miles on Motorway A-1 to Orte, National Route No. 3 *bis* to Terni, National Route No. 3 to Fano, and Motorway A-14. ▪ *Information*: 41 Via Rossini (63690). ▪ *Hotels*: Vittoria (M), 2 Piazzale della Libertà (34343), on the waterfront; Mamiani (M), 24 Via Mamiani (41041), central, Villa

Serena (M), on Monte Ardizio, southeast of Pesaro (0721-79347), recon-verted seventeenth-century villa with garden. ▪ *Restaurants*: Carlo al Mare (M), 267 Viale Trieste (31453), on the waterfront (closed from October to April); Il Castiglione (M), 148 Viale Trento (64934), in a former majolica factory, with garden; Taverna del Pescatore (M), at Castel di Mezzo on Panoramic Road, 7.5 miles northwest of Pesaro (0721-607100), seafood, panorama of the Adriatic Sea. ▪ *Museums*: Civic Museums, 29 Piazza Mosca (31213); Archaeological Museum, 96 Via Mazza (33344).

PIACENZA ▪ ZIP code 29100; telephone area code 0523. By rail from Rome in 7 hours; from Milan in 50 minutes. By car from Rome, 320 miles on Motorway A-1; from Milan, 40 miles on Motorway A-1. ▪ *Information*: 10 Piazzetta dei Mercanti (29324). ▪ *Hotel*: Grande Albergo Roma (M), 14 Via Cittadella (23201). ▪ *Restaurants*: Antica Osteria del Teatro (M), 16 Via Verdi (23777); Ristorante Gotico (M), 26 Piazza dei Cavalli (21940). ▪ *Museums*: Civic Museum and Archaeological Museum, Palazzo Farnese, Piazza Cittadella (20742); Ricci Oddi Gallery of Modern Art, 13 Via San Siro (20742); Alberoni Gallery of Art, 77 Via Emilia Parmense (63198).

PIENZA ▪ ZIP code 53026; telephone area code 0578. By rail from Rome to Chiusi in 2 hours, from Florence to Chiusi in 1 hour 50 minutes; from Chiusi to Pienza, 22 miles by public bus or cab. By car from Rome, 118 miles on Motorway A-1 to Chiusi–Chianciano Terme, and National Route No. 146; from Florence, 83 miles on Motorway A-1 to Val di Chiana, provincial road to Torrita di Siena, and National Route No. 146. ▪ *Hotel*: Corsignano (P) (748501). ▪ *Restaurant*: Il Prato (P) (74601). ▪ *Museums*: Piccolomini Palace (74503); Museum of Sacred Art (74549).

PISA ▪ ZIP code 56100; telephone area code 050. By rail from Rome in 3 hours; from Florence in 55 minutes. By car from Rome, 228 miles on Motorway A-1 to Florence and Motorway A-11, or Motorway A-12 to Civ-itavecchia and National Route No. 1 (Via Aurelia). ▪ *Information*: Piazza del Duomo (23535). ▪ *Hotels*: Dei Cavalieri (T), Piazza della Stazione (43290), near railroad station; Ariston (P), 42 Via Cardinale Maffi (24255), near Leaning Tower. ▪ *Restaurant*: Sergio (T), 1 Lungarno Pacinotti (48245). ▪ *Museums*: National Museum, Lungarno Mediceo (23750); Campo Santo and Museum of Sinopias, both in Piazza del Duomo (both 22531); Galileo House, 26 Via Santa Maria (23726).

PISTOIA ▪ ZIP code 51100; telephone area code 0573. By rail from Florence in 35 minutes. By car from Florence, 23 miles on Motorway A-11. ▪ *Information*: 110 Corso Gramsci (34326). ▪ *Hotel*: Appennino (P), 21 Viale

Venti Settembre (32244), near railroad station. ▪ *Museums*: Civic Museum, City Hall, Piazza del Duomo (367871); Cathedral Museum, Piazza del Duomo (21059); Ospedale del Ceppo, Piazza Giovanni XXIII (367821).

PORTOFERRAIO ▪ ZIP code 57037; telephone area code 0565. By rail from Rome to Piombino Marittima, with change of trains in Campiglia Marittima, in 4 hours 15 minutes; navigation Piombino-Portofino, 1 hour by boat, 30 minutes by hydrofoil (*aliscafo*). By rail from Florence to Piombino Marittima, with change of trains in Campiglia Marittima, or in Pisa and Campiglia Marittima, in 3 hours 15 minutes to 4 hours; navigation Piombino-Porto-ferraio, as above. By car from Rome, 165 miles on Motorway A-12 to Civitavecchia, National Route No. 1 to Venturina, and National Route No. 398 to Piombino; from Florence, 101 miles on Motorways A-11 and A-12 to Livorno, National Route No. 1 to San Vincenzo, and provincial highway to Piombino; navigation Piombino-Portoferraio, as above. ▪ *Information*: 26 Calata Italia (92671). ▪ *Hotels*: Ape Elbana (P), 7 Via Cosimo de' Medici (92245), central; Touring (P) (915851). ▪ *Restaurants*: Da Oreste La Strega (P), Piazza Vittorio Emanuele (962211); Da Gino (P), 1 Via Verdi (962116). ▪ *Museums*: Napoleon Museum, Casa dei Mulini (93846); Museums in the Villa Napoleone and Villa Demidoff, San Martino, 4 miles south of Portoferraio (92668).

PORTOFINO ▪ ZIP code 16034; telephone area code 0185. By rail from Rome to Santa Margherita Ligure–Portofino in 6 hours; from Genoa to Santa Margherita Ligure–Portofino in 40 minutes; from Santa Margherita to Portofino, 3 miles by public bus or cab. By car from Rome, 305-315 miles either on Motorway A-12 to Civitavecchia, on National Route No. 1 to Livorno, and on Motorway A-12 to Rapallo, or on Motorway A-1 to Florence North, Motorway A-11 to Viareggio via Lucca, and Motorway A-12 to Rapallo; from Rapallo to Santa Margherita Ligure and Portofino on National Route No. 227. ▪ *Information*: 35 Via Roma (69024). ▪ *Hotels*: Splendido (T) (69195); Piccolo Hotel (P) (69015). ▪ *Restaurants*: Stella (M) (69007); Delfino (M) (69081).

PORTO SANTO STEFANO ▪ ZIP code 58019; telephone area code 0564. By rail from Rome to Orbetello–Monte Argentario in 1 hour 55 minutes; from Orbetello station to Porto Santo Stefano by public bus in 15 minutes. By rail from Florence, with change of trains in Pisa, in 3 hours 45 minutes to Orbetello–Monte Argentario, and 15 minutes by bus to Porto Santo Stefano. By car from Rome, 102 miles on Motorway A-12 to Civitavecchia, National Route No. 1 (Via Aurelia) to Orbetello Scalo, and National Route No. 440; from Florence, 121 miles on Motorway A-11 to Pisa, Motorway A-12 to

Livorno, National Route No. 1 to Orbetello Scalo, and National Route No. 440. ▪ *Information*: 55a Corso Umberto (814208). ▪ *Hotels*: Vittoria (M), 65 Strada del Sole (818580); Villa Domizia (M), Santa Liberata (812735), 2.5 miles east of Porto Santo Stefano. ▪ *Restaurants*: La Bussola (M), 11 Piazza Facchinetti (814225); Armando (M), 1/3 Via Marconi (812568).

PORT'ERCOLE ▪ *Hotel*: Il Pelicano (T), Strada Panoramica (0564-833801), 2 miles southwest of Port'Ercole.

GIGLIO ISLAND ▪ ZIP code 58013; telephone area code 0564. Daily boat service from Porto Santo Stefano, sailing time 1 hour. ▪ *Information*: 1 Via Umberto, Giglio Porto (809265). ▪ *Hotel*: Saraceno (M), Giglio Porto (809006).

POSITANO ▪ ZIP code 84017; telephone area code 089. By rail from Rome, with change of trains in Naples, in 3½ hours to Sorrento; from Naples in 1 hour to Sorrento; from Sorrento to Positano, 11 miles by bus or cab. By car from Rome, 167 miles on Motorway A-2 to Naples, Motorway A-3 to Castellamare di Stabia, and National Routes Nos. 145 and 163 to Sorrento and Positano; from Naples, 36 miles on Motorway A-3 to Castellamare di Stabia, and National Routes Nos. 145 and 163 to Sorrento and Positano. ▪ *Information*: 2 Via del Saracino (875067). ▪ *Hotels*: Le Sirenuse (T) (875066); Poseidon (M) (875014); Buca di Bacco (M) (875699); all three with views of the sea. ▪ *Restaurants*: Le Tre Sorelle (M) (875452); Chez Black (M) (875036); side by side on street overlooking the beach.

RAVELLO ▪ ZIP code 84010; telephone area code 089. By road, 3.5 miles from Amalfi; for travel from Rome or Naples, see *Amalfi*. ▪ *Information*: 10 Piazza del Duomo (857096). ▪ *Hotels*: Palumbo (T) (857244); Rufolo (M) (857133); Parsifal (M) (857144); all three with views of the sea. ▪ *Restaurant*: Garden (M) (857226), with terrace and view. ▪ *Museums*: Antiquarium in the Villa Rufolo (archaeological collection); Cathedral Museum (medieval sculptures and precious objects).

RAVENNA ▪ ZIP code 48100; telephone area code 0544. By rail from Rome, with change of trains in Ferrara, in 6½ hours; from Venice, with change of trains in Ferrara, in 3 hours. By car from Rome, 239 miles on Motorway A-1 to Orte, National Route No. 204 to Terni, National Route No. 3 (Via Flaminia) to Fano, Motorway A-14 to Rimini, and National Route No. 16; from Venice, 92 miles on National Route No. 309. ▪ *Information*: 7 Piazza San Francesco (36129). ▪ *Hotels*: Centrale-Byron (M), 14 Via Quattro Novembre (22225); Jolly (M), 1 Piazza Mameli (35762), near railroad station. ▪ *Restaurant*: Bella Venezia (M), 16 Via Quattro Novembre (22746), central. ▪ *Museums*: National Museum of Antiquities, 17 Via San Vitale (28317); Archiepiscopal Museum, 1 Piazza dell'Arcivescovado (28559); Dante

Museum, Via Guido da Polenta; Picture Gallery of the Academy of Fine Arts, Via Roma (23935).

RIETI ▪ ZIP code 02100; telephone area code 0746. By rail from Rome with change of trains in Terni, in 1 hour 50 minutes. By car from Rome, 49 miles on National Route No. 4 (Via Salaria). ▪ *Information*: Piazza Vittorio Emanuele (43220). ▪ *Hotels*: Quattro Stagioni (M), Piazza Cesare Battisti (43306); Miramonti (M), 57 Piazza Oberdan (41333). ▪ *Restaurant*: Da Checco (M), 10 Via Marchetti (44271).

RIMINI ▪ ZIP code 47037; telephone area code 0541. By rail from Rome, usually with change of trains at Falconara Marittima, in 4½ hours; from Milan in 3 hours 10 minutes. By car from Rome, 210 miles on National Route No. 3 (Via Flaminia) to Fano, and Motorway A-14; from Milan, 202 miles on Motorway A-1 to Bologna, and Motorway A-14. ▪ *Information*: Piazzale Cesare Battisti (27927). ▪ *Hotels*: Napoleon (M), 22 Piazzale Cesare Battisti (27501), near railroad station; Duomo (M), 28d Via Giordano Bruno (24215), in old city center. ▪ *Restaurant*: Vecchia Rimini (M), 7/9 Via Cattaneo (26610), near railroad station. ▪ *Museums*: Civic Picture Gallery, 34 Via Tempio Malatestiano (23667); Archaeological Museum, 27 Via Gambalunga (23667).

ROVERETO ▪ ZIP code 38068; telephone area code 0464. By rail from Rome in 7 hours; from Milan in 3 hours. By car from Rome, 352 miles on Motorway A-1 to Modena North, and Motorway A-22; from Milan, 135 miles on Motorway A-4 to Verona, and Motorway A-22. ▪ *Information*: 63 Via Dante (30363). ▪ *Hotel*: Rovereto (M), 82 Corso Rosmini (35222) ▪ *Restaurant*: Cinghiale Blu (M), 8 Piazza Malfatti (33088). ▪ *Museums*: Civic Museum, 18 Via Calcinari (25487); Italian Museum of War History, 7 Via Castelbarco (38100).

SALERNO ▪ ZIP code 84100; telephone area code 089. By rail from Rome in 3 hours; from Naples in 1 hour. By car from Rome, 163 miles on Motorways A-2 and A-3; from Naples, 35 miles on Motorway A-3. ▪ *Information*: Piazza Vittorio Veneto (231432). ▪ *Hotel*: Jolly (M), 1 Lungomare Trieste (225222), on the seaside promenade.

PAESTUM ▪ ZIP code 84063; telephone area code 0828. By rail from Salerno in 30 minutes. By car from Salerno, 30 miles on National Route No. 18. ▪ *Information*: Zona Archeologica (811016). ▪ *Hotels*: Le Palme (M), on the waterfront (843036); Villa Rita-Nettuno (P), with view of the temples (811081). ▪ *Museum*: National Archaeological Museum, Via Nazionale (811023).

SAN GIMIGNANO ▪ ZIP code 53037; telephone area code 0577. By rail from Florence to Poggibonsi–San Gimignano, with change of trains in Empoli, in 1 hour 10 minutes; by public bus from Poggibonsi–San Gimignano to San Gimignano in 15 minutes. By rail from Rome, with change of trains in Chiusi and Siena, in 4 hours 20 minutes to Poggibonsi–San Gimignano; by public bus to San Gimignano in 15 minutes. By car from Florence, 35 miles on Florence-Siena Motorway to Poggibonsi exit and provincial highway; from Rome, 168 miles on Motorway A-1 to Val di Chiana exit, National Route No. 326 to Siena, Siena-Florence Motorway to Poggibonsi exit, and provincial highway. ▪ *Hotels*: La Cisterna (M), Piazza della Cisterna (940328), with restaurant; Bel Soggiorno (M), 35 Via San Giovanni (940375); Leone Bianco (M), Piazza della Cisterna (941294). ▪ *Restaurant*: La Stella (M), Via San Matteo (940444). ▪ *Museums*: Civic Picture Gallery (Pinacoteca Civica), Piazza del Duomo (940340); Museum of Sacred Art, 1 Piazza Pecori (940687); Etruscan Museum, 1 Piazza del Duomo.

REPUBLIC OF SAN MARINO ▪ ZIP code 47031 Repubblica de San Marino; telephone area code 0541 from Italy, 39541 from outside Italy. By rail from Rome in 4½ hours to Rimini, and public bus from Rimini to San Marino in 20 minutes; from Milan to Rimini in 3 hours 10 minutes, and bus to San Marino. By car from Rome, 223 miles on National Route No. 3 (Via Flaminia) to Fano, Motorway A-14 to Rimini South exit, and National Route No. 72; from Milan, 217 miles on Motorway A-1 to Bologna, Motorway A-14 to Rimini South exit, and National Route No. 72. ▪ *Information*: Palazzo del Turismo (0541-992101). ▪ *Hotels*: Titano (M), 21 Contrada del Collegio (991007), near Government Palace; Grand Hotel San Marino (M), 31 Viale Onofri (992400), outside the old town; Tre Penne (P), Via L. Marini (992437), below the summit of Mount Titano. ▪ *Restaurants*: La Taverna (M), Piazza della Libertà (991196), central; Diamond (M), 72 Contrada del Collegio (991003), near the basilica, with rooms.

SAN REMO ▪ ZIP code 18038; telephone area code 0184. By rail from Rome in 7 hours; from Genoa in 1 hour 50 minutes; from Nice, France, in 1 hour. By car from Rome, 408 miles on National Route No. 1 (Via Aurelia); from Livorno (Leghorn), also on Motorway A-12 to Genoa, and on Motorway A-10; from Genoa 100 miles on Motorway A-10 or National Route No. 1; from Nice, 38 miles on Motorway A-10. ▪ *Information*: 1 Largo Nuvolini (85615). ▪ *Hotels*: Miramare (T), 9 Corso Matuzia (882381), with garden; Nazional (M), 5 Via Matteotti (77577), opposite the Municipal Casino. ▪ *Restaurant*: Da Giannino, 47 Via Roma (70843).

SANSEPOLCRO ▪ ZIP code 52037; telephone area code 0575. By rail from

Rome, with change of trains in Terni and Perugia Ponte San Giovanni, in 4 hours 15 minutes; from Florence, with change of trains in Terontola-Cortona and Perugia Ponte San Giovanni in 4 hours 40 minutes; or by rail to Arezzo in 1 hour, and bus from Arezzo to Sansepolcro (frequent departures), about 1 hour. By car from Rome, 163 miles on Motorway A-1 to Orte, National Route No. 204, and Superhighway No. 3 *bis* (E-7); from Florence, 72 miles on Motorway A-1 to Arezzo, and National Route No. 73. ▪ *Hotels*: La Balestra (M), 29 Via Montefeltro (73515); Fiorentino (M), 60 Via L. Pacioli (76033); Taverna (P), 27 Via Anconetana (76575). ▪ *Restaurants*: Nuova Stella (M), 2 Via Venti Settembre (76541); Romano (M), 178 Via Venti Settembre (75340). ▪ *Museum*: Civic Museum, 65 Via Aggiunti (76465).

MONTERCHI ▪ By car from Sansepolcro, 12.5 miles on National Route No. 73 to Le Ville, and National Route No. 221.

CAPRESE MICHELANGELO ▪ By car from Sansepolcro, 19 miles on Superhighway No. 3 *bis* to Pieve Santo Stefano, and provincial highway. Michelangelo Museum (0575-793912).

SASSARI ▪ ZIP code 07100; telephone area code 079. By train and boat from Rome, 1 hour by rail, Rome-Civitavecchia, and 7 hours' navigation, Civitavecchia-Olbia; by rail from Olbia to Sassari, with change of trains in Chilivani, in 2 hours 10 minutes; or by car from Olbia to Sassari, 65 miles on National Routes No. 127 and No. 199 to Oschiri, and National Route No. 597. By boat from Genoa to Porto Torres, 12–13 hours' navigation; by rail from Porto Torres to Sassari in 30 minutes, or by car, 12 miles on National Route No. 131. By air from Rome or Milan to Olbia, proceeding to Sassari by train or car, as above; or to Alghero-Fertilia, proceeding to Sassari by bus or car, 18 miles on provincial roads and National Route No. 291. ▪ *Information*: 19 Piazza d'Italia (275395). ▪ *Hotels*: Jolly Grazia Deledda (M), 47 Viale Dante (271235), in the city's modern east; Giusy (P), 21 Piazza Sant'Antonio (233327), near railroad station. ▪ *Restaurant*: Gallo d'Oro (M), 3 Piazza d'Italia (230044). ▪ *Museum*: National Museum G. A. Sanna, 64 Via Roma (272203).

ALGHERO ▪ ZIP code 07041; area code 079. By air, Rome or Milan to Alghero-Fertilia, by bus or car to Alghero, 7 miles on provincial roads. By car from Sassari, 22 miles on National Route No. 127 *bis*. ▪ *Information*: 9 Piazza Porta Terra (979054). ▪ *Hotel*: Carlos V (M), 24 Lungomare Valencia (979501). ▪ *Restaurant*: Riu (M), 2 Piazza Civica (977240).

SIENA ▪ ZIP code 53100; telephone area code 0577. By rail from Florence in 1 hour 15 minutes; from Rome, with change of trains in Chiusi–Chianciano Terme, in 3 hours 30 minutes. By car from Florence, 43 miles on National Route No. 222; from Rome, 150 miles on Motorway A-1 to Val di Chiana, and National Routes Nos. 326 and 73; also from Rome to Siena, 143 miles on National Route No. 2 (Via Cassia). ▪ *Information*: 55 Piazza del Campo (280551). ▪ *Hotels*: Jolly Excelsior (T), Piazza La Lizza (288488), near a park within the ramparts; Park Hotel (T), 16 Via de Marciano (44803), in a Renaissance building in a garden on the northwestern outskirts. ▪ *Museums*: National Picture Gallery, 29 Via San Pietro (281161); Cathedral Museum and Library, Cathedral Square (283048); Palazzo Pubblico (city hall), Piazza del Campo (280590); Etruscan Archaeological Museum, 3 Via della Sapienza (44293); House of St. Catherine, 15 Vicolo del Tiratore (44177).

SORRENTO ▪ ZIP code 80067; telephone area code 081. By rail from Rome, with change of trains in Naples, in 3½ hours; from Naples in 1 hour. By car from Rome, 160 miles on Motorway A-2 to Naples, Motorway A-3 to Castellamare di Stabia, and National Route No. 145; from Naples, 30 miles on Motorway A-3 and National Route No. 145. ▪ *Information*: 35 Via de Maio (8782104). ▪ *Hotels*: Excelsior Vittoria (T), 34 Piazza Tasso (8781900); Bellevue Syrene (M), 5 Piazza della Vittoria (8781024); both with gardens and view of Gulf of Naples and Mount Vesuvius. ▪ *Restaurants*: Cavallino Bianco (M), 11a Via Correale (8785809); La Favorita–O'Parrucchiano (M), 71 Corso Italia (8781321); both central. ▪ *Museum*: Palazzo Correale Museum, 50 Via Correale (8781846).

SPOLETO ▪ ZIP code 06049; telephone area code 0743. By rail from Rome, direct or with change of trains in Orte, in 2 hours. By car from Rome, 82 miles on Motorway A-1 to Orte, National Route No. 204 to Narni, and National Route No. 3 (Via Flaminia). ▪ *Information*: 7 Piazza della Libertà (28111). ▪ *Hotel*: Dei duchi (M), 2 Via G. Matteotti (35241), fine view. ▪ *Restaurant*: Sabatini (P), 56 Corso Mazzini (49617). ▪ *Museums*: Civic Museum, 3 Via del Duomo (22209); Municipal Picture Gallery, Piazza Municipio (32141); Theater Museum, 1 Via Filitteria (24161); Collection of Theatrical Designs, Convent of San Nicolò, Via Gregorio Elladio (28131); Diocesan Museum, Episcopal Palace, 13 Via A. Saffi (23140).

SUBIACO ▪ ZIP code 00028; telephone area code 0774. By public bus from Rome (Via Castro Pretorio, near central railroad terminal) in 1½ hours. By car from Rome, 45 miles on Motorway A-24 to Vicovaro-Mandela exit, National Route No. 5 (Via Tiburtina) and National Route No. 411 (Via Sublacense). ▪ *Information*: 59 Via Cadorna (85397). ▪ *Hotels*: Roma (P), 38 Via Francesco Petrarca (85239), with restaurant; Belvedere (P), 33 Via dei Monasteri (85531). ▪ *Restaurant*: Aniene (P), 7 Piazza Sant'Andrea (85565).

On Mount Livata, at altitude 4,428 feet, 10 miles from Subiaco: Hotel Livata (P), Monte Livata presso Subiaco (0774-86032), open during the winter months and from June 15 to September 15.

SULMONA ▪ ZIP code 67039; telephone area code 0864. By rail from Rome in 2½ hours. By car from Rome, 97 miles on Motorways A-24 and A-25. ▪ *Information*: 21 Via Roma (53276). ▪ *Hotel*: Costanza Park (M), Strada Statale Nord (34641), 1.5 miles from town, with swimming pool. ▪ *Restaurants*: Italia–Da Nicola (M), 24 Piazza Venti Settembre (33070), central; Cesidio (M), 25 Piazza Solimo (52724). ▪ *Museum*: Civic Museum, Piazza dell'Annunziata.

SYRACUSE (Italian: *Siracusa*) ▪ ZIP code 96100; telephone area code 0931. The quickest way from Rome to Syracuse is by Alitalia to Catania, and from there by rail, in 1 hour 10 minutes; or by car, 37 miles on National Route No. 114. By car from Palermo, 210 miles on Motorway A-19 to Catania and from there on National Route No. 114. (Avoid the Palermo-Syracuse railway trip if you can help it.) ▪ *Information*: 92c Corso Gelone (67710). ▪ *Hotel*: Villa Politi (M), 2 Via Politi (32100) in a park near the Latomía of the Capuchins. ▪ *Museums*: National Archaeological Museum, 14 Piazza del Duomo (68791); National Museum of Palazzo Bellomo, 14 Via Capodieci (65343) (ancient, medieval, and Renaissance art).

TAORMINA ▪ ZIP code 98039; telephone area code 0942. By air from Rome to Catania in 1 hour 20 minutes. By rail from Catania to Taormina-Giardini in 1 hour; by car, 30 miles on Motorway A-18 from Catania South or Catania North to Taormina South. By rail from Rome to Taormina-Giardini in 11 hours; public bus, hotel coach, or cab from Taormina-Giardini to Taormina, 3 miles. By car from Rome, 433 miles to Villa San Giovanni on Motorway A-2 to Naples and Motorway A-3; car ferry to Messina; and 30 miles from Messina to Taormina North on Motorway A-18. ▪ *Information*: 144 Corso Umberto (23751). ▪ *Hotels*: San Domenico Palace (T), 5 Piazza San Domenico (23701); Timéo (T), Via Teatro Greco (23801); Excelsior Palace (T), 8 Via Toselli (23975); Villa Fiorita (M), 39 Via Pirandello (24122); Villa Belvedere (M), 79 Via Bagnoli Croce (23791). At Giardini Naxos, below Taormina: Arathena Rocks (T) (51349). At Mazzarò, below Taormina: Mazzarò Sea Palace (24004). ▪ *Restaurants*: La Griglia (M), 54 Corso Umberto (23980). At Mazzarò: Il Pescatore (M) (23125). ▪ *Museum*: Archaeological Museum (Antiquarium), Via del Teatro Greco (23220).

TARQUINIA ▪ ZIP code 01016; telephone area code 0766. By rail from Rome in 1 hour 50 minutes. By car from Rome, 60 miles on Motorway A-12 to Civitavecchia, proceeding on National Route No. 1 (Via Aurelia). ▪ *Information*: 1 Piazza Cavour (856384). ▪ *Hotels*: Tarconte (M), 19 Via Tuscia (856141); at Lido di Tarquinia: Helios (88618). ▪ *Museum*: National Etruscan Museum, Palazzo Vitelleschi (856036).

TERRACINA ▪ ZIP code 04019; telephone area code 0773. By rail from Rome, with change of trains at Priverno-Fossanova, in 1½ hours. By car from Rome, 68 miles on National Route No. 7 (Via Appia). ▪ *Information*: 156 Via Lungolinea (727759). ▪ *Hotel*: Palace (M), 6 Lungomare Matteotti (727285). ▪ *Restaurant*: La Capannina (M), at the beach near the harbor (727339).

TIVOLI ▪ ZIP code 00019; telephone area code 0774. By rail from Rome (Termini or Tiburtina stations) in 40–50 minutes. A Rome-Tivoli bus leaves every 10 minutes from the northeast corner of Piazza dei Cinquecento in front of the Termini Station. By car from Rome, 19.5 miles on National Route No. 5 (Via Tiburtina). ▪ *Information*: Piazzale Nazioni Unite (20745). ▪ *Restaurants*: Eden Sirene, 4 Piazza Massimo (21352), with a terrace near the Villa Gregoriana; at Hadrian's Villa: Adriano (530206). ▪ *Museum*: Museum of Hadrian's Villa, Villa Adriana (530203).

TODI ▪ ZIP code 06059; telephone area code 075. By rail from Rome, with change of trains in Terni, in 2 hours 10 minutes; public bus from Todi-Ponte Rio station to town center, 1.7 miles. By car from Rome, 82 miles on Motorway A-1 to Orte, and National Route No. 3 *bis*. ▪ *Information*: 19 Via Mazzini (883395). ▪ *Hotels*: Villaluisa (M), 147 Via Cortesi (883940), outside the town walls, with garden; Cavour (P), 12 Corso Cavour (882417), central. ▪ *Restaurant*: Umbria (M), 13 Via Buonaventura (882390), with terrace. ▪ *Museums*: Civic Picture Gallery and Etruscan-Roman Museum, Palazzo del Popolo, Piazza del Popolo (883541).

TRENT (Italian: *Trento*) ▪ ZIP code 38100; telephone area code 0461. By rail from Rome in 8 hours; from Milan in 3 hours; from Venice in 3 hours 10 minutes. By car from Rome, 368 miles on Motorway A-1 to Modena North, and Motorway A-22; from Milan, 151 miles on Motorway A-4 to Verona, and Motorway A-22; from Venice 134 miles on Motorway A-4 to Verona, and Motorway A-22. ▪ *Information*: 4 Via Alfieri (983880). ▪ *Hotel*: Accademia (M), 6 Vicolo Colico (981011). ▪ *Museums*: Diocesan Museum, Piazza del Duomo (34419); Museum of the Risorgimento, Castello del Buon Consiglio (26142); Provincial Museum of Ancient, Medieval, Modern and Contemporary Art, Castello del Buonconsiglio (21324); Museum of Natural Sciences, 14 Via Calepina (26543).

TREVISO ▪ ZIP code 31100; telephone area code 0422. By rail from Rome, with change of trains in Venezia Mestre, in 7 hours; from Venice in 30 minutes. By car from Rome, 338 miles on Motorway A-1 to Bologna, Motorway A-13 to Padua, Motorway A-4 to Venice-Mestre, and National Route No. 13; from Venice, 19 miles on National Route No. 13. ▪ *Information*:

41 Via Toniolo (47632). ▪ *Hotels*: Continental (M), 15 Via Roma (57216); Carlton (M), 15 Largo Porta Altinia (46988); Campeol (P), 11 Piazza Ancilotto (40871), central, with good restaurant. ▪ *Restaurants*: El Toulà (T), 26 Via Collalto (40275); Beccheria (M), 11 Piazza Ancilotto (40871). ▪ *Museum*: Civic Museum, 22 Borgo Cavour (51337).

TRIESTE ▪ ZIP code 34100; telephone area code 040. Trieste's airport at Ronchi dei Legionari, 20 miles northwest of the city, is used for Italian domestic flights only; international flights land at Venice's Marco Polo Airport. By rail from Venice in 1 hour 40 minutes to 2 hours 10 minutes. By car from Venice, 99 miles on Motorway A-4 ▪ *Information*: 4 Piazza dell'Unità d'Italia (750297). ▪ *Hotels*: Savoia Excelsior Palace (T), 4 Riva del Mandracchio (7690), on the waterfront; Jolly (T), 7 Corso Cavour (7694); San Giusto (M), 3 Via Belli (764824), on the cathedral hill. ▪ *Restaurants*: Granzo (M), 7 Piazza Venezia (762322), with outdoor terrace; Buffet Benedetto (M), 19 Via Trenta Ottobre (62964). ▪ *Museums*: Civic Museum of History and Art, 15 Via Cattedrale (741708); Revoltella Museum, 27 Via Diaz (750436); Marine Museum, 5 Via Campo Marzio (733051); Miramare Castle (224143). ▪ Aquarium, 1 Riva Sauro (36448).

UDINE ▪ ZIP code 33100; telephone area code 0432. By air from Rome or Milan to Ronchi dei Legionari (Trieste airport), 23 miles to the southeast. By rail from Rome in 7–8 hours; from Venice in 1 hour 40 minutes. By car from Rome, 399 miles on Motorway A-1 to Bologna, Motorway A-13 to Padua, Motorway A-4 to Palmanova, and Motorway A-23. ▪ *Information*: 4 Piazza Venerio (204205). ▪ *Hotel*: Astoria (M), 18 Piazza Venti Settembre (207091). ▪ *Restaurant*: Vitello d'Oro (M), 4 Via Valvason (291982). ▪ *Museum*: Civic Museum, Via Ampezzo (295891).

URBINO ▪ ZIP code 61029; telephone area code 0722. By rail from Rome, with change of trains in Falconara Marittima and Fano, in 5 hours. By car from Rome, 170 miles on Motorway A-1 to Orte and National Routes Nos. 3 *bis*, 3, and 73 *bis*. ▪ *Information*: 35 Via Puccinotti (2441). ▪ *Hotels*: San Giovanni (P), 13 Via Barocci (2827); Montefeltro (M), 2 Via Piansevero near Via Gramsci (38324), outside the city walls, with restaurant. ▪ *Restaurants*: Bramante (P), 52 Via Bramante; Nuovo Coppiere (M), 20 Via Porta Maia (4135). ▪ *Museum*: National Gallery of the Marches, Ducal Palace (2760, ext. 4014).

VERONA ▪ ZIP code 37100; telephone area code 045. By rail from Milan in 1 hour 50 minutes; from Venice in 1½ hours; from Rome in 7 hours. By car from Milan, 98 miles on Motorway A-4; from Venice, 71 miles on

Motorway A-4; from Rome, 315 miles on Motorway A-1 to Modena North, and Motorway A-22. ▪ *Information*: 10 Piazza Bra (30086) ▪ *Hotels*: Due Torri (T), 4 Piazza Sant'Anastasia (595044); Italia (M), 58–64 Via Mameli (37126). ▪ *Restaurants*: Dodici Apostoli (T), 3 Corticella San Marco (596999); Nuovo Marconi (T), 4 Via Fogge (595295); Re Teodorico (M), Piazzale Castel San Pietro (49990), with view. ▪ *Museums*: Castelvecchio Museum, Via Cavour (594734); Archaeological Museum, Convent of San Girolamo, near the Arena (23360).

VICENZA ▪ ZIP code 36100; telephone area code 0444. By rail from Venice in 1 hour; from Milan in 2–2½ hours; from Rome, with change of trains in Verona, in 7½–8 hours. By car from Venice, 39 miles on Motorway A-4; from Milan, 128 miles on Motorway A-4; from Rome, 379 miles on Motorway A-1 to Modena North, Motorway A-22 to Verona, and Motorway A-4. ▪ *Information*: Piazza Matteotti (28944). ▪ *Hotels*: Jolly (M), 21 Viale Roma (24560); Due Mori (P), 26 Contra Rode (21886). ▪ *Restaurants*: Tre Visi (M), 6 Contra Porti (23964); Al Pozzo (P), 1 Via Sant'Antonio. ▪ *Museum*: Civic Museum, Piazza Matteotti (39534).

VITERBO ▪ ZIP code 01100; telephone area code 0761. By rail from Rome, Termini Station, in 2 hours 15 minutes; from Rome, Piazzale Flaminio Station, in 2 hours 45 minutes. By public bus from Rome, Piazzale Flaminio, in 1 hour 20 minutes. By car from Rome, 50 miles on National Route No. 2 (Via Cassia). ▪ *Information*: 14 Piazza dei Caduti (34795). ▪ *Hotels*: Mini Palace (M), 2 Via Santa Maria della Grotticella (39742); Leon d'Oro (P), 36 Via della Cava (31012). ▪ *Restaurants*: Scaletta (M), 45 Via Marconi (30003); Aquilanti (M), at La Quercia (31701). ▪ *Museum*: Civic Museum, 2 Piazza Crispi (30810).

VOLTERRA ▪ ZIP code 56048; telephone area code 0588. By rail from Rome, with change of trains in Cecina, to Volterra-Saline-Pomarance, and by bus to the town center, in 4½–5 hours; from Florence, with change of trains in Pisa and Cecina, in 2 hours. Frequent bus service from Florence (inquire at railroad terminal); the bus trip takes about 1 hour. By car from Rome, 178 miles on Motorway A-14 to Civitavecchia, National Route No. 1 to Cecina, and National Route No. 68; from Florence, 47 miles on National Route No. 2 to Poggibonsi, and National Route No. 68. ▪ *Information*: Piazza dei Priori (86150). ▪ *Hotel*: Nazionale (M), 2 Via dei Marchesi (86284). ▪ *Restaurant*: Etruria, 8 Piazza dei Priori (86064). ▪ *Museums*: Guarnacci Etruscan Museum, 1 Via Don Minzoni (86347); Municipal Picture Gallery, Palazzo dei Priori (86025); Diocesan Museum of Sacred Art, 13 Via Roma (87654).